READING THE ROOM

Reading the Room
Lessons on Pedagogy and Curriculum from the Gender and Sexuality Studies Classroom

EDITED BY
Natalie Kouri-Towe

Concordia University Press
Montreal

Unless otherwise noted, all text and photographs copyright the authors.
CC BY-NC-ND

Every reasonable effort has been made to acquire permission for copyright material used in this publication, and to acknowledge all such indebtedness accurately. Any errors and omissions called to the publisher's attention will be corrected in future printings.

Cover design: Allen's Cruz, OTAMI-Design and typesetting: Garet Markvoort, zijn digital
Proofreading: Saelan Twerdy
Index: Judy Dunlop

The body text of *Reading the Room* is set in JJannon, designed by François Rappo and released in 2019 by Swiss foundry Optimo. JJannon revives the letters cut by seventeenth-century Swiss printer Jean Jannon, whose work was misattributed to Claude Garamond for nearly 300 years until scholar Beatrice Warde rectified this error in the 1920s.

Printed and bound in Canada by Imprimerie Gauvin, Gatineau, Quebec

This book is printed on Forest Stewardship Council certified paper and meets the permanence of paper requirements of ANSI/NISO Z39.48-1992.

Concordia University Press's books are available for free on several digital platforms. Visit www.concordia.ca/press

First English edition published in 2024
10 9 8 7 6 5 4 3 2 1

978-1-988111-53-7 | Paper
978-1-988111-54-4 | E-book

Library and Archives Canada Cataloguing in Publication

Title: Reading the room : lessons on pedagogy and curriculum from the gender and sexuality studies classroom / edited by Natalie Kouri-Towe.
Names: Kouri-Towe, Natalie, editor.
Description: Includes bibliographical references and index.
Identifiers: Canadiana (print) 20240438000 | Canadiana (ebook) 20240438035 | ISBN 9781988111537 (softcover) | ISBN 9781988111544 (EPUB)
Subjects: LCSH: Sex differences in education. | LCSH: Gender identity in education. | LCSH: Education, Higher—Curricula. | LCSH: Classroom environment. | LCSH: Teaching. | LCSH: Learning.
Classification: LCC LC212.9 .R43 2024 | DDC 370.81—dc23

Concordia University Press
1455 de Maisonneuve Blvd. W.
Montreal, Quebec H3G 1M8
CANADA

Concordia University Press gratefully acknowledges the generous support of the Birks Family Foundation and the Estate of Tanneke De Zwart.

This book has been published with the help of a grant from the Federation of the Humanities and Social Sciences through the Awards to Scholarly Publications program, using funds provided by the Social Sciences and Humanities Research Council of Canada. Support has also been received from Concordia University's Aid to Research Related Events, Publication, Exhibition and Dissemination Activities Program.

CONTENTS

Foreword and Acknowledgements   xi

Introduction | Learning to Read the Room   3
Natalie Kouri-Towe

Part I | Contending with Accountability: Power and Vulnerability in Higher Education   21

1 | Wielding the "Empowered Student" Narrative: Examining How the Responsibility for Anti-Racism Is Assigned and Denied in Higher Education   27
Meghan Gagliardi

2 | Desiring Disability in Our Learning Communities: Fostering a Crip Culture of Access   45
Kelly Fritsch

3 | "Hi Professor, Am I a Sex Worker?": Adapting to the Shifting Culture around Sex Work in Higher Education   61
Megan Rivers-Moore

4 | Mirrors in the Classroom: 75
The Power of Autobiography as Pedagogy
S. Trimble

5 | Ecstatic Pedagogies: Navigating Desire and 91
Pleasure across the Boundaries of the Classroom
Dan Irving

6 | Pedagogy of Implication: 107
Complicity as Difficult Knowledge
Susanne Luhmann

Part II | The Classroom as a Problem: 125
The Challenges Facing Teachers and Students

7 | The First Teaching Experience: 129
Failure as a Strategy for Critical, Anti-Oppressive,
and Queer Approaches to Pedagogy
Alexis Poirier-Saumure

8 | "Are We Still Talking about This?": 145
Racism and Settler Colonialism in the Feminist
and Queer Studies Classroom
Gulzar R. Charania

9 | The Classroom as a "Safe Space" for Anti-Racism 163
Work: Reflections on Racism in the Canadian
Classroom and the Roles of Students and Teachers
*Mitchell Rae Yang, Rebecca Gaëlle Joachim,
and Kimberley Ens Manning*

10 | Reflections on the "Trigger Warning" Debate: 177
Divergent Strategies for Warnings in the Classroom
Hannah Dyer, Natalie Kouri-Towe, and Michelle Miller

11 | Teaching Trans: Pedagogical 195
Implications of Embodying Course Content
Julia Sinclair-Palm

Part III | Classroom Strategies and Applied Pedagogy: 211
How to Take Risks and Seek Pleasure with Learning

12 | Kink and Pedagogy: A Case for Peer Teaching 215
Nathalie Batraville

13 | On Levity and Subversive Comedy: 231
Feminist Humour as Critical Pedagogy
Gada Mahrouse

14 | Teaching through Digital Intimacies: 247
A Strategy for Critical Cross-Disciplinary Pedagogy
Nathan Rambukkana

15 | Risking Uncertainty: In Defence 263
of Play in the Classroom
Dina Georgis

Part IV | Pedagogies for Care: Building Communities 275
for Transformative Encounters in Education

16 | Kanawenjigewin: Learning to Care 279
for One Another in Circle
Jenn Cole

17 | Collaboration Pedagogy: Co-creating a Handbook and Toolkit for Teaching the Intro Course   295
Sabina Chatterjee and Kristine Klement

18 | Pedagogies of Abolition: Community-Engaged Learning, Struggles for Change from the Prison to the Classroom   313
Chandni Desai

19 | Regional Perspectives on Gender and Sexuality in the Classroom: A Roundtable   331
Carol Lynne D'Arcangelis, Mylène Yannick Gamache, Nicholas Hrynyk, and Suzanne Lenon

20 | Education for All: Open Access and Community-Based Pedagogy through the Toronto Queer Film Festival   347
Kami Chisholm

Conclusion | The Classroom as a Coalition: A Pedagogical Manifesto   361
Natalie Kouri-Towe

Contributors   381

Index   391

FOREWORD AND ACKNOWLEDGEMENTS

This project came out of my experiences developing curricula for sexuality programs, including helping to design a new minor focused on sexuality at the University of Pittsburgh's Gender, Sexuality, and Women's Studies program and as the inaugural program director, and later practicum director, for the newly launched major in Interdisciplinary Studies in Sexuality at Concordia University. Propelled by both student interest and institutional encouragement to build sexuality as a field for undergraduate education, I have grappled with what it means to build curriculum in an area that has grown exponentially across disciplines, and where many of our students are at the forefront of new language, knowledge, and theories of gender and sexuality as practices of everyday life. Interrogating the various ways that faculty teaching in sexuality may or may not be "on trend," and how students are caught between new normalizing structures and the institutionalization of discourses on diversity and inclusion, it became clear to me that developing a sexuality program required more than simply identifying a canon of literature and structuring knowledge into a coherent curriculum. Alone in the work of implementing the new major, I wanted collaborative encounters and spaces to help me navigate the cultural, ideological, social, and political differences that shape critical scholarship within higher education. This book is a result of my desire to better understand the role of faculty and students within institutional structures, to interrogate how power functions through everyday educational interactions, and to model a vision of education as a vehicle for social and political transformation, grounded in and informed by experiences in the classroom.

Feminist and queer pedagogy scholars have highlighted the importance of critical analytic skills alongside an understanding of the embodied and material effects of structures of power on education. Reading this body of work, I began to interrogate how we think about classroom practices and the feminist and queer academic positioning of critique vis-à-vis praxis. Faced with the real challenges of our contemporary moment, critique and analysis alone felt inadequate for the urgent concerns emerging in my classrooms and in my program. Despite the dangers of codifying critical pedagogies, I needed pragmatic tools and supports for both students and faculty. Grappling with what it meant to put into practice justice-based pedagogical and curricular techniques in an interdisciplinary field,[1] I wanted to interrogate the often contradictory and sometimes troubling ways that sexuality was theorized and taught. I spent part of my early years at Concordia University developing a teaching resource and guide for our faculty, working at one point alongside a former undergraduate student, Myloe Martel-Perry, who became my co-author for an open-access self-published resource in 2021, which I revised and republished in 2024: *Better Practices in the Classroom: A Teaching Guidebook for Sustainable, Inclusive, and Equitable Learning from a Gender and Sexuality Studies Framework*. *Better Practices* became a living document for reflecting on and coalescing emergent approaches to pedagogy and curriculum alongside well-established strategies for inclusive and justice-based approaches to education.

Despite the risk of advancing didactic methods for teaching that reduce learning to a series of universalizing metrics and tools, or

---

1. Justice-based approaches to education include gender inclusive (Airton and Koecher 2019) and anti-normative approaches (Britzman 1998), anti-oppression education (Kumashiro 2000), anti-racist and feminist education (hooks [1984] 2000, 1994), and other social justice approaches such as disability justice, decolonial and anti-colonial praxis.

succumbing to the fantasy that gender and sexuality pedagogies are radical or transformative by their very nature,[2] *Better Practices* became a site for connecting with others around how to navigate teaching within our contemporary context.[3] My own hesitations were mirrored in many of my conversations with colleagues over the critiques of the neoliberalization of higher education and the centralization of power within our institutions, on the one hand, and the challenge of contending with how power, violence, complicity, and accountability take shape within the classroom, on the other. Within this context, the early vision for this book first came about in conversation with Concordia University Press editor Ryan Van Huijstee. After sharing my ideas around *Better Practice*s with him, I decided to assemble a space for collaboration among scholars from Canadian institutions teaching across disciplines in the areas of gender and sexuality. Looking at institutionalization within higher education, alongside the state of education more broadly, as well as the everyday challenges facing our contemporary classrooms, this collection took shape as a strategy for collectivizing, sharing skills and resources, debating, and strategizing around how to teach within a context where the terms around justice implicate us differently across our individual and institutional locations.

Guiding this work are a set of questions that I have been asking myself since starting my first appointment as a faculty member. Can the classroom, despite its limitations, provide students and teachers alike with tools for transformation? Why do some classrooms just

---

2. For critiques of institutionalization and diversity see Ahmed 2012, Ferguson 2012, Thomsen 2016, and Wiegman 2016.
3. I have shared and connected with colleagues on the *Better Practices* document through organizing a workshop, plenary discussion, and then digital presentation on the guide with the Sexuality Studies Association between 2020 and 2022. Additionally, I have spoken publicly on the guidebook, including during Concordia University's Open Access Week in 2022, and through regular workshops starting in 2024.

work, while others feel impossible? How do we move through conflicts that arise within the classroom and our institutions? And lastly, how do we grapple with complicity when we are situated within a field that aspires to transformative and radical potential?[4] Like all institutions, education has a culture (or cultures), and higher education especially so—with struggles over resource allocation, administrative ideologies, and elitism. Within this context, fields that grapple with gender, sexuality, race, and what Roderick Ferguson (2012) calls "minority differences," must contend with what Robyn Wiegman describes as:

> the cultivation of the political imaginary of the alternative [that] has been institutionalized in left oriented disciplines as a pervasive disciplinary rule. In the process, the very power we wield in the domains of everyday university life we can call our own—curricular programs, publishing venues, editorial boards, admittance committees, conferences, professional organizations, grading practices, doctoral supervision, etc.—has been obscured, if not actively ignored…Being political is itself a critical convention, no matter how affectively genuine. (2016, 85)

Because institutions of higher education are spaces filled with people—people who make choices around how they communicate, how they navigate structures, and how they wield institutional and administrative power—I drew on the principles of collective organizing as a framework to approach the exercise of writing and editing this book, inviting the contributors to reflect in dialogue on the ways they grapple with the above challenges.

Drawing on my background in popular education and activism, and my graduate training in feminist and social justice praxis, this project centres on pedagogical practices in gender and sexuality

---

4. Susanne Luhmann addresses this question directly in this collection.

studies in collaboration with students and faculty alike. Between January and June 2021, I invited a group of almost forty Canadian faculty and graduate students teaching in the areas of gender and sexuality to participate in a series of workshops on contemporary pedagogies. My goal was twofold. First, I wanted to bring together scholars who work across disciplines but who contend with similar pedagogical questions to discuss some of the pressing topics facing our classrooms. These discussions included topics such as: decolonizing pedagogies; strategies for inclusive and accessible education; navigating call-out culture; tackling student criticism of curriculum; mediating divisiveness and ostracization within the classroom; developing classroom ethics; discussing sexuality in the #MeToo era; and practising effective strategies for fair and transparent supervisory relationships. Second, I wanted to create a space for collaborative reflection and writing on the strategies and approaches we each use in our own teaching. Beginning with paper abstracts and outlines, we developed our drafts through a weekly writing group and then workshopped our chapters through feedback in a second workshop and peer feedback with other participants. The outcome of this work can be found within the pages of this edited collection, where half the participants have written, revised, and re-revised chapters in collaboration with me and the other authors.

This book would not have been possible without the championing of Concordia University Press's acquisitions editor Ryan Van Huijstee, who saw the vision for this project from start to finish and who provided regular thoughtful and engaging feedback on the book's development and funding for over three years. Many thanks also go to our copyeditor, Joanne Muzak, Judy Dunlop for help with the index, and the rest of the Concordia University Press team, including Geoffrey Robert Little, Saelan Twerdy, and Natalie Greenberg and the members of the editorial board. I owe much gratitude to the research assistants who worked on parts of this project throughout the process, including Alexis Poirier-Saumure, one of the contributors in this collection; Myloe Martel-Perry, my co-author for the open access teaching resources and guide we published in 2021; and Rhys McKay, who helped with the transcription and editing of my interview with Kami Chisholm. I could not have developed this work without the collaborations and conversations I had with my colleagues, Genevieve Renard Painter and Kimberley Manning, with whom I co-organized multiple departmental pedagogy retreats. I am thankful for my trusted friends, family, and colleagues who gave me feedback on my own chapters in the book, including Sharlene Bamboat, Eric D. Bernasek, Lisa Brush, Kelly Fritsch, and Elina Penttinen and the participants in the Christina Lecture at the University of Helsinki in January 2024, where I workshopped my conclusion. I also owe much gratitude to the contributors in this book, who joined me in a participatory process for writing during a period when everyone struggled with heavy workloads and depleted energy due to the global pandemic—a point that emerges in many of the chapters included within. Missing within this collection, however, are the dozen other scholars who participated in this project at various stages but had to withdraw due to the challenges of overburdened workloads, personal and family illnesses, loss, and the strain of living and working through the early years of a pandemic. I want to acknowledge their role in helping to shape this book and to also express my gratitude for their participation. I don't name these contributors here, but hope their work and ideas that developed in conversation with this collection can soon find homes for publication elsewhere.

This work was supported by funding from the Social Sciences and Humanities Research Council of Canada's Connection Grant program, the Federation for the Humanities and Social Sciences Scholarly Book Awards Publication Grant and Open Access supplemental grant, funding from Concordia University's Office of Research and Office of the Vice-President, Research and Graduate Studies Aid to Research Related Events, Publications, Exhibition and Dissemination

Activities Program, and in-kind support from Concordia University Press.

References

Ahmed, Sara. 2012. *On Being Included: Racism and Diversity in Institutional Life.* Durham, NC: Duke University Press.

Airton, Lee, and Austen Koecher. 2019. "How to Hit a Moving Target: 35 years of Gender and Sexual Diversity in Teacher Education." *Teaching and Teacher Education* 80 (April): 190–204. https://doi.org/10.1016/j.tate.2018.11.004.

Britzman, Deborah P. 1998. "Is There a Queer Pedagogy? Or, Stop Reading Straight." In *Curriculum: Towards New Identities*, edited by William F. Pinar, 211–31. New York: Garland Publishing.

Ferguson, Roderick. 2012. *The Reorder of Things: The University and Its Pedagogies of Minority Difference.* Minneapolis: University of Minnesota Press.

Kouri-Towe, Natalie, and Myloe Martel-Perry. 2024. *Better Practices in the Classroom: A Teaching Guidebook for Sustainable, Inclusive, and Equitable Learning from a Gender and Sexuality Studies Framework.* Montreal: Concordia University Library Pressbooks. https://opentextbooks.concordia.ca/teachingresource/.

Kumashiro, Kevin. 2000. "Toward a Theory of Anti-Oppressive Education." *Review of Educational Research* 70 (1): 25–53. https://www.jstor.org/stable/1170593.

Thomsen, Carly. 2016. "Becoming Radically Undone: Discourses of Identity and Diversity in the Introductory Gender and Women's Studies Classroom." *Atlantis: Critical Studies in Gender, Culture and Social Justice* 37.2 (2): 76–82. https://journals.msvu.ca/index.php/atlantis/article/view/76-82%20PDF.

Wiegman, Robyn. 2016. "No Guarantee: Feminism's Academic Affect and Political Fantasy." *Atlantis: Critical Studies in Gender, Culture and Social Justice* 37.2 (2): 83–95. https://journals.msvu.ca/index.php/atlantis/article/view/83-95%20PDF.

READING THE ROOM

INTRODUCTION

Learning to Read the Room

NATALIE KOURI-TOWE

> There was no way to critique the university without tacitly affirming it, which made it important to retreat from the romance of non-complicity long enough to consider what aspects of the university we might want to cultivate and defend.
>
> —Robyn Wiegman, "No Guarantee: Feminism's Academic Affect and Political Fantasy" (2016)

While I edited this book, the province I teach in passed a controversial law on academic freedom that aimed, among other things, to discourage universities from enforcing trigger warnings in academic activities.[1] Some speculated that the law, under the guise of academic freedom, was introduced as a campaign promise to appease a cultural backlash against "woke culture" in the province. This is just one example of a much wider trend within North America where countless states and provinces, municipalities, school boards, and other offices have taken action to restrict what is taught in schools and what kinds of knowledge and subjectivities can remain visible within education. This kind of political interference in education illustrates the

---

1. In June 2022 the Quebec government passed Bill 32, an Act Respecting Academic Freedom in the University Sector. While this bill does not prohibit the use of trigger warnings outright, it requires that trigger warnings not be included in university policies on academic freedom when referring to material that might "offend."

important role that education plays in shaping public life, as both a vector of state control and scene of contestation over divisive ideological battles in society more broadly.[2] Yet the pedagogical debates happening *within* higher education do not necessarily mirror popular debates *on* education. Turning to the points of contention, reflection, and friction within academic pedagogical discussions can illustrate a different set of concerns over what is at stake in education and society more broadly. Debates over what language we use in the classroom, what topics we can or should learn, and how we grapple with difference permeate all classrooms across disciplines. Those of us teaching in the areas of gender and sexuality studies often find ourselves on the front lines of many of these debates.[3] From attacks on "gender ideology" and teaching about critical race theory,[4] to debates over

---

2. In his work on the institutionalization of minority difference in higher education, Roderick Ferguson argues "power enlisted the academy and things academic as conduits for conveying unprecedented forms of political economy to state and capital, forms that would be based on an abstract—rather than a redistributive—valorization of minority difference and culture" (2012, 8).

3. I use the phrase "areas associated with gender and sexuality studies" as a shorthand to refer to the interdisciplinary fields of research and teaching that span feminist theory, gender studies, queer theory, sexuality studies, trans studies, trans theory, and women's studies. These are fields that are at the forefront of debates and strategies for grappling with the "crises" in higher education, including navigating shifting gender and sexuality identities in the classroom setting, debates about pronoun go-arounds, trigger and content warnings for class content, diversifying classroom curriculum, decolonizing pedagogies and curriculum, navigating accessibility and disability justice, and responding to social movements within our campuses, such as #MeToo and the Movement for Black Lives. The authors span multiple fields, including child studies, communication studies, English literature, equity studies, geography, sociology, and most commonly, women's, gender, and sexuality studies.

4. "Gender ideology" is a term taken up by both anti-feminist men's-rights thinkers and activists, *and* transphobic feminists, commonly referred to as TERFS (trans-exclusionary radical feminists), a term that was originally used to describe a particular branch of radical and separatist feminism from the late 1970s and early '80s that been applied to contemporary liberal feminists who attack trans people.

the use of the "n-word" in the classroom, from "cancel culture" and "trigger warnings," to labelling students who demand social justice as "snowflakes," the political disputes playing out within and about higher education reflect the wider ideological battles shaping our contemporary world, as liberation and far-right movements further intensify divisions—and at times even disturbingly converge—within the neoliberal context. However, these sites of contestation over education often mask the crisis within higher education that is shaped by the neoliberalization of education, including increases in tuition costs for students, precarious working conditions for teachers, administrative workloads for faculty, and the expansion of upper administrative roles that create a divide between the professorial and managerial classes within institutions. If we follow the controversies emergent in social media and in op-eds, we might be left with the impression that education is at a crossroads in the battle between critical thinking and right-wing ideologies. However, many of these debates are missing an understanding of the thoughtful, adaptive, reflexive, and reflective techniques that faculty have been developing and incorporating into their classrooms in light of the concerns and issues that have been taken up in public forums. Much of this work is performed invisibly by faculty within their classrooms, shared at times under the auspices of teaching innovation in job market "teaching philosophy" statements and in tenure and review files. Occasionally, scholars share their strategies in trade publications and journals, such as *University Affairs, Radical Teacher, The Chronicle of Higher Education*, and *Inside Higher Ed*. Yet those of us teaching in the areas of gender and sexuality have grappled with the role of the classroom as both a microcosm of the outside world, and as a scene of possibility for envisioning, experimenting with, thinking through, and applying transformative ways of responding to the ongoing problems of injustice.

Long before the trigger-warning debates came into popular forums, people teaching in women's and gender studies grappled with the ethics of teaching about sexual violence in a context where one in three women and one in eight men have experienced sexual violence in their lifetime (Cotter and Savage 2019). Likewise, those teaching about race and racism have contended with what it means to learn about racial violence when both teachers and students may be victims of interpersonal and systemic racism, such as in the case of Black feminist scholars in the classroom (hooks 1994; Nash 2019). Although studies in higher education, teaching, and learning have long established research on pedagogy and curriculum, the interdisciplinary fields of gender and sexuality have developed their own cultures and norms around classroom pedagogy and curricular development—anchored on intersectionality, anti-oppressive and inclusive principles in the classroom, and teaching practices developed in conjunction with popular education and justice-based approaches.[5]

Scholars teaching in the areas of gender and sexuality studies often grapple with the conditions of foundational knowledge and learning outside of disciplinary canons, including the challenge to build "intersectional," "anti-racist," "decolonial," and inclusive pedagogy without clear consensus over what such pedagogy entails or aims to achieve (Ahmed 2012; Alexander and Mohanty 2005; Ferguson 2012; Gaztambide-Fernández 2012; Gaztambide-Fernández et al. 2022; Malatino 2015). How do we integrate respectful and inclusive strategies in our teaching while navigating a political landscape where the terms of what practices are "best" may not correspond to a set of interventions in the classroom that actually accomplish their intended goal? For instance, do territorial acknowledgements or inclusion of Indigenous material in our classrooms effectively "decolonize" our classes?[6] Do trigger warnings effectively prepare students to grapple with learning

---

5. For example, see Jennifer C. Nash's critique of the way intersectionality has been used as "women's studies primary program-building initiative, as its institutional and ethical orientation" (2019, 2) and the popular use of Paulo Freire's (1970) *Pedagogy of the Oppressed* as the canon for critical praxis.
6. See Tuck and Yang's (2012) critique of the use of decolonization as a concept in education.

about violence? Do we risk cultivating a culture of dogmatic and didactic, rather than thoughtful and adaptive, thinking when we institute "best practices" in our courses? What is the threshold between harm and academic freedom, particularly when debate is framed around the violence, injuries, and identities shaping the experiences of our students, our colleagues, and ourselves? These foundational questions animate not only our field but many other classrooms, workplaces, organizations, and communities today. As concepts such as intersectionality, critical race theory, and trauma travel across academic and popular usage, the institutionalization of these concepts into the structure of education (Ahmed 2012; Nash 2019)—from diversity, equity, and inclusion initiatives to sexual assault support services—have made those fields working on topics of gender and sexuality ripe for critical engagement, as well as vulnerable to the bad-faith arguments that aim to dismiss and undermine the work of student organizers, unions, and social movements trying to make our institutions less harmful (Ferguson 2012, 5).

Interrogating pedagogical practices from a gender and sexuality framework follows foundational work published in recent years, such as Melissa Autumn White and Jennifer Musial's (2016) important special issue of *Atlantis*, "Belaboured Introductions: Inspired Reflections on the Introductory Course in Gender and Women's Studies," which assembles works reflecting on the field's introductory course; Tracy Penny Light, Jane Nicholas, and Renée Bondy's (2015) edited collection *Feminist Pedagogy in Higher Education: Critical Theory and Practice*; the edited collection by Amber Dean, Jennifer L. Johnson, and Susanne Luhmann (2019), *Feminist Praxis Revisited*, on community engagement in women's and gender studies education; and Susan Hillock's (2021) edited collection, *Teaching about Sex and Sexualities in Higher Education*. This work accompanies a wider development in scholarship coming from gender and sexuality on pedagogy that begins with feminist approaches to the classroom and moves to critiques over the neoliberalization of education. Building on the long history of feminist work that reflexively examines pedagogies and praxis inside and outside of the classroom,[7] new generations of scholars and teachers have had to contend with a different landscape of economic precarity, individualism, and rapidly changing discourses around gender and sexuality (Drabinski 2014; Malatino 2015; Stryker, Currah, and Moore 2008).

Even within the fields of gender and sexuality, many faculty struggle with the integration of the wider cultural shifts that are shaping education in the twenty-first century, such as

- gender diversity and campus barriers that cause exclusion (e.g., lack of gender-neutral washrooms, gendered ID cards, and class lists);
- calls for racial and disability justice in the classroom (beyond reliance on university services and anti-discrimination policies);
- student demands for accountability and accommodations (e.g., requests for professors to adjust their teaching and assessment models to meet student needs, and critiques of students-as-consumer models of education);
- a supposed "mental health crisis" on campus (juxtaposed against the limited availability and resources of counselors and therapists);
- campus sexual violence scandals; and
- debates over the meaning of consent in workplace and learning contexts (e.g., university policies on disclosure and prohibited relationships).

---

7. With growing institutionalization, feminist scholars began examining the role of feminist praxis, community engagement, and experiential learning that had become integral to women's studies programs. For examples, see Balliet and Heffernan 2000; Bojar and Naples 2002; Dean 2007; Dittmar and Annas 2017; Hyman and Lichtenstein 1999; Jones 2017; Light, Nicholas, and Bondy 2015; Mayberry and Rose 1999; McNeil, Wermers, and Lunn 2018; Naples 2002; Peet and Reed 1999.

It is often hard for those of us with expertise in these areas to know how to respond to the above conditions of teaching and learning in the context of our classrooms. Many teachers across disciplines are afraid of saying or doing the wrong thing (Kumashiro 2000, 39). Fear of facing upset students, of being called out or publicly shamed, make the choices we make in our classrooms much bigger challenges than simply the pedagogical and curricular objectives we lay out in our syllabi. Conversely, student experiences of harm within higher education illustrate the pervasive nature of structural violence that shapes the choices we make as teachers, and the risks associated with our decisions.[8] Given all this, how can we better *read the room* and adapt to the conditions shaping higher education, our classrooms, and society more broadly? Coming from a place of sustained hope and cautious optimism over the role of education, this book invites a wide range of academic readers to join us in thinking through how to adjust our teaching to the students in our classrooms and the world around us.

The central problem that this collection attempts to make sense of is how teachers put into practice the transformative and liberatory values of justice in the everyday pedagogies of the classroom in higher education. Beyond a model of inclusive learning, where subjects and people historically excluded are "added in" to the curriculum,[9] the authors across this book attempt to make sense of their teaching practices amidst the challenges facing contemporary education, including important critiques of the racial and colonial structures of education, its violent exclusions and expulsions, and the limits of institutional change alongside the collective desire for transformation.

---

[8]. For examples of structural harm in classroom contexts, see Bedera 2021; Wentling 2015.

[9]. The inclusive model of education has been critiqued by psychoanalysis and education scholar Deborah Britzman, who questions the "plea to add marginalized voices" through inclusion. For example, in the case of anti-homophobic education, where "arguments for inclusion produce the very exclusions they are meant to cure" (1998, 219).

The chapters that follow contend with the contradictions inherent in working within institutional systems and take up the challenge to envision models of education that are both transformative and pragmatic for the conditions facing our working and learning environments. Drawing on autoethnographic, dialogic, critical analytic, self-reflexive, and self-reflective methods, the chapters each consider a set of concerns around the contemporary classroom and provide insights for a general reader outside of gender and sexuality studies to engage in the questions and discussions those in our field are grappling with.

The book is organized across four thematic parts. The first part, "Contending with Accountability: Power and Vulnerability in Higher Education," assembles chapters that confront the violence embedded within institutional structures and explores our attempts to compensate for this violence in the classroom. From systemic racism to ableism, confronting our own projections and desire for innocence, the authors of this section ask us to think about our role as teachers in navigating injustice in higher education. The second part, "The Classroom as a Problem: The Challenges Facing Teachers and Students," looks at the anxieties, conflicts, and difficulties that shape the experience of teaching and of learning. Each chapter in this part asks us to reconsider what we might usually take for granted about the classroom. The third part, "Classroom Strategies and Applied Pedagogy: How to Take Risks and Seek Pleasure with Learning," offers approaches to teaching that aim to bring pleasure into the space of learning by grappling with the challenge of taking risks in the classroom. Outlining concrete strategies for the classroom, the authors share insights into what works, and doesn't work, in their own classrooms. Lastly, the fourth part, "Pedagogies for Care: Building Communities for Transformative Encounters in Education," offers a visionary approach to learning by transforming the very foundations of education through care, collaboration, and activism. The changes that these chapters make viable illustrate the capacity of education to be a scene for wider social transformation. The book ends with a conclusion/manifesto, which invites readers to rethink the classroom through coalition by drawing on five pedagogical approaches illustrated by the work and arguments shared throughout the contributing chapters of the book.

Written as an invitation for scholars across disciplines to join us in conversation, each chapter illustrates how faculty teaching in the areas of gender and sexuality have navigated many of the same challenges faculty face across disciplines: from trying to respond to conflict in the classroom (Dyer, Kouri-Towe, and Miller; Irving; Poirier-Saumure; Yang, Joachim, and Manning), to the challenge of understanding ourselves as embodied in our roles as teachers (Charania; Trimble; Sinclair-Palm), the chapters draw on self-reflection and self-reflexion (Kumashiro 2000, 45), classroom experimentation, subject expertise, and research to offer pragmatic solutions or points of entry for anyone teaching in higher education, regardless of their field. Likewise, those who are interested in looking critically at the role and function of education as both a vehicle for the circulation of knowledge and a site through which the ideals of transformation come to a head with the structures of power shaping education will find their counterparts in many of the chapters.[10] From critiques over the role of complicity in education (Chatterjee and Klement; Gagliardi; Luhmann) to models that call for a radical reorientation of power in the classroom (Batraville; Chisholm; Cole; Fritsch), many of the authors share compelling ways of rethinking our classrooms as spaces of experimentation and play (Desai; Georgis; Mahrouse; Rambukkana). A number of chapters engage with concepts relating to pedagogies of discomfort (Dyer, Kouri-Towe, and Miller; Luhmann; Poirier-Saumure), a concept coming out of both psychoanalytic approaches to education and

---

10. The desire for transformation through education must also contend with the fundamental question over whether curriculum can transform learners through education when we rely on the fantasy that "the truth of the minority might persuade the normative folks to welcome the diversity of others" (Britzman 1998a, 220).

theories of emotion in education (Boler 1999; Britzman 1998b; Felman 1991). Throughout the book, authors also engage with a wide variety of strategies, techniques, and approaches to pedagogy to grapple with the challenges they face in their teaching, including pedagogical techniques, such as peer learning, relational knowledge, and public pedagogy; the politics of pedagogy, such as anti-racism, decolonization, and allyship; and pedagogical innovations in the form of tools and approaches to learning outside of common instructional methods, such as kink, play, humour, desire, emotion, and intimacies.

At its core, this book interrogates what it means to confront our fantasies of the classroom as well as the lived reality of teaching. Despite our best efforts, there are risks in assuming that what we intend pedagogically will be legible in the classroom. As both the epigraph by Robyn Wiegman (2016) and Susanne Luhmann's chapter in this collection remind us, we are all subjects of wider systems and structures of power. As such, our best efforts might be betrayed by our complicity with power, through the unconscious and conscripted ways that the tacit function of violence and exclusion are threaded throughout institutional structures. Although teaching is one of many forms of labour conducted by faculty in higher education, the desire or fantasy of being a good teacher compels many of us to place substantive effort, care, and thought into our teaching. However, scholars looking critically at what happens within education have challenged the ideals and fantasies of education as well as its practices within the institutions that structure encounters with learning.

Deborah Britzman argues, "pedagogical thought must begin to acknowledge that receiving knowledge is a problem for the learner and the teacher, particularly when the knowledge one already possesses or is possessed by works as an entitlement to one's ignorance or when the knowledge encountered cannot be incorporated because it disrupts how the self might imagine itself and others" (1998a, 220). Referring to the challenge of multicultural education, Britzman continues by explaining that the problem is not so much a "resistance to knowledge" (i.e., the student doesn't want to learn), but "knowledge as a form of resistance" (i.e., the student's existing knowledge is the basis of a resistance to learn otherwise) (220). Put this way, she challenges her readers to consider how it is precisely through knowledge that we entrench normative ideas that reinforce hegemonic ways of knowing. Likewise, in "Toward a Theory of Anti-Oppressive Education," Kevin Kumashiro argues there are two challenges of education: "the teacher can never really know (1) whether the student learned what he or she was trying to teach, and (2) how the student will be moved by what was learned" (2000, 38). This feature of education poses a central challenge to the very premise of critical education, because it means whatever strategies we employ in the classroom may not have a corresponding effect in what is learned. Kumashiro's survey of the models of anti-oppressive education precisely illustrates the array of limitations that undermine the goals of critical pedagogies. Instead, he argues for a series of strategies that build on practices and approaches rather than sets of knowledge. These strategies include disrupting normative repetitions and transforming discourses (42), creating space for resistance and crisis in curriculum (44), self-reflection (how one is implicated) and self-reflexivity (how knowledge informs one's sense of self) (45), "changing how we read normalcy and Otherness" (45), drawing on strategies that are situated, and recognizing "that teaching involves unknowability and that learning involves multiple ways of reading" (46).

Rather than try to teach the correct "critical" material, the authors in this collection grapple with how to reorient the relationship of learning in the classroom by interrogating the problem of knowledge and learning through attention to power, harm, accountability, and adaptation. Because the classroom is co-implicated in the wider institutional cultures of our schools and the political debates shaping our societies, we cannot assume that our classrooms will be separate from pre-existing knowledge, power, or violence. This is why pedagogical practices around creating "safe space" in the classroom have come under heavy criticism, including from many of the contributors in this book (see Batraville; Charania; Dyer, Kouri-Towe, and Miller). Despite these critiques, all the contributors contend with how to make their classrooms better spaces—both for student learning and for the experiences of teachers in their roles as educators. While teaching innovations have become part of the metrics used for assessing faculty performance and program review within higher education, faculty teaching in the areas of gender and sexuality often experiment with and innovate pedagogical strategies. These strategies illustrate the adaptive potential of the classroom to build different and perhaps even better ways of learning by disrupting education's entrenched norms. At the same time, the imperative to innovate burdens individual faculty in the neoliberalized metrics of performance, evaluation, and exceptionalism. Instead of drawing on the language of institutional innovation, the authors in this collection draw on a reflexive prompt (Thorpe et al. 2016) to rethink their approaches, strategies, and practices within the classroom.

What motivates and inspires learning differs from teacher to teacher, student to student. As such, this book asks, What happens if our approach to teaching adapts to who enters our classrooms? Reflexivity is an important intervention in the practice of education because we cannot assume how and why our students enter into the work of learning. What knowledge shapes students' desire to learn our subjects, and how do our students' social locations and life experiences shape their approaches to learning, as much as these very same considerations shape our approaches to teaching?

The imperative to incorporate equitable, diverse, and inclusive teaching is not only administrative policy but correlates to the calls for justice and accountability in our institutions coming from historically excluded groups (e.g., the Movement for Black Lives and anti-racism work; Idle No More and the Truth and Reconciliation Commission Report; trans inclusivity and gender advocacy groups; accessibility on campus and disability justice groups). From the adoption of respectful practices around gender pronouns (e.g., they/them; ze/hir) to the vicious attacks on trans people by "gender critical feminists," we have seen an intensifying array of divergent positions coming up in our classrooms that require ethical intervention; and yet, what that intervention should be is hotly contested even within the fields of gender and sexuality. For instance, should teachers invite students to share their pronouns in a "pronoun go-around" or do such activities single out trans and non-binary students in the classroom, or worse, risk inviting transphobic comments from others in the class? These questions are challenging to grapple with as faculty attempt to provide thoughtful and considerate ways of centring respect and dignity in the classroom. Alongside these challenges, we also encounter attempts to appropriate critiques of systemic violence by using the language of "diversity and inclusion" to justify articulations of homophobic, transphobic, racist, and other violent discourses. We have seen institutional anti-discrimination policies used as a way to harass and target queer and women of colour faculty, and our departments continue to be targeted by misogynistic, racist, and homophobic vitriol (Calixte et al. 2017; Savic 2020).

The authors in this book all examine the transformative strategies and approaches used to create inclusive and experimental classrooms by addressing systemic forms of violence and harm, challenging the normative space of the classroom, and grappling with our pedagogical choices. Rather than aiming to find the "best" practice (Kumashiro 2000, 46), as if there can be a universal practice that works best in every classroom, the chapters that follow assemble a set of reflections on the practices that scholars have used both inside and outside of the classroom to address the contemporary challenges facing us pedagogically and institutionally.

Ferguson argues that we should resist institutionalization and the formalization of administrative infrastructures by turning to informal spaces, such as cross-departmental coalitions, and by making what he calls "effective institutional practice" (2015, 51). The turn to coalition has a long history in both feminist and queer activism (Cohen 1997), and if we consider what strategies might allow us to hold the tension between the limits of formalization and the transformative potential of critical education, then we must take seriously the role of building coalition as the basis for our pedagogical work. This means developing concrete strategies to confront what it means to practice education under the conditions of neoliberalization and institutionalization without falling prey to a nihilistic view of the role of education as a vehicle for governmentality. Like the process that went into the creation of this book and its chapters, this work entails centring collaboration in learning—not only students collaborating together or teachers working collaboratively—but envisioning the project of education as one that requires our intentional engagement and collaboration across our fields and across our social locations both inside and outside the classroom.

Turning to Wiegman's reflection on the affective and political fantasies of gender and sexuality studies, she argues in favour of shifts in our disciplinary approaches that offer "pedagogies of correction that renew the possibility of a transformed future by locating the field's value in detecting the scenes in which feminism's political compass has failed" (2016, 90). Drawing on this notion of pedagogies of correction, I see this collection of works as an invitation to participate in a coalition of scholars who use strategies of self-reflexion and self-reflection, critical analysis, and transformative praxis as a basis for transforming higher education from the classroom to our wider institutions. Rather than falling prey to the desire to trust in the formalization of our institutions, the works that follow all grapple with the everyday practices of our classrooms as a way "to engage the university as a contradictory but resonant scene of political desire" (93). This involves taking seriously the ways faculty and students alike have tried to adapt the classroom to the changing political needs surrounding gender and sexuality both inside and outside of educational contexts. My hope is that the works included within this collection will offer our readers a series of voices to be in dialogue with, a space for the coalitional possibility of education as we navigate the challenges of teaching beyond our own classrooms and across disciplines.

Taken together, the chapters throughout this collection ask us as teachers to resist the desire to control the outcome of learning while simultaneously putting into practice different strategies for making the classroom a better space: a space that develops critical skills in our students; a space that is more inclusive and welcoming of both teachers' and students' differences; a space that holds the potential for experimenting with ideas and ways of envisioning the world differently; and a space that can hold the discomforts of resistance to learning and unlearning. "Teaching…like learning, cannot be about repetition and affirmation of either the student's or teacher's knowledge, but must involve uncertainty, difference, and change" (Kumashiro 2000, 44). The impossible task of education means not only learning how to teach our subject areas but also learning how to help students cultivate a capacity for their own learning. Challenging ourselves as teachers to disrupt the impulse and desire to transmit knowledge, while we navigate the burdens of labour under the neoliberalization of our institutions, is a seemingly impossible task. My hope is that this invitation to read and think alongside the scholars and thinkers in this collection can help collectivize that work in ways that alleviate the challenges of teaching today and make possible more fluid transformation of our classrooms, departments, institutions, and communities.

References

Ahmed, Sara. 2012. *On Being Included: Racism and Diversity in Institutional Life*. Durham, NC: Duke University Press.

Alexander, Jacqui M., and Chandra Talpade Mohanty. 2005. "Cartographies of Knowledge and Power: Transnational Feminism as Radical Praxis." In *Critical Transnational Feminist Praxis*, edited by Amanda Lock Swarr and Richa Nagar, 23–45. Albany: SUNY Press.

Balliet, Barbara J., and Kerrissa Heffernan, eds. 2000. *The Practice of Change: Concepts and Models for Service-Learning in Women's Studies*. Washington, DC: American Association for Higher Education.

Bedera, Nicole. 2021. "Beyond Trigger Warnings: A Survivor-Centered Approach to Teaching on Sexual Violence and Avoiding Institutional Betrayal." *Teaching Sociology* 49 (3): 267–77. https://doi.org/10.1177/0092055X211022471.

Bill 32, An Act Respecting Academic Freedom in the University Sector. 2022. 2nd session, 42nd Legislature, National Assembly of Québec. http://www2.publicationsdu quebec.gouv.qc.ca/dynamicSearch/telecharge.php?type=5&file=2022C21A.PDF.

Bojar, Karen, and Nancy A. Naples, eds. 2002. *Teaching Feminist Activism: Strategies from the Field*. New York: Routledge.

Boler, Megan. 1999. *Feeling Power: Emotions and Education*. New York: Routledge.

Britzman, Deborah. 1998a. "Is There a Queer Pedagogy? Or, Stop Reading Straight." In *Curriculum: Towards New Identities*, edited by William F. Pinar, 211–31. New York: Garland Publishing.

—. 1998b. *Lost Subjects, Contested Objects: Toward a Psychoanalytic Inquiry of Learning*. Albany: SUNY Press.

Calixte, Shana, OmiSoore Dryden, Jennifer L. Johnson, Natalie Kouri-Towe, and Aven McMaster. 2017. "Statement on Anti-Feminist and Anti-Black Vandalism at Thorneloe University from the Department of Women's, Gender, and Sexuality Studies (Located at Laurentian U)." March 3, 2017. http://www.thorneloe.ca/wp-content/uploads/2017/03/WGSX-Statement-on-Anti-Black-and-Anti-Feminist-Vandalism_1.pdf.

Cohen, Cathy J. 1997. "Punks, Bulldaggers, and Welfare Queens: The Radical Potential of Queer Politics?" *GLQ: A Journal of Lesbian and Gay Studies* 3 (4): 437–65. https://doi.org/10.1215/10642684-3-4-437.

Cotter, Adam, and Laura Savage. 2019. "Gender-Based Violence and Unwanted Sexual Behaviour in Canada, 2018: Initial Findings from the Survey of Safety in Public and Private Spaces." *Statistics Canada*. December 5, 2019. https://www150.statcan.gc.ca/n1/pub/85-002-x/2019001/article/00017-eng.htm.

Dean, Amber. 2007. "Teaching Feminist Activism: Reflections on an Activism Assignment in Introductory Women's Studies." *Review of Education, Pedagogy & Cultural Studies* 29 (4): 351–69. https://doi.org/10.1080/10714410701454065.

Dean, Amber, Jennifer L. Johnson, and Susanne Luhmann, eds. 2019. *Feminist Praxis Revisited: Critical Reflections on University-Community Engagement*. Waterloo, ON: Wilfrid Laurier University Press.

Dittmar, Linda, and Pamela Annas. 2017. "Introduction: Toward Public Pedagogies: Teaching Outside Traditional Classrooms." *Radical Teacher* 109 (Fall): 1–3. https://doi.org/10.5195/rt.2017.414.

Drabinski, Kate. 2014. "Identity Matters: Teaching Transgender in the Women's Studies Classroom." *Radical Teacher* 100 (Fall): 139–45. https://www.jstor.org/stable/10.5406/radicalteacher.92.0010.

Felman, Shoshana. 1991. "Education and Crisis: On the Vicissitudes of Teaching." *American Imago* 48 (1): 13–73. https://www.jstor.org/stable/26304031.

Ferguson, Roderick. 2012. *The Reorder of Things: The University and Its Pedagogies of Minority Difference*. Minneapolis: University of Minnesota Press.

—. 2015. "University." *Critical Ethnic Studies* 1 (1): 43–55. https://www.jstor.org/stable/10.5749/jcritethnstud.1.1.0043.

Freire, Paulo. 1970. *Pedagogy of the Oppressed*. Translated by Myra Bergman Ramos. New York: Herder and Herder.

Gaztambide-Fernández, Rubén. 2012. "Decolonization and the Pedagogy of Solidarity." *Decolonization: Indigeneity, Education & Society* 1 (1): 41–67.

Gaztambide-Fernández, Rubén, Jennifer Brant, and Chandni Desai. 2022. "Toward a Pedagogy of Solidarity." *Curriculum Inquiry* 52 (3): 251–65. https://doi.org/10.1080/03626784.2022.2082733.

Hillock, Susan. 2021. *Teaching about Sex and Sexualities in Higher Education*. Toronto: University of Toronto Press.

hooks, bell. 1994. *Teaching to Transgress: Education as the Practice of Freedom*. New York: Routledge.

Hyman, Colette A., and Diane Lichtenstein, eds. 1999. "Expanding the Classroom: Fostering Active Learning and Activism." Special issue, *Women's Studies Quarterly* 27 (3–4).

Jones, Cara E. 2017. "Transforming Classroom Norms as Social Change: Pairing Embodied Exercises with Collaborative Participation in the WGS Classroom (with Syllabus)." *Radical Teacher* 107 (Winter): 14–31. https://doi.org/10.5195/rt.2017.322.

Kumashiro, Kevin. 2000. "Toward a Theory of Anti-Oppressive Education." *Review of Educational Research* 70 (1): 25–53. https://www.jstor.org/stable/1170593.

Light, Tracy Penny, Jane Nicholas, and Renée Bondy, eds. 2015. *Feminist Pedagogy in Higher Education: Critical Theory and Practice*. Waterloo, ON: Wilfrid Laurier University Press.

Malatino, Hilary. 2015. "Pedagogies of Becoming: Trans Inclusivity and the Crafting of Being." *TSQ: Transgender Studies Quarterly* 2 (3): 395–410. https://doi.org/10.1215/23289252-2926387.

Mayberry, Maralee, and Ellen Cronan Rose, eds. 1999. *Meeting the Challenge: Innovative Feminist Pedagogies in Action*. New York: Routledge.

McNeil, Elizabeth, James E. Wermers, and Joshua O. Lunn, eds. 2018. *Mapping Queer Space(s) of Praxis and Pedagogy*. Cham: Palgrave Macmillan.

Naples, Nancy A. 2002. "Negotiating the Politics of Experiential Learning in Women's Studies: Lessons from the Community Action Project." In *Women's Studies on Its Own: A Next Wave Reader in Institutional Change*, edited by Robyn Wiegman, 383–415. Durham, NC: Duke University Press.

Nash, Jennifer C. 2019. *Black Feminism Reimagined: After Intersectionality*. Durham, NC: Duke University Press.

Peet, Melissa, and Beth Glover Reed. 1999. "Activism in an Introductory Women's Studies Course: Connected Learning through the Implementation of Praxis." *Women's Studies Quarterly* 27 (3–4): 21–35. https://www.jstor.org/stable/40004474.

Savic, Lela. 2020. "Des messages suprémacistes en amont du Mois de l'histoire des Noirs." *Journal Métro* (blog). February 6, 2020. https://journalmetro.com/actualites/montreal/2417353/des-messages-supremacistes-en-amont-du-mois-de-lhistoire-des-noirs/.

Stryker, Susan, Paisley Currah, and Lisa Jean Moore. 2008. "Introduction: Trans-, Trans, or Transgender?" *Women's Studies Quarterly* 36 (3–4): 11–22. https://www.jstor.org/stable/27649781.

Thorpe, Jocelyn, Sonja Boon, Lisa Bednar, Glenda Tibe Bonifacio, Marg Hobbs, Rachel Hurst, Krista Johnston, Heather Latimer, Marie Lovrod, Carla Rice, and Alissa Trotz. 2016. "The Intro Course: A Pedagogical Toolkit." *Atlantis: Critical Studies in Gender, Culture and Social Justice* 37.2 (2): 54–67. https://journals.msvu.ca/index.php/atlantis/article/view/54-67%20PDF/54-67.

Tuck, Eve, and K. Wayne Yang. 2012. "Decolonization Is Not a Metaphor." *Decolonization: Indigeneity, Education & Society* 1 (2): 1–40. https://jps.library.utoronto.ca/index.php/des/article/view/18630.

Wentling, Tre. 2015. "Trans* Disruptions: Pedagogical Practices and Pronoun Recognition." *TSQ: Transgender Studies Quarterly* 2 (3): 469–76. https://doi.org/10.1215/23289252-2926437.

White, Melissa Autumn, and Jennifer Musial, eds. 2016. "Belaboured Introductions: Inspired Reflections on the Introductory Course in Gender and Women's Studies." Special issue, *Atlantis: Critical Studies in Gender, Culture and Social Justice* 37.2 (2).

Wiegman, Robyn. 2016. "No Guarantee: Feminism's Academic Affect and Political Fantasy." *Atlantis: Critical Studies in Gender, Culture and Social Justice* 37.2 (2): 83–95. https://journals.msvu.ca/index.php/atlantis/article/view/83-95%20PDF.

PART I

Contending with Accountability

Power and Vulnerability in Higher Education

At the core of many sites of friction, tension, and conflict in the classroom are considerations over the wider conditions of systemic and structural violence and inequality that shape our institutions of higher education, and society more broadly. While the systemic and structural set the stage for many of our encounters with injustice, as well as our complicity within these, manifestations of violence can also be found in the everyday interactions and functions of our institutions. Part I explores the various ways that both students and faculty contend with power in education. From calls for accountability from students, to experiences of vulnerability to systemic, structural, as well as interpersonal harm, the authors in this section attempt to make sense of how we hold ourselves, our colleagues and peers, and our students accountable; and how we respond to student demands for change.

How faculty negotiate power and desire in the classroom can illustrate the limits and possibilities of what happens in education. If we follow the arguments made by critical education scholars, such as Deborah Britzman (1998a, 1998b) and Kevin Kumashiro (2000) (discussed in the introduction), the challenge teachers face is not so much student refusals to learn, but our own (and their own) attachments to ways of knowing. How do our own standpoints and positionalities impact the classroom? And how, in turn, are they impacted by the classroom? Grappling with the contradictions between the pedagogical content of gender and sexuality studies, wherein intersectional approaches highlight the interconnected nature of oppression, the authors in this part discuss the struggle of working for institutional transformation and the failure of the classroom as a space to protect students *and* teachers from harm. Instead, the classroom and higher education more broadly are scenes where students are compelled to mobilize and call for transformation despite institutional barriers and punitive effects of doing this work, and minoritized faculty are overburdened with carrying the weight of this harm through their positionality within institutions of higher education. One such scene can be found in the role placed on students to self-advocate. In one model of education, developing skills around resilience and self-advocacy are seen as beneficial outcomes of higher education; however, critiques of the way institutional harm is upheld by complicity with structures of power that render those most vulnerable responsible for calling for change put into question whether self-advocacy has its own limits.

Meghan Gagliardi's work opens this part by taking up precisely the above concern: What happens when we rely on student empowerment and advocacy for institutional change work? Drawing on her graduate research examining student anti-racism on campus, she provides a damning investigation into the violence done to racialized students through institutional anti-racism work. As Gagliardi makes clear, racialized students are made responsible for leading anti-racism initiatives within higher education precisely because white faculty, staff, and students fail to enact anti-racism within their roles. The conundrum that racialized students face is compounded by the contradiction that emerges between the critical feminist, intersectional, anti-oppressive, and anti-racist pedagogies that are integral to gender and sexuality curriculum, and the institutionalized structure that renders faculty members, departments, administrators, and peers complicit with institutional violence through the status quo of systemic racism, as well as other forms of oppression despite university policies around anti-discrimination or equity, diversity, and inclusion. Gagliardi challenges the assumed power configurations in institutional anti-racism work by interrogating how the implicit reliance on racialized student self-advocacy reinforces institutional white supremacy by relinquishing white faculty, students, and staff from taking responsibility for systemic racism.

Next, Kelly Fritsch's chapter on disability and collective access offers a critique of institutional ableism in higher education. Her chapter outlines the persistent failure of institutions and the people within them to contend with the reality of disability in the classroom beyond institutional accommodations, which renders disabled people as a problem for institutions to manage. She argues instead for a model of access that can "anticipate, welcome, and desire disability in our learning communities" by turning to the collective, reframing our relationship to disability from an inclusive to a transformative model of education. Fritsch's proposal to re-envision access through desire for disability offers a visionary approach to transforming our institutions by rendering the work of access and inclusion a matter that everyone can be implicated in and seek meaning in. Further, her model of collective access through crip culture provides concrete strategies for building inclusive communities in our classrooms and our institutions.

The question of visibility and inclusion continues in the next chapter with Megan Rivers-Moore's work on the growing public presence of sex worker students in higher education. Tracing the shifts around visibility of sex workers on campus, her chapter proposes that we approach the classroom from a place that begins by challenging the foundational assumptions of who constitutes a student by flipping our understanding of sex work as external to the classroom. Instead, her proposition to assume that every classroom has student sex workers can help us integrate a shift in our broader assumptions around the figure of the student in the classroom. Taken together, these three chapters highlight the importance of disrupting our normative assumptions of who is in the classroom and holding ourselves and our institutions accountable to the way systemic and structural harm manifest through the everyday conditions of higher education.

The second half of this part looks more closely at the self-reflective and self-reflexive approaches that open up new ways of thinking about power and vulnerability in the classroom. S. Trimble's[1] work centres on thinking about the embodiment of the gender and sexuality professor—particularly when the professor's body becomes an object of classroom pedagogy, a theme that returns later in Julia Sinclair-Palm's work. Trimble grapples with her own vulnerability in their reflection on their experience of embodiment through student encounters with her gender. Reflecting on their own autobiography in which their disavowal of gendered embodiment became a tool of survival, Trimble examines how disciplinary norms situate faculty differently in front of a classroom. Calling for teachers to render themselves as embodied, Trimble argues for a pedagogical approach that centres rather than disguises vulnerability by making transparent the genealogy of learning that opens us and our students to the risks of learning, "to show how you arrived at your work and how your life experiences shaped—and still shape—your relationship to ideas."

Building on the autobiographic approach, Trimble's chapter is followed by Dan Irving's work on desires for the classroom. Revisiting his own history of desire around learning, he contends with the challenge of recognizing how students and teachers may want different things from the classroom. Learning to listen, Irving introduces ways of reorienting oneself in the classroom by learning through

1. Both gender-neutral and gendered pronouns are used with reference to Trimble, who uses "she/they" pronouns.

desire and pleasure and by grappling with student resistance through understanding how vulnerability and harm might emerge in the classroom. He writes, "regardless of our intentions, when we project our desires onto the classroom as faculty, we threaten to further expose already vulnerable students to violence when we fail to consider the implications around power in the classroom." He offers a model of ecstatic pedagogy as a method for overcoming the risk around harm between teacher and student, and instead reorients the classroom towards an approach that encourages students and teachers alike to follow their passions for learning. This turn to pleasure is echoed in the third part of the book in Nathalie Batraville's chapter on "Kink and Pedagogy."

The part ends with the problem of complicity in Susanne Luhmann's confrontation with the difficult knowledge of learning about one's implication in systems and structures of violence. Critiquing the impulse to innocence that foregrounds much work in critical pedagogies, Luhmann turns to her own history as a learner to uncover the discomfort of learning that she is implicated in systems of power and hierarchy. Introducing a pedagogical approach that centres on implication rather than critique, her chapter provides insight into how we can confront defensive responses in the classroom. She argues, "if recognizing one's oppression and victimization can be painful, learning about and from the oppression and suffering of others can undo students even more." Luhmann offers concrete strategies for how to overcome this classroom challenge by developing approaches that rely on accountability through self-reflection rather than innocence or expertise. Holding room for difficult feelings that emerge through these encounters in learning makes possible more sustained responses to systemic and structural forms of violence. In this way, Luhmann's "pedagogy of implication" provides teachers from across disciplines a way of thinking about our orientation to power and emotion in the classroom that centres on moving past the desire to imagine ourselves as good or innocent.

1

Wielding the "Empowered Student" Narrative

How the Responsibility for Anti-Racism Is Assigned and Denied in Higher Education

MEGHAN GAGLIARDI

Introduction

Universities across Canada are increasingly confronted with the demands of anti-racist and anti-colonial organizers, activists, students, and faculty to address the crises of racism, colonialism, and anti-Blackness in institutions of higher education. Institutional attempts to respond to these demands have accelerated in recent years in response to Indigenous anti-colonial activism surrounding and beyond the publication of the *Final Report of the Truth and Reconciliation Commission of Canada* in 2015 and following international Black Lives Matter organizing up to and since 2020. While universities have long adopted a myriad of initiatives and policies ostensibly designed to promote equity, diversity, and inclusion, the efficacy and purpose of these institutional responses has been questioned by scholars (Ahmed 2012; Dua and Bhanji 2017; hampton 2020; Henry et al. 2017; Walcott 2019). Critical race scholars argue that the "expansion of equity initiatives...not only obscure[s] the ongoing racism in higher education but also help[s] perpetuate the neoliberal university" (Henry et al. 2017, 205). This chapter is concerned with how the responsibility for anti-racism in higher education is assigned, and what these assignments obscure and perpetuate in increasingly neoliberal universities. Through a case study conducted with anti-racist student organizers, I examine a phenomenon that I term the "empowered student narrative," a racialized and racializing narrative that assumes when students encounter racism in the university they are, and should be, responsible for addressing it. I consider how this narrative is wielded in the university to assign the responsibility for anti-racism to student organizers—specifically, to Black, Indigenous, and racialized student organizers—while simultaneously exempting white students and faculty from this same responsibility.

I situate this case study in the neoliberal university through scholarship that describes how higher education is embedded within logics of individualism and privatization. Drawing from Boone Shear and Susan Brin Hyatt, I position "neoliberalism" as a "relatively open signifier" (2017, 7) to capture its "ethos of individualism, colour blindness, metrics, competition, and entrepreneurship" (Henry et al. 2017, 68), whereby neoliberalism and racism interlock in the university to constrain and undermine meaningful anti-racist efforts. Indeed, the co-authors of the *Equity Myth* argue in their concluding chapter that there is "evidence that anti-racism efforts are at best stalled and at worst receding in a climate of neoliberal managerialism, where audits, accountability, austerity measures, and public relations feel-good tactics have outpaced dedication to equity, fairness, inclusiveness, and human rights" (Henry et al. 2017, 298). This receding of meaningful anti-racist work is a dual and sinister effect of neoliberalism in that it justifies the withdrawal of resources from anti-racism work while it "functions to conceal 'the effects of power, politics and racial injustice' (Giroux 2006, 161)" (Henry et al. 2017, 14). As Canadian higher education attempts to respond to institutional racism, I seek to demystify the racialized labour and responsibilities of actors in the university so that our efforts towards anti-racism do not continue to "reify" racist institutions (Ahmed 2007, 157), nor tax already overtaxed racialized students.[1] In this chapter, I ask, if the empowered student narrative is wielded to assign and deny the responsibility for anti-racism, is it possible to redistribute this responsibility to amplify instead of undermine meaningful anti-racist organizing in the university?

I approach this question through ethnographic research conducted between September 2017 to December 2018. During this period, I conducted semi-structured interviews with eleven anti-racist student organizers who designed and coordinated a range of anti-racist projects in one urban Canadian university. These projects represent a number of responses to structural and interpersonal racism in the university, including a collective working towards the creation of a Black studies program; an online platform fostering Black representation in media; a student paper re-establishing an annual race issue; student associations organizing anti-racism workshops in their departments; and working for anti-racist practices in hiring, in the classroom, and on syllabi reform. Participants sought funding from their departments or other institutional bodies, self-funded, or led their projects without funding. Only two research participants were paid by the institution: one former undergraduate student working full-time coordinating a university-wide project addressing inequities in gender and sexualities with an anti-racist lens, and one graduate student working part-time co-coordinating an anti-racist equity project on campus (Gagliardi 2022, 598).

I recruited my research participants through my roles as a full-time graduate student and student organizer, and part-time university staff and paid student coordinator for a university-wide equity project (Gagliardi 2022, 598). My interest and stakes in demystifying

---

1. By "tax" I gesture to the well-documented experiences of Black, Indigenous, and racialized students who encounter and navigate racism and coloniality in their learning environments (see hampton 2020 and Mahtani 2004 for examples). This in itself is a taxing experience, compounded and amplified by the expectation or demand that racialized students then respond to these forms of racism in order to necessarily access spaces of learning.

the university stem from my participation in this environment as a white settler and first-generation student from a working-class family. I designed this project to make better sense of how whiteness has continuously conferred and affirmed my legitimacy in university spaces while I simultaneously navigate its elitism and classism. Through this project, I seek to contribute to the dismantling and complete transformation of higher education, which necessarily targets the neoliberal reproduction of the university's interlocking racist, colonial, and classist foundations in tandem.

This chapter is organized in three parts. I first draw on open-ended interviews with participants to trace the emergence of the empowered student narrative within neoliberal working conditions. I then consider how this narrative is wielded to assign the responsibility for anti-racism to racialized students, while exempting white actors from the same responsibility. Finally, I conclude by reflecting on the stakes of redistributing this responsibility to consider the possibility of meaningful anti-racist work in increasingly neoliberal universities.

Generating the Empowered Student Narrative

I use the empowered student narrative to capture the many overlapping conditions and effects that research participants shared in describing their experiences as anti-racist student organizers in higher education. I employ this narrative as an analytic that can help to make sense of these cumulative descriptions in their neoliberal context. This analytic describes a contemporary phenomenon in the long legacy of effective and subversive student anti-racist organizing in higher education: in the neoliberal university, student organizers are expected to produce the forms of anti-racism they demand from their institutions.

The empowered student narrative is anchored in and perpetuates the assumption that students are responsible for addressing the expressions and enactments of racism that their university claims to seek to redress. During a student union meeting "about race intervention and oppression on campus," research participant A critiqued the student union for asking the students in attendance "What could students do? What do students have to do?" During our interview, A resisted the suggestion that the student union was making that "some students are too scared to approach their professors" and "that's why they don't say anything [about racism in the classroom]." A countered that "it's not that students are shy" to confront professors about racism in the classroom, rather that students recognize the labour and attendant risks of confrontation and thus strategically navigate engagement and disengagement in their learning environments. A argued that the student union "is not going to accomplish much of anything when they just keep circulating that same narrative." This narrative assumes that students have the capacity, resources, and agency to address interpersonal and structural forms of racism and that racism in the university can, and should be, remedied by student action. Students can be empowered agents of change in the university and have demonstrated a significant capacity to transform the institution through anti-racist organizing and work. However, the expectation that students are responsible for this work conceals and perpetuates the power hierarchies that both emerge from and generate racism within the institution. This narrative demonstrates how the responsibility for anti-racism is consigned to students while simultaneously denied and refused elsewhere.

Neoliberal working conditions in higher education play an integral part in the generation and proliferation of the empowered student narrative. Participants described their work as embedded in conditions that dually justified and undermined their anti-racist labour. Participant P was hired to coordinate a project that had been selected from a pool of special project proposals and awarded funding by their institution to address inequities in their university. P explained that the project was dependent on uncompensated student labour from the outset and that the project had also proposed expected deliverables to the granting body within one calendar year. Six months into their one-year contract it became clear that the workload of the project had expanded beyond P's capacity, while the project supervisors became concerned with the promised project deliverables. P proposed the option to split their role into two positions based on the scale of the project; this proposal was rejected. Given the unsustainable working conditions and the organization's refusal to revise the distribution of workload, P left the project. P emphasized how structural issues informed this experience:

> This is less a condemnation of the small organizations funded by student fee-levies[2] and grants and basically bloated with the work of trying to make the university a more equitable place, and more a condemnation of the structural issue of the university outsourcing vital equity work to unpaid, underpaid, and precarious labour contracts…Unlike longer-term paid positions, the contract worker is unsupported, confined by objectives set before there is a clear understanding of the backlog of issues, and then not given the breadth or trust to respond according to what arises. Things have been festering, that's the rush. But it's an unwise approach and there is a crisis of people burning out in these positions as a result.

Research participant X, a graduate student and one of P's former collaborators, discussed how P's experience illustrated the working conditions anti-racist student organizers encounter and navigate more broadly. According to X, unsustainable working conditions are common in institutional anti-racism work and manifest in a number

---

2. Student fee-levies fund student groups through a per-credit fee. On-campus initiatives addressing structural inequities at the university led by fee-levy groups are thus funded by students themselves.

of structural problems, including inflexible deadlines determined without an understanding of the scope of the work and based on the project's precarious funding structure rather than institutional needs; the prioritizing of individualized work and writing over collaboration; the lack of project sustainability, where one person is expected to design and complete a project on a tight timeline; unrealistic expectations of coordinator skills, where just one person is expected to be a supervisor, a financial coordinator, a facilitator, and a consultant; prioritizing "innovation" and results over grounded relationship building; and the lack of investment in process or project longevity. Several other research participants, including P, discussed the problems associated with this lack of investment in project longevity. P argued that "to create such a far-reaching project to be exercised within a timeline of one calendar year, you generate superficial results without structural change." T, a research participant and member of a collective working to establish a Black studies program, described this lack of investment as a strategic temporal orientation, where power holders in the institution will "kind of indulge these initiatives knowing that most of these people are going to graduate in two or three years. So, it's very easy for them to be confident that this will wear out." Because student organizers are impermanent, the university can strategically wait out the anti-racist work that students engage in, or indulge and even exploit student labour without structural commitments of long-term support and investment.

Research participant M, in the context of their anti-racist work for their department, described how this temporal orientation intersects with uncompensated labour to ultimately benefit the institution by exploiting the overworked student: "We do all this work [for free] and there's all this resistance and it's only for [the institution], we leave." Indeed, institutions of higher education rely on and absorb student labour to foster anti-racism, albeit superficially, in lieu of formal institutional efforts, initiatives, and services. This dependence on student labour to address structural racism is part of a devolution of responsibility for anti-racism, while it simultaneously undermines students' efforts towards transformative change. Students are tasked with the work of anti-racism because, unlike the university, students cannot wait out the crises of racism they encounter in their learning environments. Conversely, neoliberal working conditions foster student burnout and project failure while power holders can depend on student impermanence to limit threats of long-term success in the form of financial or structural impacts on the institution. But these assignments do not affect all students equally, and the following section examines how the empowered student is wielded strategically to assign the responsibility for anti-racism predominately to Black, Indigenous, and racialized students.

Assigning the Responsibility for Anti-Racism

Actors and processes that mobilize the empowered student narrative assign the responsibility for anti-racism predominately to racialized students in two ways. First, by demanding that racialized students engage in interpersonal confrontation across power hierarchies entrenched in, exacerbated by, and expressed through racism. Second, by leaving the marginalization of Black, Indigenous, and racialized knowledge production in the university to students from these communities to redress. While working on departmental anti-racism work, Z illustrated the demands made of Black students specifically: "I'm the only Black woman in that program, I'm very used to people interpreting my resting face as angry and hostile and interpreting my shy behavior in certain ways and I'm very much cognizant of how I come off to people as far as attitude goes—or what is perceived as my attitude." When Z would highlight racism, faculty and staff routinely said things like "just stand up for yourself," and thus demand that racialized students self-advocate in the face of institutional and interpersonal forms of racism. Z shared that "it's pretty much a known

known that confrontation does not come off well for the student." The expectation that students engage in interpersonal confrontation in response to structural racism has particularly high risks and violent consequences for Black, as well as Indigenous and racialized, students. In many interviews, students described how faculty, peers, and staff respond to confrontation with hostility and defensiveness, and so racialized students risk these relationships in pursuing anti-racist work and advocacy in the university, which could foreclose institutional access.

Research participant A echoed how the risk of retaliation from faculty members impacts the ostensibly empowered student: "The idea of putting all the power on me as a student to keep speaking up—do you understand the actual labour? Stop with this whole narrative of 'you have power.' I don't...I could submit all of those [accounts of racism in the classroom] to [the student paper] and then get failed." Here A describes how the unequal power relations between professors and students make retaliation a risk for racialized students. Both A and Z describe how the empowered student narrative does not empower racialized students and rather obscures how institutional power hierarchies are embedded in and expressed through intersecting structural and interpersonal racism. The expectation that students confront racism can have serious emotional and psychic impacts on student well-being. For instance, Z described the empowered student experience as "exhausting":

> I want to make these people understand what being there is like for me, but I've realized it's far too much work to get that done and it was really making me unwell. I really fell off my school work and the toxicity of academia was something that I had thought about before but I went through a period where I was like, "Right, it makes perfect sense why academics commit suicide, I totally understand it." And it was just a sad realization that

what I was experiencing was par for the course and how could I ever expect anything else? I became very pessimistic and just checked out eventually.

Z's account parallels research on the experiences of racialized faculty within higher education, and women of colour especially, who document higher instances of mental and physical illness as a result of institutional racism (Dua and Lawrence 2000; Gonzalez and Harris 2014; Mahtani 2004). The legacy of this narrative has lasting and compounding effects on the well-being and careers of scholars historically excluded from academia and may be one reason for the attrition and even absence of racialized students and faculty in higher education.

Turning to this second effect of the empowered student narrative, X described how the responsibility to represent their community in and through their scholarship is specific to racialized students: "My community is not represented in the space so I'm constantly feeling like I'm trying to sneak in people that wouldn't normally be talked about or cared about. And then I'm trying to create new knowledges, and then on top of that they're asking me to justify these knowledges via people who don't acknowledge these people in the first place."

Because X's community is structurally underrepresented in and beyond the university, X works to represent their community through their intellectual labour. Additionally, X described how racialized students are dually tasked with making these representations legible to the university. X argues that this responsibility falls on racialized graduate students, and Black students specifically: "But when you're a racialized person you're coming at it from a very different perspective, an experience of: I need this theory to work. I can't make something that ten people are going to read. Because I come from a community who needs me in the sense that, I am extremely privileged to be where I am and I am the only person out of twenty-five people in this program who is thinking about Black communities in [my city]." This responsibility to perform intellectual labour to address institutional racism at the structural level adds to the workload of students from historically excluded communities, and this additional workload is not shared by their white student peers.

The empowered student narrative assigns Black, Indigenous, and racialized students the responsibility to produce racial justice in the academy through their intellectual labour, while simultaneously navigating hostility from faculty and peers and subsequent risks of retaliation. My findings illustrate that this narrative has an opposite but equally active effect on white actors in the university. By assigning this responsibility to racialized students, white students, faculty, and staff are exempt from the responsibility for anti-racism.

Denying Responsibility: The Active Work of White Actors in the University

The empowered student narrative structures the responsibility for anti-racism in ways that further entrench racial hierarchies within higher education. This process also relinquishes white actors from expectations and demands to undertake anti-racist work, or makes it remarkable and thus rewardable when they do so. During our interview, X described their experiences with white members in their department, who were neither expected nor required to undertake research related to race or racial justice: "If you don't feel like your identity is being attacked, it's not very central to your life, you can do projects on whatever because you're not constantly being questioned as a human being." X described how white faculty and students within higher education avoid responsibility for anti-racism by leaning on the false notion that research topics are neutral choices. Dána-Ain Davis describes this neutralization as a process of "unmarking" by applying Lisa Duggan's examination of neoliberalism to the university context. Davis works through Duggan to explain how "neoliberalism glosses over difference in the interest of having particular political identities fade into the distance and in order to reassert or maintain the power and privilege of people who are ostensibly 'unmarked' (but who actually are marked by virtue of their location in positions of power)" (2017, 164). The effect of the empowered student narrative is that it "unmarks" the multi-scalar processes that generate and circulate these assignments of responsibility. The empowered student narrative perpetuates the misconception that racialized students choose justice-oriented research agendas as a matter of personal preference rather than a necessary response to racism, and that white students and faculty do not likewise actively choose whether or not to undertake anti-racist work or research. Thus, this narrative manifests as an interlocking of neoliberalism and racism to conceal the active decisions of white students, faculty, and power holders in the university to deny responsibility for anti-racism.

Racialized research participants described anti-racism as a responsibility imposed on them in the absence of wider institutional anti-racism, while simultaneously made optional for white scholars. When white students and faculty choose to take on anti-racist work that has not been imposed upon them, this responsibility positions them differently. This difference is described by Lori Patton and Stephanie Bondi as the ability for white actors to "walk away" from anti-racism when it no longer feels beneficial (2015, 507). T observed the ability of white actors to "walk away" when "you can come in and go—you can be an ally but sometimes you don't have to be." Likewise, E, a research participant working on anti-racism in departments through a student association, reflected on how their whiteness facilitated the option to "walk away" or "come in and go" in institutional anti-racism work through procrastination and stepping back:

> I think procrastination was one of the ways that [white guilt] showed up…I did have a tendency to kind of try to put, maybe not more work, but more responsibility of project direction on the people of colour I was working with. Because I was afraid to make decisions and not confident in my capacity to make

decisions. I think that my whiteness was and continues to be a really bizarre factor in all of the work that I was doing...I think I was pushing people in the school to do things that they didn't want do and that was maybe helpful for the dynamics of it not having to be a racialized person pushing all the time—but then again, at some points when I didn't know what I was supposed to be doing I would just back off and not push at all and then leave that for other people to do.

Here, E demonstrates how the option to not push, to "walk away" or to "come in and go" means that white actors may be present in anti-racist work—and even gain social, cultural, and intellectual capital from this engagement—but are not made equally responsible for the work of anti-racism.

The roles and responsibilities of white and racialized actors in the university are co-constituted by a cycle wherein white actors deny this responsibility by actively assigning it to racialized members of the university. E's explanation helps illustrate the wider institutional processes at play in the empowered student narrative, where reliance on the leadership of racialized students assigns responsibility for anti-racism on those who are both historically excluded from and already burdened by the violence of racism. The reliance on empowered students in turn allows institutions of higher education to avoid making formal and consistent institutional commitments to fostering anti-racism.

Conclusions: Redistributing the Responsibility for Anti-Racism

Addressing racial injustice in the neoliberal university requires a redistribution of the assignment of responsibility for anti-racism across every level of higher education—from students to faculty to staff and upper administration. In failing to take on this responsibility, white actors guarantee the preservation and reproduction of institutional racism by relying on the false notion of neutrality when they actively choose not to work on anti-racism. I have argued that the empowered student narrative serves an important and overlooked role in perpetuating institutional racism by unfairly assigning the responsibility of anti-racism to Black, Indigenous, and racialized anti-racist student organizers. This process illustrates the interlocking relationship between neoliberalism and racism in higher education, and actively implicates white students, staff, and faculty by releasing them from the same responsibilities expected of racialized students. There are serious consequences, both at the individual and institutional level, to reinforcing the empowered student narrative. For instance, racialized students carry the undue burden of remedying the legacy of institutional racism in higher education, and in the process their labour is exploited and they become targets of resentment and retaliation by members of their shared environment, they suffer from burnout and face barriers in pursuing careers in higher education. Meanwhile, institutions of higher education remain hostile spaces for racialized people, reinforcing institutional racism through approaches that actively exempt white actors from the labour of anti-racism, and showing only superficial signs of change through nominal efforts to recruit racialized faculty and co-opt and showcase exploited racialized student labour.

The experiences shared by participants in this case study reveal how ostensibly empowered students are tasked with attending to the violence they experience in institutions embedded in racism, while simultaneously working towards racial justice for those around them and those who will follow. Despite the injustice of this responsibility, student organizers accomplish incredible feats with few resources while simultaneously experiencing wider societal racial violence circulating within and beyond the institution. The empowered student narrative is not a story of student empowerment, but a consequence of active decisions within institutions of higher education made by those who are unwilling to take on the labour of anti-racism.

Alternative configurations are possible but require a reorientation of how we understand and enact our interconnected roles in perpetuating the university's racist and neoliberal arrangements.

Taking seriously the anti-racist work of students requires that we intervene in the neoliberal working conditions that undervalue student labour and compromise student organizers' transformative capacity. If we are as serious about racial justice as our institutions increasingly claim to be, we must confront the empowered student narrative as a technique used by white actors to evade responsibility for racism and preserve whiteness and racism by allowing only those student initiatives that are constrained by neoliberal working conditions. To do this, white actors must reckon with how we deny responsibility for anti-racism through procrastination, stepping back, and accepting and preserving conditions in which racialized colleagues, peers, and students are expected to take sole responsibility for producing racial justice in shared spaces of higher education. We must recognize and divest from the ethos of neoliberalism, which justifies the embedding of students' anti-racist work in conditions that guarantee failure and exploitation.

Taking responsibility for racism in higher education requires reorienting the ways we understand and respond to institutional racism in its structural and interpersonal forms at every level of education. Acknowledging how the responsibility for anti-racism is strategically assigned and denied can help us to understand how access, opportunities, and commitments remain racially stratified over time in higher education. Instead of presuming neutrality in the university, students, faculty, and staff can ask themselves the following questions: How does my work contribute to the unmarking of whiteness in the university and the perpetuation of racism? How does my role specifically perpetuate structural and interpersonal forms of racism circulating in my institution and how do I refuse and reorient these effects? How can I materially support and compensate the necessary work of student anti-racist organizers who cannot afford to wait for racial justice?

How can I respond to the demands of anti-racist student organizers in my particular role and scale these responses up without further exploiting racialized student labour? Undoing the empowered student narrative requires reconstituting our active roles in the reproduction of racism by refusing to rely on racialized students to carry the burden of addressing institutional racism, and instead taking responsibility for our interconnected roles as teachers, researchers, administrators, and students to share in anti-racism work. And this task dually demands that we organize ourselves against the exploitative working conditions that continue to facilitate and justify the exploitation of racialized student labour.

References

Ahmed, Sara. 2007. "A Phenomenology of Whiteness." *Feminist Theory* 8 (2): 149–68. https://doi.org/10.1177/1464700107078139.

—. 2012. *On Being Included*. Durham, NC: Duke University Press.

Davis, Dána-Ain. 2017. "Constructing Fear in Academia: Neoliberal Practices at a Public College." In *Learning under Neoliberalism: Ethnographies of Governance in Higher Education*, edited by Susan Brin Hyatt, Boone Shear, and Susan Wright, 151–77. New York: Berghahn Books.

Dua, Enakshi, and Bonita Lawrence. 2000. "Challenging White Hegemony in University Classrooms: Whose Canada Is It?" *Atlantis: Critical Studies in Gender, Culture & Social Justice* 24 (2): 105–22.
https://journals.msvu.ca/index.php/atlantis/article/view/1595/1356.

Dua, Enakshi, and Nael Bhanji. 2017. "Mechanisms to Address Inequities in Canadian Universities." In *The Equity Myth: Racialization and Indigeneity at Canadian Universities*, edited by Frances Henry, Enakshi Dua, Carl E. James, Audrey Kobayashi, Peter Li, Howard Ramos, and Malinda Smith, 206–38. Vancouver: UBC Press.

Duggan, Lisa. 2004. *The Twilight of Equality? Neoliberalism, Cultural Politics, and the Attack on Democracy*. New York: Beacon Press.

Gagliardi, Meghan. 2022. "Counterclaims: Examining and Contesting White Entitlement to the Space of the University through the Labour of Anti-Racist Student Organizers." *Canadian Geographies / Géographies canadiennes* 66 (3): 595–606. https://doi.org/10.1111/cag.12734.

Giroux, Henry A. 2006. *America on the Edge: Henry Giroux on Politics, Culture, and Education*. New York: Palgrave Macmillan.

Gonzalez, Carmen G., and Angela P. Harris. 2014. "Presumed Incompetent: Continuing the Conversation (Part I)." *Berkeley Journal of Gender, Law & Justice* 29 (2): 183–94. http://scholarship.law.berkeley.edu/bglj/vol29/iss2/1.

hampton, rosalind. 2020. *Black Racialization and Resistance at an Elite University.* Toronto: University of Toronto Press.

Henry, Frances, Enakshi Dua, Carl E. James, Audrey Kobayashi, Peter Li, Howard Ramos, and Malinda Smith, eds. 2017. *The Equity Myth: Racialization and Indigeneity at Canadian Universities.* Vancouver: UBC Press.

Mahtani, Minelle. 2004. "Mapping Race and Gender in the Academy: The Experiences of Women of Colour Faculty and Graduate Students in Britain, the US and Canada." *Journal of Geography in Higher Education* 28 (1): 91–99. https://doi.org/10.1080/0309826042000198666.

Patton, Lori, and Stephanie Bondi. 2015. "Nice White Men or Social Justice Allies? Using Critical Race Theory to Examine How White Male Faculty and Administrators Engage in Ally Work." *Race Ethnicity and Education* 18 (4): 488–514. https://digitalcommons.unl.edu/cehsedadfacpub/10/.

Shear, Boone, and Susan Brin Hyatt. 2017. "Higher Education, Engaged Anthropology and Hegemonic Struggle." In *Learning under Neoliberalism: Ethnographies of Governance in Higher Education*, edited by Susan Brin Hyatt, Boone Shear, and Susan Wright, 1–30. New York: Berghahn Books.

Walcott, Rinaldo. 2019. "The End of Diversity." *Public Culture* 31 (2): 393–408. https://doi.org/10.1215/08992363-7286885.

2

Desiring Disability in Our Learning Communities

Fostering a Crip Culture of Access

KELLY FRITSCH

Our university classrooms include disabled, chronically ill, neurodivergent, and mad students and teachers, many of whom are multiply marginalized. Yet, all too often, our course syllabi, classroom spaces, teaching practices, institutional policies, and collegial relations continue to anticipate and privilege nondisabled instructors, teaching assistants, support staff, and students. Anticipating our learning communities to be nondisabled, or in only expecting disability to appear and be contained in institutionally sanctioned ways, ignores not only the many ways ableism and saneism function in higher education institutions but also elides the promise of desiring disability in our learning communities, a desire that can radically transform our communities, institutions, and pedagogical practices for the better. Even though one in five Canadians aged fifteen years or older identify as having a disability (Morris et al. 2018), I continue to witness at all levels across the Canadian university sector how higher education institutions render disabled people as unexpected and anomalous community members.

In this chapter, I reflect on the need to anticipate, welcome, and desire disability in our learning communities as an opportunity to counter the structural ableism embedded within contemporary academia. Drawing on practices of collective access and accessibility grounded in crip theory, disability justice, and disability culture that push against the barriers inherent to individualistic forms of medicalized accommodation and inclusion, I engage with examples of academic ableism, forced intimacy, access fatigue, and inaccessibility in the university. Bringing together my own experiences as a visibly disabled white settler professor, teaching, supervising, and mentoring disabled and nondisabled students in inaccessible and ableist institutions alongside the scholarly literature examining the complex of ableism in higher education, I suggest some ways to foster a crip culture of access across our campuses. Crip culture expresses the defiance and pride of politicized disabled people who push back against ableism, seeking not to become assimilated or made the same as nondisabled people. To crip is to welcome how disability culture and politics disrupts ableist social relations and normative ways of being and doing things, sparking new ways to transform how we engage with each other, impacting our pedagogical practices, collegial and administrative relations, as well as the design of our shared spaces.

Academic Ableism and Access Fatigue

Despite claims to accessibility and inclusion, I would not describe any of the institutions I have worked at as outstandingly accessible. Although the barriers I have encountered have not been uniform nor static across institutions, as I moved from being a student to becoming faculty, new encounters with the inaccessibility of the university have become apparent to me. For example, none of the classrooms I have been scheduled to teach in have been fully accessible to me. Often, if there are accessible features in a classroom, they are designed to take into consideration the presence of a disabled student but not that of a disabled instructor. As a wheelchair user, I have been scheduled to teach in a room that had stairs leading up to the lecture podium and technology controls. This room was designated by the scheduling system as accessible because there was a specific place for a student wheelchair user to sit in the room and an accessible pathway leading to that spot. Frequently, there is heavy furniture blocking my access to parts of the classroom. In most rooms, the controls for the lighting or classroom technology (computer, projector, projection screen, etc.) have not been easy to access from a seated position. Seminar rooms intended for discussion-based small classes are often too small to comfortably facilitate one or more user of assistive devices such as walkers, wheelchairs, or scooters; nor do these rooms easily welcome one or more service and support animal.

Across campus, I have had to wait for someone to pass by in order to ask them to open a heavy door that either did not have an automated button, had a broken button, or as happens all too often, has a working button but the power switch for the button (usually located at the top of the door) had been turned off. I have had to learn circuitous routes to classrooms or offices because the direct route involved a flight of stairs, out-of-service elevators, or navigating multiple heavy doors. I've missed teaching a class because the only elevator in the building was out of service. In another instance, I had to be carried down a flight of stairs when that very same elevator went out of service while I was teaching and no technicians were available to repair it in a timely way. In my current position, I waited over a year until I was able to locate the right person to talk to on campus to address bathroom access; there was only one bathroom on campus that was accessible to me. During that period, I spent a significant amount of time waiting outside of this busy bathroom to use it and came to learn that it was a popular destination for students (and occasionally also staff and other faculty members) to take time to themselves, talk on the phone, eat lunch, use drugs, change clothes, do hair and make-up, or, as happened on more than one occasion, have sex. Clearly, there are insufficient spaces on campus for community members to do what they need or want to do, and there are also insufficient all-gender accessible bathrooms, making this bathroom particularly in high demand. Access intersects with many other important social inequity issues.

To simply do my job has involved the "forced intimacy" of disclosing and discussing all these experiences (and more) with multiple people at different levels of the university, often multiple times. Disability justice activist Mia Mingus (2017) uses the term "forced intimacy" to describe the ways disabled people have to "share personal parts of ourselves to survive an ableist world." To simply gain basic forms of access can require not only emotional labour and vulnerability by sharing intimate details about our bodily abilities and needs, but can also include forced physical intimacy when needing physical help in inaccessible settings. "Forced intimacy" Mingus writes, "is a cornerstone of how ableism functions in able bodied supremacist world...We are the ones who must be vulnerable—whether we want to or not—about ourselves, our bodyminds and our abilities." Because some accessibility needs were not well anticipated before my arrival, forced intimacy has been a requirement for getting some of my basic needs met. Access-related email threads span months and years, and many issues remain unresolved. The requirement of disclosure, and anticipation of the many conversations and emails that will follow, make me reluctant to start the process of getting access. At times, when I can already anticipate that there is no easy solution to solve a complex access issue, it does not seem worth pursuing. Some scholars have referred to this kind of work as "access fatigue" (Konrad 2021), because documenting barriers and finding solutions is significant additional labour added onto our everyday workload.

As Annika Konrad spells out, disabled people "are often encouraged to advocate for their own access without consideration for the mental and emotional labor required to do so" (2021, 180). Access fatigue, Konrad argues, "reveals how a lack of familiarity with disability and practices of accessibility places pressures on disabled people to teach others how to participate in access" (183), naming "the everyday pattern of constantly needing to help others participate in access, a demand so taxing and so relentless that, at times, it makes access simply not worth the effort" (180). Access fatigue exposes the underlying assumption that disabled people "automatically or instinctively know how to—or always want to—advocate for their own access" (180). As Adam Hubrig and Ruth Osorio comment, "access requires vulnerability, the vulnerability of disclosing, of asking for help, and of exposing embodied needs and/or traumas...The ability to be vulnerable (especially in professional spaces) is a function of positionality, privilege, and power" for which "not all folks can ask for help in straightforward ways or at all" (2020, 93). Seeking access demands navigating power relationships and often entails "managing how other people feel about disability" (Konrad 2021, 184), including "making disability and inaccessibility 'okay' for other people" by "performing a disabled self that helps others feel more at ease" (187).

Navigating how nondisabled people feel about disability can be tricky business given that higher education is structured by what Jay Dolmage refers to as "academic ableism," which mandates compulsory "able-bodiedness and able-mindedness, as well as other forms of social and communicative hyperability" (2017, 7). As Rebecca-Eli Long and Albert Stabler note, this positions disability "as the inverse of higher education and incompatible with its logics" (2022, 289). Like other institutions, education is also foundationally built on ableism, saneism, and disability oppression, which are "historically interwoven with white supremacy, settler colonialism, capitalism, [and cis] heteropatriarchy" (Shelton 2020, 194). Academic ableism is thus informed by ubiquitous conceptions of "normality, intelligence, excellence, desirability, and productivity," which "are deeply rooted in anti-Blackness, eugenics, misogyny, colonialism, imperialism, and capitalism" (Lewis 2021).

The barriers I have encountered in academia are by no means unique (or even the worst of it), and there is a significant body of literature documenting the many ways academic ableism is experienced and reproduced in higher education. I draw attention to my experiences not to single out any particular university I have attended or worked at, but because higher education all too often deems accessibility relevant only when there is an individual request for accommodation, and more often than not considers access as falling under the purview of individual disabled people, disability studies programs, or the student accommodation centre (if there is one). Yet, as Long and Stabler note, academic ableism is not an individual experience but "part of a broader complex of ableism," suggesting that to "examine academic ableism, many disabled scholars have offered their own personal experiences as testimonials to experiences that are often overlooked...Rather than just serving as memoir or reflection, writing about experiences of disability in higher education helps other disabled people understand their own experiences as part of a broader complex of ableism" (2022, 289). This broader "complex of ableism" has been traced by Margaret Price in a study of disabled faculty, which found that "disabled faculty members often seem to inhabit a different reality than their nondisabled colleagues" (2021, 263). Disabled faculty members are asked "how badly they actually need the requested accommodation" (266), illuminating how the individualized institutional requirement "to assert and reassert access needs becomes a kind of repetitive stress injury" (272). Institutional accommodation processes also frequently require disability "to be constant and certain" (270), despite the fact that disability and access needs are often experienced as relational, shifting, or unstable. Once articulated, implementing access "may take a long time to put in place" (265) and "when processes move slowly, academic workers experience material costs," including "paying for one's own accommodations, giving up research and creative opportunities, or even having to leave one's job" (264).

Stigma also contributes to a broader complex of ableism. Researchers at the US-based National Center for College Students with Disabilities found that "even after addressing physical and structural barriers, the campus environment may be inhospitable for students, faculty, and staff with disabilities due to ableist attitudes about disability, as well as curricular, programmatic, and policy barriers" (Harbour and Greenberg 2017, 4). Long and Stabler note that shame and stigma may stop those with less visibly apparent disabilities from disclosing. As one professor in their study noted, "I go to great lengths to make sure that my colleagues do not know about my disability. They are generally hostile to students with disabilities, so I am certain they would be uncomfortable with a colleague who has accommodations" (2022, 303).

Stigma and ableism are not limited to collegial relations, of course, but also extend into classroom dynamics as well as graduate supervision. For example, Long and Stabler recount the ableist attitudes students experienced, including professors telling disabled students that their disability and access needs are "an 'exaggeration'" (2022, 303). In my own experience as a faculty member, I have witnessed colleagues respond to student writing by telling students they are "terrible writers." Highlighting grammatical errors in draft writing and requiring that students manually "fix the errors" to "learn from their mistakes" places disabled students, such as those who use voice recognition software, in a burdensome situation, since even if software can be used to edit grammar in a text, it is difficult and time consuming. I have had students ask me, "How do I get my access needs met when professors refuse to recognize my needs?" This refusal to recognize students' needs is especially punishing when professors mistakenly assume students already have their access needs met by university services.

Many of the actors involved in higher education understand accessibility as a narrowly defined individual right to accommodation that can be operationalized via a technical checklist that is institutionally standardized and resourced. The existence of the checklist, and often wrongly assumed accompanying institutional resources, leads people to believe that access is an issue that has already been resolved or is already being taken care of with nothing more that needs to be done or changed. As disability studies scholar Tanya Titchkosky (2011) notes in her research on access at her inaccessible university campus, people saw the international wheelchair access symbol appear on signs around campus and thus assumed that the university must already be accessible. As Konrad asserts, "in the public imagination, access is largely a procedural matter—one that happens by procuring resources for qualified individuals in the appropriate times and places" (2021, 181). While standardized institutional accommodations such as receiving increased time to complete exams, having access to classroom note takers, ensuring accurate captions on media, making PDFs screen-reader accessible, providing visual descriptions of images, or having access to ASL interpretation can all be crucial to creating a baseline of institutional access, such forms of inclusion operate as a way of including disabled people into the structures as they already are, eliding the transformative potential of disability and accessibility to subvert ableist relations. As Desiree Valentine puts it, "too often in practice rights-based frameworks fall short of the radical transformative potential of disability activism by allowing legalistic, accommodationist inclusion to be its pinnacle achievement. Such accommodationist inclusion allows for change only insofar as the central structures and values of society are maintained. For example, independence remains valorized and so 'access' amounts to disabled individuals independently accessing those spaces that non-disabled individuals can now access" (2020, 79). Focusing on individual inclusion rather than radical alteration "assumes independence as a condition of equality and then presumes equality as a matter of sameness, thus leaving intact fundamental pillars of an ableist society" (79).

Disabled people "know that they have the right to access, in principle and in law, but that they must work, continuously, in order to claim this right...[This] invisible work is, at heart, the high cost of living in a disabling world," disability studies scholar Jan Grue (2021) writes. "The question is never simply 'Am I being discriminated against?' In practice, it is also 'How much of my invisible work can reasonably be shifted on to society?'" This is no small challenge as the scholarly literature shows again and again that in an ableist world, anticipating disabled people in our communities and providing even basic forms of accessibility are frequently deemed unreasonable. In part, this unreasonableness stems from the way access as a right is understood within a "vertical framework" where "access is given by someone with more power to someone with less power" (Hubrig and Osorio 2020, 92). This approach can erase the relational aspects of accessibility, "and flatten disability into an individual legal and medical problem" (Long and Stabler 2022, 306–307). As Valentine outlines, rights-based accommodationist accessibility frameworks "ultimately fail to envision the depths of transformation necessary to address our current ableist world" (2020, 77). Documenting academic ableism and access fatigue is one way to "to identify the habits and structures that need to change to support more inclusive public life" (Konrad 2021, 185). To further enact the kind of change necessary to counteract the habits and structures that sustain ableism requires building on the baseline of accommodation and individual rights to foster a crip culture of access informed by disability justice practices and disability culture, as well as crip and mad social theory.

Fostering a Crip Culture of Access

In *Care Work: Dreaming Disability Justice*, Leah Lakshmi Piepzna-Samarasinha asks, What would it mean to "shift our ideas of access" away from "an individual chore" towards "a collective responsibility that's maybe even deeply joyful" (2018, 33)? Expansive access practices can create new epistemologies and ontologies, including innovative pedagogical and aesthetic practices as well as theoretical articulations that have the power to radically transform the ways we do things and how we engage with each other, making access, as disabled artist Alice Sheppard puts it, "a creative force" (quoted in Whalen and Krieger

2021). Reorienting the question of access away from accommodation can expand beyond the predetermined checklist towards access as a creative force of togetherness. As Valentine notes, "If our social world is not comprised of individuals conceived of as bounded units for accessibility programs to 'bring into' its existing organization, then accessibility can be expanded to include attention to some of the most fundamental elements of our ways of living, acting, and being. Accessibility would thus be about intervention at the level of our sedimented patterns of relating and belonging" (2020, 77). Access can be continually re-created in the pursuit of togetherness. Approaching access as a form of relational togetherness renders institutional standardized accommodations and technical access checklists as crucial to create a baseline of togetherness but not an end in itself. Access is not an "isolated *thing* or *event*. It is not about what one person or institution can do for another person but involves an ongoing, interpersonal process of relating and taking responsibility for our inevitable encroachment on each other" (Valentine 2020, 78). As Titchkosky suggests, "access leads us to ask how access can be an interpretative move that puts people into different kinds of relations with their surroundings" (2011, 13), where such relations with our surroundings can include human and more-than-human obligations, responsibilities, and accountability towards people, communities, and environments. Access can both enable togetherness and can be kind of attack on ableist social relations, disrupting naturalized ableist ways of doing things (Fritsch 2016).

Because of the myriad ways ableism is entrenched within our social structures and institutions, the access needs of disabled people can seem to be an overwhelming encroachment on naturalized ways of teaching, learning, relating, and belonging. Working to undo this naturalization at all levels of higher education—from our pedagogical practices to collegial and administrative relations, to the design of our shared spaces—is the work of cripping academic ableism, of undoing ableism, and of opening ourselves up to welcoming, anticipating, and desiring disability as part of our communities. To crip is to open up desire for how and what disability disrupts; for example, the ways disability disrupts the naturalization of academic forms of productivity, meritocracy, or what counts as effective communication. In denaturalizing normative ableist social relations, crip cultural practices of access emphasize relations of togetherness, how we move, learn, and collaborate together, informed largely by the disability justice principle of collective access.

Over the last twenty years, disability justice has shaped social movements and scholarship across North America and beyond. Emerging out of conversations and collective access making practices happening within social movement spaces and disability arts communities in the early 2000s, and led by disabled people of colour and queer and trans disabled people, disability justice emphasizes disability as a political and creative transformative force in the world. Built on the ten core disability justice principles popularized by theorists and social movement builders such as Mia Mingus (2014, 2017, 2018), Leah Lakshmi Piepzna-Samarasinha (2018), Patty Berne, and US-based disability performance group Sins Invalid (2016), disability justice includes collective access and emphasizes social, political, economic, and infrastructural transformations that centre the flourishing of diversely embodied people in design and implementation. Much of this work makes important linkages across movements, emphasizing how, for example, disability and accessibility are deeply entangled with issues related to policing, prisons, institutionalization, pathologization, deviance, and criminalization.

Collective Access Practices for the Classroom

Collective access deindividualizes access needs, emphasizing the shared responsibility of creating access and the ways our capacities function differently in various contexts. This work begins with becoming aware of our own access needs and communicating what resources and capacities we have for meeting the access needs of others; collective access is relational and requires our interdependence. It may not be possible to enact access in all forms needed because of a lack of resources, insufficient help, or material barriers that cannot be quickly or easily changed, such as the design of a classroom. However, communicating our needs, capacities, and limits can contribute toward building collective strategies that can include working together for longer-term changes or finding creative ways to negotiate around barriers. For example, in one classroom where several physical barriers were present as a wheelchair user, I invited students to participate in collective access measures such as turning on and off the light switches, or rearranging tables and chairs. Rather than frame this as benevolent volunteer work, these access practices became part of a whole suite of actions that counted as a valid way for students to earn class participation marks. In this situation, students who had shied away from oral participation in the class came to feel more comfortable and connected to the classroom community by having their contributions recognized as important aspects of our togetherness.

Another way of simultaneously building community and collective access has been through creating a shared Google doc for students to contribute crowdsourced lecture notes, which also counts as a form of participation. Collective access in the classroom can also look like deciding to end class early so that everyone has a break before their next class or meeting; providing nonpunitive flexible deadlines for the submission of work; the ability for students to receive extensions without requiring specific reasons or documentation; options for hybrid or online participation; or including multimodal alternative assignment or course readings formats. Collective access practices can model that there is no shame in having access needs, that we are all implicated in creating access to be together, and that medicalized documentation is not required to get what we need. We can ask for what we need to be together without the forced intimacy of needing to disclose too much, and we can also expect that our needs for being together will change because access needs are not static.

Collective access is also enacted with the practice of incorporating audio description for visual images, such as describing images used in lecture slides. Not only does describing images provide better access for classroom participants who may be blind, visually impaired, or who otherwise have difficulty cognitively processing visual materials, but it also opens a unique opportunity to engage with students. Pausing lecture to ask students to describe an image gives classroom participants a moment to think critically and reflexively about what they see and how they see and invites the instructor to likewise think critically and reflexively about which images are used and how they relate to the material presented.

Practicing collective access can also help us learn to navigate access frictions, when one or more access needs of togetherness conflict or requires creative responses. For example, Remi Yergeau et al. (2013) note that there is "no such thing as a text that meets everyone's needs." However, "to say that no text will be universally accessible is not a justification for failing to consider what audiences are invited into and imagined as part of a text. It matters who reads, it matters who engages, and it matters who is conceptualized as a reader" (Yergeau et al. 2013). While no text may be universally accessible to all, instructors can work towards including a wide variety of styles and formats of writing, prioritize texts that have alternative formats available (such an audiobook version) as well as incorporate multimodal sources of knowledge such as podcasts, graphic novels, or documentary films.

Engaging a crip culture of access can also help us push back against the neoliberal and ableist expectations of quick thinking, hyperproductivity, overwork, and hurried scholarly production. Such expectations not only foster negative health effects but can also exclude disabled people who are not able to sustain such intense demands or who experience brain fog, chronic illness, or debilitating pain at unpredictable intervals (Lau 2019; Helms, Kirby, and Merrill 2022). As Travis Lau notes, academia's "culture of speed individualizes failure as a student's inability to do good work...Students frequently internalize the struggle to 'keep up' in fear of being seen as less capable or unfit for the profession by mentors or peers" (2019, 15–16). Instead, we can collectively work towards mitigating fatigue and overwork by building rest breaks into our syllabi, reducing the required number of readings and assignments, providing multimodal choices in activities, assignments, and forms of participation, and being flexible about deadlines.

Collective access supports the building of a crip culture of access that is grounded in disability culture, disability justice principles, and crip social theory. Such a culture can be transformative in approaching access as "dynamic, relational, intersectional, and political" (Hubrig and Osorio 2020, 91), such that it goes "beyond ensuring individuals can enter a space" to "also cultivate intimacy and love" (93) for disabled people that can be world building and transformative. As Mingus (2018) describes, the world remaking powers of access as love can move us beyond inclusion: "Access for the sake of access is not necessarily liberatory, but access for the sake of connection, justice, community, love and liberation is. We can use access as a tool to transform the broader conditions we live in, to transform the conditions that created that inaccessibility in the first place. Access can be a tool to challenge ableism, ablebodied supremacy, independence and exclusion." "Access can bring people together and move them toward liberation," Hubrig and Osorio (2020, 93) write. "But for that liberation to occur, disabled scholars need to feel safe in communicating their access needs to the community" (93). For Konrad, such liberation can be fostered by intentionally creating openings for "inviting engagement with difference, embracing unfamiliar relationality, exercising a notion of agency that includes disability and use of assistive technology, and uptake and transfer of access-oriented practices from one situation to another" (2021, 196).

Broad structural and systemic changes are desperately needed across higher education to dismantle ableism and better anticipate and address the needs of disabled, chronically ill, neurodivergent, and mad students and teachers. While we work towards long-term transformation, we can also begin fostering a crip culture of access immediately in our collegial relations, classroom policies, course structure, forms of grading, and ways of participating and communicating.

References

Dolmage, Jay T. 2017. *Academic Ableism: Disability and Higher Education.* Ann Arbor: University of Michigan Press.

Fritsch, Kelly. 2016. "Accessible." In *Keywords for Radicals: The Contested Vocabulary of Late Capitalist Struggle*, edited by Kelly Fritsch, Clare O'Connor, and AK Thompson, 23–28. Chico, CA: AK Press.

Grue, Jan. 2021. "The High Cost of Living in a Disabling World." *The Guardian*, November 4, 2021. https://www.theguardian.com/society/2021/nov/04/the-high-cost-of-living-in-a-disabling-world.

Harbour, Wendy S., and Daniel Greenberg. 2017. "Campus Climate and Students with Disabilities." *NCCSD Research Brief* 1, no. 2 (July). https://files.eric.ed.gov/fulltext/ED577464.pdf.

Helms, Nic, Cait Kirby, and Asia Merrill. 2022. "Designing for Fatigue." *Hybrid Pedagogy*. January 27, 2022. https://hybridpedagogy.org/designing-for-fatigue/.

Hubrig, Adam, and Ruth Osorio. 2020. "Enacting a Culture of Access in Our Conference Spaces." *College Composition and Communication* 72 (1): 87–117. https://doi.org/10.58680/ccc202030892.

Konrad, Annika M. 2021. "Access Fatigue: The Rhetorical Work of Disability in Everyday Life." *College English* 83 (3): 179–99. https://doi.org/10.58680/ce202131093.

Lau, Travis Chi Wing. 2019. "Slowness, Disability, and Academic Productivity: The Need to Rethink Academic Culture." In *Disability and the University: A Disabled Students' Manifesto*, edited by Christopher McMaster and Benjamin Whitburn, 11–19. New York: Peter Lang.

Lewis, Talila A. 2021. "Working Definition of Ableism." *Talila A. Lewis* (blog). January 1, 2021. https://www.talilalewis.com/blog/january-2021-working-definition-of-ableism.

Long, Rebecca-Eli M., and Albert Stabler. 2022. "'This Is NOT Okay:' Building a Creative Collective against Academic Ableism." *Journal of Curriculum and Pedagogy* 19 (4): 288–314. https://doi.org/10.1080/15505170.2021.1926374.

Mingus, Mia. 2014. "Reflection toward Practice: Some Questions on Disability Justice." In *Criptiques*, edited by Caitlin Wood, 107–14. N.p.: May Day Publishing.

—— 2017. "Forced Intimacy: An Ableist Norm." *Leaving Evidence* (blog). August 6, 2017. https://leavingevidence.wordpress.com/2017/08/06/forced-intimacy-an-ableist-norm/.

—— 2018. "'Disability Justice' Is Simply Another Term for Love." Opening keynote speech presented at 2018 Disability Intersectionality Summit, Cambridge, MA. *Leaving Evidence* (blog). November 3, 2018. https://leavingevidence.wordpress.com/2018/11/03/disability-justice-is-simply-another-term-for-love/.

Morris, Stuart, Gail Fawcett, Laurent Brisebois, and Jeffrey Hughes. 2018. "A Demographic, Employment and Income Profile of Canadians with Disabilities Aged 15 Years and Over, 2017." Statistics Canada, November 28, 2018. https://publications.gc.ca/collections/collection_2018/statcan/89-654-x/89-654-x2018002-eng.pdf.

Piepzna-Samarasinha, Leah Lakshmi. 2018. *Care Work: Dreaming Disability Justice*. Vancouver: Arsenal Pulp Press.

Price, Margaret. 2021. "Time Harms: Disabled Faculty Navigating the Accommodations Loop." *South Atlantic Quarterly* 120 (2): 257–77. https://doi.org/10.1215/00382876-8915966.

Shelton, Samuel Z. 2020. "Disability Justice, White Supremacy, and Harm Reduction Pedagogy: Enacting Anti-Racist Crip Teaching." *Journal Committed to Social Change on Race and Ethnicity* 6 (1): 191–208. https://www.jstor.org/stable/48644516.

Sins Invalid. 2016. *Skin, Tooth, and Bone: The Basis of Movement Is Our People: A Disability Justice Primer*. N.p.: Sins Invalid.

Titchkosky, Tanya. 2011. *The Question of Access: Disability, Space, Meaning*. Toronto: University of Toronto Press.

Valentine, Desiree. 2020. "Shifting the Weight of Inaccessibility: Access Intimacy as a Critical Phenomenological Ethos." *Puncta* 3 (2): 76–94. https://doi.org/10.5399/PJCP.v3i2.9

Whalen, Kelly, and Isara Krieger. 2021. "Kinetic Light Dancers Take Disability Arts to New Heights." *KQED*, November 3, 2021. https://www.kqed.org/arts/13905452/kinetic-light.

Yergeau, Remi, Elizabeth Brewer, Stephanie Kerschbaum, Sushil K. Oswal, Margaret Price, Cynthia L. Selfe, Michael J. Salvo, and Franny Howes. 2013. "Multimodality in Motion: Disability & Kairotic Spaces." *Kairos* 18 (1). https://kairos.technorhetoric.net/18.1/coverweb/yergeau-et-al/pages/access.html.

3

"Hi Professor, Am I a Sex Worker?"
Adapting to the Shifting Culture around Sex Work in Higher Education

MEGAN RIVERS-MOORE

Jeremy showed up to my office hours today, with this question: "Am I a sex worker?"

He proceeded to tell me that my class from the week before when we had discussed the multiplicity of work arrangements that exist in the sex industry had shaken him: "I texted my buddy after class and said 'dude, are we sex workers?' and we've been texting back and forth ever since. We think we probably are, even though we never thought about it that way before." Jeremy told me about his participation in a niche activity involving nudity and cash remuneration that I had never heard of (and made a note to look up later). He was genuinely interested in talking through how we define sex work, what it would mean for him to identify as a sex worker, and how the label might change, or not change, the way he understood this particular income-generating activity. This was a first for office hours. But we're only three weeks into the term and I've already had two students come out in the classroom as sex workers, and now this conversation with Jeremy.

—Teaching notes, Winter 2020

In reflecting on the ways that teaching sex work has changed over time, this chapter examines how adaptation and flexibility in our approaches to teaching can help us respond to the shifting cultural contexts we find ourselves facing in higher education today. Drawing on my first attempts to engage students around the topic of sex work in 2009 during a gig as a contract instructor at the University of Costa Rica, a sexuality studies course taught at the University of Toronto during a postdoctoral fellowship in 2011, and then finally to many years of teaching a course specifically focused on sex work as a tenure-track and then tenured professor at Carleton University, I consider how student reactions and their openness to engaging in discussions about sex work have changed significantly, and how these changes might connect to the wider political economy of sex work. Given the important change that has come with the increasing presence of sex workers in the university, we cannot assume that sex workers are external to higher education. This chapter looks at how shifts in sex work research reach education, and how teaching can adapt to shifting cultures both inside and outside the classroom. Since students at all levels of higher education may be sex workers, this chapter proposes that we rethink our classrooms as spaces where sex work may be the norm, rather than the exception, in the lives of our students and proposes ways of adapting our teaching to this context.

I did my PhD in the UK and was distinctly aware that I had received significantly less teaching training and experience than my colleagues who had done PhDs in North America. As a result, I started the habit of taking notes about teaching immediately after each class, and when something of particular interest happened (like the above conversation with Jeremy), in the interest of trying to make sense of what was working and not working. Sometimes the notes are short and quick ("never use this reading again"), and sometimes they are longer considerations of particular dynamics or moments. I will draw on these notes throughout this chapter, changing any details that could make students identifiable. Given the shifts and changes in how students respond to sex work and how sex work is talked about and represented in public, I have found it useful to return to my teaching notes as a pedagogical method, allowing me to trace more clearly how different, and more productive, kinds of framing of the issues can be adapted in my pedagogy than when I first started teaching. Our pedagogy must be flexible enough to adapt to changes in the student body and the political climate. In *Pedagogies of Crossing*, Jacqui Alexander writes that "we need to become fluent in each other's histories" (2005, 269). The classroom is not a comfortable place, and that is now something I address directly with students at the beginning of each term, in every class I teach. Learning is difficult and sometimes it hurts, but becoming fluent in each other's histories is necessary work and can be deeply rewarding. Finding and transforming ourselves, understanding our connections to each other and the world, is also a joyful experience.

(Sex) Workers in the Classroom

When I first taught my course specifically on sex work at Carleton, it was small. Some students shared that they were taking the course to better understand the industry and the experiences of people working as sex workers, especially when these were students' friends. That first year, I very deliberately did not invite any sex workers to speak to the class. I was still trying to think through how to find a balance between the importance of centring the voices of sex workers and not fetishizing them. The size of the class later tripled and then quadrupled when I changed the name from "Feminist Studies of the Sex Industry" to "Sex for Sale." With each passing year, I found more and more students wanting to talk about selling sex. At first, I wondered whether students were drawn to the topic because of its explicit nature. It reminded me of Elizabeth Bernstein's (2018) argument about young evangelicals in the United States who were attracted to work on sex trafficking because it allowed them some proximity to a risqué topic, without becoming contaminated by it. Was this just a way for young people to rub up against sex work without experiencing any stigma? It may be partly that, but this explanation did not properly account for the rapid increase in student interest in this topic. Instead, I speculate that the reason may be connected to the increasing visibility that comes from the cultural shifts that make sex work a more present part of life on campus and the experiences students share as sex workers in our classrooms.

Research has demonstrated that more and more students are sex workers, and sex workers are students. Even as early as 2007, Bernstein identified the growing middle-class presence in sex work through a trend of white, relatively class privileged, university-educated men and women moving into more upscale sectors of the industry. This kind of sex work often involves providing specialized services such as tantric sex (a slow, meditative, and healing practice) and the girlfriend experience (sexual-economic exchange that includes more intimate activities typically associated with courtship, like kissing). The increasing cost of university education, higher student loan debts, and the privatization of those costs to families, along with reduced public funding for education, has led many students to seek out comparatively high paying but flexible work options, which often include sex work (Brents and Sanders 2010; Gbagbo and Gbagbo 2021; Roberts, Jones, and Sanders 2013; Sanders and Hardy 2015). Sex work may also be a more viable form of work for students because of online options ranging from websites designed to connect workers and clients, like Seeking Arrangements, to spaces that facilitate digital connections, like Only Fans and various cam sites. This increasing access to platforms that can facilitate sex work in recent years has also been accompanied by journalistic fascination (and often handwringing) about this phenomenon (Miller 2011; Motyl 2013; Nayar 2017).

While the academic literature focused on student sex work is still relatively small, research to date shows that students largely move into sex work out of economic necessity (Ernst et al. 2021; Roberts, Bergström, and La Rooy 2007; Roberts et al. 2010; Roberts, Jones, and Sanders 2013). This is, of course, the same reason that virtually all of our students now work full-time or part-time while also attending university. The appeal of sex work, as Teela Sanders and Kate Hardy

(2015) demonstrate in their study of student dancers, is that participants can maintain a steady income and still have enough flexibility to get to class. While much of this literature comes from the UK, small scale studies in Canada (Hammond 2019; Lavoie et al. 2010; Sinacore and Lech 2011; Sinacore et al. 2014) and Australia (Lantz 2005; Simpson and S. Smith 2019; Simpson and C. Smith 2021) present similar conclusions. It is worth noting Emily Hammond's (2019) important finding that despite the fact that sex work's flexibility remains appealing to students, her interviewees described having to rely on sex work along with other sources of income generation because the earnings from sex work were too irregular to rely on. More research is needed to determine if this is a widespread phenomenon, and what the causes and consequences might be.

Over the last decade of teaching, I have seen a shift in how students self-disclose their status as sex workers. At first privately in office hours, students now increasingly come out in front of everyone in a class as large as 150 students. Student sex workers participate in a range of sex industry activities, including working as escorts, burlesque dancers, and on cam sites. I often start the semester by doing a brainstorm with the class of all the different kinds of sex work that exist. I invite students to explain the various parts of the industry to me to help break the ice on a topic that can be deeply personal for some of the students in the class. Although my expertise on this topic means that I often know more about sex work than most of the students entering the class, my students have sometimes introduced me to new sex work spaces and variations that weren't yet on my radar. When disclosures happen in my class, no matter how nonchalant or comfortable my students who identify as sex workers seem when they self-identify, I always make a point to check in with them after class, to make sure they are feeling okay about having disclosed. Despite the evidence that a growing number of students participate in sex work, universities typically don't have policies to acknowledge or protect students who are sex workers, and our institutions largely fail to offer any kind of services that are specific to the needs of sex workers, such as access to emergency funds when irregular income is lost, or sex-work-informed counselling. Further, institutions of higher education do not make any efforts to combat the stigma that student sex workers might encounter when accessing existing student campus services (Cusick, Roberts, and Paton 2009; Hammond 2019; Sagar et al. 2015). Indeed, studies demonstrate that universities seem to be mainly concerned with the reputational consequences that come from acknowledging that their students are also sex workers (Sagar et al. 2015). One important exception is the University of Leicester's *Student Sex Work Toolkit* (2020) that offers students information about the legalities of the sex industry in the UK and the various supports available, on campus and off. The toolkit also offers information for staff about how to engage with sex working students with respect. While certainly groundbreaking, the toolkit has been met with backlash from anti-sex-work feminists, including an online petition to have it removed from the university's website.

Despite the continued stigma that sex work faces, there has been a notable shift in the views on sex work that students share vocally in the classroom. This shift is partly due to the increase in the visibility of sex work in popular culture, as representations of the industry have grown, and at least in some cases improved. Sometimes when I teach the class, I ask students to choose an example from popular culture and analyze its depiction of the sex industry, using the theoretical frameworks we studied in class. Although the views of sex work exclusionary radical feminists (or SWERFs) still emerge in my classroom, their voices are significantly quieter now, and students on the whole are critical of frameworks that shame and stigmatize sex workers, even if they remain critical of power and exploitation in sex industries. I suspect this goes hand in hand with the increasing visibility of sex workers and their openness in disclosing their identities. It becomes harder to imagine them as silent victims when they are sitting right beside you sharing their ideas, experiences, and perspectives.

Another factor that might explain the cultural shift around sex work in the classroom is that virtually all of my students work while they attend school. Many of them have had multiple jobs in various sectors, and are interested in comparing notes with one another about exploitative and unfair working conditions. When I invite them to talk about their work, they all have stories about shitty bosses and shitty customers. They compare notes about having been sexualized and harassed in uncomfortable ways on the job. They have an implicitly anti-capitalist analysis through their fundamental understanding from experience that work is exploitative. Rather than romanticize sex work, students see connections between different kinds of labour and their aim is to improve the conditions of all workers. Thinking comparatively about work de-exceptionalizes sex work. Students start to see sex work as a job like other forms of labour, one that in some contexts and conditions is great and in others less so. They can see sex work as ordinary rather than extraordinary, as something that is mundane as often as it is titillating.

Because sex workers are not external to the classroom, a number of years ago I started bringing in a guest speaker to class, a friend and comrade who is a sex work activist. Talking about her experiences as an activist and the impact that Canada's most recent legislation has had on sex workers opened up different kinds of pedagogical possibilities for the classroom. This is what I think Alexis Poirier-Saumure (this volume) is getting at in his discussion of pedagogical allyship. Guest speakers can become important anchors for student learning when the groundwork has been laid for them to speak as experts in a conversation that can be open and non-fetishizing. But there are also risks when bringing in a guest speaker, especially if we turn to guest speakers to avoid accountability for having to engage across differences in a responsible way. For example, when white faculty bring a racialized guest speaker to avoid having to speak to race and racism themselves, they remove themselves from the realities of living in a world structured by racism that we all participate in and are implicated in in complex ways. This approach strikes me as pedagogically and intellectually lazy, and a deeply problematic example to enact for students. My experience of introducing guest speakers in my class more recently has illustrated the power of supporting student learning as they become fluent in each other's histories, and most importantly, as they come to an understanding that there are multiple ways that those histories in fact overlap and connect.

While the presence of sex workers in the classroom has opened up conversations in productive ways and allowed students to connect across difference from a place of curiosity and empathy, they have thus far been unable to extend the same level of interest to the clients of sex workers. The stigma around purchasing sex has ended up being the more intractable theme as the years go by, despite my efforts to assign various studies that emphasize complexities and humanize people who buy sex (Khan 2015; Rivers-Moore 2016). The vitriol from students is such that bringing in a guest speaker, finding someone who buys sex and is willing to speak about it with my students, would be a deeply irresponsible decision pedagogically. I have been assigning Chester Brown's graphic memoir about paying for sex, called *Paying for It* (2011), for many years, despite frequent expressions of discomfort from students. It will be interesting to see if the cultural and political economic shifts around sex work eventually broaden enough to include interest in and understanding of clients.

On "Balance" and "Objectivity": Adapting to a Cultural Shift

> I think I'm done with teaching SWERF readings. I have been so careful about wanting to be "balanced," as if it were possible to present an objective view of sex work to my students (or of anything, in fact). I have included less and less content from writers who consider sex work to be violence, but next time I'm including none at all. I'm done with them and done with pretending that I am in any way objective on this topic.
>
> —Teaching notes, Winter 2019

The last time I taught my "Sex for Sale" course, I didn't assign any readings by anti-sex-work authors. I certainly presented the arguments: I put key quotes on slides and made lots of space to discuss anti-sex-work positions. But assigning the actual texts stopped feeling appropriate when there were more and more sex workers in the room. Why was I asking sex workers (and, for that matter, everyone else) to read works that question their value and, often, their humanity? It was starting to feel uncomfortable and epistemologically violent. I have stopped thinking about the classroom as a place where I am supposed to provide an unbiased, objective, balanced view of the world, especially when perspectives are harmful and invalidating for students. I try to demonstrate to students the ways that my own thoughts have shifted, to highlight the fact that our ideas are not set in stone, and can change over time. One way to do this is actually to underscore my own specific point of view. I tell my students that I am not the final word on this topic; that I have a particular interpretation, based on seventeen years of research, but that it is a position that I have crafted carefully and with attention to alternative positions. Students may disagree with the arguments that I present in the class, but my pedagogical focus is on working with students so they can learn how to identify an argument, make connections, and communicate their own ideas through the careful crafting of their own positions.

One concrete way to work toward this kind of approach is to talk about the importance of methods, and then pay attention to the methods used by all the authors we read together. As a class, we are constantly returning to the question, How did this author come to this particular understanding? Who are they in conversation with? This pedagogical practice is not just about reading work by sex workers, but considering how the people who talk with and about sex workers are positioned in relation to the topic as well. While we read first-person accounts by sex workers, we also read lots of non-sex-worker academic scholarship, too. Reading across first-person and scholarly work on the topic means asking whether the author talks to and listen to sex workers, as either peers or research subjects.

The main goal I share explicitly with students is that I hope that we will end up in pragmatic and realistic common ground for grappling with the complex experiences, lives, and systems shaping sex work. This is important for helping students who are also sex workers to have space to locate themselves within the material, while also not presuming that being a sex worker means you can understand or speak on behalf of all sex workers. While it may be easy to search for and find sex workers who will confirm the view one already holds of the world, we must return to the harder philosophical question about our discomfort around links between sex and money, and the role of wider institutional and social structures that shape and constrain the choices we are able to make. We might ask whether our goal should be to envision a world free of sex work—where all labour is separate from systems of exploitation and violence, and all people can access resources to sustain themselves and explore sex free of the coercive economic systems that cause exploitation. Asking the question is an absolutely important and valid one, but it's something to discuss over wine with nerdy, earnest friends rather than something that we will find a definitive answer for together in class. Instead of wishing sex work were not a reality in higher education, we should consider that in every classroom, in every library, in every institution, there are sex workers taking classes, using institutional resources, and trying to navigate life as students. I want us to ask, How can we support these students, regardless of whether they disclose the kind of work they're doing while in school? At the very least we can commit to treating sex workers as beloved comrades and valued members of our communities, whether we know they're there or not.

Adapting to the shifting culture around sex work in higher education involves acknowledging that we all already have student sex workers in our classrooms. To develop more inclusive classrooms for our students, both those who are sex workers and those who are not, we can adopt the following practices in our teaching. Get comfortable using non-stigmatizing and non-judgemental language (for example, *sex work*, *sex workers*, and *clients*, rather than *prostitution*, *prostitutes*, and *johns*). If students disclose that they are sex workers, allow them to speak about their experiences and don't ask inappropriate or probing questions. Do not ask students to self-disclose their status as current, former, or potential sex workers; self-disclosure should be at a person's discretion and not the result of being prompted. Understand that stigma is real and intense, so check in with students if they have disclosed publicly in your classroom. Do not share your knowledge of a student's involvement in sex work with other students, faculty members, or staff. Do not assume you know why students are involved in sex work, what their experiences might be, or that they need you to help or save them. Treat sex working students (and indeed, all students) with respect and acknowledge that they are the experts on their own lives. Advocate for your university to adopt resources to support sex workers on your campus, including hiring professional support staff specialized in working with sex workers in affirming ways; encouraging the adoption of flexible deadline policies without requiring official documentation or disclosure; making emergency funds available for all students, especially those with irregular incomes. Some of these strategies are sex-worker-specific, but others reflect the basic principles of respectful engagement with students both inside and outside of the classroom, and inclusive campuses more generally. When in doubt, ask yourself whether you've listened to what your sex worker students are asking for; they likely know what kind of support they want and need from their faculty and their institutions.

References

Alexander, M. Jacqui. 2005. *Pedagogies of Crossing: Meditations on Feminism, Sexual Politics, Memory, and the Sacred*. Durham, NC: Duke University Press.

Bernstein, Elizabeth. 2007. *Temporarily Yours: Intimacy, Authenticity, and the Commerce of Sex*. Chicago: University of Chicago Press.

—. 2018. *Brokered Subjects: Sex, Trafficking, and the Politics of Freedom*. Chicago: University of Chicago Press.

Brents, Barbara G., and Teela Sanders. 2010. "The Mainstreaming of the Sex Industry: Economic Inclusion and Social Ambivalence." *Journal of Law and Society* 37 (1): 40–60. https://www.jstor.org/stable/25622007.

Brown, Chester. 2011. *Paying For It*. Montreal: Drawn and Quarterly.

Cusick, Linda, Ron Roberts, and Susan Paton. 2009. "Higher and Further Education Institution Policies on Student and Staff Involvement in Commercial Sex." *Journal of Higher Education Policy and Management* 2 (31): 185–95. https://doi.org/10.1080/13600800902825876.

Ernst, Felicitas, Nina Romanczuk-Seiferth, Stephan Köhler, Till Amelung, and Feliz Betzler. 2021. "Students in the Sex Industry: Motivations, Feelings, Risks, Judgments." *Frontiers in Psychology* 12 (February): 1–10. https://doi.org/10.3389/fpsyg.2021.586235.

Gbagbo, Fred Yao, and Josephine Akosua Gbagbo. 2021. "Commercial Sex Work among University Students: A Case Study of Four Public Universities in Ghana." *BMC Women's Health* 21 (1): 103–16. https://doi.org/10.1186/s12905-021-01251-2.

Hammond, Emily. 2019. "The Labour of Paying for Education: An Exploration of Student Sex Work in Canada." MA thesis, Carleton University.

Khan, Ummni. 2015. "'Johns' in the Spotlight: Anti-Prostitution Efforts and the Surveillance of Clients." *Canadian Journal of Law and Society* 30 (1): 9–29. https://doi.org/10.1017/cls.2014.27.

Lantz, Sarah. 2005. "Students Working in the Melbourne Sex Industry: Education, Human Capital and the Changing Patterns of the Youth Labour Market." *Journal of Youth Studies* 8 (4): 385–401. https://doi.org/10.1080/13676260500431669.

Lavoie, Francine, Caroline Thibodeau, Marie-Héléne Gagné, and Martine Hébert. 2010. "Buying and Selling Sex in Québec Adolescents: A Study of Risk and Protective Factors." *Archives of Sexual Behavior* 39 (5): 1147–60. https://doi.org/10.1007/s10508-010-9605-4.

Miller, Alex. 2011. "Sugar Dating: A New Take on an Old Issue." *Buffalo Journal of Gender, Law and Social Policy* 20 (1), art. 4, 33–68. https://digitalcommons.law.buffalo.edu/bjglsp/vol20/iss1/4.

Motyl, Jacqueline. 2013. "Trading Sex for College Tuition: How Sugar Daddy 'Dating' Sites May Be Sugar Coating Prostitution." *Penn State Law Review* 117 (3): 927–57. https://www.pennstatelawreview.org/117/3/Motyl%20final.pdf.

Nayar, Kavita Ilona. 2017. "Sweetening the Deal: Dating for Compensation in the Digital Age." *Journal of Gender Studies* 26 (3): 335–46. https://doi.org/10.1080/09589236.2016.1273101.

Rivers-Moore, Megan. 2016. *Gringo Gulch: Sex, Tourism, and Social Mobility in Costa Rica*. Chicago: University of Chicago Press.

Roberts, Ron, Sandra Bergström, and David La Rooy. 2007. "Sex Work and Students: An Exploratory Study." *Journal of Further and Higher Education* 31 (4): 323–34. https://doi.org/10.1080/03098770701625720.

Roberts, Ron, Amy Jones, and Teela Sanders. 2013. "Students and Sex Work in the UK: Providers and Purchasers." *Sex Education* 3 (13): 349–63. https://doi.org/10.1080/14681811.2012.744304.

Roberts, Ron, Teela Sanders, Ellie Myers, and Debbie M. Smith. 2010. "Participation in Sex Work: Students' Views." *Sex Education* 10 (2): 145–56. https://doi.org/10.1080/14681811003666507.

Sagar, Tracey, Deborah Jones, Katrien Symons, Joanne Bowring, and Ron Roberts. 2015. "Student Participation in the Sex Industry: Higher Education Responses and Staff Experiences and Perceptions." *Journal of Higher Education Policy and Management* 37 (4): 400–412. https://doi.org/10.1080/1360080X.2015.1056604.

Sanders, Teela, and Kate Hardy. 2015. "Students Selling Sex: Marketization, Higher Education and Consumption." *British Journal of Sociology of Education* 36 (5): 747–65. https://doi.org/10.1080/01425692.2013.854596.

Simpson, Jessica, and Cassandra Smith. 2021. "Students, Sex Work and Negotiations of Stigma in the UK and Australia." *Sexualities* 24 (3): 474–90. https://doi.org/10.1177/1363460720922733.

Simpson, Jessica, and Sarah Smith. 2019. "'I'm Not a Bloody Slave, I Get Paid and If I Don't Get Paid Then Nothing Happens': Sarah's Experience of Being a Student Sex Worker." *Work, Employment and Society* 33 (4): 709–18. https://doi.org/10.1177/0950017018809888.

Sinacore, Ada L., Beheshta Jaghori, and Shohreh M. Rezazadeh. 2015. "Female University Students Working in the Sex Trade: A Narrative Analysis." *Canadian Journal of Counselling and Psychotherapy* 49 (1): 40–56. https://cjc-rcc.ucalgary.ca/article/view/60991.

Sinacore, Ada L., and D. Lech. 2011. "Canadian University Students and the Sex Trade." In *Global Perspectives on Prostitution and Sex Trafficking: Europe, Latin America, North America, and Global*, edited by Rochelle L. Dalla, Lynda M. Baker, John DeFrain, and Celia Williamson, 255–74. Lanham, MD: Lexington.

Trueman, Gaynor, Saskia Hagelberg, and Teela Sanders. 2020. *Student Sex Work Toolkit*. University of Leicester. https://le.ac.uk/-/media/uol/docs/academic-departments/criminology/student-sex-work-toolkit-for-staff-in-he.pdf.

4

Mirrors in the Classroom

The Power of Autobiography as Pedagogy

S. TRIMBLE

In January of 2016, I walked into a lecture hall at the University of Toronto prepared to talk about Alison Bechdel's 2006 graphic memoir *Fun Home*. It was the same room where I'd been teaching the same course at the same time for years, so I was calm and comfy as I worked my way into the space, greeting students on my way to the front. Then one of them caught my eye and pointed to the author's photo on the back of the book. "She looks like you!" the student exclaimed. Bechdel and I do share something of a "family" resemblance: we're both butch white queers with short hair and neat specs. This wasn't a wholly new experience for me. As a gender-nonconforming person, I'm recognized and misrecognized in weird ways. A return visit to a shop or restaurant can elicit an unexpectedly familiar hello, a reminder I'm memorable because I look different. But sometimes it happens on a first meeting. Why does the waiter seem to know me? I wonder if we've met before—until I realize I've been mistaken for someone else, that another white butch was there before me.

This has happened at academic conferences as well, though I experience it with neither the same frequency nor force as my racialized colleagues do. As Nadine Attewell observes in "Not the Asian

You Had in Mind" (2016), such misrecognitions derive from practices of looking shaped by ongoing legacies of colonialism and racism, by logics that separate humans into subtypes and anchor those separations to the body and the skin. For Asian subjects, Attewell writes, racist practices of looking reanimate histories of "yellow perilism," when white settler states such as Canada and the United States enacted discriminatory policies spurred by demographic panic, laying the groundwork for ongoing constructions of "Asianness as a racial form defined by likeness, by, that is, sameness and interchangeability" (183). Attewell notes, too, "the misrecognition of 'all look the same' works differentially for (East) Asian and African diasporic subjects in North America" (183). As Black feminists from Sylvia Wynter (1994) to Simone Browne (2015) have argued, the white gaze frames Black subjects as interchangeably threatening, inciting modes of surveillance and capture with injurious, often deadly consequences consequences (see also hooks 1992). My whiteness shields me from much of the violence of these ways of seeing. But the experience of being seen as "like" (some) others marks me as abnormally human. That day—the Bechdel day—it forced me to reckon with some ghosts.

My student's observation made me confront the fact of being a body in the classroom, a reality I tried to disavow in my early years as a teacher. I understood some of my queer and trans students saw themselves reflected in me; that I represented the possibility of a queer life. But while I knew they were reading queerness off my body, I evaded the role embodiment played in their identifications. The evasion was enabled by decades of practice, years of aspiring to invisibility as a solution to the problem of being seen as different. "She looks like you!" popped that bubble. With my student's remark ringing in my ears, I walked to the front of the room, turned around, and saw a hundred pairs of eyes looking at me. I stumbled into the material I'd planned and spent the whole lecture searching for a rhythm. I don't think it was apparent to my students, but inside I was unravelling and

I didn't know why. It was my first time teaching Bechdel's account of growing up queer and gender nonconforming in a family filled with secrets, but haunted houses and the troubled white families they house are my thing. What I didn't anticipate was being haunted by my own embodiment, disturbed by the awakening of what Sara Ahmed might call the "histories of arrival" (2006, 38) that brought me into that classroom in the first place.

My Bechdel moment sent me tumbling down a psychic rabbit hole. Back in a twelve-year-old version of myself, I remembered how I was bullied for being butch and first learned that classrooms are risky spaces for gender-nonconforming bodies. I didn't know it at the time, but teaching *Fun Home* broke a bargain I'd struck with my younger self on my way to becoming a teacher: No mirrors in the classroom. No representations reflecting my genderqueerness to the room, confronting me with matters I was busily evading. The first part of this chapter is about how I struck a fresh deal with my vigilant young ghost by incorporating some of my coming-out story into a new version of the *Fun Home* lecture. This was the silence subtending my illusion of invisibility. Breaking it allowed me to show up for my students in new ways, to let them in on how I came to be that person standing at the front of the lecture hall. And once I realized my journey matters—that it gives students insight into my pedagogical choices and analytical strategies—another untold tale raised its hand. The second part of this chapter is about how I arrived at my field: feminist cultural studies. It's about why it took me a long time to recognize myself as doing cultural studies, why the feminist genealogies of cultural analysis with which I was working didn't cohere for me, until recently, as a formation of cultural studies.[1] It didn't occur to me this story might be of value to my students, that it might have a

---

1. I owe the phrase "doing cultural studies" to Paul du Gay et al.'s *Doing Cultural Studies: The Story of the Sony Walkman* (1997). Designed as a textbook, it attests to the role of pedagogy in the development of the field.

place in the classroom, until I learned to speak autobiographically as a teacher.

This chapter is a reflection on what I've learned and am still learning from the unravelling recognition that I appear, that my body signifies, in the classroom. It's about some of the pedagogical implications of what Stuart Hall, in his memoir, calls "the connections between 'a life' and 'ideas'" (2017, 10). To be honest, these thoughts feel belated. I'm a forty-something feminist who's been teaching in women and gender studies for a decade, and here I am feeling like "the personal is political" is a fresh insight. But this is the messiness of the nexus Hall names: ideas land differently at different times in our lives; learning is not linear, even (maybe especially) for the teacher. In my case, something I had not-known for a long time—the fact of being a body in the classroom—made itself known, and some foundational feminist insights came alive with this surfacing. This is the story of how a student's comment forced me to reckon with where I know from, which prompted me to reflect on how I arrived at the questions and methods that shape my scholarly work. It's the story of how a comment led to a crisis and, in the end, helped me find my way (back) to my field.

Our Bodies, Our (Past) Selves: On Identity and Storytelling

After my *Fun Home* fiasco, I came to two realizations. First, there wasn't enough queer and trans content in my course on pop culture. Faced with this gap in my teaching material, I did some soul-searching. I realized I was in constant negotiation with twelve-year-old me, a kid who was on red alert when I stood in a lecture hall in front of all those eyes. I came to understand the bargain I'd struck with myself—no mirrors in the classroom—as a holdover from an old survival strategy that was no longer serving me. Changing the terms of our deal would mean inhabiting the classroom differently, because that's where I first learned to pretend I was invisible.

I got into gender trouble in grade seven. I learned from a passing remark on the playground that lesbians were a thing, that girls could have girlfriends. Though I kept this new knowledge to myself, it rewrote most of what I thought was possible. At the same time, I was experiencing the social and psychic costs of doing gender badly in the early 1990s, a decade that inherited articulations of queerness with death and disease forged in the early years of the AIDS crisis. The knowledge of lesbian existence arrived alongside the nickname bestowed upon me that year: Manwoman. I understood from my peers that Manwoman was smelly and clumsy with a low, growly voice and aggressive disposition. I was too ashamed of my gender-bent alter ego to turn to anyone for help. Susan Stryker's (1994) brazen call to trans subjects to embrace our monstrosity hadn't reached my preteen ears.[2] My solution was to pretend I wasn't catching the stage whispers and knowing looks that swirled around me each day. School became a scene where I learned to separate my body from the gazes of others, granting myself the illusion of invisibility by unseeing and unhearing my peers. Turns out this is a strategy with a long afterlife. The Bechdel moment taught me a young part of myself was still in survival mode, wrapped in an invisibility cloak every time I walked into a lecture hall.

The next year, as I planned another iteration of the *Fun Home* lecture, I had a hunch I could do things differently. Something I love about Bechdel's first memoir is the tension between the author's reflections on the slipperiness of language, on the one hand, and the seeming stability of the coming-out statement, "I am a lesbian," on the other. I wanted to linger with that tension, to explore ways of thinking about identity that reflect the complexities of identification as an endless process shaped by conditions that exceed our control.

2. My grade-seven year was 1993–94. Stryker's "My Words to Victor Frankenstein above the Village of Chamounix: Performing Transgender Rage" began as a 1993 performance piece at an academic conference in California.

I paired Bechdel's text with two critical theory works: Judith Butler's 1991 essay "Imitation and Gender Insubordination," in which Butler reflects on the stakes of writing "as a lesbian" and insists, "I would like to have it permanently unclear what precisely that sign signifies" (14); and Stuart Hall's 1989 lecture, "Ethnicity: Identity and Difference," which outlines how identities are formed in historical conditions we didn't choose, spoken in a language that doesn't belong to us, refracted through outside perspectives, and shaped by a psychic life that is mostly unconscious. Choosing texts from the 1980s and '90s helped contextualize debates on "identity politics" in a longer trajectory than undergraduates are usually familiar with, so I used my own story to give them a sense of the texture of the times, plotting my coming-out process on a 1990s timeline punctuated by queer pop culture moments.

That morning, as I drank my coffee and organized my thoughts and anecdotes, I remember asking myself, "How much will I tell them?" It would only be ten minutes near the end of a two-hour lecture. I knew I could talk about grade seven in general terms, that I could concentrate on Melissa Etheridge's coming out and how the news reached me. Could I do this without telling them the name I'd been called? "Manwoman" was the sticking point—the point where all the shame was. It was a name I'd shared with only a few people in my adult life. It wasn't essential to the main idea, but some part of me knew it was the heart of the story. "I was a very queer child," I said, projecting some photos on the screen. In one of them I'm about twelve. I'm wearing loose jeans with high-tops, a white printed tee, a cowboy hat, and a sweat cuff on my wrist (Figure 4.1). I told them I got into trouble at school for "doing girlness" badly, and I almost left it there. But as I looked around, I could see the story resonated. "They called me Manwoman," I said. "It was...weirdly insightful?"

We laughed and I continued with my story. I told them I came out as a lesbian in the '90s because that was the language available;

Figure 4.1
Photograph of the author with past-shoulder length blond hair standing against a nature backdrop and wearing a white t-shirt, blue jeans, and a brown cowboy hat with a canine family friend sitting on the right (image courtesy of the author)

that I read Leslie Feinberg's *Stone Butch Blues* in my early twenties and wondered if I might be trans; that, in my thirties, I liked the word "non-binary," which is comedically close to capturing the both/and, neither/nor-ness of Manwoman. And I only arrived at non-binary, I added, because I noticed my students using the term—often in reference to me—so that the newness wore off and it started to feel like a fit. I tied things back to Butler, to Hall, bringing theoretical quotations to life by noting how my identity has shifted through time, language, cultural change, and the perspectives of others. But something was happening inside me as I carried on with my work. A pressure valve had released and the silence—the void into which I'd dropped the name "Manwoman"—had lost its gravitational pull. The child I was and her monstrous alter ego had both appeared in the classroom, and they did so on my terms. Something inside me that was clenched let go. Stories were simmering where before there had been silence.

The autobiographical turn is an old feminist strategy for interrogating the conditions that shape the making of knowledge, including the cultural and academic norms that disavow the personal and the contextual as constitutive of "theory." From standpoint theory to "situated knowledge" to "the oppositional gaze," feminist thought counters the supposed universality of heteropatriarchal, white supremacist, colonial ways of knowing by raising questions about who knows what and from which perspective(s) (see Harding 2004; Haraway 1988; and hooks 1992; see also Fournier 2021 and Miller 1991). The epistemological intervention of "the personal is political" includes but also exceeds the now common practice within gender studies classrooms of prefacing ideas or questions with a statement of social location. As my own coming-out story suggests, speaking "as a" is always more fraught, more contingent than it seems. It's a way of temporarily settling, perhaps, the shifting articulations of what I know, what I'm curious about, and what has happened to me. What kinds of stories might convey the texture of the times and experiences that have shaped me? And how—and why—does it matter in my teaching?

Fieldwork: On Finding Lifelines in the Academy

I didn't see myself in cultural studies right away. I was formally introduced to the field during my doctoral course work in the department of English and Cultural Studies at McMaster University, where I took a seminar on cultural politics and radical pedagogy. I was a graduate student writing on the cultural politics of apocalypse films. I took a cultural studies course taught by a big name in the field in a department with "cultural studies" right there on its letterhead. But, somehow, I didn't see myself reflected in the field. I finished my course work and wrote my dissertation and came away with what it says on my degree certificate: PhD in English.[3] Nearly a decade later, after years of teaching a pop culture course housed within a gender studies department, I realized I was doing cultural studies. More specifically, I was introducing my students to something called "feminist cultural studies." I had felt like an academic misfit for a long time: too visual-culture for English; too literary for cinema studies; too humanities for women's studies. Finally, I had arrived at a name and a cluster of intellectual genealogies that helped me understand what I was doing and why. But why had it taken me so long? Looking back at my training, I wondered, What was missing? And what did I miss?

What follows is an account of how I arrived, belatedly, at the recognition that I have been doing feminist cultural studies all along. The insight took a while to land because I was immersed in the work of feminist cultural analysis long before I knew about fields and disciplines; because I was (re)introduced to feminist analyses of culture in my undergraduate women's studies courses—and none of those genealogies reappeared in the cultural studies seminar I took as a doctoral student; because those feminist genealogies *did* shape my doctoral training, just not in the place I was looking. It's an account of my training that begins with my mother rather than the university; with feminist thought rather than cultural studies; and with the undergraduate classes in which I learned to be a teacher rather than the graduate seminars in which I was a student.

I began learning the skills of feminist cultural criticism long before I attended university. My mom is a feminist, a film buff, and a voracious reader with a keen sense of how stories enliven our personal mythologies. So, despite growing up amid the anti-feminist backlash of the 1980s and '90s, I learned in childhood to examine pop culture

---

3. There was an MA program but no PhD in cultural studies when I was at McMaster from 2007 to 2012. For those of us doing doctoral work in the department at the time, English was the only program available, though, in practice, there was plenty of overlap between the fields.

through a feminist lens. I also learned that autobiography and critical analysis are intertwined. My mom's first marriage was violent. In the '70s, her husband's drinking sent her fleeing into the night, running through neighbours' backyards to avoid being caught in the streetlights. One night she made her way to the local police station, where she was locked in a cell "for her own protection" while the cops had a men-to-man chat with her abuser. I always imagine my mom coming out of that cell pulsing with feminist questions—queries that, years later, she brought to our conversations about books, movies, and TV. That's how her stories came to life for me. She didn't share many details of her experiences of domestic violence, but through our discussions of Stephen King's horror writing, I came to understand the terrors of white men wrestling with their demons. My mom was my first cultural critic.

This childhood immersion in feminist cultural analysis shaped my undergraduate studies at York University in the early 2000s. Many of the gender studies courses I took centred Black and woman of colour feminisms, genealogies through which I encountered cultural criticism that was both inspiring and unsettling. I read Toni Morrison, bell hooks, Patricia Hill Collins, and Audre Lorde, learning from them the strategies and stakes of Black women's storytelling as well as some terrible truths about whiteness. Black feminist thought helped me make sense of the contradictions I felt between the white family as cultural ideal and my own experiences of its cold spots, evasions, and monsters in the closet. It also alerted me to the colonial histories and transnational formations that are typically suppressed in the stories white people tell about ourselves. I didn't know it at the time, but this was my academic gateway into cultural studies. Writers like Morrison, hooks, Collins, and Lorde represent a genealogy often sidelined by dominant accounts of American cultural studies. Sylvia Wynter introduced me to Caribbean and transatlantic itineraries of feminist cultural analysis. And Hazel Carby pointed me toward Black and feminist genealogies within British cultural studies.

Black feminist work on culture in the context of race, empire, and diaspora helped me locate myself as a child of the British Empire, implicated in the racial classifications, capital extractions, and territorial claims that made and still make colonial nation-states rich. These genealogies also served as "lifelines," to borrow another term from Ahmed. In an essay that considers this concept in the context of citational politics and field formation, Sarah Brophy writes, "if bodies usually find themselves compelled to orient themselves in relation to received heteronormative and imperialist directions, then these alternative resources offer 'the gift of the unexpected line that gives us the chance for a new direction and even a chance to live again'" (Ahmed quoted in Brophy 2017, 100). My mom had thrown me a lifeline in the form of popular feminism. I followed it to university, where lifelines multiplied, each one the expression of feminist labour, survival, and creativity—of the writers themselves, and of the teachers who brought them to me.

Most of these writers and the genealogies they represent were missing from the graduate seminar that explicitly introduced me to cultural studies a few years later, but they did feature in my doctoral training, especially when I worked as a teaching assistant for two of my feminist mentors at McMaster, Nadine Attewell and Sarah Brophy. It was here that I explored histories of slavery, heteropatriarchy, colonialism and settler colonialism, and migration and diaspora through everything from poetry to film to calypso. I became a teacher by learning to guide students through nuanced examinations of the entanglements of culture and power. Along the way, I strengthened my own engagements with feminist, Black, Asian, Indigenous, queer, and trans scholars I would later identify as doing cultural studies. In those classes in which I learned to become a teacher, I encountered the frameworks, genealogies, and citational practices my mentors mobilized to explore their questions about reproduction and capital, intimacy and kinship, empire and embodied difference. All this work informed my own research into apocalyptic storytelling, pushing me to deepen my sense of where and when a story takes place, to notice the transnational linkages that make their presence felt in something as intimate as touch, as mundane as sugar. It just took me a while to connect this to cultural studies.

This delay is partly due to the hierarchies we internalize, even when we "know better." I first learned how and why to do feminist cultural analysis from my mother, who didn't attend university until she was in her fifties. I didn't grasp the epistemological value of what we were doing, so I didn't look for its academic reflection because it didn't occur to me there might be one. Where I did encounter resonances of my mom's training in the academy, I named it as feminist studies without considering the specifically cultural dimensions of the work. My introduction to cultural studies further entrenched this way of (un)seeing what I was doing, widening the gap between the diverse genealogies assembled by my feminist mentors and the (dominantly white male) American tradition I encountered in that doctoral seminar. All of this was happening in a larger institutional context that separates—and hierarchically arranges—research and teaching. Today, I identify first and foremost as a teacher and take great pride in that job description. But first I had to unlearn what my early observations of university life had taught me: that research is prestigious, and teaching is a side hustle. I understood myself as a researcher-in-training in that graduate seminar; that was where I expected to find the outline of a field called "cultural studies." My training as a teacher taught me something different about the field, even if those lessons took time to land.

"How We Come to Knowing, and How We Share What We Know"[4]

In a 1992 lecture titled "Cultural Studies and Its Theoretical Legacies," Stuart Hall said "cultural studies has multiple discourses; it

---

4. Sentence fragment from Katherine McKittrick's (2021) essay on Black studies and citation work, "Footnotes (Books and Papers Scattered about the Floor)."

has a number of different histories. It is a whole set of formations; it has its own different conjunctures and moments in the past. It included many different kinds of work. I want to insist on that!" (72). This is typical of Hall, who was known to begin his reflections on the field with a cascade of qualifiers, all aiming to quash simplistic origin stories in which he figures as a founding father. In this lecture he absolves himself of that representational burden and then elaborates: "That means, paradoxically, speaking autobiographically. Autobiography is usually thought of as seizing the authority of authenticity. But in order not to be authoritative, I've got to speak autobiographically" (72). Informed at least in part by the insights of his feminist colleagues at the Centre for Contemporary Cultural Studies, Hall refuses a "grand narrative" or cultural studies canon and offers, instead, his own journey through the field. He locates its beginnings in work he encountered before cultural studies was named as such and, in a correlated move, characterizes the field as "a project that is always open to that which it doesn't yet know, to that which it can't yet name" (73). This insistence on multiplicity and openness does not lead to an anything-goes account of the field.[5] But it makes room for how my cultural studies story is different from Hall's even as it invites me into a set of questions, methods, and projects we might share.

I began this chapter with a story about disavowed knowledge—a not-knowing that allowed me to evade the fact of my embodied presence in the classroom—which opened onto a story about suspended knowledge, about how feeling lost and finding my way in the academy were both happening at once. But this is not a story that ends with stable truths. I still wonder, am still curious about how our embodied experiences shape our relationship to learning and knowledge. And it

---

5. Hall is insistent on this point, too: "It does matter whether Cultural Studies is this or that. It can't be just any old thing which chooses to march under a particular banner...Here one registers the tension between a refusal to close the field, to police it, and, at the same time, a determination to stake out some positions within it and argue for them" (73).

is the wondering, more than the knowing, that I hope my stories convey to my students. Katherine McKittrick asks, "What if we read outside ourselves not *for* ourselves but to actively unknow ourselves, to unhinge, and thus come to know each other, intellectually, inside and outside the academy, as collaborators of collective and generous and capacious stories?" (2021, 16). I started speaking autobiographically in the classroom not to share the truth of who I am or stabilize the field in which I work, but to set both in motion. The unhinging McKittrick speaks of can, she acknowledges, feel awful and lonely. It is also inherent in the learning process, which Dina Georgis describes as "the crisis of not being able to hold on to what you think you know and bearing it enough to make way for insight" (2013, 17). If this is what I'm asking of my students, then there's pedagogical value in my own stories of unknowing myself and finding my way (again and again). Autobiographical storytelling is one of the ways I bring feminist cultural studies and its many points of entry, its many genealogies, to life; it's how I activate lifelines instead of presenting a canon to be mastered.

Whatever your field or disciplinary training, autobiography can help students connect to your own genealogy of learning, to show how you arrived at your work and how your life experiences shaped—and still shape—your relationship to ideas. Sharing autobiographically requires vulnerability, but this vulnerability can encourage students to take similar risks in the classroom. It can invite them to collaborate with us in the hard, scary work of unravelling what we think we know to make room for knowing otherwise.

References

Ahmed, Sara. 2006. *Queer Phenomenology: Orientations, Objects, Others*. Durham, NC: Duke University Press.

Attewell, Nadine. 2016. "Not the Asian You Had in Mind: Race, Precarity, and Academic Labor." *English Language Notes* 54, no. 2 (Fall/Winter): 183–90. https://www.muse.jhu.edu/article/711453.

Brophy, Sarah. 2017. "Paris–Boston–Berkeley–The Mexico/Texas Borderlands 1949–1990; or, Gender and Sexuality." In *A Companion to Critical and Cultural Theory*, edited by Imre Szeman, Sarah Blacker, and Justin Sully, 91–113. Hoboken, NJ: Wiley-Blackwell.

Browne, Simone. 2015. *Dark Matters: On the Surveillance of Blackness*. Durham, NC: Duke University Press.

Butler, Judith. 1991. "Imitation and Gender Insubordination." In *Inside/Out: Lesbian Theories, Gay Theories*, edited by Diana Fuss, 13–30. New York: Routledge.

du Gay, Paul, Stuart Hall, Linda Janes, Hugh Mackay, and Keith Negus. 1997. *Doing Cultural Studies: The Story of the Sony Walkman*. London: Sage Publications in association with the Open University.

Fournier, Laura. 2021. *Autotheory as Feminist Practice in Art, Writing, and Criticism*. Cambridge, MA: MIT Press.

Georgis, Dina. 2013. *The Better Story: Queer Affects from the Middle East*. Albany: SUNY Press.

Hall, Stuart. 1989. "Ethnicity: Identity and Difference." *Radical America* 23 (4): 9–20.

—(1992) 2018. "Cultural Studies and Its Theoretical Legacies." In *Stuart Hall: Essential Essays*, vol. 1, *Foundations of Cultural Studies*, edited by David Morley, 71–99. Durham, NC: Duke University Press.

—2017. *Familiar Stranger: A Life between Two Islands*. Durham, NC: Duke University Press.

Haraway, Donna. 1988. "Situated Knowledges: The Science Question in Feminism and the Privilege of Partial Perspective." *Feminist Studies* 14 (3): 575–99. https://doi.org/10.2307/3178066.

Harding, Sandra, ed. 2004. *The Feminist Standpoint Theory Reader*. New York: Routledge.

hooks, bell. 1992. *Black Looks: Race and Representation*. Boston: South End Press.

McKittrick, Katherine. 2021. *Dear Science and Other Stories*. Durham, NC: Duke University Press.

Miller, Nancy K. 1991. *Getting Personal: Feminist Occasions and Other Autobiographical Acts*. New York: Routledge.

Stryker, Susan. 1994. "My Words to Victor Frankenstein above the Village of Chamounix: Performing Transgender Rage." *GLQ: A Journal of Lesbian and Gay Studies* 1 (3): 237–54. https://doi.org/10.1215/10642684-1-3-237.

Wynter, Sylvia. 1994. "'No Humans Involved': An Open Letter to My Colleagues." *Forum N.H.I.: Knowledge for the 21st Century* 1 (1): 42–73.

5

Ecstatic Pedagogies

Navigating Desire and Pleasure across the Boundaries of the Classroom

DAN IRVING

Our future is queer, or at least that is what I, as a critical sexuality studies educator, profess to my students. Urging students to approach their studies of sex, gender, and sexuality with in-depth precision, critical sexuality studies pedagogy takes a multifaceted approach to analyzing systemic power relations, including our desires to disrupt and eradicate oppression and its everyday manifestations in our lives. Our area of study draws students whose embodied sex and gender expressions and sexualities exclude them from the "charmed circle" (Rubin 1998, 109) of mainstream society and culture. These students bring passionate energies to the classroom via their desires to find themselves and their communities reflected in education. Regardless of their gender identities and sexualities, students crackle with the energy of untapped potential for critical reflection concerning governing bodies, pleasures, and pain to make sense of their own lives. Students play with their own unruly genders and sexualities in ways that are often unintelligible to mainstream society, dismissed as irresponsible and frivolous youthful experimentation, bounded by time (i.e., a four-year bachelor degree) and space (the university campus as gated community). Despite the expectation that students will "grow up" and enter the "real world" by abandoning this kind of experimentation and play, I propose that turning to the role of pleasure and desire in education can help us think about teaching and learning differently. Celebrating trans and non-binary genders, embodied sexual pleasures, and asexual intimacies can help us move beyond strict parameters of "the" sexual and see how ecstatic pedagogies can make learning a transformative process.

As a white trans and queer educator who transitioned, divorced, and cannonballed into the deep end of "polymorphous perversity" during graduate school,[1] I have experienced the enlivening potential of the sexuality studies classroom. Since becoming a tenured professor, however, I find myself longing for a classroom that provides ecstatic grounds for the kinds of intellectual communion that helps us endure the shame, depression, anxiety, and fear that grips so many of us tightly. The generative possibilities that I found as a student in the sexuality classroom does not seem to be mirrored in my classes today as a professor. I am perplexed by many of my students who refuse to engage in the intellectual labour of reading assigned materials thoroughly. There seems to be a resistance to problematizing their lived experiences and I seem to grow increasingly frustrated with this dynamic. Perhaps the cause of this friction is that sexuality studies was my lifeline, but it may not be so for my students. Current undergraduates often articulate their desire to learn about marginalized subjects in ways that affirm their own experiences, but in doing so, miss the possibility of pleasurable intellectual trysts that coursework provides. This chapter is dedicated, in part, to interrogating my melancholic relationship to the classroom. What does my approach to teaching and

---

1. In *A Dictionary of Psychology*, Andrew Colman defines *polymorphous perversity* as a term used in psychoanalysis describing "the earliest libidinal stage of psychosexual development, during the oral stage, characterized by undifferentiated sexual desire that finds gratification through any erotogenic zone. The term is also used to denote the varied bodily sources and styles of libidinal gratification in the course of early psychosexual development" (2015, 318).

increasing frustration with many of my students reveal about my own personal longings and investments in the classroom? Reflecting on my own desires as a teacher, I want to interrogate how the personal, institutional, and social barriers that produce the classroom can be a prohibitive and treacherous space for students, as much as it can be a space of self-discovery, passion, and pleasure.

Introducing the concept of ecstatic pedagogies, an approach that begins with refusing the institutional hierarchy where professors dominate students, and focuses instead on the role of pleasure and desire in shaping learning, the chapter is structured around three guiding questions. (1) What does my approach to teaching, and increasing frustration with many of my students, reveal about my own personal longings for the classroom to be a queer space? This is primarily a question about the relationship of power and desire between students and teachers. (2) What can be gained by a willingness to pervert the dominant (white, Western, and masculinist) logic framing academic institutions? This involves looking at possibilities that can come from changing positions and submitting to a different teaching practice, where I read student desires as closely as I demand they engage with course materials to better understand students' needs and wants. Because students come from multiple social locations vis-à-vis race, gender, sexuality, ability, there is much that they already bring to the classroom about bodies and power. (3) How can we harness our collective potential and passionate pleasure-seeking energies to produce opportunities that disrupt exploitative, oppressive, and extractive power regimes within our institutions? Following these questions, I propose that ecstatic pedagogies can help us think about the pedagogical entanglements that provoke personal transformation and reverberate into social spaces, contributing to broader and deeper transformations. This chapter is divided into three sections. The first section focuses on critical self-reflection concerning my personal longings and relationship to academia as an institution and how this impacts my teaching. The second section offers suggestions concerning how faculty can interpret students' lives and how they may experience the classroom. In the third section, I concentrate on ecstatic pedagogy as a passionate form of learning where the dangerous, pleasurable, messy, and contradictory bodily sensations and experiences held by each student play a central role in their engagement with learning.

Inner Longings: Exploring the Teacher's Desire

I came into myself in the university classroom during my undergraduate years. Raised in a small conservative city in the Maritimes, while I grew up middle class, both my parents had come from working poor families and were not university educated. The classroom quickly became my refuge and served as the gateway to an identity and political consciousness that I could claim as my own. It was here that I established intellectually intimate mentorship and friendships with faculty members who shared a worldview that transformed the possibility of what my life could look like. These were faculty who not only called for cooperative democracy, anti-capitalist revolution, and Indigenous sovereignty, but were also part of initiatives, organizations, and movements that worked concretely on projects for change. The classroom and broader university were spaces where I also found community with peers who shared in the struggle to unlearn the colonial, racial, linguistic, xenophobic, misogynist, and homophobic underpinnings of our lived environments. We learned from each other through sharing ideas from our courses, we rubbed up against each other's values and ideas, worked through the conflicts that often erupted, and witnessed each other's awkward integration of theory into practice.

During my doctoral studies, I found myself through ideas, texts, an incredible supervisor and mentor, as well as the challenges and support offered to me by my intellectual and social community. My own understanding of my gender was transformed after my supervisor said to me in passing, "you're so butch," which sent me on a quest to a gay bookstore to find out what butch meant. Delving into the area of sexuality, I voraciously read the most influential texts of the time: Joan Nestle's (1992) *The Persistent Desire: A Femme-Butch Reader*, Jack Halberstam's (1998) *Female Masculinity*, Leslie Feinberg's (1998) *Transgender Liberation: Beyond Pink or Blue*, and Jason Cromwell's (1999) *Transmen and Other FTMs*. Cromwell introduced me to the concept of the "female-bodied man," a term that shook me so ferociously that I blew apart. I went to my supervisor's office and proclaimed, "I'm a man." She responded with two words grounded in decades of erotic intellectual praxis: "I know." I began transitioning that year; it was 1999.

In 2007 I began my faculty appointment as the first faculty member of sexuality studies at Carleton University, as part of the new sexuality studies minor program. This opportunity simultaneously created space to bolster my intellectual development and stifled the nature of this development. The vulnerability I felt as a queer, visibly trans, and untenured academic tapered my approach to teaching. I relied on formal lectures for my classes, which conveyed my authority on a topic so easily dismissed as frivolous, but this blunted the dynamism and sexuality behind the theoretical frameworks, key concepts, and works that I was teaching. I benefitted from my white privilege, and my surgically and hormonally produced passable masculinity enabled me to deliver the kind of disembodied teaching performance that garners academic success. I resembled my male colleagues more than the provocative and performative playfulness of my supervisor, who delighted in disrupting the reserved status quo of higher education.

My move from Toronto to Ottawa, from graduate student to professor, shifted my experience from visible and embodied sexual subject to a professionalized expert. Unlike in Toronto, where many LGBTQ+ and BDSM community members attended university and could expose or strip me of my thin garb of professionalism at any time,[2] no one knew me in Ottawa. My promotion to associate professor further dulled my edges. I harboured a deep longing to reawaken my inner "trans monster" or radical storyteller whose interactions with others reveals the artificiality of the embodied identities often taken for granted as natural (Stryker 1994). I struggled with the inner turmoil, vulnerability, pleasures, and pain that professionalized embodiment and demeanour demanded. I envied the playfulness of embodied exploration that my students enjoyed and longed to join them, to escape the crushing alienation of my position as professor, and co-constitute intellectual space with them. Sexuality studies students' defiant desires and wanton urges for pleasure seeking can send pulsating surges of energy vibrating throughout the classroom. I wanted to rush to meet them on intellectual grounds and fantasized that they were mutually hungry for a terrain to meet me in the shared exchange of learning.

By 2020 I was intellectually lonely and starving for connection. I introduced a fourth-year seminar titled Queer R/evolutions: Embodied Pleasure and Political Possibility. Designed to centre sexual desire, bodily pleasures, and spiritual longing as a way to return to the radical political potential of sexuality studies, the course drew heavily on queer theory and queer of colour critique to create what I hoped would be a semester of vibrant connections. I wanted us to commune, to open up our books, minds, hearts, and souls. I longed for classroom dynamics filled with deep discussions about the materials, a dynamic that crackled with the energy that comes from injecting personal experience into our engagement with the assigned texts, to save the ideas from becoming abstractions. But this communion did not happen.

---

2. My first Trans Studies class at the University of Toronto as a contract instructor ended with a student exclaiming, "*Doctor* Irving, huh? Last time I saw you was at the Black Eagle at a holiday bash kneeling shirtless beside your Mistress with a basket of candy canes in your mouth!"

Before the Pleasure, Is the Pain: How to Read Students' Desires and Embodiment

Many of the assignments in Queer R/evolutions required students to reflect critically on their subject positions, such as their race, sexuality, class, and dis/ability (to name a few). These assignments asked them to contend with the tension between normative and marginalized elements of their existence. The radical *potential* of sexuality studies praxis lies in the slippery, messiness of queer theory and the refusal to be tied down or contained in definitive categories. I stressed to students that queer world-making praxis emanates from one's embodied daily experiences. Bodily sensations, emotions, words spoken, interactions with the natural and social worlds are the primary texts informing our analysis of gender and sexuality. However, rather than meet me and the texts in an exchange of ideas, curiosity, exploration, play, and energy, my students came to class with what felt like disinterest and apathy. Students often refused to read, their silence during class time thwarted seminar discussions, they made random comments diverting conversation away from the topics of discussion, and failed to submit written work. I was crestfallen. Were such refusals anti-intellectual, entitled, or lazy? Or, akin to a selfish lover, did I fail to read the student body and instead project my own desires onto them?

I had assumed my classroom would be a refuge for students seeking out embodied knowledge. But contained within the hierarchies of academic institutions, the fantasy of coming together to witness the pleasure and pain of our gender and sexual subjectivities may not be possible. The ruling pillars of academe—whiteness, masculinist, and a middle-class social location—demarcate the classroom as a space where students should engage in abstract (read disembodied) theoretical and rational analysis. The ability to approach topics of learning with dispassion requires a student subject who has not come to the classroom with a history of embodied violence and trauma. For many students, the university classroom is not a place of refuge or freedom; rather, it is another site of violence. My longing for students to open their minds, hearts, and spirits to intellectual exchange does not mesh with the reality that for Indigenous students, students of colour, those raised in poverty, students with disabilities, queer, and "international students" such openness can increase their vulnerability in higher education.

How can students interrogate the ways that power structures their subjectivity and make meaningful connections to their lived experiences when the classroom is already a coercive space shaped by the power dynamics of grades, canons, and dynamics that privilege settler logic, whiteness, and middle-class social locations? Marginalized students must fight to defend themselves against a hostile environment in higher education that structures knowledge through systems that disregards their lives and experiences, or worse, builds expertise by producing knowledge about the lives and experiences of historically excluded people in ways that alienate them from this knowledge. Student disengagement in the classroom cannot be seen as a lack of desire to learn, grow, and enrich their own lives and communities; instead, forced to steel themselves against oppressive institutional and classroom dynamics, their refusals may be ways for them to survive, perhaps in an unexpectedly similar way to the way I turned to the classroom and to texts to survive during my own time as a student. Vulnerable to an economy of participation, their silence during class discussions leaves them vulnerable to assumptions that they have not done the readings or cannot articulate their analysis of the assigned materials. Such silences are often "D graded" (e.g., for seminar attendance and participation) in my classes, since silence offers little room for assessment.

Reflecting on the failure of my seminar to generate the kind of embodied knowledge and world-making that I desired from the classroom, I can now see that the failure was mine for not trying to understand how those silences might signal an active engagement against further alienation for them. Caught between the competing desire to break my own alienation through intellectual exchange with my students, and my students' desires to survive the power structures of higher education, I had projected too much onto the classroom as a space for my own transformation. Many students are attracted to sexuality studies courses because they serve as fertile grounds to think through power, bodies, and desire. Similar to my own longing, students also seek a witness for their embodied sex, gender identities, and sexualities. However, for Indigenous students, people of colour, students attending university from non-Western regions, students with disabilities, as well as those who grew up in poverty, witnessing the ways that intersecting power relations mediate their embodied gender and sexual subjectivities can mean a heightened sensitivity to the ways that sex, gender, and sexuality have deep intergenerational roots in histories of violence. These are identities and subject positions deployed and used as part of the projects of settler colonialism, white supremacy, patriarchy, and class oppression.

Regardless of our intentions, when we project our desires onto the classroom as faculty, we threaten to further expose already vulnerable students to violence when we fail to consider the implications around power in the classroom. As educators, we may strive to "guide students to the forest" (hooks 1994, 197), to interrogate how knowledge is produced and engage with the exchange of ideas. However, since learning is already constrained by the struggles and experiences that are brought into the classroom, we must consider how the classroom is not experienced uniformly, especially given difference amongst students' subject positions and lived experiences. When the subject matter comes to experiences of oppression, many of us cannot open ourselves to the "pleasure[s] and danger[s]" (Vance 1984) of sexuality studies scholarship. However, learning is not simply a defensive experience for students and teachers alike, engaging in ecstatic pedagogies *is* possible and involves initial efforts to establish common grounds for the classroom encounter.

Towards Ecstatic Pedagogical Practices

The first step towards ecstatic pedagogies is to reorient teaching practices away from the professional pedagogue—who, for example, *grades* students' academic performance—and move towards reciprocity—*marking* and *being marked* by them. In *Teaching to Transgress* bell hooks's concept of Eros (1994, 198) provides a model for ecstatic pedagogical practices grounded in passionate love for learning from, and with, each other. In this approach, faculty and students come together to work together through assigned texts in ways that resist the hierarchical structure of the institutionalized relationships of teachers and students, towards relationships of mutual exchange. Intergenerational relationships have a long history within queer communities, and these relationships model ways of sharing knowledge and other resources to empower both older and younger generations. While we cannot escape the institutionalized faculty-student power relations that structure higher education, we can nevertheless approach pedagogy through a model of intergenerational friendship, which creates opportunities to build mutual benefit for students and teachers. Rather than uphold the dispassionate model of the professionalized teacher, I consider the possibility of intergenerational queer friendships as a model for rethinking the teacher-student relationship in ecstatic pedagogy. These relationships require attentiveness and care to the role of power by not shying away from contending with the role of power hierarchies in shaping all relationality. With attention to the unique dynamic established between professors and students, the classroom can be a space where the specific bonds developed make possible new ways of learning.

The next step to establish ecstatic pedagogy is to show up for our students, not simply to be available over email and office hours, but to be accountable and responsive to their learning. When students thank me for a lecture, a course, a reference letter, I always respond with "there is no need to thank me, I am doing my job." The same attitude applies when I listen to students and try to provide them with academic guidance and personal reassurance during office hours, a practice we often frame as "emotional labour." Much has been written about the added workload burden placed on marginalized faculty, who are asked to perform emotional labour for their students and colleagues, in addition to the regular workload of teaching, research, and service. Rather than critique this labour, I argue that we should expand our focus on performing this kind of role in higher education, normalizing it over the dispassionate model of the academic. As a trans queer professor, like most marginalized faculty members, performing emotional labour is a facet of our jobs that won't go away simply because we devalue this kind of work. While I hate the term *emotional labour*—and never use it in my personal life because listening, witnessing, and supporting one's friends and family is an expression of love for them, not a commodity for exchange—showing up emotionally for our students and sharing our vulnerability can humanize the classroom and teacher-student dynamics. What would happen if faculty let their guard down and rejected the professional barrier that separates students from teachers and reinforces those institutional hierarchies? The possibility that education and learning can reverberate in many directions, exceeding even the time and space of the classroom or a single semester, builds on the notion that learning cannot be contained in a quantified and guarded way.

Far exceeding course design, the next step to establish ecstatic pedagogy is building on self-reflection and mutual introspection. This involves continual introspection on both the part of the teacher and the students. In my classes, I like to remind students that their bodies and lived experience are the most important texts with which they will be working. Through reading responses and by encouraging them to discuss their feelings concerning the subject matter shaping the seminar, we explore elements of each other's lives that impact our capacities to process ideas and subjects. Developing grounds to establish trust and a caring relationship with students demands that we continue to consider our own investments projected onto the classroom. For me, that involves interrogating my desires to find my passion for the material mirrored in them. The university introduced me to a world of ideas and possibilities that provided an escape from the small city conservatism and Christian fundamentalism that I grew up with. It was through scholarship that I learned about trans subjects and the possibilities of living queerly. My students, however, come from different contexts. Many of them learn about gender and sexuality through friends, family, social media, and popular culture. While my intentions are to support my students by sharing my own love of scholarship, students may not share my feelings of alienation from society and may not seek release through intellectual stimulation or unlearning. Building on self-reflection and mutual introspection means sharing with my students what my own encounters with these texts have meant for me, and inviting them to bring the objects and texts that hold meaning for them into conversation with the readings I've assigned.

We must interrogate how the codes of professionalization can both protect people from abuse (by creating boundaries around abuse of power) *and* be vehicles for abuse (by objectifying those with less access to power). We don't protect our students by assuming that emotional distance will keep these relationships safe. Instead, we should listen to our students and take seriously their concerns about how power works, and work with them as collaborators to respond to the challenges we face and the violent systems being navigated. Providing opportunities for students to feel empowered in the classroom is one way of helping to build this dynamic. Innovative assignments that empower students to participate in discussions concerning systemic power relations also signals to students that we care for them. The generational gap between myself and my students bars a robust appreciation for the significance of social media in their lives; despite this, I invite them to teach me how to understand their frameworks and experiences.

Ecstatic pedagogy involves the exchange of ideas infused with understandings tied to life experiences across different social locations. While readings, films, and other scholarly materials are central to learning in my classes, it is vital to explore other ways to grapple with key concepts in the classroom. Students have responded well to an assignment that requires them to apply particular concepts and key questions by creating a meme. Memes have become a tool of popular education, knowledge creation, and transmission. The meme assignment provides an escape from the familiar rhythms and more traditional reading response I typically assign. Moreover, this assignment opens space to foster multiple and intergenerational relationships, as students teach me about elements of pop culture that have traction with their generation. They also support and encourage each other by posting responses to memes uploaded to the course platform or shared in class, and often use these forms of engagement to spark conversations within their families and wider social networks.

Decentring my own desires in the classroom is a key part of how I practice ecstatic pedagogy. Instead, I approach teaching and learning about theory, methodology, and key concepts through work and approaches that centre on collaborative knowledge transfer and personal empowerment, which can be meaningful for students both inside and outside of the classroom. Ecstatic pedagogy is not restricted to the classroom, which for many students remains a gated and guarded community and can be treacherous grounds. Instead, I try to focus on the way the classroom can be a place that overlaps with the grassroots movements, non-profit organizations, artistic collectives, small independently run businesses, and informal mutual aid and sharing economies that students often lead, own, or depend upon for their survival. To put this into practice, one year, students worked together to organize a public symposium to showcase their research and facilitate discussion and networking opportunities with managers, staff, and members of local organizations, as well friends, family, and anyone within the wider community who wished to attend. We met off campus in a community space and spoke in accessible language to create space for robust discussion. Another example involved extending students the opportunity to receive partial credit for the organizing and activist work they were already doing, such as decolonial, anti-racist, disability justice, im/migrant justice, and other social justice projects. It is in these spaces outside the classroom that many students feel safer to be vulnerable, amidst their chosen community, rather than in class where common grounds can be hard to build. Instead of demanding student attention in the traditional structure of the classroom, by inviting students to bring their outside lives into their learning, the ecstatic pedagogical approach can help ease the pressure that so many marginalized subjects face when forced to divide their attention and limited time into fragments across school and the rest of their lives. Desires for the classroom, queer fantasies of transformative encounters with ideas, are tempered with the exhausting reality of having to work, live, and love in multiple directions. More akin to polyamorous ethics than curriculum theory, ecstatic pedagogy means releasing students to engage in scholarly, creative, activist, and other work in ways that cannot be contained in a single class syllabus.

Ecstatic pedagogies exceed educational mandates to establish empirically measurable learning outcomes and demonstrations of value-added contributions to the economy (e.g., percentages of students that obtain jobs in their desired fields after graduation). By making room for students to guide their own passionate and loving practices, this pedagogical approach can help us to reach for our students deeply on a personal and social level while respecting their autonomy to determine what learning is ecstatic for them. By interrogating my own fantasies and desires for the classroom, projected onto my students, as well as letting go of the classroom as the definitive scene where learning occurs, I discovered that learning can be fostered between and amongst us, as well as elsewhere—in places where students from marginalized communities feel much safer to enact what adrienne maree brown calls "pleasure activism," that affirm their "deepest cravings"

(2019, 32), and slip into "a practice of saying an *orgasmic* yes together, deriving our collective power from our felt sense of pleasure" (12).

References

brown, adrienne maree. 2019. *Pleasure Activism: The Politics of Feeling Good*. Chico, CA: AK Press.
Colman, Andrew. 2015. "Polymorphous Perversity." In *A Dictionary of Psychology*, 4th ed., 318. Oxford University Press.
Cromwell, Jason. 1999. *Transmen and FTMs: Identities, Bodies, Genders, and Sexualities*. Urbana: University of Illinois Press.
Feinberg, Leslie. 1998. *Trans Liberation: Beyond Pink or Blue*. Boston: Beacon Press.
Halberstam, Jack. 1998. *Female Masculinity*. Durham, NC: Duke University Press.
hooks, bell. 1994. *Teaching to Transgress: Education as the Practice of Freedom*. New York: Routledge.
Nestle, Joan, ed. 1992. *The Persistent Desire: A Femme-Butch Reader*. 1st ed. Boston: Alyson Publications.
Rubin, Gayle. 1998. "Thinking Sex: Notes for a Radical Theory of the Politics of Sexuality." In *Social Perspectives in Lesbian and Gay Studies: A Reader*, edited by Peter M. Nardi and Beth E. Schneider, 100–33. London: Routledge.
Stryker, Susan. 1994. "My Words to Victor Frankenstein above the Village Chamounix: Performing Transgender Rage." *GLQ: A Journal of Lesbian and Gay Studies* 1 (3): 237–44. https://doi.org/10.1215/10642684-1-3-237.
Vance, Carole S., ed. 1984. *Pleasure and Danger: Exploring Female Sexuality*. Boston: Routledge & K. Paul.

6

Pedagogy of Implication

Complicity as Difficult Knowledge

SUSANNE LUHMANN

> Critical pedagogues are always implicated in the very structures they are trying to change.
> —Elizabeth Ellsworth, "Why Doesn't This Feel Empowering? Working through the Repressive Myths of Critical Pedagogy" (1989)

> If we want a world with less suffering and more flourishing, it would be useful to conceive complexity and complicity as the constitutive situation of our lives, rather than things we should avoid.
> —Alexis Shotwell, *Against Purity: Living Ethically in Compromised Times* (2016)

Teaching in gender and sexuality studies is commonly invested with teaching for social change, with producing knowledge that fosters greater social justice, and with a liberating pedagogy. Three decades ago, Elizabeth Ellsworth's (1989) challenged these and similar aspirations when she provocatively called out the "repressive myths" of critical pedagogy in what consequently became a field-defining article. Needless to say, this article produced what we now, in rather non-academic terms, call a "shitstorm." I found myself returning to Ellsworth's work as I was trying to trace how I had arrived at my own approach to teaching. Across decades of my teaching in women's and gender studies,[1] at the centre are questions of complicity and implication. More recently, I have come to think of what I do in the classroom in terms of a distinct "pedagogy of implication." To make the case for such a pedagogy, I begin this chapter by tracing how complicity and implication figured in my own formation as a feminist scholar and teacher. Next, I discuss the challenges that emerge when teaching under the sign of implication, and I conclude by demonstrating through classroom strategies how a sustained engagement with complicity can help develop a classroom environment where both students and faculty alike can grapple with the difficult knowledge of our role and responsibility vis-à-vis historical, epistemological, and structural violence.

Genealogies of Implication

Despite a profound commitment to social justice in the classroom, my work on implication begins with a critique of the very assumption that we actually know what social justice in education entails. Ellsworth (1989) explores the underlying assumptions that long have shaped ideas of critical pedagogy, what she calls "myths," and which may inadvertently undermine the very goals that social justice education claims for itself. One of the central myths of critical pedagogy, according to Ellsworth, is the assumption that the "radical" educator knows what constitutes injustices, and, thus, can help students not only to name these injustices but also to develop capacities to counter their own oppression and that of others (300). This myth is based in the presumption that students and teacher are "fully rational sub-

---

[1]. The name of the field I teach has been hotly contested since its inception. Initially called women's studies, over the last decades, many programs changed their name to Women's and Gender Studies (WGS), Gender and Sexuality Studies (GSS), or some other variation.

jects" (300), and that by theorizing justice, freedom, and oppression, students and teachers can turn "conflict into rational arguments" (301) and foster analytical and critical thinking to interrogate dominant culture. The problem, Ellsworth suggests, is that this focus on rationality and well-reasoned critique submits students to the very logics (scientism and rationalism) that historically have been the grounds of exclusion of those who are always already socially constructed as irrational Others: women, people of colour, Indigenous people, people with disabilities, queers, non-human animals, and the natural world. Another way to describe what Ellsworth calls myths is to call them persistent fantasies, fantasies that I find myself still attached to, even while I subject them to critical reflection, such as the conviction that gender and sexuality teaching can effect social transformation and that "critical thinking" will liberate the oppressed. Ellsworth's trenchant critiques of this and other "repressive myths" in critical pedagogy, and my own and others' persistent attachment to these, may constitute another example of what Lauren Berlant (2011) calls forms of "cruel optimism," attachments we hold even though they constitute obstacles to our flourishing—or the flourishing of others.

Thinking with Berlant, questions arise as to what kinds of flourishing—and, more importantly, whose flourishing—are hindered by stubborn attachments to rationality and criticality as the path towards social change. Further, does foregrounding partiality, imperfection, limited knowledge, unknowability, and conflict, as Ellsworth alternatively suggests, have greater potential for more equitable flourishing? Admittedly at times like ours, when widespread disinformation, distortion, and outright lies have become the status quo of big business and full-time jobs for some, to question a pedagogical insistence on rationality and criticality feels dangerous. However, what is at stake in my reading of Ellsworth is a larger concern over a type of purity that critical pedagogy claims. The purity of critique and of critical thought strikes me as a wish for innocence and as the refusal to grapple with the difficult insight that, for example, despite our critiques of the institution of education, and its traditional and exclusionary forms of knowledge production, we as self-identified critical or radical scholars and teachers are also *in* and *of* the institution, whose histories and current practices we might condemn. This being in and of the institution is especially the case for tenured faculty and those of us holding positions of power as administrators.[2] Indeed, in the introduction for this volume, Natalie Kouri-Towe turns us to a related point through Robyn Wiegman. Wiegman suggests there is "no way to critique the university without tacitly affirming it, which made it important to retreat from *the romance of non-complicity* long enough to consider what aspects of the university we might want to cultivate and defend" (2016, 84; my emphasis). The pedagogy of implication that guides my teaching takes seriously the challenge involved in giving up the "romance of non-complicity"—while also considering our attachment to this place we call the university or the classroom.

Interestingly enough, *complicity* has recently become a hot analytical term in both North American humanities and social sciences scholarly literature, but also in popular culture. In 2017 *complicit* was voted "word of the year" by dictionary.com.[3] For Merriam-Webster that same year, *complicity* was second only to *feminism*.[4] The renewed interest in questions of complicity resonates with much of my own feminist training. During my undergraduate studies in Germany in the mid-1980s, the German feminist thinker Christina Thürmer-Rohr exploded feminist orthodoxy, which, at the time, sought to establish

---

2. To unfold how this plays out differently for those in precarious teaching positions requires more space than I have here, but needless to say different ambivalences are at stake for these two groups.
3. The ranking is based on the frequency of terms used in internet searches and the US media.
4. For context, 2017 followed the inauguration of Trump, and the popular use of *complicity* and *feminism* may correlate to the ways white people, specifically white women, had brought him to power.

women exclusively as victims of gender violence under patriarchy (Thürmer-Rohr 1987).[5] Thürmer-Rohr's so-called *Mittäterschaftthese* ("complicity" thesis, but better translated as "with the perpetrator" thesis) argued that women become accomplices to heteropatriarchal oppression through compliance with gendered expectations for which they are rewarded. Her nuanced analysis of how women are not only victimized but also become complicit with patriarchy was shaped by the very public national reckoning with the Nazi past in Germany. Gender historians in the late 1980s were also beginning to flesh out in more detail how "ordinary" (non-persecuted) women had become accomplices in Nazi violence in gender-conforming ways, in their roles as mothers, wives, and consumers, but also professionally as nurses, midwives, social workers, and leaders of women's organizations. This work challenged the then-common view that Nazism had subjected non-persecuted German women to a repressive gender ideology. At the same time, feminist scholars in Germany, the UK, and the United States had also begun tracing (white) women's complicity in colonialism and slavery.

In 1991 a graduate studies scholarship took me to the University of Alabama, where the literature on complicity with systemic gender and racial violence became even more textured. I especially remember the difficult conversations in a hybrid undergraduate/graduate seminar on Women in the South in which white women descendants of slave-owning families sat next to women whose ancestors had been enslaved. As we were reading then-newly published scholarship about white women's role in the slave economy, classroom discussions—and their silences—let us feel and understand how violent pasts bear down on the present to affect relationships among feminists today, and demand that we grapple with our respective entanglements with this historical violence. I began to realize more fully how, even though

5. Published in English translation in 1991 (Thürmer-Rohr 1991).

I was born nearly two decades after the Holocaust, as a descendent of a non-persecuted German family I was linked genealogically to Germany's perpetrator past. The systematic murder and eradication of Jewish life and culture during the Nazi period meant that until I left Germany in 1991, to the best of my knowledge, I had never met a Jew, let alone studied side by side with Jewish women.

Especially poignant during my studies in the Southern United States was encountering the writing of the late Minnie Bruce Pratt, a white US feminist poet and essayist and alumna of the University of Alabama. In her now-classic essay "Identity: Skin, Blood, Heart" (1988), Pratt traces in great nuance her shifting identity: from growing up white in the segregated Southern United States, becoming a wife and graduate student in a small town of North Carolina, coming out as a lesbian and subsequently losing custody of her children, to her life as a lesbian feminist activist and poet in the inner city of Washington, DC. Pratt closely observes how white supremacy, class privilege, homophobia, sexism, racism, and anti-Semitism intersect across her life to show how identities are constructed and reconstructed in the intersections of discourse and materiality, history, and daily social interactions. Towards the end of her essay, she describes a dream of her dead father appearing in her bedroom carrying a heavy box, which, despite her protests, he sets on her desk before leaving:

> The box was still there, with what I feared: my responsibility for what the men of my culture have done, in my name, my responsibility to try to change what my father had done, without even knowing what his secrets were. I was angry. Why should I be left with this? I didn't want it; I'd done my best for years to reject it; I wanted no part of what was in it—the benefits of my privilege, the restrictions, the injustice, the pain, the broken urgings of the heart, the unknown horrors.
>
> And yet it is mine: I am my father's daughter in the present, living in a world he and my folks helped to create. (Pratt 1988, 71)

The dream poignantly calls her to a past and to white culture from which she had tried so hard to distance herself geographically, relationally, emotionally, and politically. Pratt contends with the understanding that neither geographic distance nor feminist political "disloyalty" to the white patriarchal, heteronormative culture of her childhood sets her free from the responsibility for the unwanted inheritance bestowed upon her by her father and her people. She is implicated in her father's (and her family's) history and accountable for a legacy of oppression and trauma because she continues to live "in a world he and [her] folks helped to create" (53).

Pratt offers here a methodology of responsibility that is grounded in feminist consciousness-raising that understands the personal as political. While Thürmer-Rohr's (1987) complicity thesis focuses on the complicity and rewards of women's compliance with a heteropatriarchal order, Pratt shows how even active non-compliance and refusal does not free one from one's implication in the effects of these histories of violence and oppression in the present. Pratt recognizes her desire to disassociate from the white supremacist heteropatriarchal culture of her birth, which has both punished her—for coming out as a lesbian feminist activist—and protected her—based on her whiteness and social class—throughout her life. This approach to thinking about oppression and complicity mirrors other parallel developments in feminist thinking at the time, where concepts such as complexity, complicity, and implication became central to the development of intersectional analysis.

First coined in 1989 by African American legal scholar Kimberlé Crenshaw, the concept of intersectionality builds on more than a century of Black, women of colour, and queer feminist thought and activism. Intersectionality captures approaches to knowledge production and social justice practice that attend to how different vectors of identity (race, gender, class, sexuality, disability, and so on) are produced and maintained through structurally determined, situationally experienced, and relationally enacted shifting conditions of power—privilege and oppression. Now widely used both inside and outside of higher education, intersectionality is often regarded as gender and sexuality studies' key scholarly contribution to contemporary thinking (Nash 2019). Crenshaw's initial (1989) analysis demonstrated how racism and sexism work together to produce employment discrimination for Black women that is distinct from both opportunities and discriminations experienced by white women and Black men, respectively. Intersectionality has since proliferated as an analytical framework for social justice–oriented theory and research that seeks to overcome the limits of single-axis analysis and the privileging of one single form of oppression at the expense of others. However, despite widely declared commitments to intersectional analysis, examples of single-vector analysis still abound. For instance, studies of gender inequities frequently focus primarily (or entirely) on white, cisgender, middle-class women; anti-racism work frequently ignores the intracategorical difference gender, sexuality, or disability make to the way racism is experienced; and arguably, many disciplines privilege humans over non-human animals and remain inattentive to environmental and planetary social justice issues.

When it comes to classroom applications of intersectionality, we must grapple with what is often a competitive model of oppression informed by zero-sum logics. Zero-sum logics are based on the fear that attention to any one axis of oppression not only competes with but diminishes others. Such logics risk erasing, making invisible, and denying a wide variety of suffering and inequality. Fear of erasure is not unwarranted, given a long history of single-vector social movements and theory. When developing my approach to a "pedagogy of implication," I had to contend with the admission that truly intersectional analyses are still more aspiration than norm. Such admission seems preferable to a competitive and single nodal model of oppression and privilege that risks missing meaningful opportunities for building multidirectional solidarities. Asking which axes of power are centred and which are marginalized can help us acknowledge the partiality, partisanship, and limits of our analyses. Once we can admit to the partiality of our scholarship and teaching, applying intersectionality becomes more possible.

Pedagogies of Implication

Complicity has been an implicit framework for my teaching about feminism for two decades or longer, but recently I made it the explicit framework for a hybrid undergraduate/graduate course I teach. While curricular decisions matter, a pedagogy of implication is not just about different content and *what* we teach. It is also about *how* we teach. My thinking has long been animated by the understanding of implication offered by Deborah Britzman (1998) as "difficult knowledge." "Difficult knowledge" captures the complex feelings that arise from the understanding that one is implicated in knowledge, especially knowledge concerning historical and present violence and social injustices. Britzman's work turns attention to the internal conflicts and crises that arise from learning from traumatic events, "the psychical defences against knowing that learners erect as they become un-done by the difficult stories of others" (Di Paolantonio 2018, 1). I have written elsewhere about how these dynamics sometimes play out in the classroom (Luhmann 2012, 2017). If recognizing one's oppression and victimization can be painful, learning about and from the oppression and suffering of others can undo students even more. Being confronted with how one's well-being and flourishing might benefit from, even rest on, the suffering of others, raises profound ethical dilemmas. This difficult knowledge challenges students' self-understanding as good and innocent subjects.

Most of us who teach in the area of gender and sexuality are familiar with the conflictual quality of learning difficult knowledge. An especially difficult dynamic in the classroom happens when the encounter with difficult knowledge animates defensiveness. Students may reject arguments and evidence, express doubt, withdraw noisily, quit quietly, or enact various forms of aggression. When this happens, it is helpful to remember Shoshana Felman's insights into learners' "passion for ignorance" (1987, 79) and the core challenge of teaching, which is not the lack of knowledge but how to overcome resistance to knowing. The insistence on ignorance and the refusal to understand is about the difficult knowledge of one's implicatedness, of coming to understand how one is a beneficiary of the suffering of others. Quite a bit of instructor attention tends to be on the students who resist knowledge or refuse insights, who remain unpersuaded by rational arguments and sound evidence, which is also Ellsworth's earlier point. In my teaching, I have been trying to shift from reacting to resistance and refusal of knowledge to listening more carefully for how and where students (and I, too) are refusing implication. When listening works, we are less likely to be merely reactive. If the problem is not resistance to knowledge per se but the refusal of implication, then responding with even more rational arguments and evidence is futile. Instead, the task is to help students to make a relationship to the complex and uncomfortable feelings that being implicated in knowledge can unleash.

One strategy I use in my teaching is to begin by studying contexts other than our own to analyze the dynamics of implication and complicity in genocide, colonialism and settler colonialism, slavery, racism, sexism, transphobia, and other mass violence and forms of oppression. After looking elsewhere and learning that other nations also live with denial in the aftermath of histories of state-sponsored violence, students are often more willing to consider their own contexts as sites for learning about violence. Working through literature on complicity also helps the class engage with how violence continues in the present, especially in their own lives. We read texts by feminist and other social justice writers, activists, and artists to see their struggles with the complex knowledge of their family and communities' involvement in state-sponsored and state-endorsed violence.[6]

Initially looking elsewhere constitutes what I call a mode of "multidirectional learning," a pedagogical approach I conceptualize by drawing on Michael Rothberg's (2009) "multidirectional memory." Multidirectional learning works through indirection: by looking first at contexts where students by and large are not personally implicated because these are the struggles of people elsewhere.[7] When students have less direct investment, learning tends to activate less defensiveness. Although students in gender and sexuality studies today are less likely to encounter Canada's violent history and present for the first time in my classes, confrontations, for example, with settler-colonial violence through the lens of Indigenous and decolonial texts can be challenging, especially (but not only) for white settler and other non-Indigenous students. These approaches ask students to reconsider what they already know about the nation-state, both past and present, and to re-evaluate the very institutions they may have been raised to trust—including the state, the church, education, the legal system, the police, and the family.[8] Because trust in the state and its institutions is a feature of complicity and implication in structures of violence, students can confront how trust is associated with the privileges of being white, middle-class, heterosexual, and cisgender, which grants safety and support to some, while putting others at risk.

---

6. In my most recent course, this has included autobiographical texts such as Pratt 1988 and Teege and Sellmair 2015, as well as documentary films: Moll 2006; Wilkerson 2017.
7. I qualify this statement with a "by and large" because of the diversity of students in our classrooms who collectively connect us to diverse global, national, and local crises.
8. It's worth keeping in mind that for some, especially for Indigenous communities, education itself has been nothing less than a scene of genocide.

In recent years, at least in the upper-year courses that I have been teaching, I have noticed a shift in students' responses to learning about complicity and implication: less resistance but more feelings of guilt and shame. This may be related to the broad commitments to social justice that enable many students to understand themselves as privileged. Feelings of shame and guilt are understandable in response to learning about the genocidal intentions and actions of one's nation. For instance, public responses to the discovery of hundreds of unmarked graves on the grounds of former residential schools in Canada brought to the forefront guilt and shame over Canada's settler-colonial violence, both past and present. These feelings can be signs of public recognition for the systemic violence of what Driftpile Cree Nation poet and scholar Billy-Ray Belcourt calls "death schools" (2022, 34). Guilt and shame arise when non-Indigenous students begin to understand that the deadly conditions of residential schools—such as diseases, malnourishment, and abuse—were known at the time, yet nothing was done to stop this. Residential schools required the quiet support of many, not only abusers in the schools but also politicians, civil servants, and the general public. Learning about the widespread support for genocidal policies and practices in residential schools can be a difficult knowledge for students who believe that education is fundamentally good.

However, shame and guilt can only be the beginning and not the end-point of engaging with collective culpability in historic and contemporary violence. Indeed, lingering on guilt, shame, and other bad feelings risks recentring once again the dominant group and their emotional states, rather than actual justice. Shame and guilt must not be pedagogical objectives. When learning about residential schools, shame risks redirecting attention away from the intergenerational trauma of residential school survivors, their descendants, and the ongoing re-traumatization that discoveries of mass graves can animate in the present. A focus on settlers' shame diverts attention away from

Indigenous people and from taking responsible action, such as supporting the sovereignty of the affected communities over the search for the bodies of their stolen children.

When feelings of shame and guilt surface in my classes, I try to acknowledge them and encourage students to turn an analytical eye onto their feelings so as to make them an object of study and insight. Shame, as Ruth Leys (2007), argues in *From Guilt to Shame: Auschwitz and After*, is about exposure, feeling exposed in front of others, and poses a challenge to one's sense of self and identity. Learning about residential schools challenges the notion of the good and benevolent Canadian. The task of a pedagogy of implication is to help students to not get too stuck in feelings of shame and guilt, and to recognize their implication and find paths towards responsibility. That is not a small task. A pedagogy of implication requires students to challenge their attachment to what, with Ellsworth, we can identify as the repressive myth that social justice studies should feel "liberatory." Although it is not possible to work in detail through the affective and conceptual complexities of shame and guilt, in the classroom we discuss the important distinction between *feeling morally guilty* and *being criminally culpable*. Focusing on questions of implication further facilitates the distinction between guilt and responsibility. Rothberg offers this helpful distinction: "Guilt," he writes, "is contemporaneous with the life of the perpetrator of the deed," while responsibility is "a diachronic as well as a synchronic phenomenon" (2019, 47). Meaning, we settler students and faculty are not criminally nor morally *guilty* for the crime of residential schools; however, we may still *feel guilty* when learning about this form of historical violence. We are *structurally implicated* in how past settler-colonial, genocidal, and racist policies and practices continue and play out in the present—even if we are not genealogically connected to those responsible for the creation, enforcement, or political support for residential schools. We, however, are *politically accountable* for how these structures continue today, and we may even be complicit in their flourishing in the present—especially when we are the beneficiaries of dispossession through wealth inheritance, land ownership, and resource extraction of Indigenous lands.

Conclusion

A pedagogy of implication challenges our deeply rooted desire for innocence, which can be especially pronounced in students and faculty with firm commitments to social justice. Intersectional analyses that consider multiple axes of oppression and their intersections add complexity to discussions of implication and complicity, past and present, because students and faculty find themselves complexly situated: subjected to discrimination and oppression in some instances; beneficiaries, bystanders, or even agents of harm in others. As students begin to grasp the full extent to which violence is sewn into the very fabric of our lives, I do encounter some modes of refusing the difficult knowledge that course readings present. However, this refusal happens less frequently as students develop an awareness of their implication in systems of violence, even if this awareness is coupled with feelings of guilt and shame around such knowledge. I continue to worry about what we might call over-identification with difficult knowledge, which finds students seeking to distance themselves from the messiness and painful feelings that recognizing implication produces. Over-identification takes many different forms, and may include sanctifying specific authors, texts, or political positions to make them unassailable; anxiously vying for "correct" language and analysis; self-righteously calling out others; hurrying into claiming an ally identification; and distancing themselves from, and dismissing, the university, their department, feminism, the nation, and a host of other positions and institutions they have come to understand as complicit in colonialism and racism. All or many of these forms of over-identification can be understood broadly as "moves to innocence" (Tuck and Yang 2012; Mawhinney 1998; Fellows and Razack 1998). Such moves to innocence seek to evade the "discomforting forms of belonging" (Rothberg 2019, 9) that implicate us in the very structures of inequality and violence that we critique.

One of the most challenging lessons we grapple with in my courses is the insight that there is no innocent position. Innocence is not an option, especially when we take a comprehensive intersectional view that also attends to the entangled relations between human and non-human animals, and environmental and planetary justice. The most shocking discovery for many students in my recent course On Complicity and Being Implicated was probably Alexis Shotwell's piercing observation that "our existence as embodied beings is predicated on the suffering of other beings" (2016, 127). Shotwell unfolds this claim in a discussion of food and energy use practices. Creating conditions that allow me to work with students to begin reckoning with the complex knowledge of our non-innocence is the goal of a pedagogy of implication. As we grapple with how specifically we each are implicated, differently so, in various forms of oppression and inequality, we also begin to ask how to make change. Once we truly understand ourselves as "entangled, impure subjects of historical and political responsibility" (Rothberg 2019, 35), we might begin considering what interrupting and refusing the continuation of domination might look like, how to do so without seeking to re-establish a false sense of our innocence, and how to be in solidarity with those in whose suffering we are implicated.

References

Belcourt, Billy-Ray. 2022. *A Minor Chorus*. New York: W.W. Norton & Company, Inc.

Berlant, Lauren. 2011. *Cruel Optimism*. Durham, NC: Duke University Press.

Britzman, Deborah P. 1998. *Lost Subjects, Contested Objects: Toward a Psychoanalytic Inquiry of Learning*. Albany: SUNY Press.

Crenshaw, Kimberle. 1989. "Demarginalizing the Intersection of Race and Sex: A Black Feminist Critique of Antidiscrimination Doctrine, Feminist Theory and Antiracist Politics." *University of Chicago Legal Forum* 1989 (1): 138–67. https://chicagounbound.uchicago.edu/uclf/vol1989/iss1/8.

Di Paolantonio, Mario. 2018. "The Other Other in Difficult Knowledge: Thinking with Jim Garrett's Learning to Be in the World with Others." *Journal of the American Association for the Advancement of Curriculum Studies* 12 (2). https://doi.org/10.14288/jaaacs.v12i2.190371.

Ellsworth, Elizabeth. 1989. "Why Doesn't This Feel Empowering? Working through the Repressive Myths of Critical Pedagogy." *Harvard Educational Review* 59 (3): 297–325. https://doi.org/10.17763/haer.59.3.058342114k266250.

Fellows, Mary, and Sherene Razack. 1998. "The Race to Innocence: Confronting Hierarchical Relations among Women." *Journal of Gender, Race & Justice*, no. 1, 335–52. https://scholarship.law.umn.edu/faculty_articles/274.

Felman, Shoshana. 1987. *Jacques Lacan and the Adventure of Insight*. Cambridge, MA: Harvard University Press.

Leys, Ruth. 2007. *From Guilt to Shame: Auschwitz and After*. Princeton, NJ: Princeton University Press.

Luhmann, Susanne. 2012. "Pedagogy." In *Rethinking Women's and Gender Studies*, edited by Ann Braithwaite, Catherine Orr, and Diane Lichtenstein, 65–81. New York: Routledge.

—. 2017. "Un-Settling Queer Pedagogy : The Illusion of 'Safe Space.'" In *Queering MINT: Impulse für eine dekonstruktive Lehrerinnenbildung*, edited by Nadine Balzter, Florian Cristobal Klenk, and Olga Zitzelberger, 73–88. Leverkusen: Opladen.

Mawhinney, Janet Lee. 1998. "Giving up the Ghost, Disrupting the (Re)production of White Privilege in Anti-Racist Pedagogy and Organizational Change." MA thesis, University of Toronto. https://tspace.library.utoronto.ca/handle/1807/12096.

Moll, James, dir. 2006. *Inheritance*. Los Angeles: Allentown Production.

Nash, Jennifer C. 2019. *Black Feminism Reimagined: After Intersectionality*. Durham, NC: Duke University Press.

Pratt, Minnie Bruce. 1988. "Identity: Skin, Blood, Heart." In *Yours in Struggle: Three Feminist Perspectives on Anti-Semitism and Racism*, edited by Ellen Bulkin, Minnie Bruce Pratt, and Barbara Smith, 27–77. Ithaca, NY: Firebrand Books.

Rothberg, Michael. 2009. *Multidirectional Memory: Remembering the Holocaust in the Age of Decolonization*. Stanford, CA: Stanford University Press.

—. 2019. *The Implicated Subject: Beyond Victims and Perpetrators*. Stanford, CA: Stanford University Press.

Shotwell, Alexis. 2016. *Against Purity: Living Ethically in Compromised Times*. Minneapolis: University of Minnesota Press.

Teege, Jennifer, and Nikola Sellmair. 2015. *My Grandfather Would Have Shot Me: A Black Woman Discovers Her Family's Nazi Past*. Translated by Carolin Sommer. New York: The Experiment.

Thürmer-Rohr, Christina. 1987. *Vagabundinnen: Feministische Essays*. Berlin: Orlanda-Frauenverlag. Translated by Lise Weil as *Vagabonding: Feminist Thinking Cut Loose* (Boston: Beacon Press, 1991).

Tuck, Eve, and K. Wayne Yang. 2012. "Decolonization Is Not a Metaphor." *Decolonization: Indigeneity, Education & Society* 1 (1): 1–40.

Wiegman, Robyn. 2016. "No Guarantee: Feminism's Academic Affect and Political Fantasy." *Atlantis: Critical Studies in Gender, Culture & Social Justice* 37.2 (2): 83–95. https://journals.msvu.ca/index.php/atlantis/article/view/83-95%20PDF/83-95.

Wilkerson, Travis, dir. 2017. *Did You Wonder Who Fired the Gun?* New York: Grasshopper Film.

PART II

The Classroom as a Problem

The Challenges Facing Teachers and Students

While the classroom can be an exciting and exhilarating space for faculty and students alike, it can also be the scene of conflict and anxiety, or worse, a site of violence. At times, the classroom is a space where subject matter is weaponized, where appropriation and exploitation go unchallenged, or a crisis unfolds in ways that make it difficult to bring everyone back together for learning. While one formulation positions teachers and students as separate figures in the classroom, the reality can often be much different. Students can align with a teacher in co-creating an environment for learning; however, there also exists a dynamic where students and teachers can entrench a culture of exclusion, where insider and outside status are delineated through ideological, political, or discursive divides that render students at odds in the classroom. Worrying about what culture we're cultivating in our classrooms can become a part of the anxiety and fear that goes into teaching, while for others the classroom is a scene for the enactment of the teacher's power and authority. This contradiction between styles and approaches to teaching render it difficult to know how we should approach teaching and what the classroom is for, and what our roles as teachers can or should be.

The classroom is a problem because there is no universal model for the classroom. It is a problem because problems arise in the classroom. From student admissions processes to the infrastructure of the classroom's design and accessibility features, there is so much that we do not control but that nonetheless informs who is in the room with us when we teach. One of the greatest mysteries of the classroom is how from section to section and year to year we can find wildly different classroom experiences. What works for one set of students doesn't work for another. The authors in this part all grapple with the problems that come from teaching and how to respond to the challenges that arise, from knowing how or what to teach to situating ourselves within the space of the classroom. While there is no definitive way to make sense of the relationship between students and teachers in the classroom beyond the artificial boundaries set by the structure of education, it can be helpful to interrogate what happens in the classroom across these different positions and roles.

The following chapters grapple with the impact of institutional power and structures of violence that implicate students as both subjects of harm and agents of change, as consumers with desires and expectations that challenge the pedagogical goals of faculty curriculum, and the role of embodiment and positionality that shapes the teacher's experience within the classroom. Part II begins with Alexis Poirier-Saumure, who reflects on his first experience teaching as a graduate student. Drawing on a reflexive approach, Poirier-Saumure confronts his anxieties and desires for the classroom by interrogating the ideals that shaped his own encounters in the classroom as a student and the kind of classroom he envisioned creating. Pressing into the source of anxiety, he turns to failure as a technique for developing the skills to teach. This reframing of anxiety into self-reflection and self-reflexion through failure invites established and emerging teachers alike to think about how revision, rather than assumed expertise, can open possibilities for reworking curriculum and pedagogical approaches.

In the next chapter, Gulzar R. Charania discusses the challenges of teaching gender and sexuality studies through critical race and Indigenous scholarship. Here, we find a familiar scene of friction emerge when the teacher's subject position and student desires for specific kinds of learning are confronted in the classroom. Reflecting on student expectations that learning about queer theory should be an exercise in learning about sexuality as separate from race and racialization, Charania confronts the way that racial logics underlie the foundations of hegemonic disciplinary systems. Pressing her students with compassion while challenging their attachment to knowledge as resistance in the logics of education's foundation in white supremacy, she proposes that a way forward through this friction is through slow and consistent interventions in the ways of knowing that students bring into the classroom. Similarly, we find more friction between students and teachers in a conversation between a professor, Kimberley Ens Manning, and her former students, Mitchell Rae Yang and Rebecca Gaëlle Joachim. Their narrative unfolds as the co-authors revisit and contend with how institutional racism renders the classroom a space that begins from a place of exclusion. Grappling with the limitations of presuming that the classroom can be inclusive through common techniques, such as establishing classroom "ground rules," the three co-authors struggle with the implications and limits of what constitutes harm versus comfort in the classroom. Confronting the fantasy that the classroom can or should be a "safe space," their work illustrates the wider challenges of how power manifests itself in the classroom and how teachers can adapt to these conditions through collaboration with students, both current and former.

Next, we continue with the dialogic form by turning to a discussion on trigger warnings between co-investigators of a SSHRC-funded national study on trigger warnings in higher education in Canada with Hannah Dyer (co-investigator), myself (co-investigator), and Michelle Miller (principal investigator). The conversation travels across the disciplinary differences of how the norms and culture around trigger warnings play out in our respective fields (child and youth studies, sexuality studies, and English literature) and how we have grappled with the challenges of giving (or not giving) warnings in our own classrooms. The discussion provides a set of strategies we have each used, as well as a set of ethical considerations for how or why warnings are incorporated into our teaching, or not. This work also considers how we position ourselves as teachers in the classroom, and how we consider our roles vis-à-vis students. Lastly, the section concludes with Julia Sinclair-Palm,[1] who reflects on their strategy of self-disclosure within the classroom, asking "What happens when the professor becomes the object of knowledge and part of the curriculum?" Like S. Trimble's work in the previous part, Sinclair-Palm takes seriously the role of embodiment in learning. She argues that teachers can help students learn by embracing the vulnerability of being embodied. Reflecting on their decisions to "come out" as queer and trans in the context of the classroom, she interrogates the normative structure of knowledge within institutionalized settings that naturalize gender in the classroom, whereby only trans subjects are rendered visible, and by extension, a problem to interrogate. Sinclair-Palm disrupts this impulse in the classroom by encouraging students to understand the classroom as a space where all subjects are gendered and embodied. Their chapter provides concrete strategies for helping students through the process of learning and unlearning, and ends with a set of prompts for faculty across disciplines to consider about their own gender and the genders of their students in the classroom.

1. Both gender-neutral and gendered pronouns are used with reference to Sinclair-Palm, who uses "she/they" pronouns.

7

The First Teaching Experience

Failure as a Strategy for Critical, Anti-Oppressive, and Queer Approaches to Pedagogy

ALEXIS POIRIER-SAUMURE

The graduate student's first teaching experience has seldom been documented or interrogated, with some exceptions (Meanwell and Kleiner 2014; Smollin and Arluke 2014). There are even fewer cases that allude to the first teaching experience in a critical gender and sexuality studies courses (Allen 2009, 2015), the field in which I first taught an undergraduate course called Media and Gender in January 2021, at the height of a global pandemic. While my interdisciplinary academic training had prepared me well theoretically, I was considerably less prepared to teach in this area pedagogically. Using a reflexive approach, I explore what I learned about teaching during an unprecedented time, and what this can tell us about strategies for teaching—both for those who are teaching for the first time and seasoned instructors.

There is a common assumption among graduate students, and within academia more generally, that you learn to teach as you go, rather than through training (Smollin and Arluke 2014). As a result, self-reflexive discourse about early teaching experiences is more rarely a topic within mentorships and collegial relationships. Through the pedagogical self-reflection that I deploy in this chapter, I have two goals: to reflect on the craft of teaching, as a form of self-training after the fact; and, following Erika França de Souza Vasconcelos, to contribute to a more robust collective thinking about beginning to teach by looking "inward and study myself in order to create a reflexive dialogue with the readers of this piece, in the hope that the meanings embedded in my life story might have relevance to other teachers" (2011, 418).

I begin by outlining the contexts shaping my experience teaching for the first time, followed by a reflection on my pedagogical standpoint, and conclude by examining two scenes from my experience in 2021 that offer a discussion on allyship—or how to teach within an ethical/political relationship—and a reflection on how to teach critically about critique. Reflecting on these formative scenes, I interrogate the ways that my position as a graduate student and first-time instructor shaped and enabled my approach to teaching from a standpoint inspired by critical, anti-oppressive, and queer pedagogies. Through this reflection, I examine how I navigated the complex power dynamics that characterize the relationship between students and an inexperienced new instructor. In a class where matters of violence, power, identity, justice, oppression, and privilege were discussed, and where the pedagogical imperative was arguably to subvert received knowledges about sexuality and gender, I found that the norms I was aiming to deconstruct with my students were already somewhat deconstructed. Teaching critical thought for the first time, then, offers insight about how pedagogical subversion is shifting and how we might use that shift to re-energize critical pedagogies.

Starting from Failure as a Pedagogical Standpoint

As a graduate student teacher, liminality heavily marks my institutional position: not a student, not yet a professor. Leandra Smollin and Arnold Arluke (2014) argue that liminality is one of the structuring conditions of a first teaching experience in graduate school. As a spatial and phenomenological condition, liminality points to the uncertainty of first-time experiences, where we don't quite know how to inhabit new subject positions, but hope to arrive there. This complex configuration gets even harder to navigate as it becomes clear that it is a one-sided experience: students are generally unaware of academic hierarchy and positions and see us as equivalent to tenured professors. This dynamic can add a layer of anxiety to the experience of liminality, since student instructors may be judged on the same basis as full-time instructors or tenured professors, without the same experience or institutional status. Teaching for the first time is seen as a "rite of passage" (Smollin and Arluke 2014, 28), a "key step toward a professional academic identity" (Meanwell and Kleiner 2014, 19). It is a stepping stone in the process of teacher identity formation, and for that reason, precisely because this new role is not only a matter of professional accomplishment but of professional identity, it is an event that can be saturated with overwhelming emotions.

The emotional aspect of a first teaching experience is a central element to consider (Meanwell and Kleiner 2014; Smollin and Arluke 2014). There is, of course, the sheer joy and pleasure associated with new kinds of understandings attained through teaching: no matter how long or deeply you have explored a conceptual or theoretical area in your studies, teaching transforms your relationship to ideas and knowledge. For example, after years of learning to critique in graduate school, returning to the disciplinary canon can be an energizing experience, bringing new insights into old ideas through the classroom. However, emotional turmoil is also an overwhelming part of the experience. Acute anxiety has been identified as a central element of a first teaching experience. According to Smollin and Arluke's study of sociology instructors, the anxiety experienced by grad students teaching for the first time encompasses five main themes: "feelings of unpreparedness, seemingly unrelenting time demands, a lack of confidence, issues with students, and insufficient support" (2014,

31). I can attest to the fact that these are all on point; however, in the context of teaching for the first time during a pandemic, this anxiety can be amplified by the rupture in the status quo of the teaching environment caused by the rapid shifts between remote and in-person teaching. How things were done "before" don't map evenly onto a first-time experience, and so the fear of failure can be especially acute.

In *The Queer Art of Failure*, Jack Halberstam (2011) proposes a framework to think through the generative potential of failure, an argument that emerges from queer politics as a critique of neoliberalism's toxic positivity. One of Halberstam's main arguments posits that there are kinds of failures that can offer "more creative, more cooperative, more surprising ways of being in the world" (2) as well as "to escape the punishing norms that discipline behavior and manage human development with the goal of delivering us from unruly childhoods to orderly and predictable adulthoods" (3). Halberstam's critique of developmental norms lends well to a discussion on the temporality of education and pedagogy, where failure is largely seen negatively rather than a productive force for subject formation and world-making. Pursuing a similar thread in the field of disability studies and pedagogy, David Mitchell et al. suggest that deploying failure might offer the possibility to "undertake pedagogical practices suppressed (or, at least, devalued) by normative neoliberal educational contexts" (2014, 300). What could happen if, instead of fearing a teaching experience structured by liminality and anxiety, we became aware of what failure allows and what ideals of success and performance foreclose? What if we actually sought out the failure of some canonical ideals of teaching? Liminality implies the "failure" of a stable, total position, and anxiety foregrounds the "failure" of preparedness and confidence. Both are inescapable modalities of the first teaching experience; therefore, we must become curious about the pedagogical potential of failing at being prepared, confident, or stable. Looking back at my first teaching experience, I propose failure as a pedagogical standpoint to start from.

My exploration of critical, anti-oppressive, and queer pedagogical approaches reveals many ways that pedagogy asks us to look at failure. Because critical pedagogies foreground an engagement with subversion and political agency, they approach knowledge through the deconstruction and unlearning of normative and mainstream discourses and frameworks, prioritizing instead liberatory approaches to learning (Freire 2012; hooks 1994; Kincheloe 2008). Thinking through not only the oppressed but also the oppressor, the normal, and the structures that sustain inequalities (Kumashiro 2000, 2002; Richard 2019), critical and anti-oppressive approaches to education centre on learning through the way systems of oppression and inequality fail minority and oppressed subjects. Failure thus becomes a generative starting point for learning about violence and (in)justice by allowing us to learn through the failure of liberal ideals relating to rights, equality, and justice. Queer pedagogical approaches can further help us ground these insights in an antinormative turn: they foreground the failure of traditional pedagogical structures and aim to subvert the hierarchical ways that knowledge typically circulates in the classroom. They introduce a critique of education as normalizing and biased, as well as ways of re-envisioning the very grounds of knowledge in education (Britzman 1995; Luhmann 1998; Shlasko 2005).

In *Teaching to Transgress*, bell hooks draws on Paulo Freire's (2012) critique of the banking system of education and recounts her refusal of traditional or normative pedagogical structures: "In graduate school I was often bored in classes. The banking system of education (based on the assumption that memorizing information and regurgitating it represented gaining knowledge that could be deposited, stored and used at a later date) did not interest me. I wanted to become a critical thinker" (1994, 5). In this passage, hooks refuses a passive, linear, teleological understanding of knowledge circulation in the classroom. When I began preparing my course, the pressure to ensure students accumulate canonical learning was at odds with my critical, anti-oppressive, and queer pedagogical standpoint. Navigating this tension was a challenge, especially as I grappled with the fact that replacing hegemonic knowledge with more, supposedly better, knowledge about historically excluded subjectivities does little to address the structural root of the problem of exclusion and violence in education, and risks simply reifying difference (Britzman 1995; Kumashiro 2000; Luhmann 1998). Critical pedagogies as a whole entail a vision of knowledge circulation in the classroom that creates flourishing conditions for the work of critique, contestation, and subversion. Allowing for knowledge to flow in the classroom in ways that run counter to the establishment of a hierarchical, solipsistic, normative pedagogy is a precondition for critical pedagogy.

Despite my commitment to critical pedagogy, however, I had to contend with the possibility that my attempts to bring horizontal models for learning into the classroom were largely at odds with the university as institution, which remains in service of the state's normative educational project. As hooks reminds us, the classroom can become "the most radical space of possibility in the academy" (1994, 12), but only if we are willing to refuse—to fail—normative ideals around teaching and pedagogy. Failure comes to shape my pedagogical standpoint in two ways: first, as a praxis—failing, for example, to follow institutional norms and expectations around education, such as a rigid transmissive model, punitive grading schemes, testing, and monitoring attendance; and second, as the condition through which the promise of knowledge can emerge by rethinking failure as the possibility of a more generative engagement with critique and subversion. From here, I turn to two scenes from my first experience teaching to reflect on how failure can be a path for training as a first-time teacher.

Teaching as a Mode of Allyship

In my introduction survey for the class, I asked the following question: "Do you have any apprehensions about this class? They can be about the topics that will be covered, about evaluations, about the current context of remote teaching during the pandemic, etc." I received a response that mirrored my own anxiety: the student expressed apprehension about the fact that often, topics about marginalization on the basis of race, sexuality, and gender are taught by heterosexual, cisgender white men, who have not experienced such discrimination.

At first, part of me wanted to reply directly, to address the fact that no one can have lived experiences related to every topic they teach about, especially in terms of sexuality and gender, and at the same time recognize the importance and relevance of the student's apprehension and let them know that I had already thought of that exact critique. Instead, I decided to position myself in class, to acknowledge my identity as a white, cisgender, able-bodied queer/gay settler man who teaches from that standpoint, with awareness. I explained that I had decided to invite guest speakers precisely in order to make up for my own largely privileged positionality, and most importantly, that even though I was teaching about Blackness, about transness, about disability, about racism, and other forms of oppression, I had not experienced any of those things and thus my teaching was not enacted from an experiential standpoint.

Reflecting on my urge to justify my relationship to teaching topics outside of my lived experiences, I can see how my reaction was rooted in a desire to be an ally in the classroom. Part of me wanted my work as a teacher to be an irreproachable act of allyship (although allyship interested in avoiding reproach is always already performative and thus aimed solely at self-preservation). As someone who had never been a hands-on, frontline activist, it seemed to me that teaching was where I could most radically contribute my anti-oppressive and queer political interventions. It held the promise of a sort of self-actualization that could be generative at a community level, as well as meaningful at a more personal and psychic level, for both myself and the students in my class. Louisa Allen mirrors this experience when she writes, "in accordance with notions of consciousness raising and social transformation to which I had been exposed...I loftily viewed my teaching as 'a political act'" (2015, 772). I began to question the possibility of allyship through teaching and my desire to *succeed at allyship* in the classroom.

Allyship, whether an identity or a political relation, has been studied across diverse fields, such as social psychology (Brown and Ostrove 2013), Indigenous community activism (Indigenous Action Media 2014; Sullivan-Clarke 2019), and global solidarities (Goetz and Tobin 2018). An ally is generally understood to be a person belonging to a dominant social group "willing to take action, either interpersonally or in larger social settings, and move beyond self-regulation of prejudice" (Brown and Ostrove 2013, 2212). Further, an ally is distinct from "low-prejudice individuals" through an ally's "desires to promote social justice actively and their willingness to offer support to nondominant people" (2212). Missing from this definition, however, is an understanding of how power dynamics shape and restrict the possibility of allyship. If an ally is always assumed to belong to a dominant social group, then social hierarchies risk being unavoidable in relationships of solidarity (Sullivan-Clarke 2019, 184). Further, the above definition fails to attend to the ways allyship can also function across subjugated groups, such as in South-South solidarities.

Some Indigenous activists have disavowed the term *allyship*, calling out what they aptly term the "ally industrial complex," which they critique as the "commodification and exploitation of allyship" and "a growing trend in the activism industry" where "ally has also become an identity, disembodied from any real mutual understanding of support. The term *ally* has been rendered ineffective and meaningless" (Indigenous Action Media 2014). Indeed, it is now possible to undergo training and become a "certified ally,"[1] a badge that can be neatly applied to the fabric of one's social identity. Rachel McKinnon (2017)

---

1. For instance, organizations such as the Safe Zone Project and the Trevor Project offer certified allyship training.

also warns us against an identity-oriented understanding of allyship, precisely because as neoliberal politics flatten identities into individual claims to self-truth, the allyship badge becomes a way for variously privileged people to congratulate themselves on *who they are* and evade responsibility for their inaction towards, and complicity in, systemic oppression. Such a "neoliberal way of expressing solidarity" (Goetz and Tobin 2018, 21) calls for more radical understandings of solidarity, such as through the figure of the accomplice, and through an approach that is less self-interested and more attuned to the needs, realities, and histories of minoritized groups (Indigenous Action Media 2014).

Despite the above critiques, I am interested in how the concept can be recuperated from the presumed power inequities that shape many practices of allyship today. To do this, I interrogate the possibilities and risks of *teaching as a mode of allyship*. If allyship can be practiced by taking a step back, by relinquishing space in order to leave it open for historically excluded voices to make themselves heard, then the classroom continues to hold the possibility, even if complicated, for enacting allyship. Because the teacher-student hierarchy shapes the classroom, allyship only has the potential to happen through concrete actions guided by an ethical commitment to resisting the entrenchment of these hierarchies. Allyship must be understood *not* as an identity you attain and can thus claim as yours, but as something that is process based, never complete, always on the horizon, and dependent on mutually agreed upon actions rather than words alone. Can inviting guest speakers in a pedagogical space be a concrete example of allyship? I argue that it can be, but it must be approached with care.

I mobilize the figure of the guest speaker as it is ripe with the tensions and nuances that animate the possibilities and challenges of allyship. Can bringing in guest speakers from historically excluded communities be an effective form of allyship? Or does reliance on the guest speaker reify power in the classroom and instrumentalize diversity? The anxiety I felt as I debated my reliance on guest speakers as a way of building allyship with racialized, trans, and disabled communities became a scene where my fear of failure took hold. What if instead of worrying about failing at being an ally, my goal was simply to accept that attempts at allyship may fail, and that the work and process of building allyship is important for learning to teach? Instead of debating whether or not to bring in guest speakers, I am interested in how we invite guest speakers into the classroom as part of the process of renegotiating the hierarchies and power that structure higher education. Guest speakers can be a way for the teacher to relinquish knowledge/knowing in order to listen, take a step back, and reflect. When inviting guest speakers becomes a means to avoid accountability, the transformative potential of the role of the guest speaker is undermined. However, when guest speakers are brought in as interlocutors, as experts from their lived experiences, and as collaborators in the classroom, there is less risk of tokenization and more possibility for the classroom as a space for allyship to be built. I think that a reflexive process attuned to failure can be a good place to start interrogating the role of allyship in the classroom, especially if we hope to develop our capacity to ethically engage with lived experiences that exceed our own.

Teaching Critically about Critique

I'm chatting with an insightful friend about how the power dynamics that structure the university classroom experience intersect with the fact that I teach a critical theory class about gender and sexuality. How does my position, which is simultaneously one of teacher and student, of experience and inexperience, in other words unstable and unclear within academic hierarchies, affect my engagement with a critical discourse about gender and sexual normativity in media representations?

My friend listens to me patiently. When I finish, he rephrases bluntly: Ah! So... what you mean to ask is, How do you teach about your own opinion on these matters?!

I am surprised at first; yet, his observation touches upon something I hadn't considered. I reply that one of the goals of my class is for students to try and deconstruct "objectivity" and complicate the relationship between "opinion" and "fact" or "truth," but his remark strikes a chord: How do I teach theory that aligns with my political values without uncritically transmitting knowledge that I implicitly construe as "right" or "good"? How do I teach critically about critiques I agree with?

What my friend conveyed relates to "education's traditional fixation on knowledge transmission, and its wish for the teacher as the master of knowledge" (Luhmann 1998, 126). His comment implied a view of education where the teacher masters a body of objective knowledge that is transmitted and not interrogated, which is of course not at all how I had framed my class. I had positioned my course from the start through intersectional and feminist theoretical approaches, but I hadn't sufficiently thought about how to teach critical thinking beyond the critiques developed by critical theorists.

Reflecting on my teaching on the concept of intersectionality, I want to rethink how I introduce critique into the classroom. One way is to incorporate texts that engage critically with the mainstreaming of a given critical discourse. For example, Kimberlé Crenshaw's (1991) original concept of intersectionality has been widely taken out of its original political context and integrated into numerous branches of mainstream and white feminism (Bilge 2013). In my course, I introduced the concept of intersectionality through Sirma Bilge's (2013) work in "Intersectionality Undone: Saving Intersectionality from Feminist Intersectionality Studies." Bilge critiques how intersectionality has been used as a tool for feminist analysis in ways that flatten differences. Instead, she argues we must understand intersectionality as a concept developed to illustrate the life conditions of racialized women in an imperialist state. Her work offers a way for students to enter into critical thinking on the concept of intersectionality; however, in retrospect, reading the critique of a critical theory did not illustrate how concepts can be taken up and change in meaning over time. Without historicizing the development of critical thinking on intersectionality, students risked parroting the critique of intersectionality without ever having to think through why such a critique became necessary. Returning to the original text alongside critiques can help students learn about how ideas develop and change.

Because *intersectionality* was already a buzzword for some of my students, it was useful to teach material that asked them to interrogate the taken-for-granted assumptions around intersectionality; however, by teaching only Bilge's critique of a critical theory, I was missing a pedagogical opportunity to share with them how critical thinking develops in dialogue with social and political practices alongside theory. Failing to teach the original text by Crenshaw and the theoretical development of intersectionality illustrates something that my friend got right: in suggesting they use Bilge as a starting point because it had been a critical moment in *my* understanding of the mainstreaming of intersectionality, I was, in a way, teaching my "own opinion" instead of fostering a critical engagement with critique. In retrospect, the best way to illustrate the commodification and mainstreaming in the trajectory of a given critical discourse is to retrace the development of that discourse with students, so that they can analyze the shift in thinking that leads to changes in how ideas are taken up. This illustrates another way that attending to failure in teaching can help us become better teachers. By taking in critical self-reflection on my own impulses and desires in the way I teach, I have been able to find concrete ways of developing my teaching, with plans underway to do things differently the next time I teach this course.

Conclusion: Failure to Subvert

I might have written a different chapter if my first teaching experience had been shaped by political clashes in the classroom, but there were none. Despite the wider political and cultural backlash in Québec, where I taught, against the "woke radical left," a term that circulated regularly in the Québécois media in the 2020–21 academic year, our discussions of even the most contested current political debates remained quite consensual. We even had a class specifically about how claims that dismiss calls for justice as "woke" are often relayed by affluent white men in positions of power, who accuse the left of threatening their free speech when they in fact enjoy incommensurable reach and capacity for public expression. When I taught that class, I thought there might be a possibility for clashes, but it went smoothly. It all seemed very orthodox to me, and definitely not quite pedagogically queer. I found myself disappointed. Was I doing radical teaching if I hadn't incited something disruptive in the status quo? I sat with this ambivalence, feeling like I had somehow failed at creating epistemological discomfort. In the words of Allen, "what happens when queer pedagogy's incitement to discomfort no longer leaves some of us (students and professors) uncomfortable?" (2015, 773).

I end this chapter by reflecting on the failure to subvert. Many of the pedagogical approaches I incorporated into my first teaching experience—standpoint transparency, vulnerability, a strong anti-oppressive political position—had been subversive for me in my own undergraduate student trajectory. Yet, when applied in my classroom as a teacher, I was surprised to be met with openness and an overwhelming sense that my students and I more or less spoke the same language. Perhaps I underestimated the fact that I share more with them than I did with my own teachers when I was in my undergrad. Or perhaps there is something about an openness to failure that softened the classroom environment. Nevertheless, I am left with the question of how to teach to provoke the kind of discomfort that critical, anti-oppressive, and queer pedagogies warrant, especially from a non-experienced position. An avenue for that could be to think collectively with students around how to establish the "terms of subversion" based on critical conversations about what challenges seem needed or not. If what is assumed to be subversive no longer is, then it might be the case that we must change how we plan pedagogical subversion, especially in terms of gender and sexuality, at a moment where taboos and silences are considerably shifting. Starting from the point of failure can help separate our own expectations around what happens in the classroom from what students understand as subversive engagement with ideas that challenge the status quo. Reflecting on failure helped me learn *how* to learn how to teach.

References

Allen, Louisa. 2009. "'Sexing the Subject': Evoking 'Sex' in Teaching an Undergraduate Course about Sexuality." *International Studies in Sociology of Education* 19 (3–4): 245–56. https://doi.org/10.1080/09620210903424634.
— 2015. "Queer Pedagogy and the Limits of Thought: Teaching Sexualities at University." *Higher Education Research & Development* 34 (4): 763–75. https://doi.org/10.1080/07294360.2015.1051004.
Bilge, Sirma. 2013. "Intersectionality Undone: Saving Intersectionality from Feminist Intersectionality Studies." *Du Bois Review: Social Science Research on Race* 10 (2): 405–24. https://doi.org/10.1017/S1742058X13000283.
Britzman, Deborah P. 1995. "Is There a Queer Pedagogy? Or, Stop Reading Straight." *Educational Theory* 45 (2): 151–65. https://doi.org/10.1111/j.1741-5446.1995.00151.x.
Brown, Kendrick T., and Joan M. Ostrove. 2013. "What Does It Mean to Be an Ally?: The Perception of Allies from the Perspective of People of Color." *Journal of Applied Social Psychology* 43 (11): 2211–22. https://doi.org/10.1111/jasp.12172.
Crenshaw, Kimberle. 1991. "Mapping the Margins: Intersectionality, Identity Politics, and Violence against Women of Color." *Stanford Law Review* 42 (6): 1241–99. https://www.jstor.org/stable/1170593
França de Souza Vasconcelos, Erika. 2011. "'I Can See You': An Autoethnography of My Teacher-Student Self." *TRQ: The Qualitative Report* 16 (2): 415–440. https://doi.org/10.46743/2160-3715/2011.1063.
Freire, Paulo. 2012. *Pedagogy of the Oppressed*, 30th anniversary ed. Translated by Myra Bergman Ramos, introduction by Donaldo P. Macedo. New York: Bloomsbury.
Goetz, Camden, and Kathryn Tobin. 2018. *Intersecting Movements Resisting Authoritarianisms: Feminist and Progressive Analysis and Tactics*. Region Refocus, December 2018.

Halberstam, Jack. 2011. *The Queer Art of Failure*. Durham, NC: Duke University Press.

hooks, bell. 1994. *Teaching to Transgress: Education as the Practice of Freedom*. New York: Routledge.

Indigenous Action Media. 2014. "Accomplices Not Allies: Abolishing the Ally Industrial Complex." *Indigenous Action*, Commentary & Essays, May 14, 2014. https://www.indigenousaction.org/accomplices-not-allies-abolishing-the-ally-industrial-complex/.

Kincheloe, Joe L. 2008. *Critical Pedagogy Primer*. 2nd ed. New York: Peter Lang.

Kumashiro, Kevin K. 2000. "Toward a Theory of Anti-Oppressive Education." *Review of Educational Research* 70 (1): 25–53. https://www.jstor.org/stable/1170593.

———. 2002. *Troubling Education: Queer Activism and Antioppressive Pedagogy*. New York: Routledge.

Luhmann, Susanne. 1998. "Queering/Querying Pedagogy? Or, Pedagogy Is a Pretty Queer Thing." In *Queer Theory in Education*, edited by William F. Pinar, 120–32. New York: Routledge.

McKinnon, Rachel. 2017. "Allies Behaving Badly: Gaslighting as Epistemic Injustice." In *The Routledge Handbook of Epistemic Injustice*, edited by Ian James Kidd, José Medina, and Gaile M. Polhaus, 167–74. New York: Routledge.

Meanwell, Emily, and Sibyl Kleiner. 2014. "The Emotional Experience of First-Time Teaching: Reflections from Graduate Instructors, 1997–2006." *Teaching Sociology* 42 (1): 17–27. https://doi.org/10.1177/0092055X13508377.

Mitchell, David, Sharon Snyder, and Linda Ware. 2014. "'[Every] Child Left Behind': Curricular Cripistemologies and the Crip/Queer Art of Failure." *Journal of Literary & Cultural Disability Studies* 8 (3): 295–314. https://doi.org/10.3828/jlcds.2014.24.

Richard, Gabrielle. 2019. *Hétéro, l'école? Plaidoyer pour une éducation antioppressive à la sexualité*. Montréal: Les Éditions du Remue-Ménage.

Shlasko, G.D. 2005. "Queer (*v.*) Pedagogy." *Equity & Excellence in Education* 38 (2): 123–34. https://doi.org/10.1080/10665680590935098.

Smollin, Leandra M., and Arnold Arluke. 2014. "Rites of Pedagogical Passage: How Graduate Student Instructors Negotiate the Challenges of First-Time Teaching." *Teaching Sociology* 42 (1): 28–39. https://doi.org/10.1177/0092055X13502181.

Sullivan-Clarke, Andrea. 2019. "Decolonizing 'Allyship' for Indian Country: Lessons from #NODAPL." *Hypatia* 35 (1): 178–89. https://doi.org.10.1017/hyp.2019.3.

8

"Are We Still Talking about This?"

Racism and Settler Colonialism in the Feminist and Queer Studies Classroom

GULZAR R. CHARANIA

Twelve weeks. The length of a course on queer theory. Students, particularly trans, non-binary, and queer students, come to this course hurting, searching, angry, wanting. Wanting affirmation, representation, visibility, community. There is bound to be disappointment. I teach in majority white classrooms, in a program where there is a wide range of politicization and literacy that students bring to their studies. My teaching is guided by three abiding principles: first, there is no queer theory without Indigenous and women of colour feminisms; second, sexuality is lived and enmeshed with race, colonialism, nation, gender, embodiment, and capitalism; and finally, we are all knowledge producers, meaning that the obligation to think with and engage course materials is a shared one. The course is never the same because teaching and learning are relationships and responsibilities, shaped by the people in the room and the ideas and texts we read and think about together. These principles create opportunities and openings but also discord and uncertainty in the classroom.

A feminist orientation to queer studies insists that our fields of study become what Alissa Trotz calls "object[s] of analytic scrutiny"

(2007, 11), meaning that we learn to be reflexive about queer theory's embeddedness in institutional power and its recounting of itself as a liberatory project. I started teaching Queer Theories while on a long-term contract. The economic conditions under which teaching occurs and the precarity structuring many university teaching positions is a critical and often unacknowledged part of the pedagogical landscape and structure of institutional power. On the first day of each course, I tell students that the syllabus is an act of power, meaning it presents a particular version and vision of a field of study that necessarily centres some ideas and theorists and marginalizes others. It tells one story. As Patricia Hill Collins and Sirma Bilge (2016) explain, the disciplinary formations that students typically learn, emphasize central thinkers and origin points. They argue that these "straight-line renditions of history" (63) masquerade as universal and authoritative when they are, more accurately, specific and partial representations of knowledge and the world. Explicitly teaching students that genealogies of fields of study are contested is one way of making disciplinary norms and professorial power more transparent and available for scrutiny and discussion.

In this chapter, I reflect on two specific pedagogical challenges that I've encountered in trying to centralize critical race and Indigenous scholarship within queer theory. I begin with a discussion of how a collective approach to pedagogy sets the stage of my Queer Theories classroom, before turning to the first dilemma: students assuming in advance that queer theory is concerned with sexuality and sexual liberation. I follow this discussion with a second problem that I call "waiting for Foucault," which focuses on how racism and settler colonialism are normalized within knowledge production in the academy, shaping even our efforts to engage queer theory that centralizes the scholarship of Indigenous and racialized theorists. I conclude the chapter with a reflection on how these lessons might be translated outside of the queer theory class.

Collective Visions of Pedagogy

The collective vision shaping my approach to pedagogy has been guided by many mentors, colleagues, students, teachers, and family members who helped to anchor my own trajectory as a high school and university teacher through two areas of influence. First, the collective work of Indigenous feminist scholars teaches us that "settler colonialism is a structure, not an event" (Arvin, Tuck, and Morrill 2013, 27), an intervention that has animated much contemporary and historical analysis of settler colonialism, illustrating its embeddedness in political and social life. Following this argument, I ask how taking racism and colonialism as structures, not events, as a starting point for pedagogy, can be generative in guiding course development and teaching. In other words, what are the implications of confronting racism *and* settler colonialism as structures in our pedagogical work? Second, I teach in a feminist and gender studies program that is shaped by a commitment to anti-racist and anti-colonial scholarship. Still, how this commitment is put into practice—and the differently assumed risks that come with confronting white supremacy and Canadian national mythologies of benevolence, innocence, and exceptionalism—persist. Despite its perceived solitary nature, teaching is shaped by collective labour in countless ways. Both within my institution and across others, I benefit from generous feminist practices of sharing syllabi, collaborating on course development, co-teaching, guest lecturing, negotiating teaching dilemmas, discussions about teaching on social media, and more. I work with deeply committed feminist educators who take seriously the intellectual and political work of teaching and learning.

Dilemma 1: Queer = Sexuality

Our daughter went through a period demanding that I teach her the things I was teaching in university classrooms. This led to many hilarious, slow, and sometimes frustrating discussions. It was also a pedagogical challenge to distill ideas down to their core and communicate them to a young child. Sometimes, I took these explanations, examples, or activities to the classroom and, on occasion, they were helpful and illuminating. During discussions about queer theory, our daughter asked, "Well you can already get married. What else do you want?" She articulated a question that gets to the heart of what some students assume about the destination of queer struggle and the frameworks they bring to queer theory. This is not surprising. Few emerge from public education with more than a liberal framework of individual rights and what Lisa Duggan refers to as the "new homonormativity" (2003, 65).[1] She writes that in place of contesting heteronormativity, "we have been administered a kind of political sedative—we get marriage and the military, then we go home and cook dinner, forever" (62).

Students are shaped and formed by the above ideas and homonormative aspirations: that inclusion is the goal of movements for sexual liberation. This should not be mistaken as a critique of individual students or their political analysis; desires for liberation are carefully and methodically curtailed and excised and in their place, we are taught, seduced and coerced to strive for inclusion, recognition, individual or normative family security. This analysis follows Jasbir Puar's suturing of Duggan's *homo* from *homonormative* to the nation as "homonationalism" (2007, 2), which traces a post-9/11 war on terror configuration where the nation seeks to include and incorporate

---

1. As Duggan (2003) discusses, homonormativity is meant to signal the ways that neoliberalism as a political, cultural, and economic project committed to privatization and personal responsibility are reshaping and containing sexual politics. Same-sex marriage, the right for LGBTQ+ folks to serve in the military, and consumerism are the hallmarks of this shrunken political terrain that seeks to include respectable gays and lesbians into political life. In other words, LGBTQ+ folks are encouraged to aspire to and reproduce normative visions of the good life.

some homosexual subjects, the respectable ones, in an effort to rally its population behind endless imperial wars and occupations.[2]

While students arrive with some vocabulary and analysis of connections between gender, race, sexuality, and other forms of oppression through intersectionality, the struggle to think in sustained ways about sexuality as enmeshed in and inseparable from race, class, gender, and nation endures. The majority white classroom poses particular challenges. Students are waiting to be done with racism and settler colonialism. This expectation punctuates course evaluations and conversations in class. This again? This still? In the first weeks of the course, we read Audre Lorde (2007), Gloria Anzaldúa (1994), the Combahee River Collective ([1977] 2017), Martin Cannon (2012), Sarah Hunt and Cindy Holmes (2015), and Cathy Cohen (1997), and watch the documentary *Pride Denied* (Chisholm 2016). Engagement with these texts is intended to lay the groundwork for thinking about a particular genealogy of queer theory that emerges from Indigenous and women of colour feminisms. The settler-colonial nation, citizenship, and rights are not the political horizons of these Black and anti-colonial intellectual traditions. And while most students have come to expect Black, Indigenous, and women of colour feminisms on the course syllabus, the subtext is often that we can encounter and move on from this scholarship. It is not a dwelling place that students expect will shape the rest of the class because this is, after all, a course on sexuality, not a course on racism and settler colonialism, as some are keen to emphasize.

---

2. For Puar, the war on terror requires that the United States "temporarily suspend its heteronormative imagined community to consolidate national sentiment and consensus" (2007, 3) around imperial intervention and militarism. She refers to this as the complicity of "some homosexual subjects…with heterosexual nationalist formations rather than inherently or automatically excluded from or opposed to them" (4). Naming this formation *homonationalism*, Puar examines how the selective national inclusion of homosexuals enfolds some queers into the nation if they are sufficiently patriotic, respectable, consuming subjects.

When will we stop talking about war, white supremacy, police violence, capitalism, imperialism, and occupation and talk about queer theory? The enduring nature of the prompt from students that queer theory is *not* primarily a form of learning about racism or settler colonialism illustrates the power of wider knowledge systems shaping the classroom, which assume that sexuality is not a racial configuration and that queer theory developed autonomously of theories of race and colonization. This belief persists despite a theoretical and pedagogical map through course readings that illustrates otherwise.

Roderick Ferguson observes that the increasing domestication of homosexuality and queer sexuality as a "single-issue mode of difference divorced from race and gender" (2012, 217) is linked to the way intersectional politics, interconnected histories of struggle, and capacious critiques of imperialism, racism, and patriarchy are increasingly concealed in articulations of sexuality that align more closely with capital and state. That "one-dimensional discourses of queerness" (Ferguson 2019, 14) are assumed to be the proper object of study in queer theory speaks to its containment. In her article on how the nation-state shapes the teaching of feminist studies courses and constrains a transnational feminist analysis with feminist studies curricula, Trotz observes that an additive pedagogical approach, makes racialized Others "fleetingly visible" and compartmentalized (2007, 3). In this approach to pedagogy, one usually finds a week on various groups of women organized by identity, such as African Canadians, Indigenous, Japanese Canadians, and so on. Instead of learning to theorize interconnectedness, relationality, and historicity, students learn that the world is divided into disparate categories and cartographies of here and there, us and them, then and now. Who, Trotz continues, is the "normative female subject of the remaining 'unmarked' weeks?" (3).

In Queer Theories the pedagogical silos marked by dominant paradigms of difference play out in the desire and longing from students to return to the struggles of middle-class, white, Western queers. In other words, the "unmarked" queer who is normatively centred as the proper subject of sexuality shapes their impatience with having to engage racism, imperialism, and settler colonialism throughout the course. The struggles of non-Western or racialized queer subjects are narrowly admitted into the desired topics of sexuality studies—only if we can save them or instruct them in democracy. I am confronted with the challenge that many students have difficulty imagining that the intellectual traditions of Indigenous and queers of colour thinkers can sustain a queer theory course. Twelve weeks. Many seem anxious to leave intersectional, anti-colonial queer theory behind, but the course is organized to keep it alive. There is no moving on. Some students quarrel over the presumed loss of an imagined queer community void of confrontations around racism and inequality, to which they can unproblematically belong. In particular, students struggle with the idea advanced by Cohen (1997) that an analysis of power, rather than our sexual identities, could shape our political organizing and coalitional work.

Cohen's work challenges the "'queer/hetero divide'" (1997, 447), that is taken for granted in common understandings of sexuality, and instead insists that not all heterosexuals are empowered through their sexuality, nor are all queers marginalized. Without effacing the real and lived consequences of queer struggle, Cohen considers what kinds of transformational politics might be possible if queers live, organize, and theorize from the premise that systems of domination are never singular but interdependent. Rather than simply enumerating class, race, gender, and sexuality, she asks us to understand their enmeshment in theoretical and practical terms in people's lives and act as though this analysis matters. As Cohen elaborates, there are people who are heterosexual, such as racialized women on welfare, whose sexuality and "sexual choices are not perceived as normal, moral, or worthy of state support" (442), while some sexual minorities enjoy proximity to dominance through their race, class, and gender. For Cohen, the power of a queer analysis lies in its ability to connect the struggles of those most impacted by state power and capitalism, regardless of their sexuality. Reorienting our analysis from sexual distinctions, identities, and dichotomies (i.e., the hetero-homo divide) to "our shared marginal relationship to dominant power" (458), she argues, is promising ground for expansive, coalitional political organizing. Refusing the queer = sexuality formulation, Cohen instead redirects us to an analytic framework that insists on an intersectional analysis of power, identity, domination, and oppression.

In contradistinction to Cohen, the single issue analytic that most students are taught and bring to the classroom intensifies the tension between my pedagogical approach and their attachment to presumed knowledge on sexuality. It is hard to let go of old dreams, desires, and habits of thought. Some clench tighter. Defensive. Afraid. Some loosen, but it takes more than twelve weeks. Unlearning and learning is not apparent or immediate, but unfolding, unsure, non-linear. Some run with abandon to new ideas and their promises, having always longed for them even if they didn't have words yet because the old words were ill-fitting or eventually betrayed them. Some have lived in this expansive space for a while, having been offered them by parents or aunties or grandparents or strangers or prayers or poets or animal friends or trees or books or "other more-than-human beings" (Todd 2017, 104). Others stumble, disoriented, not knowing what to do or how to live. Office hours and emails are sometimes very long. Others give little away.

Dilemma 2: Waiting for Foucault

The second dilemma I have confronted in teaching queer theory is an orientation to reading theory characterized by a willingness, sometimes even openness and receptivity to engaging with Black, Indigenous, and racialized scholarship, but only if we also read what some consider to be the queer theory canon. The first year that I taught this class, we read Michel Foucault's *The History of Sexuality* (1990) early on in the semester, a text often posited as canonical in sexuality studies and queer theory. Something interesting and unsurprising happened. Foucault, and later Judith Butler, became the texts that students constantly referenced as the course unfolded. In other words, the genealogy of queer theory that students reproduced in the course, even when I actively taught against it, was a white one. Students carelessly and frequently universalized from Foucault in a way that they rarely did with Black, Indigenous, and racialized scholars, such as Leanne Betasamosake Simpson (2017), Rinaldo Walcott (2016), M. Jacqui Alexander (2005), or Martin Manalansan (1997).

Critiquing the tendency to universalize from particular Western frames and understandings of sexuality, Gloria Wekker argues that the unwillingness to "let go of that dominance and to imagine other sexual universes, is deeply troubling, and has all the trappings of a neo-imperial gesture" (2006, 69). As Alexander G. Weheliye (2014) observes, in addition to being ubiquitously invoked in the academy, the theoretical work of Foucault and other white European thinkers is accorded universal, credible, and rigorous standing in a way that is structurally denied to Black feminist theorists. White European theorists do not appear to be impacted by identity or geography because these are not acknowledged in their work, thus rendering Foucault and others as "proper objects of knowledge" (Weheliye 2014, 7). Students regularly reproduce the notion that white thinkers are universal, temporally and spatially unbound, unencumbered by geography, history, and situatedness. They theorize from nowhere about everything (Haraway 2003). Weheliye continues that even where minoritized and women of color scholars are writing about power, politics, and history, because this knowledge is often elaborated in relation to their "identities, the knowledge they produce is often relegated to ethnographic locality within mainstream discourses" (2014, 7). Tiffany Lethabo King similarly notes persistent devaluing of the theoretical contributions of Black feminist theory, which assumes that "Black women are too particular, too embodied and therefore not capable of producing knowledge that can transcend identity" (2015, 124).

The question of what is legible to students as theory is a persistent one across disciplines. In the classroom, this cleaving of Black and women of colour feminisms from theory shows up repeatedly in students' conceptual understandings and reading practices. For example, they regularly struggle to situate the "Combahee River Collective Statement" as an articulation of theory and social transformation, reading it instead through a lens of identity and experience, disarticulated from power and structure. Trapped in the ethnographic, experiential, and specific, most students are implicitly or explicitly taught that "minority discourses cannot inhabit the space of proper theoretical reflection" (Weheliye 2014, 9). Teaching against these deeply engrained interpretive frameworks for reading and thinking is difficult, slow, and necessary work.

Dian Million (2013) argues that theory is something that Indigenous people do in their daily lives as they reflect on personal experiences and connect them to histories and systems of power. Barbara Christian also explains that "people of colour have always theorized – but in forms quite different from the Western form of abstract logic" (1988, 68). Million and Christian remind us that poetry, memoir, story, song, feeling, narrative, riddle, proverb, and documentary are all languages of theory. Reclaiming theory from the purview of the few, they insist that developing an analysis of how the world works, doing theory, is something we all do, yet the theoretical traditions of some have been disqualified from academic knowledge through the disciplining of knowledge. Recalling her own education, Christian writes, "I was told that the minds of the world lived only in the small continent of Europe" (72). Writing about Indigenous intellectual traditions, Maile Arvin, Eve Tuck, and Angie Morrill insist that Indigenous people are the "authors of important theories about the world we all live in" (2013, 21), but too often, their scholarship is "flattened into theories of identity" (Tuck and Yang 2017, 9). For example, reflecting on the Indian Act's "management of Indigenous people's gender roles and sexuality" (15), they argue that it continues to be a challenge for some to understand that the relationship between sovereignty and sexuality for Indigenous people is inseparable. Gender and sexuality variance were commonly practiced in diverse Indigenous nations pre-contact (Cannon 2012; L. Simpson 2017); however, Indigenous genders and sexualities are often taught and understood as illustrations of sexual diversity rather than challenges to settler-colonial knowledge systems and forms of governance. As Indigenous feminist scholars argue, the point is not to integrate the struggles of Two-Spirit and queer Indigenous people into existing queer settler frameworks and knowledge systems (L. Simpson 2017) or to demand better ethnographic representation (A. Simpson 2014), but to confront dispossession and violence by settlers and the setter colonial state.

It takes constant vigilance to keep a critique of settler colonialism as a core pedagogical analysis of the structures of contemporary power at the forefront of the classroom. In other words, it is not only necessary to learn about Indigenous people and what was, and is, done to them, but also their intellectual traditions, governance systems, forms of survival, resurgence, and world-making. To start from the premise that the origin of queer theory is not found in canonical thinkers, such as Foucault or Butler, but an understanding of settler colonialism as a system that shapes knowledge of sexuality entails confronting students and faculty alike in the presumed knowledge that sexuality belongs to Western, white subjects. That non-Indigenous settlers, including those of us who are queer settlers, subject our desires for inclusion, security, and representation within structures of colonial violence requires that the classroom be a space where we examine our commitments and accountability to Indigenous sovereignty as central to queer theory. This is not easily accomplished. Every year, I sit with this responsiblity as I think about how to structure the syllabus and teach within the conditions of urgency around colonial, racial, gender, and sexuality-based violences. Using my own incomplete and compromised knowledge systems, I set my intentions for the classroom, trying to model how to move beyond canonical thinking for my students. I read, I start, I stumble, I fail, I start again. This is the work of confronting and countering racism and settler colonialism in learning. This work is made more difficult when racialized female professors have to work constantly to establish ourselves as knowledgeable in the first place. "Are you the professor?" a white student asked me on the first day of Queer Theories, slowly packing up her things and leaving, before the start of class.

Translating Lessons on Racism and Settler Colonialism across Classrooms

Trying to take seriously diverse articulations of theory and knowledge production, in one of the final course assignments I ask students to engage with memoir, poetry, or cultural critique written by Black, Indigenous, and queer of colour writers. Students are asked to put these texts into conversation with course materials and consider how they contribute to, contest, or expand queer theory. They are also given the opportunity to do a creative response to theory that engages with the materials, producing a podcast, painting, social media, or video project. This and other assignments have yielded beautiful student engagement and thinking. And yet the longer I teach, the more I worry that the university's desire for and absorption of difference leaves behind the demands of radical social movements. Analyzing how intersectionality circulates within feminist studies, Bilge (2013) traces how insurgent intellectual traditions are often domesticated as they are incorporated into the university. Observing the shifting tactics of white supremacy, Ferguson (2012) similarly insists that we pay attention to the substitution of redistribution of power with a focus on representation and institutionalization instead. I struggle with how to cultivate a position in relation to the theoretical work of Black,

Indigenous, and racialized scholars that is not about consumption or "commodity" (Christian 1988, 67), containtment, or extraction. I worry that too many students endeavour to master a language without being committed to a struggle and that learning these theories simply fortifies the power of already dominant students (Laymon 2018). Warning against the consumption of Black feminist thought, Lorde asks, "Do you ever really read the work of Black women? Did you ever read my words, or did you merely finger through them for quotations?" (2007, 68). These are not problems with quick fixes. Unlearning these ways of engaging, and instead cultivating commitments to one another's histories, struggles, and liberation (Alexander 2005), is unending work in the context of higher education, which prioritizes competition and individualism and incentivizes us to reproduce the status quo.

Working in context-specific and responsive ways with guiding principles has been generative in integrating an analysis of racism and settler colonialism into my teaching beyond theme weeks. The primary principle that guides how I structure classes, assign readings, and develop assignments is that Black, Indigenous, and women of colour feminists have contributed to knowledge about everything. While writing *Living a Feminist Life*, Sara Ahmed (2014) explains that she decided not to cite any white men as both an experiment and refusal of white men as an "institution." She elaborates that collectively, white men function as a "persistent structure or mechanism of social order," governing the norms and regulations of knowledge production in the academy. Her refusal to cite white men also teaches her how generative it is to turn to the work of Black, Indigenous, and racialized women scholars. Centring other ways of teaching and imagining institutional life outside of white men has been challenging at times but also remarkably nourishing and exciting. It has resulted in different pedagogical experiments in courses I teach. Sometimes, I organize classes to read canonical texts alongside their critiques; however, increasingly I am refusing the institutional authority of what is deemed canonical because it leaves insufficient time for doing other kinds of work and thinking in the classroom. Twelve weeks. Such a move displaces whiteness in ways that are important for all students in our learning communities. While the anger and resistance that this engenders in the classroom are real, so too are the joy, creativity, and world-making that come from sustained engagement with radical Black, Indigenous, and women of colour intellectual traditions.

I am learning, over time, to have more confidence in a slow and patient pedagogy. It is insistently iterative—circling around a core set of ideas, reading them closely and collectively and thinking with them again and again. It takes time and persistence to slowly lessen the grip of white supremacy on our knowledge systems, investments, and ways of thinking, reading and feeling in the world. It is not only white students who are shaped by these logics; for everyone, this work is always unfinished, albeit in different ways and with different stakes. Sometimes by the end of a course, a student can process or think with a previously unfamiliar idea. In this case, resistance can turn to engagement, which in turn can bring up complex emotions. Learning is deeply affective. Helping students name and reflect on the impacts of these emotional landscapes on their learning is one dimension of my pedagogical goal. I sometimes welcome and other times resent having to do this labour, and yet I know that bringing thinking and feeling closer together in the classroom is important for shifting our capacities to learn. Insisting that our teaching takes seriously the obligation to create futures where racial and settler violence are simply unimaginable is a beginning. The rest we make and create, imperfectly, together.

I started this chapter explaining that I teach in majority white classrooms. Focusing so much on whiteness risks marginalizing the students who are not waiting for Foucault, who have not inherited racial and colonial domination and for whom unlearning is not the major pedagogical task in the classroom. What are the costs of white learning and unlearning on the Black, racialized, and Indigenous students I teach? What does the continuous centring of resistance to whiteness cost? As Katherine McKittrick (2014) observes, "the site where we *begin* to teach is already white supremacist"; therefore, the work of rethinking our classrooms by centring racism and settler colonialism requires more than simply teaching about racism and colonization. Rather than rehearsing the violence of anti-Blackness and colonialism, McKittrick orients us to classroom practices that "work out how knowledge is linked to an ongoing struggle to end violence." Rethinking the authority of the canon, the interests it serves, and consequences it secures, while simultaneously resisting the limits of incorporation and demands for institutional legibility, continue to complicate and guide my teaching practices. How might it guide yours?

References

Ahmed, Sara. 2014. "White Men." *feministkilljoys* (blog). November 4, 2014. https://feministkilljoys.com/2014/11/04/white-men/.

Alexander, M. Jacqui. 2005. *Pedagogies of Crossing: Meditations on Feminism, Sexual Politics, Memory, and the Sacred.* Durham, NC: Duke University Press.

Anzaldúa, Gloria. 1994. "To(o) Queer the Writer – Loca, escritoria y chicana." In *Inversions: Writings by Queer Dykes and Lesbians*, edited by Betsy Warland, 249–61. Vancouver: Press Gang Publishers.

Arvin, Maile, Eve Tuck, and Angie Morrill. 2013. "Decolonizing Feminism: Challenging Connections between Settler Colonialism and Heteropatriarchy." *Feminist Formations* 25 (1): 8–34. https://doi.org/10.1353/ff.2013.0006.

Bilge, Sirma. 2013. "Intersectionality Undone: Saving Intersectionality from Feminist Intersectionality Studies." *Du Bois Review* 10 (2): 405–24. https://doi.org/10.1017/S1742058X13000283.

Cannon, Martin. 2012. "The Regulation of First Nations Sexuality." In *Queerly Canadian: An Introductory Reader in Sexuality Studies*, edited by Maureen FitzGerald and Scott Rayter, 51–63. Toronto: Canadian Scholars.

Chisholm, Kami, dir. 2016. *Pride Denied: Homonationalism and the Future of Queer Politics.* Media Education Foundation, 2016.

Christian, Barbara. 1988. "The Race for Theory." *Feminist Studies* 14 (1): 67–79. https://www.jstor.org/stable/1354255.

Cohen, Cathy J. 1997. "Punks, Bulldaggers and Welfare Queens: The Radical Potential of Queer Politics?" *GLQ: A Journal of Lesbian and Gay Studies* 3 (4): 437–65. https://doi.org/10.1215/10642684-3-4-437.

Collins, Patricia Hill, and Sirma Bilge. 2016. "Getting the History of Intersectionality Straight?" In *Intersectionality*, by Collins and Bilge, 63–87. Malden, MA: Polity.

Combahee River Collective. (1977) 2017. "The Combahee River Collective Statement." In *How We Get Free: Black Feminism and the Combahee River Collective*, edited by Keeanga-Yamahtta Taylor, 15–28. Chicago: Haymarket Books.

Duggan, Lisa. 2003. *The Twilight of Equality: Neoliberalism, Cultural Politics, and the Attack on Democracy*. Boston: Beacon Press.

Ferguson, Roderick A. 2012. *The Reorder of Things: The University and Its Pedagogies of Minority Difference*. Minneapolis: University of Minnesota Press.

—2019. *One-Dimensional Queer*. Medford, MA: Polity Press.

Foucault, Michel. 1990. *The History of Sexuality*. Vol. 1, *An Introduction*. Translated by Robert Hurley. New York: Vintage Books.

Haraway, Donna. 2003. "Situated Knowledges: The Science Question in Feminism and the Privilege of Partial Perspective." In *Turning Points in Qualitative Research*, edited by Yvonna S. Lincoln and Norman K. Denzin, 21–46. Walnut Creek, CA: AltaMira Press.

Hunt, Sarah, and Cindy Holmes. 2015. "Everyday Decolonization: Living a Decolonizing Queer Politics." *Journal of Lesbian Studies* 19 (2): 154–72. https://doi.org/10.1080/10894160.2015.970975.

King, Tiffany Lethabo. 2015. "Post-Identitarian and Post-Intersectional Anxiety in the Neoliberal Corporate University." *Feminist Formations* 27 (3): 114–38. https://www.jstor.org/stable/43860817.

Laymon, Kiese. 2018. *Heavy: An American Memoir*. New York: Scribner.

Lorde, Audre. 2007. *Sister Outsider: Essays & Speeches by Audre Lorde*. Berkeley, CA: Crossing Press.

Manalansan, Martin F., IV. 1997. "In the Shadows of Stonewall: Examining Gay Transnational Politics and the Diasporic Dilemma." In *The Politics of Culture in the Shadow of Capital*, edited by Lisa Lowe and David Lloyd, 485–505. Durham, NC: Duke University Press.

McKittrick, Katherine. 2014. "Katherine McKittrick, author of *Demonic Grounds*, on Trigger Warnings." Interview with Peter James Hudson. *Bully Bloggers* (blog). December 17, 2014. https://bullybloggers.wordpress.com/2014/12/17/katherine-mckittrick-author-of-demonic-grounds-on-trigger-warnings/.

Million, Dian. 2013. *Therapeutic Nations: Healing in an Age of Indigenous Human Rights*. Tucson: University of Arizona Press.

Puar, Jasbir K. 2007. *Terrorist Assemblages: Homonationalism in Queer Times*. Durham, NC: Duke University Press.

Simpson, Audra. 2014. *Mohawk Interruptus: Political Life across the Borders of Settler States*. Durham, NC: Duke University Press.

Simpson, Leanne Betasamosake. 2017. *As We Have Always Done: Indigenous Freedom through Radical Resistance*. Minneapolis: University of Minnesota Press.

Todd, Zoe. 2017. "Fish, Kin and Hope: Tending to Water Violations in *amiskwaciwâskahikan* and Treaty Six Territory." *Afterall: A Journal of Art, Context and Enquiry* 43 (Spring/Summer): 102–107. https://doi.org/10.1086/692559.

Trotz, D. Alissa. 2007. "Going Global? Transnationality, Women/Gender Studies and Lessons from the Caribbean." *Caribbean Review of Gender Studies*, no. 1, 1–18.

Tuck, Eve, and K. Wayne Yang. 2017. "Late Identity." *Critical Ethnic Studies* 3 (1): 1–19. https://doi.org/10.5749/jcritethnstud.3.1.0001.

Walcott, Rinaldo. 2016. *Queer Returns: Essays on Multiculturalism, Diaspora, and Black Studies*. London, ON: Insomniac Press.

Weheliye, Alexander G. 2014. *Habeas Viscus: Racializing Assemblages, Biopolitics, and Black Feminist Theories of the Human*. Durham, NC: Duke University Press.

Wekker, Gloria. 2006. *The Politics of Passion: Women's Sexual Culture in the Afro-Surinamese Diaspora*. New York: Columbia University Press.

9

The Classroom as a "Safe Space" for Anti-Racism Work

Reflections on Racism in the Canadian Classroom and the Roles of Students and Teachers

MITCHELL RAE YANG, REBECCA GAËLLE JOACHIM, AND KIMBERLEY ENS MANNING

> Diversity work is the work we do when we do not quite inhabit the norms of the institution.
> —Sara Ahmed, *Living a Feminist Life* (2017, 91)

Introduction

In late January 2019, three women's studies students unveiled a prominent display in the Webster Library at Concordia University. Exactly fifty years after an unprecedented protest against racism took place in the university's Hall Building across the street, the vitrine documented twentieth-century Black life in Montreal through archival photos, books, and objects. In this chapter, two of the students who created the vitrine, and one of the two professors who oversaw the project, discuss the promises and challenges of student leadership in transforming institutional forms of academic racism. This is as true of the students who occupied the Hall Building over fifty years ago, as it is of students today, many of whom are striving to remake the academy into a more equitable space of learning. But saying that student leadership is important, even vital, to institutional transformation does not render it without cost. In this chapter, we discuss the gestation, formation, and fruition of the vitrine project to explore the contours of Canadian academic racism, past and present.

This chapter draws on a collaborative autoethnographic methodology, in which the authors "turn their interrogative tools on themselves, generating and utilizing their autobiographical data to understand social phenomena" (Chang, Ngunjiri, and Hernandez 2013, 37). In this chapter, we draw upon our conversations over the course of the early winter of 2021, writings from original course assignments, and evolving reflections that emerged through the writing itself. Kim, one of the two original instructors of the course, is a white, tenured, political science professor who initiated the Feminist University Seminar (FUS) as one prong of a multiyear pilot project to address racism and other forms of injustice in the context of the university. In offering this course, Kim had hoped to provide students with a means of directly engaging with and possibly transforming inequities within the university. What Kim did not recognize until she began to work on this chapter, however, was that there were ways in which her own teaching had contributed to inequities within the FUS classroom itself. What began as a chapter focused on the vitrine transformed rapidly into an opportunity to revisit and confront how racism operates in classes shaped by good intentions. Kim's understanding of how racism shows up in the classroom has shifted dramatically as a consequence of working on this chapter with Mitchell and Rebecca.

Today, Mitchell and Rebecca have both graduated from the Simone de Beauvoir Institute having successfully completed the FUS course. Not completely divorced from academia, Mitchell went on to pursue his master's in sociology, focusing on critical race theory and critical whiteness theory while simultaneously serving as a steering committee member for the Access in the Making Lab in Concordia University's Department of Communications Studies. Despite lingering in the university alongside his critiques of it, Mitchell's concentration remains centred in community organizing. At the time of writing, he was the executive director of Project 10, a non-profit community organization that supports the well-being of LGBTQ+ youth in Montreal and is a co-founder of ChamPaintMTL, a social initiative to create safer spaces for young Black, Indigenous, and people of colour (BIPOC).

Rebecca and Mitchell: Writing this chapter has not been easy. We often found ourselves feeling frustrated at having to recount our story. As two people disenchanted with academia, the choice to co-author a chapter in an academic text is in tension with feeling exasperated by the process itself. Despite this frustration, we felt it was important to contribute to this discussion so that readers will consider our experiences as a cautionary tale of how students can be made to feel unwelcome in the classroom.

This chapter begins with a brief description of the FUS, and the larger context out of which it arose. We then offer a discussion of the vitrine project, based upon excerpts of collaborative student writing, which at the time focused on some of the challenges of obtaining access to archival materials and physically installing the project. The final part of the chapter focuses on what largely remained unwritten at the time of the course, including reflections on class dynamics that unintentionally reinforced some of the very structures that the course was attempting to undo.

The Feminist University Seminar: The Teacher's Perspective

Kim: Built on Sara Ahmed's observation that "it is through the effort to transform institutions that we generate knowledge about them" (2017, 93), the FUS was offered over two years, 2017–18, 2018–19, as one part of a larger pilot project: Critical Feminist Activism and Research (CFAR). Funded by the Faculty of Arts and Science at Concordia University, CFAR was a community-building, research, and training initiative emerging from an intersectional feminist framework anchored in anti-racist and anti-oppressive approaches to equity, inclusion, and representation on campus and across communities. At its heart, the collective work of CFAR sought to support the leadership of graduate and undergraduate students to tackle institutional inequities, while simultaneously incorporating the participation of community members in order to challenge, open, and expand upon ideas of the university. The FUS itself was a year-long, six-credit, team-taught course designed for students interested in learning about institutional transformation. The project-based pedagogy allowed students to work in small groups to learn more about themselves and the university as they sought to advance new equity initiatives at Concordia. With an original enrolment of about twenty-five students, the instructors had pre-organized four projects on which the students could choose to work. Project work was supported by the two course instructors, two research assistants, and several faculty mentors. One project, selected by the two student co-authors of this chapter, focused on Black history in Montreal and at Concordia. By actively seeking to document this history, student project participants generated new knowledge about a past that the institution itself had long occluded. We also generated knowledge about ourselves, although some of this learning did not become fully apparent until later in the course, or indeed, until work on this chapter had begun.

The Project of Historicizing Racism within the University: The Students' Perspective

Rebecca and Mitchell: On the first day of class the teachers announced to us the different projects we could work on for the next year. There were four options and one of them was an exhibition on the Sir George

Williams Affair to mark the fiftieth anniversary of the student occupation of Sir George Williams University (now Concordia University) in 1969. The occupation aimed to highlight the racism that Black students experienced in their education and in Montreal. The protest was in part a response to a white biology teacher, Perry Anderson, who was accused of systematically assigning low grades and failing Black students in his class (Austin 2007). The protest that followed was "the biggest student riot in Canadian history" (Quan 2019) and had a far-reaching impact on Black communities in Canada, including influencing Canada's human rights policies.

The significance of the protest in the history of Canadian racial inequality motivated students of colour in the class to gravitate toward this project, and (for the most part) when it was time to sit together in our group, it was easy for us because we were already all sitting together. Sitting in close proximity to one another, and even one next to the other, was no coincidence and, in fact, represents a conscious survival tactic performed by many students of colour in white-dominated spaces. After meeting with and consulting some of the principal organizers of Protests and Pedagogy, the fiftieth anniversary conference and events commemorating the Sir George Williams Affair at Concordia, our team decided to design and curate a visual display in the large showcase vitrine of the main student library on campus.

We worked in part with community members, but mostly with Concordia archivists, to build a collection of materials that would serve as visually narrative pieces under the theme of "Waves of Resistance," a symbolic leitmotif that acknowledged the ebbs and flows of what resistance and opposition looked like and to pay homage to the constant presence of this resistance, even when it wasn't as loud as a student occupation of a university building. Using a combination of both historical and contemporary books, posters, and images, our team illustrated how struggles of resistance have gone through waves across Canada's colonial history and contemporary practices.

Our exhibition was housed in a large glass cabinet that we divided lengthwise into a timeline of significant moments in history, the before and the after the Sir George Williams Affair, which all students and faculty walk through when entering the library. The entire vitrine was anchored by the visuals of water (alluding to the waves), sand, and paper birds flying towards the present-day section of the timeline. The middle of the display featured a large photo of the Hall Building where the riots took place.

Developing a project that was designed within the academy and respected the rules of pedagogy, but was intended to challenge academia and the institution, made for a complicated dynamic between students, teachers, and the university. A comprehensive understanding of our positionality as students (of colour) became necessary in order for us to navigate the intricate and oftentimes invisible power dynamics of academia in ways that could approximate feelings of safety and accessibility as we immersed ourselves in the project. In retrospect, we see how the inevitable process of working in close collaboration with faculty would have benefitted from the teachers establishing a holistic approach to the diverse points of entry that project members found themselves in. This approach would have been especially beneficial for the students, who are the most vulnerable within these sorts of unbalanced and unchecked dynamics. As people (students) of colour, our experiences were influenced by our different experiences interacting with the world and the ways that the world interacted with us. These experiences proved challenging for us as racialized students working within the university. Reflecting on that time today, we value and would prioritize the opportunity to work with enthusiastic partners who share our vision and intention for the project. Notwithstanding these gaps in the structure of the project as it existed within a seminar course, working with and within an institution will perpetually produce limitations that are unavoidable when students are challenging and interrogating the university that is grading them. Ultimately, because our project's entire essence, its ethos, was to provide a critique of the university and academia, our capacity to execute our plans for the project was often compromised in favour of facilitating the work of the institution and its focus on bureaucratic process and hierarchies of approval. Ultimately, this bureaucracy complicated the ways that we could participate together as a group without feeling policed in our proximity.

The Work: "Safe Spaces" and Racism within the Institution

Mitchell and Rebecca: The impact of systemic racism on BIPOC students is compounded in situations where the dynamic involves students and faculty, especially those who are perceived—at least by the students from their perspective—as being in higher, more powerful positions. For instance, on numerous occasions our work on the project as students required us to visit the *special* archives. Not only did this feel overwhelming on an administrative level because of the bureaucracy to simply access these archives, but the lack of transparency about the internal processes made our visits to the archives an uncomfortable experience where it felt like we were somewhere that we shouldn't have been. Moreover, it felt like we were somewhere that didn't expect us to be there (read: didn't want us there)—confirming our fears and feeding the anxiety of impostor syndrome that we were somewhere we shouldn't have been. In addition to the way the institution makes the process for accessing university resources opaque to students, it also makes clear who belongs and who does not belong in certain university spaces. Faced with restrictions while trying to access materials from the archives, it was easy to feel like our work was not welcome, and, therefore, that we were not welcome. We were all trying to navigate the same violent system the best way we could. We were all frustrated. This experience resonated with us through Ahmed's work, that "we have to persist because there is institutional resistance. The requirement to persist becomes a job requirement" (2017, 96).

> Rolling eyes = feminist pedagogy.
> —Sara Ahmed, *Living a Feminist Life* (2017, 38)

Kim: There were also real challenges within the class itself, especially during the first weeks of the course. Although I worked to establish a relationship of trust over time, I never discussed how the classroom itself reinforced whiteness until we began to work on this chapter together. Indeed, our collaborative autoethnographic method has helped me to probe how racism continues to shape the contemporary classroom, fifty years after the Sir George Williams Affair. My own lack of awareness of the racialized power dynamics embedded in the university classroom was on display early in the course. During one of the first class meetings, I was confounded, and more than a little outraged, when I spotted Mitchell rolling his eyes as I was speaking. Debriefing this moment, some two years later, Mitchell shared that my role as professor and principal of the Simone de Beauvoir Institute (where the Women's Studies program at Concordia is held) had resulted in him having a high guard in relation to how much faith he afforded to me and to my words. As Rebecca shared in later conversations, she was doubtful of the efficacy of starting the course with a declaration that we were attempting to create a "safe space" for respectful class discussions. In fact, in her final paper for the course, Rebecca discussed bell hooks's critique of the "safe" classroom, drawing on the following quote: "the unwillingness to approach teaching from a standpoint that includes awareness of race, sex, and class, is too often rooted in the fear that the classroom will be uncontrollable, that emotions and passions will not be contained" (1994, 39). Despite the fact that I had assigned the hooks reading, and read Rebecca's paper at the course end, I had not absorbed the implication of hooks's argument, and Rebecca's critique, for decentring whiteness in the classroom.

Katherine McKittrick argues that the notion of safe teaching and learning spaces is a "white fantasy that harms" (Hudson and McKittrick 2014, 237). Specifically, she argues that the kind of hate-prevention that appears on syllabi (no racism, transphobia, homophobia, ableism in the classroom) replicates rather than undoes systems of injustice. In a very real sense, when white instructors like myself mandate "respectful" participation, as was written on the syllabus and repeated in class, without acknowledging the multiple ways that racism and other forms of power are already permeating and shaping classroom interactions, we reinforce the very power we say we are trying to disrupt. Indeed, according to McKittrick, "Privileged students leave these safe spaces with transparently knowable oppressed identities safely tucked in their back pockets and a lesson on how to be aggressively and benevolently silent" (Hudson and McKittrick 2014, 238). With power invisiblized, racialized students may feel obliged to not be "disruptive" and may thus engage in alternative modes of resistance, such as an eye roll, that effectively point back to the unacknowledged power that is shaping the room.

> It is as if these problems are not there until you point them out; it is as if pointing them out is what makes them there.
> —Sara Ahmed, *Living a Feminist Life* (2017, 39)

Rebecca and Mitchell: The trouble is, in reality, that students of colour, and especially Black and Indigenous students, are often subjected to a particularly harsh and heightened level of surveillance and scrutiny. This scrutiny not only creates significant problems in the classroom, where BIPOC students are hesitant to engage with the material of the curriculum, but can also generate apathy in relation to the academy. In this context, the eye roll is not a sign of defiance; rather it is a strategy used by students to survive the very real-world consequences of being Black, Indigenous, or a person of colour in academia. On the first day of class, a racially insensitive comment was made, sparking a feeling of hopelessness in Mitchell with regards to how the next year of class was going to feel for him. As a Chinese person, the comment that had been made personally offended him, but when he looked to his other racialized friends in the classroom for comfort, this was met with scrutiny. In his case, the eye rolling was interpreted as an attack on the hierarchy of the classroom; but for him, it was a call for compassion from the people in the class he knew would understand him the most. Similar defence mechanisms in the classroom are not signs of disrespect, but logical and strategic reactions to societal conditions of being racialized and trying to navigate institutional hierarchies as a student at the same time.

On that first day in the FUS class, we were tasked as students to come up with a collective agreement to establish some ground rules to create a "safe classroom environment." When this idea was presented by the two teachers, most of the people in the class seemed content with it. Like many academic spaces, it is important to highlight that the majority of the students in the classroom were white, and even more, that all of the people of colour in the classroom chose to work together (including the teaching assistants). This self-segregation of the groups when selecting projects did not go unnoticed, and we felt that both our (white) peers and the (white) teachers were made uncomfortable by the unmistakable message being sent by the racialized people in the room about who we wanted to be around (because of who we didn't want to be around). As Ahmed argues, "inviting those who are not white to insert themselves into whiteness can be how whiteness is reinserted" (2017, 151). Indeed, the very idea of safety in the classroom is often predetermined by racial hierarchies in education. For white students, it is more likely to have white professors mirror ideas of safety that maintain the comfort of white people in the classroom (e.g., not showing anger); whereas, for BIPOC students, safety may appear as a threat to the status quo of the institution (e.g., anti-racism in the classroom, by-and-for spaces).

As a result, it was difficult to feel comfortable as racialized students when the majority of your peers are white and the teachers are also white. Made the object of white attention, surveillance, and seemingly relentless hypercriticisms, and without explicit anti-racist framing in the class, BIPOC students are left uncertain about what kind of safety will be asserted in the classroom. For example, would white students feel unsafe if racialized students expressed anger about racism? Added to the uncertainty about safety in the classroom is the very unsafe configuration of the university space itself. Our classroom was physically located in a building with no accessible gender-neutral washrooms. Further, the structure of our project often meant that we, as racialized students, had to navigate precarious dynamics with our white peers, where it felt like our grades depended in large part on our ability to be passive and cooperative (read: agreeable to whiteness). As racialized students, we end up asking ourselves, "Will they think I'm being mean?" or "Would this upset them if I brought it up?" Ultimately, left to interpret what feels like obfuscated landmines based on unspoken social cues, racialized students must navigate an intricate dance around poorly defined parameters of what kind of communication is "safe" in the classroom.

Navigating the racial dynamics of "safe space," there is a problem when this language is used as part of a classroom activity where the definition of safer space is debated and its conditions decided by "everyone," despite the uneven social locations that students come from. Ahmed argues, "you have to work not to appear as aggressive because you are assumed to be aggressive before you appear" (2017, 131). Because racism shapes the lives of BIPOC students both inside and outside of the classroom, discussions over what is safe will inevitably be informed by students' experiences. In a predominantly white classroom, whose experiences and perspectives will shape that discussion? Because racism is embedded in our institutions, safety cannot be offered to racialized students, and specifically to Black and Indigenous students in higher education. It is not possible.

In our experience, because safety for white students and white professors often translates as comfort, this simply reinforces complacency with institutional and systemic racism. We experience discussions of "safe space" as primarily vehicles to comfort white people and reassure them that they won't be judged—even as they perpetuate white supremacy and actively harm racialized people in the classroom—because classrooms should be spaces for *learning* (also known as spaces for white students to offend without consequence and to be rewarded for this "vulnerability"). Asserted by a white majority, opposition to safety as comfort is positioned as "difficult" and unreasonable in class discussion. Predictably, as students offered suggestions for rules of the classroom, the rule "not to judge" was added to the list.

Mitchell, Rebecca, and Kim: Although not everyone was familiar with women's studies classes, and the risk of being judged for not having this knowledge could make someone scared to do the wrong thing, the rule "not to judge" also impacts the ability for students and teachers alike to hold peers and ourselves accountable in the classroom. While there should indeed be room to make mistakes in the classroom, the capacity of the class to grapple with racism requires systems of accountability, not safety from judgement.

Mitchell and Rebecca: Centring the comfort of white students in the classroom does not make the space "safe"; it just protects and reinforces the racial norms of the institution. Instead of focusing on safety, classrooms should focus on accountability. Being accountable and holding others accountable also means centring the perspectives of the most marginalized and, more specifically, those most likely to face harm. Thinking about the legacy of the Sir George Williams Affair at Concordia, no one who should have been held accountable was held accountable—not the teacher, not the white students who defended institutional racism, not the university. Instead, the student protesters—primarily Black students—who spoke up and denounced racism at the university were the ones who were punished for speaking up. Despite the fifty years that have passed, this is not an uncommon experience for racialized students today. We are not allowed to say that we are not safe and instead find ourselves dismissed at best, and reprimanded at worst. If we want to dare to see the changes we want in our classrooms reflected back to us actively, then safety cannot be guaranteed to the oppressor and instead accountability needs to be guaranteed to the oppressed.

Kim: Prior to offering the FUS, I had for years facilitated collective agreements in my political science classrooms as a tool for students to set parameters around classroom discussion and interaction. I saw the agreement, in part, as a means of barring racism and sexism from the classroom—indeed, I saw it as a means for me to hold students accountable should racist and sexist comments be expressed. What I understand now is that this kind of agreement does not account for the fact that the classroom is already shaped by white supremacy, before students even walk in the door. Without a full accounting for racialized power dynamics that are already at play, no agreement among students and instructor is going to create the conditions in which those dynamics can be addressed, much less undone. This understanding, in no small part shaped through conversations with Mitchell and Rebecca, has radically shaped how I teach. Rather than try to impose an "agreement" onto differently positioned students, I teach about how fields of scholarship are racialized and gendered disciplines of knowledge production. I also teach anti-racist analysis and critique as a foundational skill, with the understanding that race and racism shapes all of our political interactions, including within the walls of the classroom.

Conclusion

> Killing joy is a world-making project. We make a world out of the shattered pieces even when we shatter the pieces or even when we are the shattered pieces.
>
> —Sara Ahmed, *Living a Feminist Life* (2017, 261)

Writing this chapter provided a new opportunity to make racism "something that can be spoken of and addressed by and with others"

(Ahmed 2017, 34). We began this chapter with the plan to discuss the vitrine project and the attempts of the students to navigate complex bureaucratic challenges, to access those histories. In the process of preparing to write together, we realized that we had just as much to say about the ongoing enactment of racism in the classroom today as we did about the racism of the past. Focusing on the dynamics of tackling the legacy of institutional racism in the classroom through "safe space" discussions, we explored what it means to take seriously the work of anti-racism in the classroom across the power dynamics of teachers and students, and across racial hierarchies. Ahmed's words from *Living a Feminist Life* became anchor for this work. Indeed, insofar as Ahmed's book served as the FUS textbook, the quotes offer reminders of how racism can be rendered invisible under the weight of the very attempts to undo it, without the scaffolding necessary to uphold it. Ultimately, we hope that this chapter recentres the voices, critiques, and contributions of BIPOC students in the classroom, not as their white professors think that they should be, but as they must be: the world-making foundations of a pedagogy of freedom.

References

Ahmed, Sara. 2017. *Living a Feminist Life*. Durham, NC: Duke University Press.

Austin, David. 2007. "All Roads Led to Montreal: Black Power, the Caribbean, and the Black Radical Tradition in Canada." *Journal of African American History* 92 (4): 516–39. https://www.jstor.org/stable/20064231.

Chang, Heewon, Faith Wambura Ngunjiri, and Kathy-Ann C. Hernandez. 2013. *Collaborative Autoethnography*. Walnut Creek, CA: Left Coast Press.

hooks, bell. 1994. *Teaching to Transgress: Education as the Practice of Freedom*. New York: Routledge.

Hudson, Peter James, and Katherine McKittrick. 2014. "The Geographies of Blackness and Anti-Blackness: An Interview with Katherine McKittrick." *CLR James Journal* 20 (1–2): 233–40. https://www.jstor.org/stable/26752069.

Quan, Douglas. 2019. "50 Years Later: How Racism Allegations against a Montreal Professor Turned into the Greatest Student Riot in Canadian History." *National Post*, January 28, 2019. https://nationalpost.com/news/canada/50-years-later-how-racism-allegations-against-a-montreal-professor-turned-into-the-greatest-student-riot-in-canadian-history.

10

Reflections on the "Trigger Warning" Debate

Divergent Strategies for Warnings in the Classroom

HANNAH DYER, NATALIE KOURI-TOWE, AND MICHELLE MILLER

Introduction

Debates about how trigger or content warnings are used in higher education have circulated in both popular culture and scholarly communities for much of the early part of the twenty-first century. "Trigger warnings" or "content warnings" are a mode of anticipatory preparation for the presentation of content or knowledge that students might feel troubling. For some, they are necessary interventions to make in the classroom (Carter 2015; Fenner 2018; Rae 2016; Spencer and Kulbaga 2018; Taylor 2017), while for others, they are undesired (Boysen et al. 2021; Duggan 2014; Halberstam 2014; Jarvie 2014; Sanson, Strange, and Garry 2019). Christina Hanhardt and Jasbir Puar, in conversation with other queer studies scholars, outline the debate as follows: "For advocates of their classroom use, they are promoted as a proactive response to student vulnerability, especially following sexual violence. For those opposed, they are often described as attacks on free speech, or as anti-intellectual and individualized forms of coddling students. Still others point out that the demand for trigger warnings can punish faculty who are themselves vulnerable as teachers" (Hanhardt et al. 2020, 50). As Hanhardt and Puar describe, the topic of trigger warnings in the classroom is a tangled field of resistance, vulnerability, and pedagogy. A discussion of trigger warnings has also to do with the very conditions of teaching and learning.

As co-investigators on the first national study examining the practices around and perceptions of trigger warnings in Canadian institutions of higher education, this chapter is a reflection on our relationship to and practices around pedagogical warnings within our own teaching practices. Coming from interdisciplinary feminist approaches to education, and situated across child studies, sexuality studies, and English, our work takes up diverse standpoints and perspectives over what constitutes safety in the classroom, how to navigate pedagogical goals across various classroom cultures, and how to approach learning from different and sometimes conflicting pedagogical perspectives. In thinking together from across our various disciplines, this chapter builds on the following questions: In relation to histories of trauma and difficult experience, what expectations do our students come to the classroom with? What priorities orient our approaches to warnings in the classroom? How do we grapple with the contradictions between safety and learning? How do we teach about violence in pedagogically useful ways? Taken together, our responses to these inquiries draw on feminist, queer, educational, and psychoanalytic approaches to learning in order to contend with the frictions that emerge through the possibilities and impossibilities of attending to individual and historical trauma in the classroom.

Introduce yourself and your relationship to the question of trigger/content warnings and your interest in this topic.

NKT: I am interested in trigger and content warnings from a curricular and pedagogical perspective. How do warnings take place within the pedagogical needs of gender and sexuality programs, and what role do they serve for student learning in the classroom? Conversely, how do performative gestures like instituting warnings risk giving students and faculty a false sense of safety in the classroom? Or worse, do warnings indoctrinate students and faculty into a practice that performs a disciplinary function around appearances of "good" and "bad" teaching, rather than as a reparative gesture to create safer or better learning environments? In their publication of a roundtable on the topic of trigger warnings, Hanhardt et al. (2020) contextualize these debates within queer studies and the critique of liberalism. In particular, I am compelled by their argument that the normalization of trauma as a pathological condition requiring individual aid obscures the systemic forms of violence that produce the conditions that traumatize (50). How can a classroom warning contend with such violence? Can our disciplines do justice to historical and contemporary forms of violence if the classroom is a space where trauma and choice are collapsed?

As a faculty member who has been teaching in the area of gender and sexuality for over a decade, it was only after I took on a more administrative role as the program director of a new interdisciplinary sexuality program that I started to think about warnings differently. What exactly are students asking for when they request warnings, and what are faculty refusing when they deny these requests? What happens in the classroom when a warning is given, and students walk away? I'm thinking here about the violence performed when white students leave a room when a trigger warning is given around a text or object that grapples with racial violence and white supremacy. If a warning can become the basis for refusing uncomfortable learning, then warnings as pedagogical tools can also serve to reinforce hegemonic power configurations, such as white innocence (Stewart, Cappello, and Carter 2014). Although not everyone is conflicted about the trigger/content warning debate, I continue to struggle with when and why warnings are necessary or appropriate as a pedagogical act as I oscillate between resisting and prioritizing giving warnings in my classes.

MM: My PhD is in language, culture, and teaching, and I teach English literature at the Ontario College of Art and Design University, in Toronto. I teach courses on comics and graphic novels, and on trans and queer literature. As such, my classes contain a lot of graphic representations of physical, sexual, social, and emotional violence. Coming up, I never really noticed content warnings in classes I took. While my professors did work to support students around difficult content, an "official" sort of warning in advance just wasn't common.

I started learning about content warnings in 2017, when all of a sudden many of my students were providing warnings before presentations or seminars, or sometimes even just comments in class discussion. I was really confused at first because I didn't understand what these warnings were for—after all, students in the classes would have already encountered the texts we were taking up in class. I was and to some degree am still a bit skeptical of whether content warnings "work." As a reader and a thinker, I have often been taken by surprise by literature in ways both inspiring and painful. And these moments of surprise have been rich sites of learning about the world and about myself. But at the same time, in my classes, I noticed and I appreciated that the students were using these warnings to express care for one another—they were conscious that some kinds of content could hurt their colleagues and they wanted to honour this. I can't be sure whether they thought their warnings, offered moments before presentations, would actually protect their classmates. Perhaps that was beside the point! Rather, these warnings were being used to articulate a desire for care and that was enough. While I still didn't really understand warnings and was skeptical about whether they might really work, I knew that I also wanted to express my care for students and to acknowledge that they bring their whole selves into the classroom, and their whole selves are at stake in reading and in learning.

My first attempts to bring content warnings into my classrooms were clumsy. Individual students complained that I hadn't effectively warned them about difficult content, when I thought I had. Working with warnings has been a study in humility for me, as I learn from my students what it looks like to show respect for them individually and as a class community. Actually, this is what I love about content warnings: if we look at the emergence of content warnings in education, they came into classrooms from students who were used to seeing and using them in online spaces (Lothian 2016). They began asking for their classes to show them the compassion they fostered in online communities.

Now I use content warnings in my classes as one tool among several that mitigates content that I know is of pedagogical value but which also has the capacity to strike students deep, making it hard for them to participate fully in my classes. I still don't know if they really "work" to prevent students being "triggered" by content, but I know that using them alongside other techniques that express care, I show students that they matter to me enough to try.

HD: I'm wading into the discussion of "trigger warnings" with some hesitancy but a history of asking determined questions about the relationship between pedagogy, care, and vulnerability. I like Sherene Seikaly's take on the topic: "The task at hand is to dismantle and repurpose trigger warnings in a way that models radical empathy and provides students with tools to enact it" (Hanhardt et al. 2020, 56). This formulation and call to action feels resonant with my approach to course instruction, which I hold all the while knowing that after being in the university for some time, I've likely internalized some of the institution's neoliberal approaches to education, which must surely restrict my radical capacities to offer collective care. I'm interested in the modes of analysis opened up when trigger warnings are always already agreed upon to fail. This failure, though, is not a reason to shirk the responsibility of convening around difficult topics, but rather to prepare for the asymmetrical ways that course material and related conversations impact students and faculty. I'm also interested in the theories of trauma and affect that get mobilized and manipulated in the notion of a trigger and how this process then becomes an organizing principle for our understanding of what happens to and for students in the classroom.

I'm now an associate professor and graduate program director in Child and Youth Studies at Brock University. I received my PhD from the University of Toronto (OISE), and, as a doctoral student, built friendships with Michelle and Natalie. We were all completing our programs at the same time and I had overlapping interests with each of them, but we've landed in programs that are quite different from each other. Unlike Natalie and Michelle, I haven't been asked much at all about trigger warnings from my current students or colleagues. The field of child and youth studies can harmonize itself with the liberal tenets of the university and can disavow difference in an attempt to propose a theory of development that describes "growing up." There are, for example, students for whom sexuality as a field of study and critique should have nothing to do with childhood. In many ways, my research has been about how theories of child development consistently and strategically deflect difficult material in order to maintain fidelity with white supremacy, heterosexism, and capitalism.

Who are the students in the classrooms you teach, and how do your students' expectations impact your relationships to warnings?

NKT: I try to think about the cultural and political contexts that shape what students come to the classroom with, and what topics, tensions, and conflicts shape their engagement with their programs of study. For instance, are my students responding to a specific set of conflicts within our department (e.g., demands for warnings from faculty, complaints about specific courses or topics), or are they responding to wider social movements (e.g., the #MeToo and Movement for Black Lives)? At my current institution, where the campus is known for its history of student activism, the classroom is not only a space for learning but also a space where students practice activism, advocacy, empowerment, and demands for transformation. The current cohort of students I am working with are exceptionally knowledgeable about sexuality. Many are part of a vanguard that sees gender and sexuality politics as intimately connected to trauma in a way that I had not anticipated. These students are committed to making the classroom a space that responds to their political demands, not only around inclusion but also attentive to their articulations of gender and sexuality in relation to histories of violence and trauma. In this way, students in my classes expect more of the classroom as a scene that is responsive to harm, trauma, and violence. At the same time, I have found that students can be prescriptive about what the classroom should look like, and this can create dissonance between students who have advanced understanding of these topics, and those who are learning about gender, sexuality, colonialism, racism, ableism, and other systems of oppression for the first time. The tension between these differential entry points into the classroom make for sometimes challenging and messy scenes for thinking about course material and content. Who is in the room can shape responses to difficult material, as much as the material itself.

HD: For many undergraduates who arrive to my courses, the notion of a universal child who needs intervention in order to properly "develop" is brought with them. Child and Youth Studies is a large program with faculty trained in and committed to many different ways of thinking and knowing things, inclusive of neuroscientists, developmental psychologists, statisticians, and those of us working from frameworks of inquiry that foreground relationality or history, for example. Students in the program take courses in each of these fields, so when they arrive to the classroom I facilitate, it might feel quite different from what they are otherwise doing in their coursework. Childhood studies and its adjacent fields of psychology and neuroscience, for example, is not quite the same political or curricular project as gender studies (even though, of course, there are interesting things that happen in their overlap). That is not to say that my students are without empathy and, indeed, many are driven towards solidarity and justice. Part of my pedagogical intervention in child and youth studies, at least the brand that is taught in my institution, is to demonstrate the ways social categories of belonging and exclusion inform not only children's realities but also our very theories of childhood. In the roundtable that Natalie previously highlighted, Kwame Holmes explains that "so-called trigger warnings" are that "which prepare students to immerse themselves in potentially activating content" (Hanhardt et al. 2020, 52). In order to request preparation, a student in child and youth studies courses must know that the study of childhood has to do with the study of race and gender, for example, and they haven't always been told this or been welcomed to make these connections. In this way, the violence of abstracting or dislocating a subject from the social locations they inhabit comes to bear on what requests students know are even possible to make.

What are your pedagogical practices around warnings? Do you use the same strategies in all classes? Why choose some kind of warnings over others?

NKT: I don't use the same strategy for every class and find myself varying my approach to giving warnings in different contexts. In a course that does not examine particularly violent texts or objects, I may prioritize a warning before a reading that deals with especially difficult topics, like sexual violence or abuse. In other contexts, however, difficult learning is embedded across the whole focus of the course, and I formulate my syllabus around learning through violence. This is especially the case when I've taught courses on race and racialized violence. In these cases, I have oriented my entire course around working through the different ways that violence creates racialized embodiment and how our own embodiment shapes our encounters with race and racialization. Our reactions to learning about and witnessing racial violence is shaped by our social location and embodiment. The emotional range of reactions to this kind of difficult learning, and expression of pain, sadness, fear, disbelief, anger, numbness, dissociation, etc. suggest that we cannot approach violence and trauma from a single standpoint.

HD: I don't have a coherent or uniform strategy for warning students about what feelings or reactions will arise in a classroom, in part because anticipating or assuming another's needs is complicated. But more so, I don't have a uniform approach because I just haven't found a way to angle it right. And yet, I do make a committed choice to teach from a site of care and I do feel a sense of responsibility for the pain and discomfort that can arise in students when confronted not only with certain material but by another student's cruelty. That is something I worry a lot about, actually—the pain students cause each other and the moments it stings but I may not know it has occurred. For me, the very conditions of teaching and learning are made from our own histories of subject formation and also the fantasies of who we are to each other. I want to be imagined and experienced as one who teaches from a site of care, but know that this is an unfinished project that requires constant accountability to students.

MM: I do use content warnings in all my classes when we are working with difficult material, but I teach one course where the material is specifically troubling. In my Trans and Queer Literature course, every representation contains physical, social, colonial, and/or sexual violence. As Sara Ahmed points out, "the histories that leave us fragile are often those that bring us to a feminist room" (2018, 59). Many students who take this class are marginalized in complex ways, experience ongoing homophobia and transphobia, and many need strong emotional and community support to participate meaningfully in class. I offer content warnings in several different ways for these students. To start, I label warnings beside the readings on the syllabus. I suggest substitute readings when the content is extremely challenging. I make it clear that students need to prioritize their well-being, and that, as adults, I trust them to make decisions about what is appropriate for them to encounter, when they may or may not be able to encounter it, and under which conditions. When we study difficult representations, I offer open office hours. Students are welcome to come and talk about specific issues or nothing at all—they can bring themselves as they are. I also link to our Student Wellness office on our course homepage. Everything I've listed above is a kind of support I think is related to the content warning, even though obviously it exceeds the warning itself. I also end every class with a "to-do" list, and I remind students of the content warnings here. And if, while preparing for class, I encounter something that might be difficult that I hadn't warned for, I send mid-week emails! I know I sound obsessed. But when I'm assigning texts, reading texts, prepping classes, I'm holding my students in my mind, and I want to offer them the kinds of support they tell me they need.

Is trauma something you are thinking about in your teaching? If so, what shapes your attention to trauma?

NKT: I never thought of myself as a scholar who taught on trauma, but the more I think about how I have learned to navigate difficult encounters in the classroom, the more I realize that a lot of this navigation is holding space for the way trauma can manifest through the classroom in discordant ways. Increasingly, I am learning from trauma-informed popular education tools to help me adapt my impulse to intellectualize difficult emotions into pedagogically informative moments, and instead support learning while also making room for feeling. I can't say that I am particularly skillful in this regard, but it's the place I am trying to learn more from. I have found that introducing vulnerability, transparency, honesty, and apology in my approach to the classroom has been helpful for navigating these kinds of encounters. Modelling these qualities in my own teaching, despite my aversion to being vulnerable in the classroom as a teacher, has helped me break down the defensive and resistant impulse that can emerge in difficult encounters in my classes, including when I've been called out, or when conflict emerges.

HD: I teach, research, and write about theories of trauma as they relate to childhood. I have other colleagues who teach about childhood trauma, though it is from a different disciplinary perspective. I'm interested in a transdisciplinary approach to trauma theory that draws from literary studies, narrative theory, and psychic life. I've written about traumatic experience as it relates to white supremacy, queer affect, Palestine, and sex education. In the large first year course I teach, which can hold more than a thousand students, I teach a unit on trauma that introduces psychoanalytic concepts such as repression, identification, and defence mechanisms. I do so alongside conversations about violence, memory, and affect. These are some of the more popular lectures I give and I think this is because a course of this size allows students to have some amount of anonymity while also potentially inhabiting course material. Another reason that students might like the topic, though, is because the notion of a traumatized child who requires saving compels many people to join the field of child and youth studies. For this reason, I begin the course with a unit on the damage and inequities contained in childhood innocence, which has also to do with whose trauma is assumed, denied, or attended to. My reading in trauma theory is brought into conversations about the usefulness of trigger warnings and the interaction between the unconscious and the knowable content of social interactions.

What is something you wish other faculty would consider about trigger/content warnings?

NKT: Instead of assuming that when students ask for warnings they're asking faculty to acquiesce to their demands (although students might use calls for warnings to exercise solidarity or self-advocacy), what if we assume that these requests are inquiries that allow students to gauge the capacity for trust and collaboration in the classroom? Thinking about the warning as a technique rather than an imperative, warnings can help us attune our teaching to thinking carefully about the pedagogical goals of using violent content or difficult material in our classes. For instance, when learning about racial violence, there is significant debate about showing graphic scenes of violence (e.g., video footage of torture victims, scenes of war that show dead bodies, documentation of police killings). Do these scenes perpetuate violence or can they serve a pedagogical role? This is a widely debated question. Rather than assume there is a "yes" or "no" answer, asking ourselves how and why we give warnings can help inform how we use these kinds of materials in the classroom. I am also interested in how responses to the warnings can themselves be instructive. As Fatima El-Tayeb has noted, warnings can serve as shorthand for wider political positionings (Hanhardt et al. 2020, 56), so that when students are asking for warnings, they're actually saying something about their political location. In some cases, therefore, the request for a warning is less about trauma than it is about a particular kind of political commitment, location, or demand for solidarity.

HD: This question leads me to ask something different but related: Is there a problem that arises when a course outline or syllabus would not warrant a conversation about the purpose or usefulness of a content warning? That is, if a syllabus is void of difficult material, how can the topic of trigger warnings be brought into proximity? Sometimes, it is not only how material is presented but whether it is presentable at all. Students might experience pain or frustration not because something is shown or read, but because there are large gaps in what is offered as viable or "real" data/method/inquiry. In this case what is painful for the student is the complete disavowal of experience or history, or avoidance of topics that might be of interest or relevance to their lives. When courses or even disciplines imagine themselves as outside of controversy, we have another sort of problem. The request for syllabi that include too often marginalized literature or content might not be solely explained by the realm of trauma or the notion of a trigger warning, as Natalie infers, but also to do with, as she states, "political commitment, location, or demand for solidarity."

MM: In "The Illusion of Safety / The Safety of Illusion," Roxane Gay (2012) writes about her own contradictory feelings about content warnings. She discusses her own resistance to being offered a trigger warning, arguing "How dare you presume what I need to be protected from?" As a person living with complex trauma, she is triggered by events that are common, specific to the ways she has experienced trauma. No one could protect her from what hurts her, because her triggers are environmental and sometimes surprising. However, for Gay, whether trigger warnings actually protect us from our complex trauma is beyond the point. She argues that it is not up to us to presume to know what others need: "Those of us who do not believe should have little say in the matter. We can neither presume nor judge what others might feel the need to be protected from." I think of this all the time. Professors *should have little say*. If our students express a need for a warning (and my research indicates that many students feel they need warnings), then that's that. We should show them we are listening to them, because we don't know as much about them as they know about themselves. When our students begin offering warnings to one another about difficult content, we can notice that their action is a request. They offer care because they value care, and they value care because they need care.

Ahmed positions the student who asks for a warning as a "killjoy" (2018, 64). She describes the feminist killjoy as an "affect alien" who turns good feelings into bad, disrupting the normal flow of things by refusing to go along with what is happening. Student killjoys who request content warnings might cause an interruption that feels bad to an instructor trying to lecture. But this is the job of a killjoy: to alert us to what is *already* bad. She writes that, contrary to the popular argument that students use warnings to avoid learning or to censor professors, "actually the killjoy here is asking for more, not less: asking us to complicate the materials; to situate the materials; to consider how the materials can create ripples in how they move us" (64). This is a generous read of what is happening when a student asks for a warning, and one that feels right to me.

In 2019 I ran a small study on content warnings. Much of what students reported was familiar to me—they desired their professors to treat them like adults who could make decisions about what was best for them, and they wanted to be able to participate meaningfully in their classes. One student, reporting a positive experience with difficult content in the classroom, detailed the techniques the professor used to contextualize the content, make space for students to prioritize their well-being, and get emotional support as needed. They said, "The material was still very difficult to encounter because of my own trauma history, but it felt manageable because I felt respected, warned so I could prepare, and the gravity of the material was acknowledged, as was my personhood because my potential reaction was validated. If the professor had sprung that material on us, I would have had to leave the room, might have dissociated or experienced flashbacks, but the way it was handled allowed for me to stay in the room and engage fully with the material." Here the student outlines a professor's strong approach to supporting students: a warning, some context to the inclusion of the material. An invitation to leave class if necessary, a gesture to available resources, an offer of support. The student felt empowered every step along the way, and thus could "engage fully." Here the student reports that they wouldn't have been able to engage the material *without* this warning, but *with* it, they can be an active participant in the class.

Conclusion

Across the responses to our study on trigger warnings, one outcome of our research is a belief that rather than a fixed set of practices, trigger warnings and their related practices lend themselves best to a reflexive approach to the classroom. Our respondents shared with us how the dynamics of the classroom, and the orientations and social locations of our students, shaped how difficult encounters were navigated beyond an imperative to use or not use warnings. Rather than presuming to know our students, or that our students know us, our work illustrates the importance of admitting uncertainty and a willingness to enter meaningful conversations with our students as we navigate classroom learning and interactions. This means entering into difficult conversations in the classroom without shying away from the possibility of discomfort while recognizing the impossibility of being able to predict or control the impact of history on the experiences and standpoints of our students and ourselves. While we have tried not to be prescriptive in our approach to trigger warnings, we might conclude with this statement: If offering trigger warnings is a strategy for caring for yourself and your students, then continue using this technique. However, we have found in our study that faculty and students use a number of different strategies for thoughtful and ethical classroom engagement. What matters most in relation to difficult encounters in learning is that the teacher approach the classroom as a site where vulnerability, honesty, and apology make new avenues possible for responding to and revising relationships between past, present, and future.

References

Ahmed, Sara. 2018. "Feminist Hurt / Feminism Hurts." In *The Power of Vulnerability: Mobilising Affect in Feminist, Queer and Anti-Racist Media Cultures*, edited by Anu Koivunen, Katariina Kyrole, and Ingrid Ryberg, 59–70. Manchester: Manchester University Press.

Boysen, Guy A., Raina A. Isaacs, Lori Tretter, and Sydnie Markowski. 2021. "Trigger Warnings Efficacy: The Impact of Warnings on Affect, Attitudes, and Learning." *Scholarship of Teaching and Learning in Psychology* 7 (1): 39–52. http://dx.doi.org/10.1037/stl0000150.

Carter, Angela M. 2015. "Teaching with Trauma: Disability Pedagogy, Feminism, and the Trigger Warnings Debate." *Disability Studies Quarterly* 35 (2). https://dsq-sds.org/index.php/dsq/article/view/4652/3935.

Duggan, Lisa. 2014. "On Trauma and Trigger Warnings, in Three Parts." *Bully Bloggers* (blog). November 23, 2014. https://bullybloggers.wordpress.com/2014/11/23/on-trauma-and-trigger-warnings-in-three-parts/.

Fenner, Sofia. 2018. "Not So Scary: Using and Defusing Content Warnings in the Classroom." *Journal of Political Science Education* 14 (1): 86–96. https://doi.org/10.1080/15512169.2017.1359095.

Gay, Roxane. 2012. "The Illusion of Safety / The Safety of Illusion." *The Rumpus* (blog). August 28, 2012. https://uwm.edu/cultures-communities/wp-content/uploads/sites/219/2018/10/The-Illusion-Of-Safety-The-Safety-Of-Illusion.pdf.

Halberstam, Jack. 2014. "You Are Triggering Me! The Neo-Liberal Rhetoric of Harm, Danger and Trauma." *Bully Bloggers* (blog). July 5, 2014. https://bullybloggers.wordpress.com/2014/07/05/you-are-triggering-me-the-neo-liberal-rhetoric-of-harm-danger-and-trauma/.

Hanhardt, Christina B., Jasbir K. Puar, Neel Ahuja, Paul Amar, Aniruddha Dutta, Fatima El-Tayeb, Kwame Holmes, and Sherene Seikaly. 2020. "Beyond Trigger Warnings: Safety, Securitization, and Queer Left Critique." *Social Text* 38.4 (145): 49–76. https://doi.org/10.1215/01642472-8680438.

Jarvie, Jenny. 2014. "Trigger Happy." *The New Republic*, March 3, 2014. https://newrepublic.com/article/116842/trigger-warnings-have-spread-blogs-college-classes-thats-bad.

Lothian, Alexis. 2016. "Choose Not to Warn: Trigger Warnings and Content Notes from Fan Culture to Feminist Pedagogy." *Feminist Studies* 42 (3): 743–56. https://www.jstor.org/stable/10.15767/feministstudies.42.3.0743.

Rae, Logan. 2016. "Re-focusing the Debate on Trigger Warnings: Privilege, Trauma, and Disability in the Classroom." *First Amendment Studies* 50 (2): 95–102. https://doi.org/10.1080/21689725.2016.1224677.

Sanson, Mevagh, Deryn Strange, and Maryanne Garry. 2019. "Trigger Warnings Are Trivially Helpful at Reducing Negative Affect, Intrusive Thoughts, and

Avoidance." *Clinical Psychological Science* 7 (4): 778–93. https://doi.org/10.1177/2167702619827018.

Spencer, Leland G., and Theresa A. Kulbaga. 2018. "Trigger Warnings as Respect for Student Boundaries in University Classrooms." *Journal of Curriculum and Pedagogy* 15 (1): 106–22. https://doi.org/10.1080/15505170.2018.1438936.

Stewart, Michelle, Michael Cappello, and Claire Carter. 2014. "Anti-Oppressive Education and the Trap of 'Good' Intentions: Lessons from an Interdisciplinary Workshop." *Critical Education* 5 (14): 1–19. https://doi.org/10.14288/ce.v5i14.184392.

Taylor, Holly. 2017. "Accessibility on Campus: Posttraumatic Stress Disorder, Duty to Accommodate and Trigger Warnings." In *Trigger Warnings: History, Theory, Context*, edited by Emily Knox, 22–36. Lanham: Rowman & Littlefield.

11

Teaching Trans

Pedagogical Implications of Embodying Course Content

JULIA SINCLAIR-PALM

Introduction

When I began my current position, I was invited to develop a fourth-year seminar on a topic of my choosing. I created a course titled Queer and Trans Youth, which, at the time of writing, I have taught four times. In the course we discuss some of the challenges queer and trans youth face, and explore how queer and trans youth have been conceptualized in research, medical and psychological discourse, media, literature, policy, and education. Drawing from Toby Beauchamp and Benjamin D'Harlingue, my course is structured to focus on "how gendered subjects are produced by institutions" (2012, 26). From the beginning of the course, I insist on the notion that we all have a gender, and that our gender is impacted by social systems and structures. I want students in the course to recognize how transphobic ideas about gender perpetuate the idea that trans people's gender identities are artificial and manufactured, while cis identities are real and natural. I also want my students to understand how transphobia hurts everyone, not just trans people.

The majority of the students who take this course are white, cisgender, and heterosexual, which reflects the demographics of the students in my program at large. Unlike many of the faculty who write about their experiences teaching courses on trans issues and trans theory, I do not teach in a gender studies or sociology department. This means that my students often lack a strong foundation in theories about gender or current terminology and practices in trans communities. They are beginners who are typically well-meaning and want to be good allies to trans folks. In class discussions about gender identity and pronouns, students express worry and fear about "getting it wrong." The anxiety students experience in the classroom is in part a reflection of the care they are offering me, their trans professor. Although I don't come out as trans until part way through the course, the queerness of my gender is visible, and this leaves me questioning the pedagogical implications of the legibility of my gender and my decision to come out as trans.

In this chapter, I draw on education scholarship on coming out, embodied knowledge, engaged pedagogy, and trans studies to explore the pedagogical implications of embodying course content. What happens when the professor becomes the object of knowledge and part of the curriculum? As more and more trans teachers enter the university, how will this impact pedagogy? University courses focusing on trans studies are relatively new and yet much has been written about how gender is taught (Beauchamp and D'Harlingue 2012; LeMaster and Johnson 2019). When classes do cover trans issues, they are often discussed as a small part of a course, where lived trans identity is leveraged to teach about trans issues (Courvant 2011)—for instance, when guest speakers are brought into courses to speak or teach about trans issues. More recently, work has been developed on the way trans embodiment impacts how trans educators discuss their pedagogy and their engagement with students, and how the trans or cis embodiment of students impacts how they engage with trans studies (Keenan 2017a; Sathiyaseelan 2014). Because everyone has a gender in the classroom, grappling with the embodiment of teachers and students can help with learning beyond the gender and sexuality classroom. I begin with my own classroom and the way I introduce gender through self-reflection; I then discuss my gender embodiment as a teacher, and conclude with a discussion of the risks and rewards of an engaged pedagogy that takes seriously the role of the teacher's embodiment in learning.

Everyone Has Gender in the Classroom

Many LGBTQ+ educators and scholars of colour insist on the importance of creating a safe learning environment for students, and yet I observe the discomfort my students face when encountering course material that confronts them with difference, and I wonder about how my own body and gender contribute to their discomfort. Some of this discomfort points to the expectation that the classroom serves as a space for white cisgender heterosexual students to feel safe, despite critiques of safe space in the classroom that point to how classrooms are already sites of harm for racialized, trans, and queer students (Hudson and McKittrick 2014). Given the above context, I am left wondering how to approach situations where white cisgender and heterosexual students feel uncomfortable in my classes when faced with the realities and violence of transphobia.

One strategy for addressing students' fears is to give them opportunities to practice new terms and opportunities to explore different ways to respond to transphobia and homophobia that they might encounter. In addition to encouraging my students to practice using terms that may be new (e.g., *genderqueer*, *cisnormativity*, *transgender*), I also use personal reflection as tool for getting students to engage with course material and put these new words and concepts into context. Freewriting exercises encourage students to think about their own gender and how they are complicit in maintaining cisnormativity.[1]

---

1. *Cisnormativity* refers to the norms and assumptions that are tied to the belief that everyone's gender identity aligns with the sex they were assigned at birth.

One of the first freewriting exercises students are assigned is based on Kate Bornstein's (1997) *My Gender Workbook*, in which she asks readers to consider how they know what their gender is. I ask them to reflect on these prompts: Do I have a gender? How do I know what my gender is? And can other people can tell what my gender is? Through these exercises, students become more acquainted with the ways they think about, navigate, and express their gender. Students often enter the class assuming they will learn about gender from the experiences of, and research about, queer and trans youth. However, through self-reflection they quickly find that they can learn about gender from their own relationship to it. This comes as a surprise to many students who have normative gender expressions. Their gender is typically something they haven't thought much about. Their gender is "normal," and they enter the class to learn about "abnormal" and "atypical" genders.

I am interested in the moment when students engage with their gender embodiment and expression for the first time. When does gender enter the classroom? What is a critical trans pedagogy that invites cisgender students to learn through their normative relationships to gender? When most cisgender students enter my class, they tend to think of gender as only remarkable and complex for queer and trans youth, and that their own relationship to and understanding of their gender cannot provide them an avenue for conceptualizing how queer and trans people experience their gender. The curiosity they bring to queer and trans youth must also be brought to their engagement with their own gender.

Gender can become a more vulnerable topic as cisnormativity is troubled. Students can feel awkward discussing their own gender in the classroom. I question whether it is invasive to ask students about their gender, while also teaching about the gender of queer and trans youth. One of my strategies is to normalize the complexity of gender. To argue and insist that we all express and explore our gender in different ways in various contexts and in relation to others. Everyone's gender is impacted by the gender binary and gender norms; none of us get to escape it.

When I began teaching Queer and Trans Youth, I was struck by the way students positioned themselves as not trans. Trans youth were cast as different and as the only ones with a complex relationship to gender. Normalizing the impacts of gender norms and expectations on all genders shifts the cisgender student's relationship to the presumed distance from trans youth. Finding common ground with trans youth is a strategy to stop students from victimizing trans youth or seeing them as always at-risk, which reduces trans youth to objects for intervention rather than subjects with agency. While I want cisgender students to hold onto the idea that they will never know what it's like to be trans, and that they have a gender, just like queer and trans youth have a gender, the tension in this seemingly contradictory approach leaves me questioning whether we can learn about difference without othering.

Despite their initial hesitation, students are usually open to share stories about the ways they are impacted by gender roles and gender expectations in class. Nonetheless, students rarely reflect on how they express their gender and how they know their gender. Comfortable in the binary understanding of gender, many students struggle to understand themselves within the messy or fluid frameworks that queer approaches to gender invite us to think about. This conflict can raise another set of anxieties in students, such as in the case when students share that they feel like they have disappointed me or failed at the course learning objectives because they think of their gender as "simple" or "boring." If my goal is to help students understand how society impacts gender, then I must also consider what Hilary Malatino calls "the lens of benign diversity: difference that doesn't, ultimately, make much of a difference" (2015, 401). Asking cisgender students to consider the complexity of their gender doesn't erase the importance of difference; instead, it helps them engage with gender differences in a way that recognizes gender diversity as real while also not completely knowable.

Coming Out as a Queer and Trans Professor

At the beginning of the course, I introduce myself and tell students that I use the pronouns *she/her* and *they/them*. I encourage them to use the pronouns *they/them* when referring to me an opportunity for them to practice using non-binary pronouns. I also acknowledge that it can take time and practice to get comfortable using different pronouns from those that are more familiar, and remind them that non-binary pronoun use is already a common English-language practice. Although I tell them about my pronouns, I don't come out to my students as queer or trans at the beginning of the course. Instead, I tell stories about my gender and sexuality throughout when it seems relevant to course learning. A part of me doesn't think that my gender and sexuality is relevant to student learning, and some scholars argue that coming out might distract from course content and that students would spend time imagining me prior to transition (Clarkson 2017). However, my approach to pedagogy centres on an awareness of who is given the authority to be an expert on a topic, which means identity is an important consideration for education.

Coming out may seem redundant because of what I wear and how I express my gender. My gender announces itself, and so I'm surprised every time my students assume I identify as a woman. In these moments, my gender is unexpected in the classroom. In the introduction to her book *Sexuality in School*, Jen Gilbert writes about the task of choosing what to wear on the first day of class, how her students will interpret her gender, and the lack of control she has over these first impressions (2014, ix). Although sexuality and gender might be apparent to some students and colleagues, a universal understanding or recognition of gender and sexuality cannot be taken for granted.

When I teach, I wear a men's button up shirt and slacks. I style my butch hair cut with pomade and take pleasure in rolling back my sleeves when I get too hot lecturing. Drawing on whiteness and masculinity to demonstrate my expertise as an educator, a facet of my gender that I also interrogate, I use my boyishness as a way to engage with ideas in a playful and curious manner. My gender is part of my pedagogy. However, gender is not neutral in the classroom and I question what my gender teaches my students, and how trans teachers are shaping the profession (Gilbert and Gray 2020). Ed Brockenbrough (2012) asks, For whom, in what ways, and in what circumstances might the closet be of use? Some theorists have pointed out that the concept of "coming out" insinuates that one might be deceiving others or concealing a part of one's identity, or that one's sexuality and gender is the most important aspect of one's identity (Rasmussen 2004; Seidman, Meeks, and Traschen 1999). In some ways, these ideas assume there is only one closet to come out of and that coming out is a singular event; whereas, for educators, coming out is a constant process as each new year brings a new group of students to the classroom.

There has been much debate about the benefits and risks of coming out in schools and how it might impact or support the relationship educators have with students (Khayatt and Iskander 2020; Matute et al. 2020; Jiménez 2007). Educators often feel pressure to come out because of the way they might be seen as a role model or source of support for young LGBTQ+ students (Russell 2010). Others note that coming out can be political, empowering, and a strategic way to combat homophobic attitudes (Rasmussen 2004; Sears and Williams 1997). Conversely, Didi Khayatt (1997) questions the necessity of coming out and explores the pedagogical function or effect of coming out in class. Educators who do not come out to their students are often cast as failing their students, whereas educators who do come out are seen as leaders and role models. People come out or stay closeted for a wide range of reasons, including racism and the fear of being fired (Rasmussen 2004).

Jonathan Silin suggests that the risks associated with coming out may be necessary for queer and trans educators to survive in the profession and asks, "How is pedagogy changed when we dismantle the wall between private and professional experience? What risks do we take? What goals do we achieve when we open our lives to public inspection?" (1999, 96). There is both pleasure and risk involved in coming out, but for some, coming out isn't always a choice. Coming out is only possible or accessible depending on the intersecting identities and forms of oppression that a teacher faces, and this makes coming out an experience shaped by difference. The safety and comfort I feel coming out in the university reflects the privileged status of whiteness and masculinity within higher education. The comfort that certain forms of privilege can render to teachers is complicated by research about queer and trans educators that highlights how their sexualities and genders sit uncomfortably inside the category of "teacher" (Connell 2014; Gilbert 2021; Gray 2013; Mayo 2008), which is partially due to discourses about LGBTQ+ teachers that cast them as pedophiles. Despite what may appear to be contradictions that shape coming out in education, I am interested in thinking about the ways that coming out might act as a bridge between professor and student. What does my gender nonconformity announce, especially to students who are learning about gender for the first time?

The Risks and Rewards of Embodied Knowledge and Engaged Pedagogy

Students and teachers enter the classroom with diverse experiences and identities, and yet teaching practices too often do not engage, invite, or account for our unique and complex lives. Engaged pedagogy allows students to draw from their lived experiences to facilitate understanding and learning (hooks 1994). For bell hooks, vulnerability must be mutual and initiated from the teacher. Reflecting on his experience as a K-12 educator, Harper Benjamin Keenan writes, "students bring their experiences into the classroom, and I do the same in developing my pedagogy. Perhaps for most of us, the classroom door operates as a screen that filters out the complexity of who we are and the communities from which we emerge" (2017b, 539). Schools only allow or invite a part of who we are, and in turn, silence and deny aspects of our identity and histories. This is as much the case for teachers as it is for students.

Coming out in the classroom raises questions about the relationship between embodied knowledge and engaged pedagogy. While I approach my teaching with an understanding that the classroom is not a safe place for a lot of students, I prioritize the vulnerable act of sharing my experiences as a pedagogical tool, so that my students might also share some of their own stories. Embodied knowledge, knowledge that comes from the experience of gender, sexuality, race, and other aspects of one's identity and social location, is foundational to the practice of engaged pedagogy. In their introduction to *TSQ: Transgender Studies Quarterly*, Susan Stryker and Paisley Currah argue that trans studies is informed by the daily life experiences of trans people: "Transgender people (self-identified or designated as such by others) can be subjects of knowledge as well as objects of knowledge. That is, they can articulate critical knowledge from embodied positions that would otherwise be rendered pathological, marginal, invisible, or unintelligible within dominant and normative organizations of power/knowledge" (2014, 9). For Kathryn Jaekel and Z. Nicolazzo (2017), this understanding and discussion of trans studies offers them the possibility of thinking about what they call teaching trans*. Teaching trans* is a way to "conceptualize how we facilitate student learning, increase trans* representations and knowledges, and center our own experiences…Teaching trans is a pedagogical approach that consists of three primary parts: teaching as, teaching about, and teaching with trans* epistemologies. For us, 'teaching trans*' holds the tensions of who we are and who we are seen to be, how we operate in the academy, and how to engage in learning…[It] means to scavenge disciplines, media, and scholarship in an effort to represent the voices of those who are most on the margins" (Jaekel and Nicolazzo 2017, 167–68). The pedagogical techniques of engaged learning through embodied knowledge offers powerful tools for teachers to connect with students, and anchor learning in the lived experiences of gender and other experiences. However, I also wonder if it is essential or necessarily beneficial to come out to my students. Because the teacher has authority, and because the status of gender, race, and other facets of identity shape who gets to stand in front of the classroom, the risk of teaching exclusively through embodied knowledge is that students may come to think of my experience as truth or final authority on the topic. I hesitate to come out because of this concern.

By drawing on my own embodiment and experiences, am I reinforcing the idea that queer and trans experiences of gender are different from my cisgender students? When the trans teacher becomes sole representative of transness in the room, what kinds of gendered experiences are erased? Conversely, despite my status as a white masculine person, I can feel especially vulnerable in moments when my gender feels like a spectacle to be studied. In those moments I am reminded that my students do not share a gendered experience with me. I become the object of the class lecture, a shift that adds distance between me and the students that expands or becomes more apparent the more I draw on my personal experiences. This distance disrupts the rapport I have with students and makes engaged pedagogy difficult, as my expertise shifts from one of authority as a professor to the personal, as a queer and trans subject. In centring learning about gender through my own embodiment, gender risks returning to the exceptional object of otherness, reinforcing the normative position of cisgender students as genderless.

The limits of embodied knowledge can be seen in the figure of the guest speaker. Nicholas Clarkson argues that the figure of the trans guest speaker reinforces "the sense that trans concerns are separate from the concerns of cis women, [where] the 'special guest' approach requires that guests display pain to elicit sympathy from cis audiences" (2017, 234; Malatino 2015; Rand 2012). Malatino argues that "special guests are often expected to deliver a 'coming-out' story documenting movement through insecurity toward a public declaration of pride and self-love" (2015, 400). The figure of the guest speaker remains at a distance and "does not require cis students to critically interrogate the ways in which they have been produced as gendered subjects and have participated in policing gender nonnormativity" (400–401). Similarly, Keenan argues, "we need pedagogies that allow us to share the complexities of our own unique embodied knowledge with one another and to question the limitations of that knowledge" (2017b, 548). Resistance to defining trans and the trans experience means "I cannot teach my students some essential meaning of the word *transgender*, nor should I. I cannot teach them what 'transgender experience' is, nor should I—because I myself don't know what it is. There is no universal definition or experience of transness, and any activity that does not actively resist the creation of false universality runs the risk of building a new script" (Keenan 2017b, 551).

Despite the impossibility of defining a universal experience, university students still desire instructions on how to engage with trans people and trans issues in a monolithic way, and deny the complexity of trans experience. This desire poses a challenge for an engaged pedagogy that does not tell students a universal truth. Because higher education still remains structured around the banking model of education (Freire 2000), students seek clear definitions that they can repeat and consume. My students want answers and they want to know what to do when they meet trans people and encounter transphobia. They care about trans youth, even if they don't understand their lives. They arrive at the subject wanting to do less harm, wanting to be an ally, wanting to get it right. The hardest part is that there are no clear answers to these questions. Self-reflection is the closest thing to a prescription or tool I can offer. I want to teach students to be okay with not knowing, and I want them to remain curious and thoughtful. I encounter student anxieties when they express their desire to get it right, and struggle to use my pronouns. I receive this as an attempt to care for me, but it's not the care I want, nor ask, from them. By trying to challenge, or at least complicate, the idea that trans people need protection because they are always at risk, I am confronting the desire to make embodied knowledge a singular conclusion for learning.

Keenan uses the metaphor of the dance floor to think about the classroom as a space where "people who may not know one another gather together and learn how to interact and relate to one another in shared space" (2021, 1). Sharing stories about one's personal experiences or coming out in these spaces can be a way to bring students and educators together (on the dance floor), but I want to leave room for and keep close those folks who aren't able, or don't want, to come out or share personal stories. It is in imagining this scene that I feel most like my students—a beginner who is worried about getting it wrong. The teacher—whose gender is always expected but not always known or understood—can embrace this vulnerability to help students learn to remain in the discomfort of not always knowing.

Drawing on Keenan's (2017b) metaphor of the dance floor and my discussion of pedagogy, I conclude by offering five recommendations for teachers as a way to rethink their engagement with students and gender. First, I think teachers can demonstrate their care for trans students and trans issues by considering their own gender and making active decisions about making that consideration visible. The more familiar teachers are with their gender (or their own dancing), the better teacher they can be for others learning about gender. Second, it can be helpful to remember that one of the ways students learn to dance (or talk about gender) is to watch someone with more power or experience do it first. The vulnerability a teacher displays in learning about gender and making mistakes can be an invaluable lesson for students. Third, it is important to remember that gender changes, just like the dance floor and the people on it, so be careful not to assume to know someone's gender and remain adaptable and welcome shifts in a person's identity. Fourth, I recommend that teachers start from the assumption that there is always a trans person in the room, rather than waiting for a student to come out as trans. We never know who is on the dance floor and we exclude people from a space when we deny their existence. Lastly, I encourage teachers to be hospitable to the uninvited and unanticipated guest (Gilbert 2006), as they lead to those moments when we learn the most. You never know when your favourite song will come on or who you might learn a new dance move from.

References

Beauchamp, Toby, and Benjamin D'Harlingue. 2012. "Beyond Additions and Exceptions: The Category of Transgender and New Pedagogical Approaches for Women's Studies." *Feminist Formations* 24 (2): 25–51. https://www.jstor.org/stable/23275103.

Bornstein, Kate. 1998. *My Gender Workbook: How to Become a Real Man, a Real Woman, the Real You, or Something Else Entirely*. New York: Routledge.

Brockenbrough, Ed. 2012. "Agency and Abjection in the Closet: The Voices (and Silences) of Black Queer Male Teachers." *International Journal of Qualitative Studies in Education* 25 (6): 741–65. https://doi.org/10.1080/09518398.2011.590157.

Clarkson, Nicholas L. 2017. "Teaching Trans Students, Teaching Trans Studies." *Feminist Teacher* 27 (2–3): 233–52. https://doi.org/10.5406/femteacher.27.2-3.0233.

Connell, Catherine. 2014. *School's Out: Gay and Lesbian Teachers in the Classroom*. Oakland, CA: University of California Press.

Courvant, Diana. 2011. "'Strip!'" *Radical Teacher* 92 (1): 26–34. https://muse.jhu.edu/article/463365.

Freire, Paulo. 2000. *Pedagogy of the Oppressed*. 30th anniversary ed. New York: Continuum.

Gilbert, Jen. 2006. "'Let Us Say Yes to What Turns Up': Education as Hospitality." *Journal of the Canadian Association for Curriculum Studies* 4 (1): 25–34. https://doi.org/10.25071/1916-4467.16993.

—— 2014. *Sexuality in School: The Limits of Education*. Minneapolis: University of Minnesota Press. https://www.jstor.org/stable/10.5749/j.ctt7zw6j4.

—— 2021. "'Ambivalent Legacies: A Response to Harper Keenan." *Occasional Paper Series*, no. 45. https://educate.bankstreet.edu/occasional-paper-series/vol2021/iss45/13/.

Gilbert, Jen, and Emily Gray. 2020. "LGBTIQ+ Teachers: Stories from the Field." *Teaching Education* 31 (1): 1–5. https://doi.org/10.1080/10476210.2020.1709943.

Gray, Emily M. 2013. "Coming Out as a Lesbian, Gay or Bisexual Teacher: Negotiating Private and Professional Worlds." *Sex Education* 13 (6): 702–14. https://doi.org/10.1080/14681811.2013.807789.

hooks, bell. 1994. *Teaching to Transgress: Education as the Practice of Freedom*. New York: Routledge.

Hudson, Peter James, and Katherine McKittrick. 2014. "The Geographies of Blackness and Anti-Blackness: An Interview with Katherine McKittrick." *CLR James Journal* 20 (1–2): 233–40. https://www.jstor.org/stable/26752069.

Jaekel, Kathryn S., and Z. Nicolazzo. 2017. "Teaching Trans*: Strategies and Tensions of Teaching Gender in Student Affairs Preparation Programs." *Journal for the Study of Postsecondary and Tertiary Education* 2 (December): 165–79. https://doi.org/10.28945/3859.

Jiménez, Karleen Pendleton. 2007. "On Late Nights: Living in My Queer Teacher Body." In *"Unleashing the Unpopular": Talking about Sexual Orientation and Gender Diversity in Education*, edited by Isabel Killoran and Karleen Pendleton Jiménez, 63–71. Olney, MD: Association for Childhood Education International.

Keenan, Harper Benjamin. 2017a. "Khaki Drag: Race, Gender, and the Performance of Professionalism in Teacher Education." In *Confronting Racism in Teacher Education: Counternarratives of Critical Practice*, edited by Bree Picower and Rita Kohli, 97–102. New York: Routledge, Taylor & Francis Group.

——— 2017b. "Unscripting Curriculum: Toward a Critical Trans Pedagogy." *Harvard Educational Review* 87 (4): 538–56. https://doi.org/10.17763/1943-5045-87.4.538.

Keenan, Harper. 2021. "Keep Yourself Alive: Welcoming the Next Generation of Queer and Trans Educators." *Occasional Paper Series*, no. 45. https://doi.org/10.58295/2375-3668.1387.

Khayatt, Didi. 1997. "Sex and the Teacher: Should We Come Out in Class?" *Harvard Educational Review* 67 (1): 126–43.

Khayatt, Didi, and L. Iskander. 2020. "Reflecting on 'Coming Out' in the Classroom." *Teaching Education* 31 (1): 6–16. https://doi.org/10.1080/10476210.2019.1689943.

LeMaster, Benny, and Amber L. Johnson. 2019. "Unlearning Gender—Toward a Critical Communication Trans Pedagogy." *Communication Teacher* 33 (3): 189–98. https://doi.org/10.1080/17404622.2018.1467566.

Malatino, Hilary. 2015. "Pedagogies of Becoming: Trans Inclusivity and the Crafting of Being." *TSQ: Transgender Studies Quarterly* 2 (3): 395–410. https://doi.org/10.1215/23289252-2926387.

Matute, Alexandra Arraiz, Luna Da Silva, Karleen Pendleton Jiménez, and Amy Smith. 2020. "The Sex Of It All: Outness and Queer Women's Digital

Storytelling in Teacher Education." *Teaching Education* 31 (1): 98–111. https://doi.org/10.1080/10476210.2019.1708314.

Mayo, J.B. 2008. "Gay Teachers' Negotiated Interactions with Their Students and (Straight) Colleagues." *High School Journal* 92 (1): 1–10. https://doi.org/10.1353/hsj.0.0007.

Rand, Erica. 2012. "So Unbelievably Real: *Stone Butch Blues* and the Fictional Special Guest." *Radical Teacher* 92 (Winter): 35–42. https://doi.org/10.5406/radicalteacher.92.0035.

Rasmussen, Mary Lou. 2004. "The Problem of Coming Out." *Theory into Practice* 43 (2): 144–50. https://doi.org/10.1207/s15430421tip4302_8.

Russell, Vanessa Tamara. 2010. "Queer Teachers' Ethical Dilemmas Regarding Queer Youth." *Teaching Education* 21 (2): 143–56. https://doi.org/10.1080/10476211003735427.

Sathiyaseelan, Sinduja. 2014. "Negotiating the Bi-Nary: Strategic Ambiguity and the Non-Nameable Identity in the Classroom." *Writing on the Edge* 25 (1): 56–61. https://www.jstor.org/stable/24871680.

Sears, James T., and Walter L. Williams, eds. 1997. *Overcoming Heterosexism and Homophobia: Strategies That Work*. New York: Columbia University Press.

Seidman, Steven, Chet Meeks, and Francie Traschen. 1999. "Beyond the Closet? The Changing Social Meaning of Homosexuality in the United States." *Sexualities* 2 (1): 9–34. https://doi.org/10.1177/136346099002001002.

Silin, Jonathan. 1999. "Teaching as a Gay Man: Pedagogical Resistance or Public Spectacle?" *GLQ: A Journal of Lesbian and Gay Studies* 5 (1): 95–106. https://doi.org/10.1215/10642684-5-1-95.

Stryker, Susan, and Paisley Currah. 2014. "General Editors' Introduction." *TSQ: Transgender Studies Quarterly* 1 (3): 303–307.

PART III

Classroom Strategies and Applied Pedagogy

How to Take Risks and Seek Pleasure with Learning

In the previous part, the contributors examined how problems and challenges arise in the classroom. In part, the pervasive culture of conflict in the classroom may be explained by the open secret within higher education that very few faculty have been trained as teachers. Instead, most of us learn how to teach through emulation, mentorship, some professional development, and a lot of experimentation. Navigating between our own desires for the classroom and the norms, conventions, practices, and models of education that are both discipline- and context-specific, teaching is an exercise in venturing into uncertainty and attempting to create coherence for the sake of learning. Knowing how to extend ourselves beyond the comfort of what is familiar, to take risks in how we approach teaching and learning, is perhaps one of the greatest challenges we face as teachers. It is easy to rely on what we think works, but because learning is not a linear process of knowledge reception, what appears to work might only be working for some contexts. While the authors throughout this collection challenge our presumptions around education and propose new ways of configuring our approaches to the classroom, the chapters in this part all provide strategies and approaches to teaching that encourage each of us to take more risks in education. Whether those risks are around letting go of the familiar assessment models we use in our teaching or venturing into unknown areas of scholarship outside of our areas of expertise, taking risks is an essential part of what makes learning possible.

Conversely, the punitive model of education that shapes the classroom through infrastructures of grading, as well as faculty assessment through scholarly productivity, makes risk-taking in learning a risky endeavour for teachers. Our mistakes can cost us, sometimes materially with the threat of job loss for precariously employed faculty, and sometimes reputationally, like when students complain about what they don't like in our classes. However, as the authors in this part all illustrate, the rewards of taking risks, of pushing ourselves as teachers outside of the comfort of what is familiar, can make teaching and learning more rewarding. This makes risk an important pedagogical approach to higher education. Part III begins with Nathalie Batraville, who takes a risk around course design and assessment by inversing the orientation of learning between teacher and students through peer teaching. Drawing on Black feminist theorization of power, violence, and pleasure, her chapter begins with an understanding of the classroom as a space imbued with power. Attending to the paradox between the self-discovery of learning and the coercive structure of education, Batraville draws inspiration from kink and play as scenes through which racial violence can be resisted and transformed to disrupt the punitive models of education that reinforce power hierarchies. She illustrates how peer teaching can reorient the classroom by challenging institutional power and making room for the playful and pleasurable possibilities of learning through the flipped classroom structure.

Next, both Gada Mahrouse and Nathan Rambukkana offer detailed examinations of the process of rebuilding course curriculum through approaches to learning that aim to transform both the teacher's and students' perspectives on course topics. Walking us through their strategies, they illustrate ways of reworking syllabi, approaching course design, and adapting to what happens in the classroom in ways that model how teaching can be a process of revisioning and reorientation. Gada Mahrouse's chapter picks up on threads introduced by Batraville's work when we consider the possibility of turning to pleasure in the classroom. For Mahrouse, "comedy opens up new possibilities of teaching" that can "be effective and engaging for exploring power relations and social issues in ways that are fresh, relevant, and fun." Using comedy as a way to enter into learning around difficult topics, such as race, racism, and colonialism, her chapter demonstrates how to develop strategies that are attentive to both experimentation and risk with material while also considering how to navigate power and harm in the classroom. Turning to a reflection on the design of two courses on digital intimacy, Rambukkana similarly experiments with class material and structure to take risks with new topics and encounters in the classroom. He asks, "What discipline does not deal, in some way, with forms of intimacy?" (247) as he walks us through class assignments and approaches to digital intimacy that make play and experimentation core approaches to his pedagogical model. In doing so, Rambukkana models how teachers can use reflection, adaptation, and revision as pedagogical approaches that render possible ventures into exploratory new areas of learning.

The part ends with Dina Georgis's work on seeking pleasure and taking risk in the classroom. Responding to what is perhaps a familiar scene of breakdown in the classroom, Georgis invites us to reconsider how to make learning a space where students and teachers alike can take risks. Interrogating her own resistance to her students' aversion to risk, she reflects on her friction with her students, such as student resistance to class structure, to examine the interplay between student desires and her own pedagogy. Drawing on psychoanalytic approaches to play, she outlines a vision of "pedagogy that does not view learning as the acquisition of knowledge but a journey of knowledge-making. Importantly, learning is not disassociated from feeling vulnerable and the risks associated with challenging certainty and predictability" (265). For Georgis, to achieve an environment that facilitates the creativity and pleasure of exploration for students requires that the teacher establishes the classroom in a way that invites play. To do this, Georgis softens her approach. By shifting her understanding of the classroom, she illustrates how adapting to the needs of the students can make space for both safety and risk in ways that allow both teachers and students to return to difficult knowledge and learning.

12

Kink and Pedagogy
A Case for Peer Teaching

NATHALIE BATRAVILLE

A few years ago, I participated in an academic conference where the chair of each panel was playfully referred to as the dominatrix. The title highlighted the chair's role in maintaining order and discipline, particularly around keeping time. I did not think of it again for some time, until I read M. NourbeSe Philip's (1988) short novel *Harriet's Daughter*. Students in the story create a role-playing game where children of different backgrounds act as runaway slaves, slave catchers, and dogs. Their school becomes the site that symbolizes slavery in the game, the place from which those playing the slaves will run, while freedom is tied to secret locations that the children must reach (Philip 1988, 15). It was during a class discussion of this novel that I first contemplated the idea of teaching a course about kink. As some of my students discussed the discomfort the game elicited for them, I pointed out that adult versions of this game also revisit historical power imbalances and relationships of domination. Linking the children's game to adult play led to connecting sadism and masochism (SM) practices to the everyday forms of racial subjection and oppression that structure many aspects of our lives, that make dependence and coercion the norm rather than the exception.[1] Linking the

---

1. Sadism and masochism are types of sexual practices commonly associated with kink.

children's game to adult play led to connecting SM practices to the classroom and to the liberatory potential that play holds.

The students were discussing Philip's novel because it was at the heart of an essay I had assigned, Katherine McKittrick's (2007) "Freedom Is a Secret: The Future Usability of the Underground." Pointing to historic landmarks tied to Black freedom seekers, McKittrick's essay challenges the idea that Black geographies are tied to fixed locations. This argument was compelling because as a Black feminist educator, I introduce students to cultural and intellectual work by Black thinkers, which they then seek to understand and to make legible to themselves and to others. McKittrick's work reveals to students why "freedom is unmappable" (111). She argues that freedom comes alive through active practices that work against "seductive and comfortable geographies of domination and ownership" (102). Her article makes an argument for the opacity of buried freedom routes and the unmappability of Black futures. My hope is that students develop their own freedom practices. I also hope that my classroom is itself a space of experimentation that challenges structures of domination and oppression. In this short essay, I explore what active practices in the classroom can work against the coercive and alienating dimensions of academic achievement, which are protected by normalized, "seductive and comfortable geographies of domination and ownership." Before detailing a proposed model based on negotiation and power exchange, I will first analyze *Harriet's Daughter* to reflect on the relevance of thinking about kink in relation to pedagogy.

Kink as Play

Published in 1988 and awarded several prizes, including a Canadian Children's Book Centre's Choice Award, Philip's short novel *Harriet's Daughter* tells the story of two schoolgirls of Caribbean descent living in Toronto. The book foregrounds themes such as friendship, power, longing, and play, filtered through the eyes of a fourteen-year-old narrator, Margaret. Margaret's world is shaped by her life at home and at school, and brightened by her friends, particularly Zulma, who just migrated from Tobago and joined her school. A sharp, adventurous spirit, Margaret resists as much as she can the stifling order her strict parents have instituted in her life. She resists creatively, using humour to challenge the main authority figure in her life. She asks, for instance, "Dad, you're always talking about Good West Indian Discipline, what is Bad West Indian Discipline?" (1988, 15). The teen finds an anchor in the kinship she feels for Harriet Tubman and her godmother Harriet Blewchamp, a Holocaust survivor. Her curiosity, critical eye, and playfulness lead her to create a role-playing game in which school children of different backgrounds act as runaway slaves, slave catchers, and dogs.

The children who play as slaves run away from school, which represents slavery, with the goal of reaching the secret locations that symbolizes freedom (Philip 1988, 15). The game brings to the surface histories and hierarchies already present in the characters' lives. The dramatization of slavery into ritualized play makes space for the children to touch wounds accumulated in schooling as well as layers of historical trauma that in many instances remain unacknowledged, buried. McKittrick points out that in Philip's narrative "the historical present is a way of considering how the past informs and shapes the present, and it is connected to the idea that historical formations (geographic organization, political desires, legal and administrative frameworks) are open to our critical engagement precisely because they are locations that connect time and space" (2007, 106). By unearthing submerged histories of white supremacist violence and juxtaposing them to the logics of coercion and discipline that still define anti-Blackness today, *Harriet's Daughter* produces a critique of the school as a colonial institution. The novel also offers a reflection on mutually constitutive structures of domination across institutions, like the school and the prison, that are born of and sustained by libidinal economies of sadism and masochism, what Christina Sharpe calls the "sadomasochism of everyday black life" (2009, 118). Highlighting the presence of everyday subjection and oppression practices challenges the "exceptional" nature of SM fantasies, and the notion that some spheres of life can exist outside of ritualized pain and subjection and power exchange.

In *Monstrous Intimacies: The Making of Post-Slavery Subjects*, Sharpe describes SM as a "set of sexual practices...that may make explicit the very master-slave configurations that haunt us, that make visible slavery within freedom and questions of consent" (2009, 148). Kink as a praxis relates to history in complex and layered ways. One salient difference between everyday masochism and sadism in the classroom on the one hand, and kink on the other, is that the latter represents a set of practices and relationships that work to be consensual, even when play includes non-consent. The "master-slave configurations that haunt us" in the classroom are different than those that animate SM since they tend to be structurally coercive and involve relatively little consent, negotiation, or collaboration. Knowledge production and pedagogy can learn from kink as a set of evolving practices, norms, and communities that foreground collaboration and cultivate agency. What distinguishes violence from kink is control and agency: the negotiation of details beforehand, the power to halt or pause a scene at any point, the possibility to include aftercare, and care more broadly. As Staci Haines writes, "choice and control remain intact in the S/M experience" (1999, 194). This is not of course to romanticize kink or to place SM outside of configurations of oppression, but rather to point out the presence of tools and mechanisms within this practice that work to create spaces that can potentially challenge harmful dynamics.

The children's search for freedom in *Harriet's Daughter* coexists with the unfreedom that permeates their everyday lives as pupils, children, and siblings. When they play in the middle of the night, the mere mention of police paralyzes Margaret: "Just thinking of cops calling my father at 3 o'clock in the morning to tell him they had his daughter...my mind went so blank, I was so scared I stopped breathing" (Philip 1988, 80). Later she explains, "everyone—slaves, guides, slave-owners and dogs—had to hide from the police. It was a strange feeling, they said, to feel that they were all on the same side, hiding from the cops" (81). Multiple systems of authority appear, with state-sanctioned violence as the suturing core, mapping the grammar of coercion. The reality of police violence and incarceration against the game's whimsy reveals how some of the configurations of enslavement and captivity live on, not only to haunt the children but as a threat to Black life. The game blurs lines between history and the present, and the anxieties that each generates. As Philip deftly explores these layered histories and traumas, the characters' questions lay bare complicated longings. When Zulma moves to share a ghost story while they are at the library doing research, Margaret suggests a more appropriate time: "I told Zulma she could tell us some other time—'like when we're in bed. I love feeling scared when I'm safe'" (28). The novel interrogates many of our impulses and the libidinal economy that conditions our probing returns not just to scary stories but to traumatic experiences and coercive institutions. Through this interrogation, Philip delivers a genealogy of kink, a way to better understand the place where pain sometimes meets pleasure. I use this genealogy to continue exploring the libidinal economies of SM present in academia.

The classroom is, on the one hand, a space of self-discovery, collaboration, knowledge production, and knowledge sharing; and on the other, a space that instills obedience, subjection, assimilation, and discipline in the mind and in the body. In many cases, the process of learning in school involves shame, humiliation, competition, punishment, alienation, and exhaustion, which often leaves students feeling defeated and powerless. In *Harriet's Daughter*, the game comes to an end when the school as an imagined symbol of slavery and the school as a real coercive institution in the children's lives collapse into one. In this scene, Pina's brother Sandro, aged seven, the youngest player in the game, decides that the game must bear on reality as he attempts to get out of school by evoking his "freedom papers": "Pina, her mother and her father were dragging Sandro kicking and screaming up the stairs—he was yelling his head off about his FREE PAPERS, and how he didn't have to go to school because he was free. They finally got him inside the school, where he lay on the floor in the lobby and screamed" (1988, 84). Having overcome slavery in the game, Sandro does not accept having to go back to school. The game and reality are collapsed in a way that questions the meaning of "freedom" by highlighting how little agency children can exert. Experiencing school as punishment is a feeling that is familiar to many. Hours spent experiencing and witnessing ableism, racism, sexism, transphobia, ageism, and other violations have broken the spirits of countless students.

The physical and psychic rigidity of education reflect a kind of sadism, an orientation towards causing suffering and being indifferent to it. Reflecting on her experience as a student, bell hooks writes, "During college, the primary lesson was reinforced: we were to learn obedience to authority. In graduate school the classroom became a place I hated, yet a place where I struggled to claim and maintain the right to be an independent thinker. The university and the classroom began to feel more like a prison, a place of punishment and confinement rather than a place of promise and possibility" (1994, 4). Schools have played a central role in the development and expansion of colonialism, most obviously through genocidal institutions such as residential schools and other carceral institutions such as juvenile detention centres. They also play a direct role in the production and dissemination of nationalist and Eurocentric narratives and frameworks. While some children do not survive schooling, some rebel, and others excel. Schools aim to produce a commitment to, and even a taste for following rules, including oppressive ones. Teachers, empowered by the institution, serve a disciplining role while children internalize submission, which can impart a deep sense of alienation, trauma, or rebellion. The archetypal roles of teacher and student, particularly as they relate to power, control, and authority, go on to be reproduced in workplaces and other social spaces.

Pleasure and Pedagogy

Of course, the truth is that many people find "something like pleasure within these constraints" (Sharpe 2009, 118). Power exchange always involves some measure of interdependence, making the borders between domination and submission somewhat porous. hooks (1994) has argued for further centring pleasure and seduction in pedagogy. Such a classroom is an embodied one, attuned to the flow of energy, if not the flow of power. In her chapter, "Eros, Eroticism, and the Pedagogical Process," hooks invites us to understand the role of desire in the pleasure we experience while learning: "Understanding that eros is a force that enhances our overall effort to be self-actualizing, that it can provide an epistemological grounding informing how we know what we know, enables both professors and students to use such energy in a classroom setting in ways that invigorate discussion and excite the critical imagination" (195). Nurturing pleasure in teaching revolves around forms of attunement, attachment, and trust that facilitate collaborative learning and growth. However, while hooks is attentive to the potentially detrimental role of power imbalances in the classroom, her evocation of eros works to sublimate the "special bonds between professors and students [that] have always existed" (198). Yet these "special bonds" remain marked by an asymmetrical structure of assessment, authority, and bureaucracy. What's more, seduction does not teach students to learn for their own sake, to please themselves, to show up for themselves and for each other.

Finally, seduction involves intent and an anticipated horizon of results; it assumes the legibility of the body, which cannot be generalized for all subjects who enter the classroom, particularly Black subjects (Daniel 2019; Johnson-Bailey and Lee 2005; Spillers 1987). Black women in academia, whether instructor or student, cannot be assumed to be read clearly throughout the multiple transactions by which knowledge is exchanged and evaluated. Notions of self-possession, rationality, and universality that are at the heart of Western ideas about knowledge were formulated and reproduced in racialized and gendered ways that place Black women squarely outside most, if not all, expectations for professorial conduct. One can of course work against these odds and against these systems, semester after semester, but at what cost? The psychic load of working against misogynoir and intersecting forms of social devaluation is enough to wear down many Black women, not to mention the added emotional labour expected and the racist and sexist behaviour and comments we might experience from colleagues and students. Jennifer Lisa Vest, having left academia, writes: "Women of Color professors experience macroaggressions as serious assaults on their physical safety while also enduring microassaults in the profession. The end result is that women of color often leave the university or are forced out. They experience chronic or life-threatening illnesses, become disabled, and sometimes they die" (2013, 485). To ignore the violence of the institution and its effects on our health is destructive. As Black women, if we are to stay in academia we must wholeheartedly engage in self-preservation and be extremely selective about what we can give.

What I take from hooks's emphasis on seduction is the importance of intent. The classroom is a space of contractual, if not consensual, role play. Even within these confines, the intention with which we approach these roles matters. Mollena Williams, in her short guide *The Toybag Guide to Playing with Taboo*, highlights the importance of transparency around motivations and intentions in kink: "I consider *intent* to be absolutely pivotal in the planning, negotiation and execution of taboo scenes. In the same way that 'intent' is the main feature that separates BDSM from abuse, intent can salvage a relationship even if a scene takes a turn for the worse" (2010, 21). Of course, intent is not always legible, and it can mean very little without accountability. Regarding intent, hooks also insists on the importance of valuing the presence of each individual, as well as the labour of care, empathy, and recognition: "To begin, the professor must genuinely *value* everyone's presence. There must be an ongoing recognition that everyone influences the classroom dynamic, that everyone contributes. These contributions are resources. Used constructively they enhance the capacity of any class to create an open learning community" (1994, 8). To establish a relationship through agreement is to create a mutually beneficial, balanced arrangement that creates a structure, boundaries, norms. This structure can potentially ensure that a radical power imbalance between individuals can exist within a relatively healthy, mutually beneficial relationship. Inspired by kink, I have adopted a teaching model that relies on negotiating power exchanges within the classroom to produce a potentially liberatory approach to education.

Peer Teaching

Because all relationships of care carry the risk of violence, the desire for a "safe space" in the classroom is illusory. Neither students nor instructors are positioned to fully negotiate all the terms of the power exchanges that occur in the classroom, since there are many contractual constraints within institutional settings. Nevertheless, as an instructor, I turn to negotiation and collaboration to create as much space as possible for agency, rather than the feeling of safety. To learn from kink with the hopes of transforming or inflecting classroom dynamics requires practical interventions in relation to agency and performance. The ideal model I have found to foreground agency is a kind of flipped classroom that asks the students to teach the course material and facilitate class discussion. Using the material I assigned in the syllabus, the students become the teachers in essence, not just for a short presentation, but for the entirety of each class and most of the course. Taking on this role means that each class, different students take turns assuming the responsibility for teaching and explaining the course material, and generating a fruitful class discussion. The instructor is present and offers insights and clarification, intervenes if it seems necessary, but mostly becomes a student in the classroom, allowing most of the instruction, discussion, and problem-solving to occur without their guidance and intervention. Each student-facilitator presents part of the assigned material by summarizing, explaining, and offering an interpretation. Following the presentations, the group facilitates an open discussion and/or activities to dive deeper into the material. Using the rubric I provide, they then grade themselves and evaluate their performance based on the expectations I outlined.

An ideal group for each class consists of three or four students who divide up the work amongst each other. The biggest obstacle I encountered is that some students, who might be anxious or introverted or feel insecure about their ability to grasp and explain the course material, can be daunted by this task, despite the incentives I offer (self-evaluation of an assignment worth 30% to 40% of the final grade). I therefore decided that within each group of facilitators, different students could have different roles based on their strengths and the tasks with which they felt comfortable. This revised structure allows one of the group's members to create the visual materials for the group's presentation instead of facilitating discussion. This same student can take notes during the class discussion to share with the whole class afterwards. The other two or three members of the group become the more outward-facing members, present the course material, and guide the discussion. All group members work together to come up with a plan for the class, discussion questions, and activities. They also support each other in making sure they fully grasp the course material and can consult the instructor for course planning or for explanations of the material.

Although some students want to learn from the instructor, not from each other, I address this issue by offering a few insights and step in if it feels like a concept isn't being explained adequately. The advantages far outweigh the drawbacks. One of the advantages of this method is that students tend to choose to teach a class to which they feel connected in some way, based on their experiences, identity, or their interests. In some cases, the students can draw on their personal experiences to teach the material in moving, evocative, and instructive ways that would have been completely out of my reach. And of course, the students control what and how much they want to share of their personal experiences, if at all. There is a great vulnerability in teaching material that is connected to one's personal experiences, but the fact that all students will have to teach contributes to producing an ethics of mutual care and solidarity.

I begin each semester by inviting students to co-create class norms and agreements that lay out the values, practices, and attitudes that—to them—are conducive to a generative and open learning environment. During this discussion, we also identify generative ways of dealing with conflict, difficult emotions, and harm. We also talk about power in the classroom, and the kinds of harm students with marginalized identities sometimes experience, how to avoid perpetuating such harm and what to do in case it happens. The fact that my classes are in gender studies and sexuality studies and relate to community in one sense or another typically means that students come to class wanting to learn how to show up for each other. I use the student-facilitator model in advanced seminars, which also means most of the students have had a chance to learn from their mistakes and from those of their classmates and instructors.

The most important benefit of flipping the classroom is that it does shift the balance of power. I typically teach the first class to model how to teach and facilitate, and, when the second class comes around, the students take control. I feel the change immediately and I remind myself to trust the students. The effect of that shift in power is that the students become more actively engaged in their collective learning experience. When a fellow student is teaching, the other students orient themselves differently. They adjust to the fact that a peer is facilitating and contribute more actively to solving problems.

This approach maximizes the agency they have in the classroom. In their guide titled "10 Ways Sex Education Can and Should Be Abolitionist," the Chicago Women's Health Center maintains that teaching "should be done with the intention of giving students as much choice and power as possible. By centering students' questions and language, we can challenge traditional, top-down approaches to education. The goal must be to share power with those who are most directly impacted by the policing structures of our educational system and to support young people in crafting their own classroom experiences" (2021, 204).

Beyond the political and interpersonal effects of power exchange, the benefits to learning are also significant. Allowing students to teach invites them to engage with the assigned course material differently than when they are all receiving instruction from their professor. Describing peer teaching, Harald Kjellin and Terese Stenfors explain, "when using this method the students become actively engaged in the production of knowledge and not only in the consumption of knowledge" (2003, 349). The unique orientation of peer teaching impacts student understanding and retention of the material. In their study published in the journal *Memory and Cognition*, John Nestojko and colleagues explained that their "findings suggest that participants processed information differently, and more effectively, when they expected to teach than when they expected to take a test" (2014, 1043). Explaining the positive results of this method, the researchers hypothesize, "The explanation we currently favor is that participants expecting to teach put themselves into the mindset of a teacher, leading them to adopt certain effective strategies used by teachers when preparing to teach—such as organizing and weighing the importance of different concepts in the to-be-taught material, focusing on main points, and thinking about how information fits together. These teaching preparation techniques are parallel to encoding strategies that are known to be powerful learning or mnemonic processes—namely, relational (organizational) and item-specific processing strategies" (1046). The collaborative learning environment created is one in which ideally all students approach the material with an expectation that they will be relying on each other and learn together. They come in expecting that the student-facilitator might not have all the answers and therefore are prepared to contribute more actively. When it is their turn to facilitate, students also learn how to collaborate with their group members, how to work with the strengths and needs of each group member, and how to facilitate conversations while honouring the course agreements named with the class.

Another major shift is that when preparing for and participating in class, students are no longer accountable to the instructor; they are accountable to each other. The instructor is no longer solely responsible for the movement of eros in the classroom, which can represent a massive shift in the amount of labour, emotional and otherwise, required to teach a class. This shift is an opportunity for students to be allies to each other, but also to their instructor. As a radical pedagogical experiment, peer teaching could transform the lives of students and, by the same token, save the lives of some of their professors with marginalized identities.

I am interested in a pedagogical practice that generates subjectivities that can wield power and agency without reproducing systemic power abuse. The classroom can be a space for experiments that actively produce solidarity, collaboration, and attunement in the face of structural dysregulation. To foreground agency in the classroom requires feminist pedagogies and modalities of collective care, friendship, and accountability. These approaches also inform the ethics of kink. When explaining, in 1981, why kink was taboo despite violence being omnipresent in society, Susan Farr wrote, "I believe that apparent paradox is due to our society's wishing to withhold experience with and knowledge about power from most people so that abuses of power by elites can be protected" (1981, 181). The same can be said about power in the classroom. The university is a dungeon for non-consensual kink. Its hierarchical structure and roles set the stage for abuses of power, including sexual abuse. Negotiating power exchange and flipping the classroom through peer teaching challenges hierarchies of domination and subjection. By learning from kink, this pedagogical model acknowledges existing social structures and creates a space for serious play and its world-making possibilities. By learning from kink, maybe some of us will still be around to see some of these possibilities play out.

References

Chicago Women's Health Center. 2021. "10 Ways Sex Education Can and Should Be Abolitionist." In *Lessons in Liberation: An Abolitionist Toolkit for Educators*, edited by Bettina L. Love, Mariame Kaba, Jay Gillen, and Education for Liberation Network & Critical Resistance Editorial, 202–10. Chico, CA: AK Press.

Daniel, Beverly-Jean. 2019. "Teaching While Black: Racial Dynamics, Evaluations, and the Role of White Females in the Canadian Academy in Carrying the Racism Torch." *Race Ethnicity and Education* 22 (1): 21–37. https://doi.org/10.1080/13613324.2018.1468745.

Farr, Susan. 1981. "The Art of Discipline: Creating Erotic Dramas of Play and Power." In *Coming to Power: Writings and Graphics on Lesbian S/M*, edited by SAMOIS, 181–89. Boston: Alyson Publications.

Haines, Staci. 1999. *Healing Sex: A Mind-Body Approach to Healing Sexual Trauma*. San Francisco: Cleis Press.

hooks, bell. 1994. *Teaching to Transgress: Education as the Practice of Freedom*. New York: Routledge.

Johnson-Bailey, Juanita, and Ming-Yeh Lee. 2005. "Women of Color in the Academy: Where's Our Authority in the Classroom?" *Feminist Teacher* 15 (2): 111–22. https://www.jstor.org/stable/40545917.

Kjellin, Harald, and Terese Stenfors. 2003. "Systematic Personal Training by Letting Students Teach Each Other." *Journal of Information Systems Education* 14 (4): 349–51.

McKittrick, Katherine. 2007. "Freedom Is a Secret: The Future Usability of the Underground." In *Black Geographies and the Politics of Place*, edited by Katherine McKittrick and Clyde Woods, 97–111. Toronto: Between the Lines Press; Cambridge, MA: South End Press.

Nestojko, John F., Dung C. Bui, Nate Kornell, and Elizabeth Ligon Bjork. 2014. "Expecting to Teach Enhances Learning and Organization of Knowledge in

Free Recall of Text Passages." *Memory & Cognition* 42 (7): 1038–48. https://doi.org/10.3758/s13421-014-0416-z.

Philip, M. NourbeSe. 1988. *Harriet's Daughter*. Toronto: Women's Press.

Sharpe, Christina. 2009. *Monstrous Intimacies: The Making of Post-Slavery Subjects*. Durham, NC: Duke University Press.

Spillers, Hortense. 1987. "Mama's Baby, Papa's Maybe: An American Grammar Book." *Diacritics* 17 (2): 65–81. https://www.jstor.org/stable/464747.

Vest, Jennifer Lisa. 2013. "What Doesn't Kill You: Existential Luck, Postracial Racism, and the Subtle and Not So Subtle Ways the Academy Keeps Women of Color Out." *Seattle Journal for Social Justice* 12 (2): 471–518. https://digitalcommons.law.seattleu.edu/sjsj/vol12/iss2/7.

Williams, Mollena. 2010. *The Toybag Guide to Playing with Taboo*. Eugene, OR: Greenery Press.

13

On Levity and Subversive Comedy

Feminist Humour as Critical Pedagogy

GADA MAHROUSE

Whether we're talking about race or gender or class, popular culture is where the pedagogy is, it's where the learning is.
—bell hooks, *bell hooks: Cultural Criticism & Transformation* (1997)

I am seriously scared of getting stuck in a "world" that constructs me that way. A world that I have no escape from and in which I cannot be playful.
—Maria Lugones, "Playfulness, 'World'-Travelling, and Loving Perception" (1987)

Australian stand-up comedian Aamer Rahman has a widely viewed joke about reverse racism: "A lot of white people say this to me…'Hey, Aamer, you get onstage and make your jokes about white people. Don't you think that's a kind of racism? Don't you think that's'—dramatic pause—'"reverse racism?"'" (Logan 2014). In response, Rahman quips that for the accusation of reverse racism to make any sense, he'd "have to get in a time machine and persuade the leaders of Africa, Asia, and the Middle East to invade and colonise Europe" (Logan 2014). He'd have to "ruin Europe over a couple of centuries so all their descendants would want to migrate [to] where black and brown people come from" (Rahman quoted in Logan 2014). He'd have to initiate social systems that privileged Black and Brown people, while intermittently bombing white people's countries, and "saying it's for their own good because their culture's inferior." The joke continues with several other examples that demonstrate the absurdity of the charge of reverse racism.

Discussing this joke in an interview, Rahman shares that he often gets emails from professors who play this clip for their classes, telling him that what he achieves in this four-minute bit is often more effective than them preparing a conventional lecture on the topic (Logan 2014). I share in this experience, since I have found using comedy in the classroom has been useful in my teaching—so much so that I decided to develop a course that uses comedy as a site for teaching about feminism, power relations, and social inequalities. This chapter reflects on the course—the reasons for it and the challenges it brings—and points to some of its limits and successes.

Why comedy in feminist classrooms? There are at least two good reasons. First, as the epigraph by bell hooks illustrates, students already learn about social inequalities from popular culture. As hooks (1997) explains, when she related popular culture to the theoretical paradigms that she was teaching, her students not only grasped theory more easily, but the lessons became more exciting and interesting. Due to the wide popularity of comedy, students are likely to encounter political commentary and critique through this genre. Comedy is, without fail, a popular topic for term papers and class presentations in my course on Critical Race Feminisms. Interest in comedy in the feminist classroom makes sense if we think of the two tenets of feminism, critical thinking and change-making, which depend on social persuasion. Comedy lends well to contemplating and assessing persuasive messaging (Brennan 2011; Krefting 2014), especially when we consider the role of representations (Hall 1997; hooks 1997), performativity, voice (or speech acts) vis-à-vis marginalization (Zwagerman 2010), and their relation to political understanding (Goldman 2013), which are all central considerations in both comedy and feminist critique.

Educators have also found that in general, humour increases learning at knowledge and comprehension levels (Hackathorn et al. 2012; Kellner and Kim 2010; Koziski 1997; Nabi, Moyer-Gusé, and Byrne 2007; Rossing 2012, 2014).

Second, and perhaps more importantly, comedy opens up new possibilities of teaching feminism in ways that are pleasurable, which is especially needed because of the difficult topics we find ourselves teaching in women, gender, and sexuality studies programs. My own courses focus on the violence of racism and colonialism. Over time, these topics can become overwhelming, provoke anguish, and take an emotional toll on professors and students alike. However, as María Lugones (1987) describes in the epigraph, there can be a profound productivity to playfulness when addressing serious topics. Building on Lugones, Chris Mayo (2014) suggests that humour can help illuminate complicities and invite more robust interactions with difference, thereby creating pleasurable encounters to work through difficult social divisions. In my experience, comedy can be effective and engaging for exploring power relations and social issues in ways that are fresh, relevant, and fun.

Not incidentally, I developed the course while two prominent discourses about comedy were circulating. First, media commentators began using the term *trigger warnings* vis-à-vis comedy, following heated public debates about whether jokes should be censored for fear they might offend certain audiences. Notions of "trigger warnings" and "political correctness" have long-established debate within feminism, and indeed much feminist work has interrogated these ideas in comedy (Flanagan 2015; Halberstam 2014; Scott 2015), despite the fear that we are currently "in the midst of a humor crisis," as one *New York Times* reporter lamented (Scott 2015).

Coinciding with trigger warning debates was "the rise of feminist comedy" and a public conversation about how performers are increasingly using comedy as a medium to promote feminism and the role of comedians as social critics. Public figures pronounced 2015 "the year of feminist comedy" (Nussbaum 2015), and many commentators observed a revived interest in comedy among young feminists (Cochrane 2013; Gay 2014; Hasselriis 2013; Kein 2015). Often focusing on the remarkable success of shows such as *Inside Amy Schumer* and *Broad City*, commentators described these women performers as "stealth" feminists who use comedy subversively to "ignite conversations about everything from body image to rape culture" (Kingston 2015). One article in *The Atlantic* stated that "people look to Amy Schumer and her fellow jokers not just to make fun of the world, but to make sense of it. And maybe even to help fix it" (Garber 2015). However, defence of Schumer has also been somewhat contentious and has provoked disagreements among feminists. For instance, while most agree that Schumer's comedy effectively tackles sexism, some commentators have critiqued what they see as her "large blind spot" when it comes to race (Donahue 2015; Sims 2015). Indeed, some of the most compelling questions that emerged out of comedy during this period were concerned with issues related to gender, race, class, and sexuality. These questions continue to influence discussions in feminist classrooms.

Building a Feminist Course on Comedy: Curricular Challenges

Logically, my first step to building the course was to explore the literature and familiarize myself with the field. As in all of my courses, I sought to develop an interdisciplinary approach underpinned by poststructural, feminist, and cultural studies frameworks that emphasize how subjects are constituted through systems of power. Given my objectives, I had to find analytical tools and readings to assign that would help students develop nuanced critiques around comedy through an intersectional feminist lens. This task was not easy. Initial broad database searches brought up psychological studies on the neurological effects of laughter, philosophical questions on whether humour is universal, and anthropological work on various literary and artistic forms of humour. While these studies helped me to better understand the field, I was mainly interested in the social and political dimensions of humour. I wanted scholarship that examined humour as social commentary and as a barometer of contemporary society.

The foundations for contemporary scholarship on the social function of humour originate from the works of Henri Bergson (1914), Sigmund Freud (Freud and Strachey 1966), and Mikhail Bakhtin (1984). These works follow three main areas of argumentation: First, superiority theory explores hierarchies between joke tellers and the subjects/objects of jokes; second, incongruity theory explains what makes things funny; and third, relief theory argues that humour is a release that allows individuals and societies to express ideas and attitudes that are otherwise repressed (Billig 2005;[1] Rozik 2011; Stott 2005; Weitz 2009). With the exception of some important feminist critiques of these canonical theories on comedy,[2] this body of literature was a far cry from what I was seeking. While relief theory corroborated my wish to teach with more levity, of the three, superiority theory was the only one that explicitly addressed questions of power; however, as a theory it lacked critical nuance and left me wanting. Furthermore, I noticed that, by and large, scholarly engagement with the topic of humour remained within disciplinary boundaries such as English and performance/theatre studies. I found very little from a critical/feminist intersectional perspective. What I did find useful, however, were

---

1. Social psychologist Michael Billig's (2005) work advances the three established theories by distinguishing between humour that is disciplinary and rebellious to show that it can be used to either maintain power dynamics or challenge them by breaking social rules.

2. For example, Brett Mills (2011) outlines the difficulties in using these theories by explaining that their foci are different, and therefore they are theories of very different aspects of humour. Mills further argues that foregrounding ideas of pleasure might be a fruitful way of thinking about comedy as a whole. Cynthia Willet and Julie Willet (2019) also explore the limitations of these theories vis-à-vis feminism.

studies that focus directly on how humour works to influence societal change. For example, Edward Brennan (2011) examines the notion that joking can create a means of connection, conflict resolution, shared understanding, and resistance, emphasizing humour's ability to grant marginalized people socially acceptable language to critique dominant groups. Nancy Goldman (2013) similarly provides an overview of how humour functions as a corrective of social injustice and the subversion of authority through the shared understanding of social norms, customs, and national ethos. Şenay Yavuz Görkem (2015) explores how the circulation and exhibition of humorous messages and visual images in social media and public spaces can be used for political persuasion and mobilization without the danger of being identified as the originator of the materials.

The role that comedy can play in advancing critiques of social division and power is one of the strengths that I wanted to draw from feminist scholarship on this genre. Drawing on Joanne Gilbert's (2004) work on "rhetorical marginality," which investigates how female comics' onstage performances reveal power relations in a broader cultural context, I was interested in how stand-up comedians are licensed social critics and that this "licence" is especially relevant when it is performed by marginalized comics (i.e., women and other minorities). Indeed, by performing their marginality at the expense of the dominant culture, marginalized comics are able to examine and subvert power dynamics. Gilbert questions how contemporary American female comics perform their marginality onstage and asks what the performance of marginality reveals about power relations in a broader cultural context (2004, 169). She argues that although female comics are marginalized, their material does not necessarily include topics that challenge the ideologies behind their marginality. Instead, like male comics, their performances address mainstream topics to entertain a variety of audiences. Furthermore, female comics generally perform marginality by constructing narratives around their femaleness. The very act of a woman standing on stage, taking up time and space can be labelled "feminist," regardless of whether what she is actually saying has anything to do with feminism. Other studies discuss feminism's uneasy relationship with stand-up comedy given that it is a male-dominated field. Some work focuses on questions of embodiment, for example challenging the "pretty vs. funny" criteria for female comics through the notion of "body-politics" (Mizejewski 2014). Similarly, Danielle Deveau (2010) has analyzed how Canadian comedian Nikki Payne's sexual aggression and emphasis on her unattractiveness empowers her on stage. Other scholarship examines how feminist politics shape performances (Kotthoff 2006), the use of self-deprecatory stand-up routines to avoid audience alienation (Russell 2002), as well as the pleasurable and economic functions of comedic acts (Mills 2011).

As an anti-racist feminist, I was especially interested in giving students readings that model critical race analyses on comedy. I found that only a small subset of studies examines race in comedy (Atluri 2009; Banjo 2011; Brayton 2011; Gillota 2013; Hirji 2009; Howitt and Owusu-Bempah 2005). The most detailed of these that I have come across is Simon Weaver's (2011) book *The Rhetoric of Racist Humour: US, UK and Global Race Joking*, which argues that racist humour is a form of rhetoric that supports racism in society, dispelling the myth that racist jokes are harmless. Weaver offers conceptual tools to help readers determine if and how comics attempt to "reverse discourses," and outlines the foundations for the emerging field of critical humour studies by identifying whether political performances are subversive. According to Weaver, we can distinguish between comedic performances that simply identify when something is stigmatized and comics who re-appropriate the stigmatized space and use it to challenge oppressive structures. Rather than concerning ourselves with the preferred meaning of a joke, he explains, "any evaluation of a reverse discourse should, therefore, be rephrased as a consideration of how the images in humour both simultaneously 'play on' and 'play off' the long-established stereotypes" (2011, 120–21).[3] Further scholarship on race and comedy (Pérez 2013) includes a small body of writing on Indigenous (often referred to as "Native") humour (Morris 2011; Taylor 2005), which includes comedy that makes a point about "playing with the stereotype versus playing up the stereotype" (Kelly 2005, 61).

Critical race humour can function as a form of public pedagogy by interrupting and transforming dominant patterns of thinking about "racial knowledge and reality," where "power relationships, institutional practices, cultural beliefs, and ideologies...shape material realities of race and racism" (Rossing 2014, 17). Building from and combining the conceptual tools from these studies, I was able to introduce frameworks that students could use to examine comedy in ways that extend beyond simply celebrating the intercultural exchange or diversity of feminist comedy, and instead examine systems of power and their multiple effects on society.

Pedagogical Challenges of Teaching a Feminist Course on Comedy

One of the challenges to developing any course is limiting the scope and setting parameters for course design. Since my course set out to examine comedy as a social commentary, I opted for readings that emphasize the social and political aspects of comedy. However, since there are so many types of comedic performance such as situational comedy or political satire, each with their own particularities, I decided to focus mainly (though not exclusively) on stand-up comedy

---

3. While Weaver's approach is useful, I also assign it with some ambivalence given my commitment to citational practices that seeks to honour the often-overlooked contributions of Black, Indigenous, and people of colour scholars (BIPOC), especially women. I also point out to students that there is a significant dearth of BIPOC scholarship on the topic of comedy.

because of the particular ways that stand-up is gendered. Although the number of women comics has increased significantly in the past decade, stand-up continues to be dominated by men, and often uses aggressive forms of humour, including sexist and misogynist humour (Mizejewski 2014). This genre offered an interesting site for analysis in my class using feminist standpoint theory. Positing stand-up comedic performances as mediated social/cultural texts (Kellner 2011), and with the main objective of prompting discussion on how comedy can be used to challenge inequalities, I set the following pedagogical objectives for the course: (1) to make connections between comedic performances and key feminist principles; (2) to consider how social and political issues can be addressed through comedy; and (3) to articulate the potential uses of comedy as a tool for social change.

Since humour often gives rise to divisive and ambivalent reactions and receptions (Bobker 2018), the biggest challenge in designing the course was my concern that the classroom could become a space where forms of violence would be enacted under the guise of comedy. Since comedy is known for being edgy and tackling "controversial" topics that can easily offend, I needed to find a way to teach the course without reproducing violence. Mayo (2014) reminds us that bringing humour into discussions of serious matters comes with risk. As a feminist educator, I work hard to minimize (and recognize that I cannot eliminate) epistemic violence in the classroom; and although I reject the notion that classrooms can be safe spaces, I do my best to reduce the harms that my students are subjected to. To this end, I cautiously structured the pedagogical aspects of the course to seek out comedy for social change. In the syllabus, I also offered the following statement: "Recognizing that much comedy is offensive, the course will attempt to limit the presentation of such material to instead identify examples that seek to challenge stereotypes, understandings, and dominant discourses on race, gender sexuality, ability, etc. Despite these efforts, however, please note that some of the course content will potentially be offensive to some."

For in-class assignments, students were asked to find examples of comedic performances in which relations of power based on gender, race, citizenship, class, and sexuality were (in their views) being disrupted through comedy. In other words, they were asked to focus on examples of *anti*-racist, *anti*-homophobia, *anti*-sexist, and *anti*-ableist comedy and to explain how it provokes and/or promotes social change. Students share myriad examples of how comedy can be used as a form of resistance, ranging from parodies on race and gender to how comedy can be used to destigmatize issues of mental health and differently abled bodies.

This approach of focusing on the comedic performances that align with feminist social justice values has worked every time I have offered the course. Certainly, we do not always agree about what is funny, or if the clips we watch are subversive. However, these disagreements provoke constructive debates about how subtle forms of power operate in discourse. The objective of finding "best practices" in comedy for disrupting hegemonic power relations works at minimizing the harms that might otherwise take place in the classroom. Through these best practices, the classroom can be transformed into a place of playfulness and laughter.

Conclusion

In this chapter, I have pieced together my own desires and struggles with using comedy as a site for teaching about feminism, power relations, and social inequalities. A significant ongoing challenge pertains to a lack of studies by BIPOC scholars. Although critical humour studies is a growing field, more anti-racist and intersectional feminist perspectives are needed to develop new methods and theories that will advance the discussions in the field. Outside of the feminist, gender, and sexuality classroom, thinking critically about humour can help teachers develop ethical ways of incorporating playfulness, laughter, and enjoying into the classroom. This work requires an approach to humour that does not replicate or reinforce systemic oppression, biases, or stereotypes but helps us shed light on the way power functions and gives voice to perspectives calling for social change. I have indeed found comedy to be a fresh, relevant, and engaging approach to teaching, especially at exposing some of the less visible and more insidious ways that racialized and gendered power relations continue to operate. Using humour in this critical way can help classrooms across disciplines confront the way education replicates inequality, despite our intentions to make equitable learning environments. Inviting humour into the classroom can empower students to share their grievances, experiences of harm, and demands for change in ways that make it possible to tackle these challenges with humility and generosity. Indeed, comedy can be a rich pedagogical site for both learning and a method for the classroom. Not only are students very enthusiastic about the subject matter, but comedy also enables them to develop new angles for social change and interesting ways of expressing themselves.

References

Atluri, Tara. 2009. "Lighten Up?! Humour, Race, and Da Off Color Joke of Ali G." *Media, Culture & Society* 31 (2): 197–214. https://doi.org/10.1177/0163443708100314.

Bakhtin, Mikhail. 1984. *Rabelais and His World*. Translated by Helene Iswolsky. Bloomington: Indiana University Press.

Banjo, Omotayo. 2011. "What Are *You* Laughing at? Examining White Identity and Enjoyment of Black Entertainment." *Journal of Broadcasting & Electronic Media* 55 (2): 137–59. https://doi.org/10.1080/08838151.2011.570822.

Bergson, Henri. 1914. *Laughter: An Essay on the Meaning of the Comic*. Macmillan.

Billig, Michael. 2005. *Laughter and Ridicule: Towards a Social Critique of Humour*. London: Sage.

Bobker, Danielle. 2018. "Toward a Humor-Positive Feminism: Lessons from the Sex Wars." *Los Angeles Review of Books Quarterly Journal* 17 (February): 48–57.

Brayton, Sean. 2011. "Race Comedy and the Misembodied Voice." *TOPIA: Canadian Journal of Cultural Studies* 22 (Fall): 97–116. https://doi.org/10.3138/topia.22.97.

Brennan, Edward. 2011. "Not Seeing the Joke: The Overlooked Role of Humour in Researching Television Production." *Media, Culture & Society* 33 (6): 819–33. https://doi.org/10.1177/0163443711411003.

Cochrane, Kira. 2013. *All the Rebel Women: The Rise of the Fourth Wave of Feminism.* London: Guardian Books.

Deveau, Danielle J. 2010. "Nikki Payne: Sexual Aggression, Speech Impediments, and the Ugly Comedienne." *Feminist Media Studies* 10 (4): 478–81. https://doi.org/10.1080/14680777.2010.514173.

Donahue, Anne T. 2015. "Amy Schumer Is Not the Feminist Voice You're Looking For." *Globe and Mail,* July 17, 2015. http://www.theglobeandmail.com/arts/film/amy-schumer-is-not-the-voice-youre-looking-for/article25552135/.

Flanagan, Caitlin. 2015. "That's Not Funny! Today's College Students Can't Seem to Take a Joke." *The Atlantic,* September 2015. https://www.theatlantic.com/magazine/archive/2015/09/thats-not-funny/399335/.

Freud, Sigmund, and James Strachey. 1966. *Jokes and Their Relation to the Unconscious.* Translated and edited by James Strachey. London: Routledge & Kegan Paul.

Garber, Megan. 2015. "How Comedians Became Public Intellectuals." *The Atlantic,* May 28, 2015. http://www.theatlantic.com/entertainment/archive/2015/05/how-comedians-became-public-intellectuals/394277/.

Gay, Roxane. 2014. *Bad Feminist: Essays.* New York: Harper Perennial.

Gilbert, Joanne R. 2004. *Performing Marginality: Humor, Gender, and Cultural Critique.* Detroit, MI: Wayne State University Press.

Gillota, David. 2013. *Ethnic Humor in Multiethnic America.* New Brunswick, NJ: Rutgers University Press.

Goldman, Nancy. 2013. "Comedy and Democracy: The Role of Humor in Social Justice." *Animating Democracy: A Program of Americans for the Arts,* November 2013. http://animatingdemocracy.org/resource/comedy-and-democracy-role-humor-social-justice.

Görkem, Şenay Yavuz. 2015. "The Only Thing Not Known How to Be Dealt With: Political Humor as a Weapon during Gezi Park Protests." *Humor* 28 (4): 583–609. https://doi.org/10.1515/humor-2015-0094.

Hackathorn, Jana, Amy M. Garczynski, Katheryn Blankmeyer, Rachel D. Tennial, and Erin D. Solomon. 2012. "All Kidding Aside: Humor Increases Learning at Knowledge and Comprehension Levels." *Journal of the Scholarship of Teaching and Learning* 11 (4): 116–23.

Halberstam, Jack. 2014. "'You Are Triggering Me!' The Neoliberal Rhetoric of Harm, Danger and Trauma." *Bully Bloggers* (blog). July 5, 2014. https://bullybloggers.wordpress.com/2014/07/05/you-are-triggering-me-the-neo-liberal-rhetoric-of-harm-danger-and-trauma/.

Hall, Stuart, ed. 1997. *Representation: Cultural Representations and Signifying Practices.* London: Sage.

Hasselriis, Kaj. 2013. "Comic Relief." *Herizons*, Summer 2013. Accessed January 24, 2016. http://www.herizons.ca/node/542.

Hirji, Faiza. 2009. "'Somebody Going to Get Hurt Real Bad': The Race-Based Comedy of Russell Peters." *Canadian Journal of Communication* 34 (4): 567–86. https://doi.org/10.22230/cjc.2009v34n4a2130.

hooks, bell. 1997. *bell hooks: Cultural Criticism & Transformation*. Produced and directed by Sut Jhally. Northampton, MA: Media Education Foundation.

Howitt, Dennis, and Kwame Owusu-Bempah. 2005. "Race and Ethnicity in Popular Humour." In *Beyond a Joke: The Limits of Humour*, edited by Sharon Lockyer and Michael Pickering, 45–62. New York: Palgrave Macmillan.

Kein, Kathryn. 2015. "Recovering Our Sense of Humor: New Directions in Feminist Humor Studies." *Feminist Studies* 41 (3): 671–81. https://www.jstor.org/stable/10.15767/feministstudies.41.3.671.

Kellner, Douglas. 2011. "Cultural Studies, Multiculturalism, and Media Culture." In *Gender, Race, and Class in Media: A Critical Reader*. 3rd ed. Edited by Gail Dines and Jean M. Humez, 7–18. Sage.

Kellner, Douglas, and Gooyong Kim. 2010. "YouTube, Critical Pedagogy, and Media Activism." *Review of Education, Pedagogy, and Cultural Studies* 32 (1): 3–36. https://doi.org/10.1080/10714410903482658.

Kelly, Don. 2005. "And Now Ladies and Gentlemen, Get Ready for Some (Ab) Original Stand-up Comedy. In *Me Funny*, edited by Drew Hayden Taylor, 51–65. Vancouver: Douglas & McIntyre.

Kingston, Anne. 2015. "Chick Wit: Comedy's New Stealth Feminism." *Chatelaine*, July 16, 2015. http://www.chatelaine.com/living/entertainment-living/chick-wit-comedys-new-stealth-feminism/.

Kotthoff, Helga. 2006. "Gender and Humor: The State of the Art." *Journal of Pragmatics* 38 (1): 4–25. https://doi.org/10.1016/j.pragma.2005.06.003.

Koziski, Stephanie. 1997. "The Standup Comedian as Anthropologist: Intentional Culture Critic." In *The Humor Prism in 20th-Century America: Humor in Life and Letters*, edited by Joseph Boskin, 86–114. Detroit, MI: Wayne State University Press.

Krefting, Rebecca. 2014. *All Joking Aside: American Humor and Its Discontents*. Baltimore, MD: Johns Hopkins University Press.

Logan, Brian. 2014. "Shock Value: How Aamer Rahman's 'Reverse Racism' Joke Saved His Career." *The Guardian*, June 4, 2014. https://www.theguardian.com/stage/2014/jun/04/aamer-rahman-reverse-racism-comedy-tour.

Lugones, María. 1987. "Playfulness, 'World'-Travelling, and Loving Perception." *Hypatia* 2 (2): 3–19. https://www.jstor.org/stable/3810013.

Mayo, Chris. 2014. "Humorous Relations: Attentiveness, Pleasure and Risk." *Educational Philosophy and Theory* 46 (2): 175–86. https://doi.org/10.1080/00131857.2012.721731.

Mills, Brett. 2011. "'A Pleasure Working with You': Humour Theory and Joan Rivers." *Comedy Studies* 2 (2): 151–60. https://doi.org/10.1386/cost.2.2.151_1.

Mizejewski, Linda. 2014. "Pretty/Funny Women and Comedy's Body Politics: Funniness, Prettiness, and Feminism." In *Pretty/Funny: Women Comedians and Body Politics*, 1–29. Austin: University of Texas Press.

Morris, Amanda Lynch. 2011. "Native American Stand-Up Comedy: Epideictic Strategies in the Contact Zone." *Rhetoric Review* 30 (1): 37–53. https://doi.org/10.1080/07350198.2011.530108.

Nabi, Robin L., Emily Moyer-Gusé, and Sahara Byrne. 2007. "All Joking Aside: A Serious Investigation into the Persuasive Effect of Funny Social Issue Messages." *Communication Monographs* 74 (1): 29–54. https://doi.org/10.1080/03637750701196896.

Nussbaum, Emily. 2015. "The Little Tramp: The Raucous Feminist Humor of 'Inside Amy Schumer.'" *The New Yorker*, May 11, 2015. http://www.newyorker.com/magazine/2015/05/11/the-little-tramp.

Pérez, Raúl. 2013. "Learning to Make Racism Funny in the 'Color-blind' Era: Stand-Up Comedy Students, Performance Strategies, and the (Re)Production of Racist Jokes in Public." *Discourse & Society* 24 (4): 478–503. https://www.jstor.org/stable/24441482.

Rossing, Jonathan P. 2012. "Deconstructing Postracialism: Humor as a Critical, Cultural Project." *Journal of Communication Inquiry* 36 (1): 44–61. https://doi.org/10.1177/0196859911430753.

——— 2014. "Critical Race Humor in a Postracial Moment: Richard Pryor's Contemporary Parrhesia." *Howard Journal of Communications* 25 (1): 16–33. https://doi.org/10.1080/10646175.2013.857369.

Rozik, Eli. 2011. *Comedy: A Critical Introduction*. Portland, OR: Sussex Academic Press.

Russell, Danielle. 2002. "Self-Deprecatory Humor and the Female Con: Self Destruction or Comedic Construction." *thirdspace: a journal of feminist theory and culture* 2 (1): 1–16. https://journals.lib.sfu.ca/index.php/thirdspace/article/view/d_russell/3117.

Scott, A.O. 2015. "Adjusting to a World that Won't Laugh with You." *New York Times*, June 5, 2015. http://www.nytimes.com/2015/06/07/movies/adjusting-to-a-world-that-wont-laugh-with-you.html?_r=0.

Sims, David. 2015. "Amy Schumer and the Growing Pains of Comedy." *The Atlantic*, June 30, 2015. https://www.theatlantic.com/entertainment/archive/2015/06/amy-schumer-race/397226/.

Stott, Andrew. 2005. *Comedy*. New York: Routledge.

Taylor, Drew H. 2005. "Whacking the Indigenous Funny Bone: Political Correctness vs. Native Humour, Round One." In *Me Funny*, edited by Drew Hayden Taylor, 67–80. Vancouver: Douglas & McIntyre.

Weaver, Simon. 2011. *The Rhetoric of Racist Humour: US, UK and Global Race Joking.* Burlington, VT: Ashgate.

Weitz, Eric. 2009. *The Cambridge Introduction to Comedy.* Cambridge, UK: Cambridge University Press.

Willett, Cynthia, and Julie Willett. 2019. *Uproarious: How Feminists and Other Subversive Comics Speak Truth.* Minneapolis: Minnesota University Press.

Zwagerman, Sean. 2010. "Like a Marriage with a Monkey: An Argument for the Use of Speech-Act Theory in the Analysis of Humor." In *Wit's End: Women's Humor as Rhetorical and Performative Strategy*, 10–41. Pittsburgh: University of Pittsburgh Press.

14

Teaching through Digital Intimacies
A Strategy for Critical Cross-Disciplinary Pedagogy

NATHAN RAMBUKKANA

For Lauren Berlant, Rest in Power

This chapter draws on my experience teaching two courses that have used a "digital intimacies" framework—the third-year lecture course Digital Intimacies and the fourth-year seminar Robotic Intimacies—to discuss how critical intimacy theory can be used to mobilize insights from gender and sexuality studies for broader analyses across disciplines. After briefly touching on how I conceptualize digital intimacies, I offer observations from my own teaching, looking at assignments and approaches that worked and didn't, to investigate how a digital intimacies focus can reorient how teachers introduce topics in the classroom, bringing a broadly rendered queer theoretical lens into critical engagement with topics that may not be apparently intimate in nature from the outset, such as robotics, digital media, artificial intelligence (AI), and platforms. Further, drawing on these insights from adapting my pedagogical approach through digital intimacies, I offer strategies for similar critical intimacy studies–informed teaching across disciplines, from sociology to engineering. What discipline does not deal, in some way, with forms of intimacy?

Critical intimacy studies emerged from an impulse to take the revolutionary theoretical and activist energy of queer theory and apply it more widely, taking in kinds of connection, affinity, and affect that go beyond gender and sexuality to comprise kinship and community, neighbourhood and nation, hobbies and fandoms, interests and obsessions. It emerged from the writing of Lauren Berlant and others—for example, in Berlant's landmark edited collection *Intimacy* (2000)—who saw in queer theoretical insights and politics something that transcended that context, a mode of engagement with "the kinds of connections that *impact* on people, and on which they depend for living" (Berlant 2000, 4). The lens of critical intimacy theory goes beyond the destabilizing and deconstruction of identities and subjectivities; its first proponents also sifted through the residue of theoretical and political encounters forged in the crucible of queer struggle and thought. The insights and intersectional approach of critical intimacy studies were something I wanted to bring more fully into conversation with my own home discipline, communication studies. It was in a focus on digital intimacies that I found a way to do this.

Digital intimacies as lens makes visible how critical intimacy studies intersects with digital culture, from algorithmic filtering of identities, to social media networks, to human–machine communication with robots and AI. A conceptual framing workshopped by many people in parallel (see Andreassen et al. 2017; Chambers 2013; Dobson et al. 2018; McGlotten 2014; Miguel 2018; Rambukkana 2015b), its emergence can be characterized by diverging yet entangled approaches. With a colleague (Rambukkana and Wang 2020), I trace how these lines of descent take in ideas from diverse fields, such as philosophy and psychoanalysis (see Bersani and Phillips 2010). Of particular note is Micheal Nebeling Peterson et al., who trace the concept through not only the theoretical lineage from Berlant but also a parallel social science one that "investigates intimacy historically by examining the way in which relationships associated with intimacy have evolved, developing from traditional intimacies carried out in proximity to local communities and families to modern or late modern intimacies, characterised by relationships of choice" (2017, 55).

The task of bridging the disciplinary and pedagogical gulfs between critical intimacy studies and digital culture studies required a new set of tools for my course. I turned to teaching texts that already straddled these fields for help; they were informative not just for their content but also for the manner in which they negotiated critical cross-disciplinary research and pedagogy (see Baym 2015; Tiidenberg 2018). Notably, this scholarship worked through the overlaps between communication studies and disciplines that attend to intimacy, kinship, and community, such as sociology and cultural studies. I also drew from my own discipline's deep engagement with Marshall McLuhan–inspired "medium theory."[1] In asking, "What are the medium qualities of digital intimacy?" and "How might this be a way into teaching this material across disciplines?" I not only reflect on my own pedagogical process and the conceptual tools it deploys but also gesture towards how that approach might be useful for further cross-disciplinary work.

These questions signal the way digital intimacies are modes of interaction with media as opposed to simply media technologies themselves. What is a medium? Surely it cannot just be the technology in a vacuum. Take, for instance, the trajectory of a book. A book, in isolation, has a history, a journey; it is the apex of a process, a singular offering that combines a complex set of ideas, referents, words, materialities (both physical and electronic), relationships (editorial, networked, distributive), and so on. All these forms of relationality, conditions, contexts, and affects contribute to the becoming of the thing itself: the book in its final form, a technological assemblage. But that isn't the end of its journey. The book as an experience and as a technology does not end with its singular coming together—unless

---

1. While theorized and elaborated by many, some even predating McLuhan (1964), his notion of "the medium" itself carrying specific "meanings" distinct and in addition to any particular content they are conveying is the most recognizable access point for what has become known as "medium theory."

perhaps it is never read. As a *medium*, its effects include how it is used and what it goes on to be part of: the experience of readers; other contexts, like the books it sits next to on shelves; the ideas it might contribute to in the minds of children, adults, scientists, politicians, and the public sphere broadly; and how it might influence what the author or others do after—in new work, in teaching, and in creation.

If a medium includes not just technologies but their uses, it is worth thinking about how we categorize media, to shift our focus between foreground and background, like playing with a camera's settings, to see what might come into focus. We already do this kind of play and adjusting with more established categories both in research and across multiple teaching disciplines, such as with "educational technologies," or "sex technologies" for that matter. More conceptionally, we write and teach about things like "democratic media" and "public sphere technologies." Despite their apparent differences, all of the above technologies can, from one way of seeing, be discussed as *intimate* technologies: as technologies of connection, contiguity, influence, and affect. And when such technologies are based in or intersect with the digital, they can be seen as enabling digital intimacies as a medium, both in their isolated potentials and in their concrete or notional uses.

Together, this previously demonstrated cross-disciplinary utility for framing technological engagement broadly, the insights from medium theory, and my experience teaching these classes led me to pin down common aspects of digital intimacies in an open and evocative way for students. What qualities define the medium of digital intimacies?

1. *They connect us.* Individually, as families, as groups, as networks, as nations, as fandoms, as factions, as ideological slices, as publics, and as a world.
2. *They sometimes divide us.* Similar to the ways they connect us, digital intimacies can function in individuating ways that

feed back into the above category of connections, and the ones below.
3 *They are agnostic to scale.* A single post could enflame a global crisis, or end a political career; a viral meme—Bernie Sanders's mittens, for example—could unite the world in a structure of feeling.
4 *They are implicated in identities.* In all ways and at all scales, from family text chains and our own personal or familial document archives on email servers and devices, to national and notional publics that form around attention to politician social media feeds or fannish interests.[2]
5 *They are material.* They matter, and also may become the matter of additional complexes and configurations.[3] When digital affordances connect us closely, we can think of those affordances as scaffolding intimacies.
6 *They are political.* They can connect us; divide us; help create, support, maintain, and transform our identities; and matter to us, sometimes deeply. Digital intimacies are sites of the political, of course they are.

I came to observe many of the above qualities through developing and teaching my third-year lecture course, Digital Intimacies. The course examined different theoretical and topical approaches

---

2. Sometimes these even connect, such as when fans of Korean boy band BTS and many in online K-pop subculture broadly used TikTok and Twitter to organize and disrupt a Trump rally by booking tickets en masse, something that in part contributed to attempts to ban TikTok in the United States (Hollingsworth 2020).
3. Or, as I have articulated elsewhere, they are "close connections that matter and subtend our lives and experiences" (Rambukkana 2015a, 28). For those less used to the broader language of materialism and affect, another way to say this would be they are impactful. The editor of this collection, Natalie Kouri-Towe, helpfully points out how digital intimacies can also (re)organize our material worlds, through new technologies, infrastructures, media objects, spaces, etc., though here I don't limit the point to physical materiality only.

to critical and digital intimacies, unpacking the wide variety of ways that people connect and build lives and experiences in digitally mediated ways. Topics covered everything from sexual subcultures over the internet—such as cybersex, sexting, the online pornography industry, and virtual spaces created for sex (e.g., within MUDs, MOOs, and *Second Life*[4]), to broader forms of intimacy in digital spaces—such as the politics of friending, hashtag publics, avatars, texting practices among tweens, digital divides, video game relationships and connections, and the politics of virtual communities. Concepts and frameworks such as intimacy, queer theory, hybridity, imagined communities, cyborg identities, the posthuman, virtuality, and affect theory were explored alongside and through considering the concrete issues above.

Mobilizing critical intimacy theory to teach digital culture studies can also help connect the intuitive and analytic dimensions of learning in the classroom. On the first day of lecture, I always ask the students, "Who here has ever gotten into a fight over text message?" In each fifty-person class, almost every hand goes up. For follow-up questions, I ask them, "What was different or weird about fighting over text versus fighting in person?" and "What was it like having a transcript of your fight that lasted after the fight was over?" These prompts connected student experiences of intimacy in the digital realm to the transformative potential of platform affordances, such as "storage" and "reach," on how personal relationships get elaborated in the digital age (Baym 2015, 7). Questions that ask students to reflect on their own experiences of mediated intimacy (for example, using dating apps) also help connect to ways sexuality, gender, and race were articulated in the early internet era, such as how text- and

---

4. MUD is an acronym for multi-user dungeon/dimension/domain, while MOO is a second-order acronym for "MUD, object-oriented." These early, mostly text-based multi-user online game and social spaces were the forerunners of later massively multiplayer online game and social spaces like *World of Warcraft* (Blizzard 2004) and *Second Life* (Linden Lab 2003).

menu-based identities acted as both constraints on, and vectors for, identity building and erotic encounters on early chat sites (Gosine 2009, 140). Working the overlap between studies of sexuality as it plays out in digital cultures, and of connection, community, and self-exploration online closed a circuit of sorts between queer theory and everyday intimacy. These insights—about identity, about binaries, about normativity, about the public/private nature of intimacy—have important implications beyond gender and sexuality studies (see Berlant 1997; Butler 1999; Foucault 1990; Warner 1999).[5]

Overall, I think the material worked well in the Digital Intimacies classroom. We covered themes as disparate as how websites can change the way we approach sexual identity exploration (Rambukkana 2009) and the ways fan fiction communities flourish on the web (Carlson 2009). We unpacked topics from online amateur porn production (Paasonen 2010), to the authenticity of digital companions (Pettman 2009; Turkle 2007), to gender representation in video games (Sarkeesian 2013a, 2013b). We approached these topics not only through academic writing but also through journalistic coverage, filmic and televisual fiction, podcasts, blog posts, and YouTube videos. Because these topics touched issues that were anything but abstract, extensive discussion forums introduced in a later version of the course also helped to elaborate student understanding through a process that was almost akin to journaling. Some students had indeed explored identities (sexual and otherwise) online; others had been

---

5. And there are even wider classroom implications around teaching and learning, such as how interpersonal communication interacts with the media of communication, and the new cultural practices that help shape how and with whom we communicate. Even in classrooms that don't tackle topics on human relationships, the very practice of teaching and learning brings questions of communication and the impact of our intimate lives into the classroom, whether we intend to or not. For example, students texting with friends or loved ones during class, distractions from focusing on lecture because of interpersonal conflicts, faculty performance impacted by wider departmental culture.

part of online fandoms; a few knew people who made online pornography; many had cared for virtual pets as kids; and many more had encountered the problematically gendered worlds of video games. Sharing and commenting on these experiences articulated well with the multimodal texts encountered, fleshing out discussions that felt organic to student experiences, and were nuanced and deepened by theoretical connections and lenses.

I turn to one assignment that students responded particularly well to as an example of how critical intimacies can help reorient teaching and learning. The "platform ethnography" assignment involved a fly-on-the-wall observation of an intimate space (for example, *Second Life*, Tinder, Facebook, r/TheRedPill[6]). The goal of this assignment was to become immersed in an intimate digital space, to observe its dynamics and rhythms for an entire month. An expanded understanding of intimacy from critical intimacy studies allowed the types of spaces engaged, as well as the types of intimacy observed, to be very broad, from sexual subcultures to anti–school mask-mandate Facebook groups during the COVID-19 pandemic. For some students, it afforded the opportunity to deepen their engagement with intimate digital spaces they already frequented, while for others it was a vector for engaging with difference. The mode of engagement that had them thinking about and with these spaces as *intimate* ones was key, and in many ways transformative, highlighting aspects of the platforms they might not otherwise have noticed or noted.

Students were also eager to engage with each other on current events and news via our class discussion forum, illustrating how connecting with each other was as much a part of learning as the assignments themselves. Their connections illustrated a type of relational dynamic that might be enabled by digital platforms, and thus the forum was meaningful as another kind of scene for digital intimacy.

6. The latter is a notorious men's rights activist subreddit on the Reddit platform, known for its open misogyny.

However, when abstract theories that were decontextualized from students' lives were introduced, such as queer aesthetics and material on the early internet, students appeared to struggle to find connections. For instance, they didn't get the point of watching *Sense8* (Straczynski, Wachowski, and Wachowski 2015) as a way into discussing "networked intimacy" (Chambers 2017) the year I tried it—though the more accessible *Her* (Jonze 2013) was very well received. Their struggle with grasping a very queered text as communication studies students highlights how there are some possible limits within cross-disciplinary pedagogy. Further, the intimacies of text-only, dial-up internet spaces were very hard for students to wrap their heads around, especially those who grew up with high bandwidth, video streaming, and smartphones, pointing to the challenges of translating historical knowledge around technology. Together, these moments suggest that disciplinary context and personal connection to the topic helped strengthen student engagement with, and understanding of, both material and complex theories.

In my fourth-year seminar, Robotic Intimacies, I explored human–machine communication, and in particular the societal prominence of robots and the emergent field of human–robot communication. While robots have long been a part of human society—especially in manufacturing, mining, sea and space exploration—we are seeing an exponential growth of robots being used for other purposes, such as military/security drones and other robotic automatons, the use of carebots in the health industry, and the commercial use of robots in the service industry. Robot companions (both animal, humanoid, and other) are proliferating across markets and for use with children, adults, and the elderly. In addition, AI, chatbots, and cyborg experiments are further blurring the lines between humans and non-humans. Through encounters with daily headlines about bionic eyes, robotic chefs, autonomous driverless cars, and ChatGPT, we find ourselves inching closer and closer to the science-fictional figurings of how societies where humans and human-like machines coexist might function. The course addressed issues related to labour, agency, sexuality, surveillance, imperialism, war, health care, and ability, with a dual focus on present discourses and possible futures.

Critical intimacy theory played the same role in this fourth-year seminar as it did in my Digital Intimacies class: as theoretical backbone. Critical intimacy studies and robotics literatures complemented each other because of the history of creating life-like and machinic entities, where the fascination with recreating life and of having relationships with those creations drives technological development. These affinities show how relationality and intimacy are always already present in robotics (see Brooks 2003; Levy 2007). Introducing critical intimacy theory helped students understand the readings from the robotics and human–machine communication literature as speaking broadly to diverse intimacies, from machinic sexuality, to labour relations, to international conflicts. While compared to my Digital Intimacies course some of the material in this seminar was less proximate to the lives of the students—such as autonomous robot soldiers, sex robotics, and meditations on the singularity[7]—other aspects had immediate impacts on students' lives, such as the looming threat of machinic job replacement and the ethics of using carebots for the elderly. Starting from a critical intimacy framework, students could more easily connect to abstract topics. For example, while "robosexuality" (Rambukkana 2021b) was a strange, unfamiliar topic for many students, looking at it through the lens of societal resistance to same-sex marriage (Levy 2007) helped students discuss the wider implications of ethics, policy, law, and other topics related to sexuality that one might not immediately consider when thinking about technology. Similarly, the entry point of intimacies within, between, and among nations helped students connect to the global

---

7. The singularity has a few definitions, but the general idea is that it is the point in history where AI becomes truly conscious and/or begins to accelerate past human consciousness with respect to complexity (see Brooks 2003).

politics of killer drones and autonomous weapons systems (Anderson and Waxman 2012; Crootof 2015), allowing them to understand the relationship between the actual military present and speculative futures of war. These conversations made visible some of the stakes in thinking intimately about technology—such as how destruction of robot soldiers doesn't carry the same domestic weight as the death of human ones, which has historically weighed into swaying public opinion about engaging in armed conflicts (Crootof 2015).

A practical example of how I used digital intimacies in the context of this seminar is how I structure the lesson "From Sex Toys to Teledildonics and Beyond" as a semi-formal debate about the societal role of sex robots. Students use an inquiry-based approach to pull examples from their readings, from material posted on the class discussion forums, and from the "Robotic Resources" archive, a trove of related digital materials (journalistic articles, websites, videos, blog posts, etc.) that I have collected and curated since I first taught the course in 2016. Over the years, these discussions have shifted with student interests and current events, covering a nuanced range of digital intimacies subtopics, including feminist defences/critiques of the sex robot industry; the reification of gender and race stereotypes in robot bodies and AI personas; sex worker rights/labour/activism; sex robots as educational/therapeutic services; robots as cures for societal loneliness and alienation; the relative benefits of banning sex robots versus regulation; the UK-based Campaign Against Sex Robots; morally grey robotics used for purposes such as sex and war; (sex) robot futures, love, and agency; robotic consciousness, consent, and rights.

The major challenge with this class was always *time*. With these issues becoming more relevant with each term I teach this, covering all the material alongside devoting some of that space to the conceptual frame of digital intimacies has proved difficult. But the trade-off has been worth it. Taking space in a term's readings and discussions to introduce and unpack critical intimacy studies and queer theory, only to apply them to an entirely different topic like robotics, takes some strategizing. The payoffs for using this lens, however, are undeniable, and not only enrich the topical discussions but can make students familiar with important concepts coming out of intimacy theory such as those around normative intimacies, or the fluid play of identities. For this class, I accomplished making space for these additional theoretical discussions largely by moving some older readings to my archive of paratexts for the course that students could mine for assignments and class activities.

Digital Intimacies and Remote Learning

One of the ironies of the COVID-19 pandemic, ongoing at time of writing, was teaching about digital intimacies remotely. The challenge of online delivery was somewhat leavened by how the format of virtual learning, not to mention the new worldwide reliance on "distant sociality" (Rambukkana 2021a), underlined a lot of my course material, both theoretical and topical. To date, my Robotic Intimacies seminar has been delivered once remotely, with the tail end of another term remote as well, and I also redeveloped my Digital Intimacies course for remote delivery. While talking about digital intimacies through an intimate digital medium has been challenging—not the least because for equity reasons I didn't make live Zoom sessions mandatory and, as a result, they were sometimes frustratingly flat before I rejigged this aspect—one windfall has been converting my classes to specifications grading (Nilson 2014).[8] I had previously used this system

---

8. Specifications (or specs) grading (Nilson 2014) is a system in which students choose the grade they wish to pursue and follow a course of work commensurate with that grade. The educational motivations, priorities, and needs of a student who just needs a C+ to remain in program; of another who wants to do well, but is also working a full-time job; and another who is gunning for graduate school are so different that they may as well be doing different courses. Rather than forcing all these students through the same course of work and then evaluating them on their success, with specs grading I can set before them diverse bundle options that must all be completed to a rigorous standard, with the completion of each

for online-only course delivery, and it relies heavily (in the format I favour) on extensive forum discussion. While Zoom classes were often blank squares and could seem, at times, like only a few of us were talking into the void, the forum discussions became in-depth and discursive, deep dives into readings, themes, and ideas in ways that both leaned into, and cast a reflective light on, the best facets of intimate digital life. Notably, at the end of the fully redeveloped version, students expressed a marked preference for learning about digital intimacies remotely (compared to the alternatives of both a fully asynchronous online class and an in-person intramural one). One argument was that it was a bit easier to talk about certain topics (such as the digital sex work industry) while not in the same room with others. While I'm not entirely convinced by this argument—I have seen the benefit of unpacking these topics in person (e.g., the in-person robosexuality debates were much better than the remote one)—something in this is worth considering, given that this new medium of pedagogy is likely not going to disappear entirely.

Conclusion: Critical Intimacies and Cross-Disciplinary Pedagogy

A critical intimacies lens can inform teaching across disciplines in a number of ways. For example, I have considered developing a graduate course called Algorithmic Intimacies, or a fourth-year seminar titled Space Intimacies—an emergent topic that grows in relevance as we reach towards Earth orbit, the Moon, and Mars as new spaces for human occupation. Classes framed around political intimacies, environmental intimacies, musical intimacies, fictional intimacies, filmic intimacies, and similar are just some ways of envisioning the

---

designating a grade they would earn. Work that does not meet the required specifications is not accepted, and students are allowed delimited opportunities to redo work through an andragogically key "process of guided trial and error" (Meyers and Nulty 2009, 566) until it meets the standard.

relationship between discipline-specific topics and the possibilities of learning through intimacy. There is much to be gained by bringing critical intimacy theory into dialogue with other-disciplinary topics. As with infusing pedagogy in general with cultural studies insights and a focus on education for social justice (Chapman and West-Burnham 2010), or using the foundational insights of critical race theory to properly inform the topics those knowledges have been erased or isolated from (Alhassan 2007), sometimes backdooring critical perspectives can be a way to build bridges to students who might not otherwise actively seek out those perspectives. They might not always buy into them, or indeed might even actively push back, but it is a way to start the conversation. While not every student will choose to take a gender and sexuality studies course as part of their learning journey, sometimes we can meet them halfway.

References

Alhassan, Amin. 2007. "The Canonic Economy of Communication and Culture: The Centrality of the Postcolonial Margins." *Canadian Journal of Communication* 32 (1): 103–18. https://cjc-online.ca/index.php/journal/article/view/1803.

Anderson, Kenneth, and Matthew Waxman. 2012. "Law and Ethics for Robot Soldiers." *Policy Review*, Columbia Public Law Research Paper No. 12-313. https://scholarship.law.columbia.edu/faculty_scholarship/1742.

Andreassen, Rikke, Michael Nebeling Petersen, Katherine Harrison, and Tobias Raun, eds. 2017. *Mediated Intimacies: Connectivities, Relationalities and Proximities*. New York: Routledge.

Baym, Nancy K. 2015. *Personal Connections in the Digital Age*. 2nd ed. Malden, MA: Polity Press.

Berlant, Lauren. 1997. *The Queen of America Goes to Washington City: Essays on Sex and Citizenship*. Durham, NC: Duke University Press.

—, ed. 2000. *Intimacy*. Chicago: Chicago University Press.

Bersani, Leo, and Adam Phillips. 2010. *Intimacies*. Chicago: University of Chicago Press.

Blizzard. 2004. *World of Warcraft*. PC.

Brooks, Rodney. 2003. *Flesh and Machines: How Robots will Change Us*. New York: Vintage.

Butler, Judith. 1999. *Gender Trouble: Feminism and the Subversion of Identity*. 10th anniversary ed. New York: Routledge.

Carlson, Christie. 2009. "Is This Because I'm Intersexual? *Law and Order, Special Victims Unit* and Internet Fan Production." In *Queer Online: Media Technology and Sexuality*, edited by Kate O'Riordan and David J. Phillips, 177–96. New York: Peter Lang.

Chambers, Deborah. 2013. *Social Media and Personal Relationships: Online Intimacies and Networked Friendship*. Basingstoke, UK: Palgrave Macmillan.

——— 2017. "Networked Intimacies: Algorithmic Friendship and Scalable Sociality." *European Journal of Communication* 32 (1): 26–36. https://doi.org/10.1177/0267323116682792.

Chapman, Laura, and John West-Burnham. 2010. *Education for Social Justice: Achieving Wellbeing for All*. London: Continuum.

Crootof, Rebecca. 2015. "War, Responsibility, and Killer Robots." *North Carolina Journal of International Law and Commercial Regulation* 40 (4): 909–32. https://ssrn.com/abstract=2569298.

Dobson, Amy Shields, Brady Robards, and Nicholas Carah, eds. 2018. *Digital Intimate Publics and Social Media*. London: Palgrave Macmillan.

Foucault, Michel. 1990. *The History of Sexuality*. Vol. 1, *An Introduction*. Translated by Robert Hurley. New York: Vintage.

Gosine, Andil. 2009. "Brown to Blond on Gay.com: Passing White in Queer Cyberspace." In *Queer Online: Media Technology and Sexuality*, edited by Kate O'Riordan and David J. Phillips, 139–53. New York: Peter Lang.

Hollingsworth, Julia. 2020. "K-pop Fans Are Being Credited with Helping Disrupt Trump's Rally. Here's Why That Shouldn't Be a Surprise." *CNN*, June 22, 2020. https://www.cnn.com/2020/06/22/asia/k-pop-fandom-activism-intl-hnk/index.html.

Jonze, Spike, dir. 2013. *Her*. Los Angeles, CA: Annapurna Pictures.

Levy, David. 2007. *Love + Sex with Robots: The Evolution of Human–Robot Relationships*. New York: Harper.

Linden Lab. 2003. *Second Life*. PC.

McGlotten, Shaka. 2014. *Virtual Intimacies: Media, Affect, and Queer Sociality*. Albany: SUNY Press.

McLuhan, Marshall. 1964. *Understanding Media: The Extensions of Man*. New York: McGraw-Hill.

Meyers, Noel M., and Duncan D. Nulty. 2009. "How to Use (Five) Curriculum Design Principles to Align Authentic Learning Environments, Assessment, Students' Approaches to Thinking and Learning Outcomes." *Assessment & Evaluation in Higher Education* 34 (5): 565–77. https://doi.org/10.1080/02602930802226502.

Miguel, Cristina. 2018. *Personal Relationships and Intimacy in the Age of Social Media*. London: Palgrave Macmillan.

Nilson, Linda B. 2014. *Specifications Grading: Restoring Rigor, Motivating Students, and Saving Faculty Time*. Sterling, VA: Stylus.

Paasonen, Susanna. 2010. "Labors of Love: Netporn, Web 2.0 and the Meanings of Amateurism." *New Media & Society* 12 (8): 1297–312. https://doi.org/10.1177/1461444810362853.

Peterson, Michael Nebeling, Katherine Harrison, Tobias Raun, and Rikke Andreassen, 2017. "Introduction: Mediated Intimacies." In *Mediated Intimacies: Connectivities, Relationalities and Proximities*, edited by Rikke Andreassen, Michael Nebeling Petersen, Katherine Harrison, and Tobias Raun, 1–16. New York: Routledge.

Pettman, Dominic. 2009. "Love in the Time of Tamagotchi." *Theory, Culture & Society* 26 (2–3): 189–208. https://doi.org/10.1177/0263276409103II.

Rambukkana, Nathan. 2009. "Taking the Leather out of Leathersex: The Internet, Identity, and the Sadomasochistic Public Sphere." In *Queer Online: Media Technology and Sexuality*, edited by Kate O'Riordan and David J. Phillips, 67–80. New York: Peter Lang.

—— 2015a. *Fraught Intimacies: Non/Monogamy in the Public Sphere*. Vancouver: UBC Press.

——, ed. 2015b. *Hashtag Publics: The Power and Politics of Discursive Networks*. New York: Peter Lang.

—— 2021a. "Is the Distant Sociality and Digital Intimacy of Pandemic Life Here to Stay?" *OUPblog*. January 30, 2021. https://blog.oup.com/2021/01/is-the-distant-sociality-and-digital-intimacy-of-pandemic-life-here-to-stay/.

—— 2021b. "Robosexuality and Its Discontents." In *Intersectional Automations: Robots, Algorithms, AI, and Equity*, edited by Nathan Rambukkana, 149–67. New York: Lexington Books.

Rambukkana, Nathan, and Keer Wang. 2020. "Digital Intimacies." In *Oxford Bibliographies in Communication*, edited by Patricia Moy. New York: Oxford University Press. https://www.oxfordbibliographies.com/view/document/obo-9780199756841/obo-9780199756841-0250.xml

Sarkeesian, Anita. 2013a. "Damsel in Distress: Part 1 – Tropes vs Women in Video Games." May 7, 2013. Video, 23:34. https://www.youtube.com/watch?v=X6p5AZp7r_Q.

—— 2013b. "Damsel in Distress: Part 2 – Tropes vs Women in Video Games." May 28, 2013. Video, 25:40. https://www.youtube.com/watch?v=toa_vH6xGqs.

Straczynski, J. Michael, Lana Wachowski, and Lilly Wachowski, creators. 2015. *Sense8*. Chicago: Anarchos.

Tiidenberg, Katrin. 2018. *Selfies: Why We Love (and Hate) Them*. Bingley, UK: Emerald.

Turkle, Sherry. 2007. "Authenticity in the Age of Digital Companions." *Interaction Studies* 8 (3): 501–517.

Warner, Michael. 1999. *The Trouble with Normal: Sex, Politics, and the Ethics of Queer Life*. Cambridge, MA: Harvard University Press.

15

Risking Uncertainty

In Defence of Play in the Classroom

DINA GEORGIS

For years, I prided myself to be the kind of teacher that managed to conduct a course without drama and without conflict. In my classroom, no one cried, no one aggressively reacted to me, and rarely did students challenge each other in disputes over conflicting political values. When trying to think about how I created a learning environment that was respectful and generative, I would be stumped to give an answer. Back then I was better at seeing what I didn't do rather than what I did do. For instance, I didn't talk down to students, I didn't shame them, I didn't drone on and on, and I didn't bore them. I knew from reading course evaluations that students found me to be a passionate teacher, skilled at exciting students with ideas. My classroom was energetic and I suppose I was vigilant at reading energy. Trained in psychoanalysis and a student of Deborah Britzman's pedagogical teachings,[1] I believed that learning is an encounter with the

---

1. It is not easy to single out any particular book or essay that captures the fullness of Britzman's influence on me with regards to the question of learning in all its risks, difficulties and joys, but I very much hold dear the first book I read, *Lost Subjects, Contested Objects: Towards a Psychoanalytic Inquiry of Learning* (1998). Her most well-cited concept in "difficult knowledge" (which appears in many of her works)

unknown and potentially with difficulty. It is a demanding pedagogy that can invoke a crisis of truth and vulnerability in students when familiar discourses collapse. But over the years, I also realized it can be a welcome surprise and discovery of new knowledge. I struggled with the feminist rhetoric of safe space as an achievable goal, and instead embraced risk, intimacy, tension, and pleasure.

When I started to notice some changes in student behaviour—resisting unfamiliar ideas,[2] becoming more sensitive to course content, feeling triggered by course material, and even challenging my course structure, I started to think that either students were changing (displaying a combination of more vulnerable and more empowered), or they were reacting to an older (more threatening?) teacher. Admittedly, my conclusions were simplistic but perhaps not entirely wrong. Conceivably, the discourse that surrounds trigger warnings has made students more attuned to their safety or lack thereof and more entitled to make demands. Of course, I cannot say one way or another if students have actually changed, but in the last decade or more, there appears to be a collective heightened awareness of vulnerabilities to social injuries and this has put pressure on teachers to create safe and predictable environments. The cultural shift is evident in the demand to want to be warned when difficult content is to be shared. There is a general assumption that content has to be scrutinized for its difficult material and not considered at all for a course if it is deemed

---

has been widely taken up by education scholars to think about how knowledge enacts a crisis in students and teachers (Pitt and Britzman 2003).

2. In my classrooms at the University of Toronto, where more than half of my students are of colour, resistance is for the most part not to the idea that we live in a white supremacist world; rather, students can resist ideas that complicate the struggles of what it means to live with present-day violences and the complex legacies of colonialism and transatlantic slavery. For instance, wearing a hijab can feel emancipatory for some women and oppressive for others. Paradox and contradiction can sometimes challenge students' political positionalities and safety in their ways of knowing.

too difficult. For me, this shift communicated a desire for predictability and certainty. Even though I have always experienced student resistance in the classroom, what felt different is an expression of risk aversion: students routinely announce that they "don't want to get retraumatized," that they "feel unsafe" and so on.[3] But the resistance is not only to being a witness to violent representation (which I tend to avoid because often those representations are either gratuitous, offensive, or not subtle enough), but also to encounters with (new, challenging) knowledge.

These changes, at least for me, have come into conflict with a pedagogy that troubles knowability, encourages curiosity, and wants students to allow themselves to have intellectual and affective encounters with difficulty and pleasure. This is a pedagogy that does not view learning as the acquisition of knowledge but a journey of knowledge-making. Importantly, learning is not disassociated from feeling vulnerable and the risks associated with challenging certainty and predictability (for scholarly works that frame learning through uncertainty and risk, see Gilbert 2014 and Dyer 2020). Students of women and gender studies very quickly become politically literate and assert their views confidently. This is a great achievement but, when combined with a discourse of injury and safety in what you know, it compromises learning. In this new cultural milieu, as I have come to view it, I found myself frustrated and recalcitrant to change my teaching practices. I refused to use the phrase "trigger warning" and would instead introduce the text as pedagogically valuable for its

---

3. For women and gender studies students, trigger warnings are demanded for sexual and gendered type violences. Even though, I have come to make it my practice to offer warnings to cultural texts, I've always combined this warning with language that troubles the idea that we can know for certain what content will trigger any of us. Psychic responses are not predictable and triggering content does not only pertain to images and scenes of sexual violences but also to histories of racial violences, of war, of poverty, etc. Often the subtlest of gestures can trigger deep, sometimes transgenerational, pain.

difficult content. I also resisted removing "difficult" texts from my syllabi, choosing risk over safety. Unbeknownst to me, I had entered into a power struggle with my students.[4] Worried that I was on the verge of becoming that teacher who refuses to learn and change, the argument of this chapter changed. Rather than write an essay that only insists that risk is necessary for learning, I also consider what makes students capacity for taking risks possible.

A good schoolmaster, says Jacques Rancière, does not "teach his pupils *his* knowledge, but orders them to venture into the forest of things and signs, to say what they have seen and what they think of what they have seen" (2009, 11). The teacher does not interact with students as though they are ignorant subjects or passive learners dispossessed of agency but rather as active contributors to knowledge. Indeed, Rancière does not even consider ignorance as a lesser form of knowledge but the opposite of knowledge. For Rancière, ignorance is a position of holding back on transmitting knowledge to students. Insisting on engagement that encourages "the poetic labor of translation [which] is at the heart of all learning" (10), he discourages any form of mastery, which distances and separates the teacher from the student. The only thing that the schoolmaster must know to do is turn something into an object of knowledge. In other words, the job of the teacher is to help incite student curiosity. The student in this classroom will learn things that the teacher may not know themselves. This shift may feel dangerous for many students who have grown accustomed to, and find safety in, the conventions of teaching and learning. While this method in teaching and learning may not be appropriate in every context, and definitely more suitable for the humanities classroom, it is an orientation not only in teaching but, more

---

4. This insight was made at the workshop associated with this publication. Special thanks goes to Natalie Kouri-Towe who gently nudged me to think about how the resistance from my students in the classroom may be related to affective power struggles. This very illuminating realization changed the course of this chapter.

importantly, in how learning happens. A student may gain knowledge but when they discover it, which is to say when it becomes an object of curiosity and play, another level of learning is underway.

Being an ignorant schoolmaster is difficult work. If it is a teacher's job is to invite students to venture out into the forest to make meaning of things they see and hear, might it also be the teacher's responsibility to prepare them for such an adventure? In the context of the women and gender studies classroom, what kind of educational adventures do we want students to have? Liberation is the adventure we are on but as Katherine McKittrick advises, "the goal is not to *find* liberation, but to seek it out" (2021, 47–48). I don't read McKittrick to say that liberation is all in the seeking but that in focusing on searching, we become more invested in learning as opposed to arriving. It requires in her view a method and method-making whose purpose is a new order of being human. This view is the antithesis of disciplinary methods. For McKittrick, academic disciplinary practices curtail creative Black ways of knowing and indeed replicate violence towards Black people in research practices that *describe* violence and in so doing reinscribe it. Method-making, she writes, "moves with curiosity (even in frustration) rather than applying a set of techniques to an object of study and generating unsurprising findings and outcomes. Methodology is disobedient (rogue, rebellious, black)" (44). A methodology that generates and gathers new ideas through curiosity—the method McKittrick is calling for—is a method that, in my view, makes space for play. Play can feel dangerous because it is, as we shall see, fundamentally disobedient to rules. In play, we abandon our attachments and let ourselves wonder.

In *An Aesthetic Education in the Era of Globalization*, Gayatri Spivak (2012) also insists that we forfeit our habits of mind and indeed offers play as the method by which this can happen. The trouble for Spivak lies in our propensity to inhabit double binds without learning how to unbind ourselves from dichotomies. Our inability to identify or learn how to live with double binds inadvertently reproduces colonial global capitalism in repetition (this is the point that McKittrick is making as well). What characterizes double binds is polarized states that are impossible to reconcile. In Spivak's words, double binds "enable and disable" (2012, 2) and learning to live with double binds is to learn to live with "contradictory instructions" (3).[5] Perhaps her most famously cited double bind is articulated in "Can the Subaltern Speak?" where she argues that postcolonial freedom and agency relies on the existence of the subaltern. If an aesthetic education "teaches that all subjects are contaminated" (Spivak 2012, 1), then critique safely distances us from the objects that come under our critical scrutiny. In the feminist classrooms, critique is a skill that is taught and practiced. Spivak asserts that cultural critique is a limited and even possibly misguided project. Instead of critique, Spivak, for instance, draws on Kant, who she heavily cites for his insights into his aesthetic philosophy, "abusing/using [his Eurocentric knowledge] from below" (11). With respect to Freud, she tells the story of how she began to read him more generously as body-mind philosopher (xii). In critique of the politics of citational practices, McKittrick asks, "What does it mean to read Jacques Derrida and abandon Derrida and retain Derrida's spirit (or specter!)? Do we unlearn whom we don't cite? And what of our teaching practice? Do we teach refusal?" (2021, 22).

Rather than teach refusal, Spivak suggests we play the double bind. Playing generates new ideas outside the terms of the binary.[6]

---

5. Consider "the tug of war" (Spivak 2012, x), as Spivak puts it, between metropolitan minority and postcolonial majority, between mother tongue and global idiom, between the individual and collective, between self and other, and between body and mind. Perhaps the most profound double bind is implicated in our relationship to babies, which, citing Levinas, positions us in "impossible ethics... the baby marked for death as it is born" (xi). These are some of the examples that Spivak identifies to help us think about the challenges of being human and living under global capitalism.

6. Notwithstanding our changing cultural relationship to "queer," consider its emergence in culture as a creative response that spoke to human sexuality in excess of the rigid terms of straight and gay/lesbian.

But she goes farther to suggest that playing has a deeper purpose and likens it to therapy in ways that exceed traumatic repetition or the propensity for mechanical and hardened impulses. For me, this is a fecund formulation that not only helps us exceed the binaries set by power but positions play as the doorway to other possibilities. It cannot be stated enough that we all struggle with remaining curious and flexible in relation to our stalwart stands. This is especially true at a time when white supremacy remains unabated and when the pandemic has made us more aware of local and global inequities. Strategic and firm assertions of right and wrong will always be necessary to address political urgencies. So to ask students, especially now, to risk safety and certainty is vulnerable-making, and this is so not just for the students but for teachers as well. The student may feel that risking uncertainty risks the real work of political change. But if we heed Spivak's assertion that desire itself needs to be rearranged (2012, 2), presumably with the effect of new sets of meaning, then dreaming is the stuff of social transformation. When we stop generating new ideas and new forms of life, we work against liberation. Liberation is the capacity to re-create life. And the classroom is a privileged space wherein students are invited to do this kind of work.

To help us understand the work of play and its relationship to re/creation of life, I turn to theorist and psychoanalyst D.W. Winnicott whose considerations on childhood learning has taught me a great deal about our creative capacity. Like Rancière, Winnicott believed that learning or knowledge is something to be "discovered," not given. In his writings on early childhood development, Winnicott (1971) observed infants' capacity to "use" objects/toys to discover their relationship to the outside world. In potential space, the term he employed to describe the space between inner and outer reality, the baby interacts with objects in free and creative play. In this space, objects are found and created in fantasy (but of course objects have to already be there to be found). Important to Winnicott's theory is the idea that instilling the capacity for creativity is necessary for human development. Winnicott believed that children needed to find their "true selfs," which in his mind is a self made freely and not in stifling compliance to the outside world. Indeed for Winnicott, an authentic self is rooted in non-compliance and "not the creativity of someone else, or of a machine" (1971, 87). Such a self is more able to grow up to withstand the pressures of social conformity, be less defended when life is challenging and more able to tolerate difficult impulses. It is also a self more able to let its guard down (able to identify and tolerate double binds?) and take creative risks. Winnicott insisted that the necessity to live creatively did not end with childhood but in fact was the only thing that made life worth living.

For Winnicott playing is "non-purposeful" and an end in of itself. Playing is therapeutic and healing not only because it outwardly expresses what is going on psychically with someone (Melanie Klein's view) but because it is fun, encourages risk, and makes way for new experiences. It is imagination at work, which has no rules or motives. If Winnicott is right, playing is fundamentally defiant.[7] That is because when we use our imagination, we are not drawing on the tried or known. With imagination, we are remaking our world through illusions, dreams, and visions. Though playing is universal and, as a capacity, is available to everyone beyond childhood, we become less inclined to engage playfully as we get older. We never actually lose the capacity; however, the demands of being an adult, accommodating and complying to the needs and rules of others, make it harder to surrender into play. Play subjects us to risk and uncertainty—feelings

---

7. Marie Lenormand's (2018) reading of Winnicott's body of work on the subject of play offers a more robust definition. Though Winnicott in his later works seems to dwell on a version of playing that is consistent with my description above, she claims that earlier work offers other versions of play, which is to say not all forms of playing are the same or tantamount to creativity. Indeed, a compulsive relationship to a toy or playing a game that has too many rules works against non-purposeful playing.

we often try to eschew. When play is or feels possible, we create and re-create our relationship to the outside world through curiosity, experimentation, and pleasure—not expectation or demand.

As educators, what does it mean to take heed of this claim? If it is incumbent upon us to cultivate creative learning, what are the conditions for making this possible? For the infant to develop a strong capacity for creativity, a safe enough environment must be provided by the parental figure. An overly fastidious and anxious parent can stifle the infant's curiosity. Conversely, an absent parent can lead to feelings of insecurity in the child. It's important to note that at this stage in the baby's development, they have experienced a loss of omnipotence. The breast is no longer under the baby's "magical control" and as such they have an awareness of their dependency on the parental figure. The baby needs to feel confident in the parent's dependability so that growing up and learning is happening in a safe environment. Indeed, the absence of a safe environment can severely compromise creative learning and living. Just as we never lose the capacity for creation, we also never stop needing a facilitating environment.

As a teacher, I may have taken for granted that I was providing a safe enough classroom environment for my students. So when I started to reflect on student vulnerabilities more generously in the last year under the trying conditions of the pandemic, I decided to soften my approach and experimented with being more attentive to student vulnerabilities. In my fourth-year seminar on psychoanalysis and race, which I taught in the winter of 2021, I immediately noticed an overall change in my students' overall disposition, which I can only describe as a softening in their affect towards me and towards the course content. It is difficult to play without some measure of safety (although we know that humans do even under extraordinary cruelty and subjugation), and indeed by the end of the course I realized that I as well had become more relaxed in the classroom, less anxious about the outcomes of exposing them to challenging content. There were many magical moments in this classroom. Playing is a subtle activity of the mind's capacity to freely notice, freely express, and freely imagine.

To create an environment that strikes a perfect balance between safety and risk is of course impossible. The objective as I see it is to create a "good enough environment," a phrase I borrow from Winnicott, that allows students to feel safe enough to take interest in and explore their vulnerabilities and curiosities. This is, in my mind, the work of liberating desire from the conscripts of racial capitalism and to live in creative rebellion, risking certainty. When epistemic certainty is agitated with the spectre of something otherwise or an unsettling affect (be it pain or pleasure), it can feel dangerously queer. For teachers to regard such moments as opportunities and adventures in learning involves not so much a position to be communicated to students in words but an affective disposition that enacts listening and witnessing and an openness to being surprised and to learn. When I finally realized my obdurate resistance to my students' demands for safety, the change in me was not new pedagogical strategies but merely what I might name as a general softening to their resistance to vulnerability.

References

Britzman, Deborah. 1998. *Lost Subjects, Contested Objects: Towards a Psychoanalytic Inquiry of Learning*. Ablany: SUNY Press.

Dyer, Hannah. 2020. *The Queer Aesthetic of Childhood: Assymetries of Innocence and Cultural Politics of Child Development*. New Brunswick, NJ: Rutgers University Press.

Gilbert, Jen. 2014. *Sexuality in School: The Limits of Education*. Minneapolis: University of Minnesota Press.

Lenormand, Marie. 2018. "Winnicott's Theory of Playing: A Reconsideration." *International Journal of Psychoanalysis* 99 (1): 82–102. https://doi.org/10.1080/00207578.2017.1399068.

McKittrick, Katherine. 2021. *Dear Science and Other Stories*. Durham, NC: Duke University Press.

Pitt, Alice, and Deborah Britzman. 2003. "Speculations on the Qualities of Difficult Knowledge in Teaching and Learning: An Experiment in

Psychoanalytic Research." *Qualitative Studies in Education* 16 (6): 755–76. https://doi.org/10.1080/0951839031000163213s.

Rancière, Jacques. 2009. *The Emancipated Spectator.* Translated by Gregory Elliott. London: Verso.

Spivak, Gayatri. 2012. *An Aesthetic Education in the Era of Globalization.* Cambridge, MA: Harvard University Press.

Winnicott, D.W. 1971. *Playing and Reality.* New York: Routledge.

PART IV

Pedagogies for Care

Building Communities for Transformative Encounters in Education

This book ends with a turn to the collaborative and collective vision of education that comes from building community through our encounters with learning, both inside and outside of the classroom. Although educational institutions hold a particular kind of authority over determining recognizable forms of knowledge acquisition and skill development, we know that learning happens in multiple ways, even without the structure of pedagogy or curriculum. As Dina Georgis illustrated previously, play can be a channel for learning, and for rendering ourselves vulnerable to one another. In the introduction, I alluded to the potential of coalition as a possible anchor for the work of pedagogy, particularly critical pedagogies that are concerned with approaches to education that both resist and transform the historical exclusions and harms that are endemic within our institutions. It is in the spirit of coalition and care that the final chapters of this book attempt to re-envision both what we do in the classroom and how we think of learning.

Rather than strive to achieve a perfect classroom, the following chapters attempt to make sense of how to work together, both within institutions of higher education and outside, in the social and political spaces of communities and society more broadly. This ending is an invitation to a different kind of opening, to co-create and collaborate in envisioning a model for education where we are less isolated, in less competition, more sustained by our work, and empowered through our collaborations. Part IV begins with Jenn Cole's approach to teaching from Indigenous perspectives, modelling an approach to the classroom that anchors on learning in circle. For Cole, the circle symbolizes a capacity to lateralize power relations in the classroom and invites knowledge sharing that does not require a singular approach to pedagogical engagement or assessment. The transformation of the space of the classroom into a space for sharing and holding embodied and relational knowledge becomes a method for decolonial teaching that Cole demonstrates through compassion, collaboration, and with students, Elders, and community members.

Next, Sabina Chatterjee and Kristine Klement map out their approach and methods for collaborating to develop a handbook and toolkit for the introductory course that Klement taught and for which Chatterjee worked as a teaching assistant. Conversational in structure and instructive as a set of tools that a reader might adapt for their own teaching, this chapter charts the skills and values at the core of their teaching. Disrupting the hierarchical relationship inherent in institutional roles, such as instructor and teaching assistant, their chapter is a model for how to work across uneven power relations in education and a call to transform those relationships through meaningful collaboration. Anchored in the seven skills they outline for critical thinking, the chapter offers tools for rethinking one's relationship to teaching as well as the relationships built in the classroom amongst students and teachers.

Similarly, Chandni Desai's chapter on pedagogies of abolition introduce another call for transforming the relationship of power in the classroom, through solidarity and coalition as central functions of community-engaged work. Bridging the classroom and solidarity activism, Desai offers a model for teaching that weaves the transformative potential of learning into practices of social change and justice. Making activism the object of study as well as the practice of classroom learning, she walks us through the steps of building an accountable model for community engagement while illustrating the potential for mutual transformation through encounters that break down the barriers between the classroom and society. Working with her students to organize in support of a trans woman of colour who was incarcerated in Ontario, Desai illustrates how abolition can be applied and integrated into class assignments, discussions, and activities. She concludes her chapter with a set of material ways that all faculty can incorporate abolition pedagogies into their teaching, including resisting the punitive models of education and building mutually accountable structures for the classroom instead.

Following this work on abolition pedagogies is a roundtable on regional perspectives on gender and sexuality pedagogies featuring Carol Lynne D'Arcangelis, Mylène Yannick Gamache, Nicholas Hrynyk, and Suzanne Lenon, working in Newfoundland, Manitoba, Alberta, and British Columbia, respectively. Their discussion on pedagogy considers the impact of rurality, the legacies of settler colonialism, and the importance of gender and sexuality education for students coming from remote communities. The chapter develops a reflexive thread around the embodied experience of teaching, especially when thinking about the relationship between the classroom and Indigenous students. Gamache, who is Franco-Métis and based in Winnipeg, shares the importance of tracing lineages of thought intertwined with lineages of familial history in her approach to teaching. Thinking about the relationship of place-based knowledge that emerges out of Indigenous knowledge systems, Gamache grapples with the importance of attending to the complexity of identity and positionality without simply reifying fantasies of knowing Indigeneity. Similarly, D'Arcangelis and Lenon both grapple with their positionalities as white settlers, and with the urgency of centring Indigenous voices and perspectives in the classroom, in tension with the risk of tokenizing or homogenizing Indigenous people through the disciplinary focus on gender-based violence. Both contributors reflect on the ethics of navigating the tension between their social locations and the pedagogical imperative to address the systemic erasure of Indigenous knowledge from our educational institutions. Alongside these concerns, the roundtable also illustrates the importance of working with students to build alliances and community through the classroom, especially when we consider, as Hrynyk notes, that for many students in rural and regional contexts the stakes of gender and sexuality exceed the classroom and are co-implicated in local communities and activist orientations to education.

Lastly, this part ends with my interview with Kami Chisholm, the co-founder and artistic director of a film-festival collective anchored in public pedagogies and the principles of justice. Thinking about the role of education outside of our institutions of higher education, Chisholm offers a provocative critique of institutional violence and illustrates how teaching and learning can happen in any space. This visionary approach to pedagogy extends the possibilities of our roles as educators to thinking about how teaching can be complicit in upholding both institutional power and resistance to it. They call on educators to take seriously the potential in community-based education, which "would be immensely transformative if we could make it more readily available and accessible. I say this to academics, because I think academics feel trapped... But we can create alternative spaces for education if we create alternative schools, classes, workshops, frameworks, and co-ops to provide education that people really want and need" (358). Ending the part with Chisholm's words serves as a call to remind us that education does not begin and end in the classroom; rather, the classroom is just another scene where learning is organized, navigated, contested, imposed, transformed, resisted, exercised, and celebrated.

16

Kanawenjigewin

Learning to Care for One Another in Circle

JENN COLE

I learned the Anishinaabemowin word *kanawenjigewin* from Elder Alice Olsen Williams.[1] She translated it for me as, "to have something inside you (like bravery is inside you) that makes you want to take care of something or someone." Spending time with Elders like Alice, in Michi Saagig territory, where I live and teach as a Two-Spirit Anishinaabekwe from Algonquin territory, has grown my intellectual worldview and profoundly changed my pedagogy. The way of relating through care that Alice articulates is part of a larger set of Anishinaabe principles that honour love, respect, bravery, truth, honesty, humility, wisdom, fluidity, curiosity, and self-determination. I often experience the living expressions of these teachings as I sit in circle with others in my communities. When we sit together, we bring our hearts, minds, bodies, and spirits together into a space of care: respectful, honest, and brave communication arises out of love, humility, and

---

1. I first met Alice Williams working with the Aging Activisms Research Collective in 2018, but she has been working with my university in one way or another for decades. I would describe her as a badass matriarch kwe.

shared curiosity. I teach in Indigenous performance studies, gender, and social justice, disciplines that amplify the importance of narratives of lived experience. In the classroom, being in circle centres Indigenous principles in education by making the space for learning non-hierarchical, where we can be in relation to one another. This involves acknowledging that the role of the teacher in the classroom is also a role of being a learner. I am learning through teaching in circle.

Taking care. Listening. Being brave enough to trust. I am learning to teach according to Anishinaabe models of reciprocity and respect. What happens when we learn together when these protocols are centred? In my courses, our learning styles reflect the material we study, which foregrounds scholarship and artistic work from many Indigenous nations across Turtle Island. This means we take care of one another, we lift up Indigenous work, we engage and communicate according to Anishinaabe circle protocols, we learn from the knowledges of many beings, we respect and trust one another's gifts and our own, and we commit to honouring the full person of each member of our classroom. This chapter draws from my experiences teaching and learning in circle since 2018. It is a practice that involves sharing what I am learning as I work to decolonize the classroom spaces that I inhabit. What follows are reflections, rather than a prescriptive list, on "how-to" decolonize the classroom. I am certainly not alone in thinking through how to bring contemporary post-secondary education into alignment with Anishinaabe and Indigenous practices, and so this reflection comes about following many teachers and authors who have elaborated on Indigenous pedagogy, including Kathleen E. Absolon (2011), Nicole Bell (2013), Margaret Kovach (2009), Linda Tuhiwai Smith (2012), and others.

This chapter is a reflection on the Anishinaabe principled pedagogy my students and I have built in relation to one another through being in circle. What does it mean to be in circle in the classroom? What are Anishinaabe principles of relating and how, in Anishinaabe cultural understandings, does knowledge move? How does learning to care for one another while we practice knowledge exchange reflect the ethics of the relations we hold with many beings outside of the classroom and vice versa? This chapter traces the pedagogical practice of unlearning the colonial constructs of patriarchy, gender binaries, heteronormativity, white supremacy, and relational subjugation with students who identify both as Indigenous and as settlers. I ask how we might learn to care for one another in relation through Indigenous epistemologies that are not extractive or coercive, that take their time, within the confines of the university institution. Learning *with* students, I examine how to study together through the pedagogical framework of care.

The Circle: A Space for Embodied and Relational Knowledge

In circle, everyone matters. Carol Greyeyes shares that in her syllabus "knowledge is a circle and it is democratic; all heads are the same height and whatever position you have in the circle is unique and has a valuable perspective. Not only do we contribute from our perspective in the circle, but we expand our collective knowledge in the process of watching others learn" (2019, 58). I have learned, from being in ceremony and in circles led by Indigenous Elders and facilitators, that we trust that everyone in the circle is there with purpose, that they have something to offer upon which the group depends. This idea follows Anishinaabe understandings of community and parenting: when a child is born, we trust that they have gifts to offer our communities, without which we would not be whole (L. Simpson 2011, 106–109). Everyone has gifts. I invite students to bring the gifts of their perspectives, their particular ways of reading, their distinctive expertise, their life experiences and stories, and I commit to offer mine as generously as possible.

Following the logic of the circle allows us to practice protocols of consent and to practice becoming better listeners. We also practice collectivity and interdependence. In circle, each student is free to speak and free to not speak if they do not wish to say anything. I will not call anyone out at random to perform "good studenthood" or muscle quiet students into demonstrating their intelligence through coercive participation. Each student knows their place in the circle, and knows that, when it is their turn, they will be allowed space and time to express themselves as they like, including if this means taking us up on the shared invitation to remain quiet or maintain privacy. In circle, we are invited to be brave enough to speak from the heart and to trust ourselves to say what is needed in the context of the group. I trust my students. Asking them to rise to the invitation to think of one another in this way and to bring their debwewin, their heart knowledge, to the conversation, especially within the context of the highly pressurized intellectual performance space of the academy, is a big ask. It takes practice and courage to connect with our hearts and bring them into the classroom when the exercise can seem at odds with entrenched academic protocols. I remember to thank students for meeting me in this generous and brave way.

A circle often begins with a check-in about how people are doing. We practice holding space for one another to arrive as we are. We might attend to a question and move that question around the circle. We might take up a practice of sharing one thing we are learning from the readings or assignments, or sharing one citation that moved us or made us curious and voicing why we think we are picking up the gift of this knowledge in particular. Dialogue builds in connection to all of the words that have been shared with focus and good intention thus far. We consciously take up a shared practice at each turn of the circle. When something is brought into the circle that does not sit well, each of us waits our turn and each person is welcomed to speak to it honestly. My experience has been that we build confidence in one another and ourselves when we know that we will be able to express ourselves in a space of collective listening and when we are invited to share out of a sense of responsibility and honesty. We keep in mind that we are practicing these things, and that we can falter and improve.

As part of the protocols of the circle, the whole person is honoured and held carefully. This applies to students indigenous to Turtle Island and students indigenous to other places. I cannot teach about the sacred medicine circle and the corresponding importance of balanced aspects of our being—body, mind, spirit, heart—and then insist that students render their bodies, hearts, and spirits invisible to me as good academic practice. The expectation that education involves leaving your lives at the door and bringing your brains to the table is a harmful colonial demand. Isolating the mind and diminishing the crucial knowledges that other parts of ourselves hold doesn't work in the classroom, where lived experiences, the bodies we inhabit, and structural injustices are theoretically and palpably intermingled. The circle is a collective of embodiments. It is an ancestral shape we can lean into that supports us. It is a resting place for the many parts of ourselves. In Anishinaabe thought, each of the aspects of our beings brings unique intelligence. For one, the body is an important site for knowledge reception and generation.

The importance of embodiment can be found across the scholarship of disability, gender and sexuality, feminist, performance, trauma-informed, and Indigenous knowledge scholars. As Stōlo performance scholar Dylan Robinson writes, "knowledge is produced, conveyed, and understood through the body" (Robinson and Martin 2016, 8–9). Likewise, feminist author Sara Ahmed elucidates our sensate embodiments of histories when she expresses that "feminism can begin with a body in touch with a world, a body not at ease in a world; a body that fidgets and moves around. Things don't seem right" (2017, 22). Sometimes body sense precedes cognitive understanding. Bodies are vortexes of complex social, cultural, and mnemonic relations. They are also among our best teachers. Marrie Mumford (Métis Chippewa Cree), former artistic director of Nozhem First Peoples Performance Space and my mentor, has told me that our senses are gifts that interpolate the world and that, when engaged, bring us deeper into relation with ourselves, our world, and one another. Marrie has taught me that when all of the aspects of our being are invited in and working together, we make stronger work.

In the classrooms I inhabit, we treat study as relational and strive to learn about reciprocity. Sam McKegney cites an anonymous residential school survivor, saying, "My story is a gift. If I give you a gift and you accept that gift, then you don't go and throw that gift in the waste basket. You do something with it" (2016, 196–97). One of our responsibilities as scholars, if we aren't going to perpetuate and teach knowledge extractivism (McKegney 2016, 210), is to learn to give back when the gift of knowledge is shared. In the classroom, this means thanking one another for showing up and finding ways to pick up what we are learning from classroom texts and knowledge workers, letting it change us, and treating our scholarly work as an offering. Letting course texts affect and transform us is heart work. This is seriously deep work and I ask that students move at their own pace when it comes to their emotional and individual beings. Being moved is an expression of relating with knowledge and depth of connection is a gift of decolonial scholarly praxis; this is also a gift that we can offer to Indigenous authors, artists, and activists.

I have learned from my teachers that if I ask someone to share a cultural practice or teaching I offer them semaa/tobacco and state my intention behind asking. This is the same when I approach the land and ask to harvest food or medicine. Tobacco first. Taking second. Potowatami botanist Robin Wall Kimmerer shares the widely held Indigenous teaching that we never harvest the first of anything we see, which teaches about consent, ethics of sustainability, and community care in human social spheres. She writes that if you ask consent to harvest leeks and they say no, you move on, no matter how badly you want them (2013, 176). I do my best to follow this Anishinaabe principle of not taking without giving something back. This is true in the classroom, where Maria Campbell says that study can be a form of giving back (cited in Dewar et al. 2013, 15–16). In scholarly spaces, we practice reciprocity by trying to offer what we are learning instead of what we know. We enact gratitude for what Indigenous scholars, creative makers, cultural keepers, lawyers, and land defenders are sharing with us. In the gender and sexuality classroom, students often come to class knowing how to be suspicious of how academic knowledge-seeking legacies are steeped in extraction. Instead of extracting knowledge, we offer thanks for scholarly articles, digital and artistic offerings—the stuff on the syllabus' reading and viewing list—by picking up something that is offered and holding it with care. We might share aloud what we are learning from the person. We might write a collective list of words that the author or artist has inspired. Our assignments are efforts to respond to what we have received. This is part of our circle practice.

Indigenous Kids in the Future

What is the living context of the circle?

In practice, learning in circle can be a decolonial pedagogy by centring Indigenous people, principles, thinkers, and artists. Decolonizing my classroom includes both working from Anishinaabe paradigms as much as possible and prioritizing course content with diverse Indigenous voices. This chapter is an example of the citational practices we invoke by also tracing the knowledge sharing of Elders and other teachers. In the justice-seeking classroom, we focus so much on work to be done, and we absorb so much information about the legacies of ongoing harm and violence. Indigenous students in my class have expressed being further traumatized in their education when discussions of "Indigenous issues" focus on violence. As I teach about the importance of nourishing our whole beings by being in good relationship, about the ethics of consent and respect embedded in Anishinaabe social and political practice, and about resurgence and the reclamation of healing going on in many Indigenous nations, part of my responsibility is to do as little harm as possible and to celebrate Indigenous thinkers and creators. In my classes, we foreground

Indigenous Peoples and their voices across territories, with emphasis on Indigenous women and Two-Spirit/Queer (2SQ) people as creative makers, vibrant thinkers, and vital members of our communities. We study Indigenous/feminist acts of resistance to colonial heteropatriarchy, continued resilience, and cultural resurgence. What are Indigenous women and 2SQ people saying that we might listen to? What can we learn from how they are saying it? As we spend time studying storytelling, remembering, community building, performance, literature, slam poetry, land defence, visual art, media work, DJ video mixing, acts of commemoration, and so on, we ask, What do we hear? What do we notice? What are we being asked to learn?

As a way of inviting Indigenous students to the front, part of our collective class agreement is to celebrate the work being done to render the world more just. We celebrate the generative, creative awesomeness of Indigenous justice work. For instance, we pair learning about colonial legal systems that have been designed to continue to oppress Indigenous people with the celebration of Anishinaabekwe Morrison's culturally grounded legal practice in "Coming for Everything Our Ancestors Were Denied: Indigenous Lawmakers Forging Pathways Ahead" (2021). Tuning to resistance with a sense of celebration is not always easy and is not always appropriate, but I want to create a space where Indigenous students can see themselves at the forefront, to sense their cosmologies and modes of expression as the strong forces of decolonization and cultural reclamation. For example, I show Halluci Nation's music video "Sisters" in nearly every class. In the video, three Indigenous women prepare to go out to a Tribe Called Red show. They dress up, laugh, and try on sunglasses on the road. They fly a Mohawk flag from the car as they cruise to their destination. The tone is carefree and joyful. Kwewag[2] relaxing and

---

2. *Kwewag* refers to women, but conceived outside of hard binaries and within the context of living gender fluidities maintained in Anishinaabemowin.

having fun. No one gets wasted. No one gets hurt. This is respite from common trauma narratives.

Mi'kmaq poet Rebecca Thomas was the first person to bring to my attention WD4, the media analysis tool for Indigenous content wherein a viewer can ask themselves if they are witnessing five of the strongest stereotypical representations of Indigenous people (McCue 2014). Are the people represented as warriors (W), or are they shown as one of the four D's—drumming, dancing, drunk, dying, or dead? A decolonizing classroom draws on a multiplicity of Indigenous narratives to move outside of WD4 representations. In class, we address colonialism but also highlight the importance of Indigenous futurities. We commit to the future for generations to come by opening our own imaginations and attuning to works that articulate Indigenous presence. Filmmaker, writer, and artist Cara Mumford articulates the power of imagining futures from a place of narrative sovereignty: "I was inspired to reconsider my own views of the future, turning away from the dystopian fiction that I love so much, to imagine my utopia for this region...imagining a world where much of this territory has been returned to the Michi Saagiig, becoming a province of the sovereign Anishinaabeg Nation. Where gender is no longer binary, where the earth is respected, where the salmon thrive again" (2016, 33).

As students and I collectively imagine livable futures for all living beings and for Indigenous women, genderqueer, and Two-Spirit people in particular, we retell narratives of the past, rethinking progress frameworks for social justice work on these lands. One of the things that tuning to Anishinaabe ways of knowing has brought to the gender and sexuality classrooms I inhabit is to dismantle heteropatriarchal normativity from within Indigenous contexts. Gender binaries, misogynist relationship structures, and homophobia were not traditionally part of Anishinaabe language, kinship structures, or cosmologies. These arrived via colonialism (Carter 2008; A. Simpson 2014; L. Simpson 2017; TallBear 2016). Not taking the Canadian colonial nation state for granted (Green 2017, 4) offers up some gems!

For millennia, in Anishinaabeg territory, there was no core belief that sex or gender fell into two hierarchical binaries. The gender fluidity of Creator, spiritual beings/manitous, and figures in our stories, was prominent. Anne Taylor (2021) has taught me and my students that, while many languages gender their words, in Anishinaabemowin we are much more focused on whether a word signifies a being who is animate or an inanimate object. Animacy is conceptually privileged over sex and gender. Do you have a spirit? Then we have certain responsibilities towards you. And we recognize the gift of you.

Kim TallBear (2016) teaches that non-monogamous kinship structures have traditionally been culturally appropriate means of relating across Turtle Island. Certainly, for the longest part of Anishinaabeg history as I understand it, no person could ever possess another person or possess land. The link between colonial marriage law enforcement and property ownership has been well established by TallBear and Sarah Carter (2008). I particularly love a statement Audra Simpson (2016) makes, in her discussion of body and nation sovereignties, that if a woman wanted to divorce a man, she simply "put his belongings outside the longhouse." To me, this gesture illustrates a matter-of-factness about the fluidity of love affairs and family structures, this time in Mohawk territory. We do not restrict one another's bodies. We do not shame people because we understand that there is no sense in undermining their road. We practice the ethic of giving space (L. Simpson 2011, 54–56). We trust one another.

There are many words, teachings, stories, and protocols in many Indigenous languages and nations connected to Two-Spirit or gender-nonconforming people. Trans health doctor and advocate James Makokis (2020) elucidates Cree teachings surrounding Two-Spirit giftings and tells trans patients that the story of their being is written in the land. Students and I navigate through brief histories of sacredness of all people and the non-monogamous, non-hierarchical, non-possessive, queer-positive, consenting, and fluid relationships Indigenous communities have nourished over time, for a long time. We tilt away from the idea that society has continually been moving away from oppression of the most vulnerable as it becomes more equitable, more just, more open, more progressive. Millenia-old political, ethical, and relational structures that are deeply anti-oppressive are held in Anishinaabe territory. As Laguna Pueblo scholar Paula Gunn Allen argues, if American society modelled "the traditions of the various Native nations...the place of women in society would become central...The elderly would be respected, honored, and protected as a primary cultural resource...[and] the destruction of the biota, the life sphere, and the natural resources of the planet would be curtailed" (1984, 35). To this list, I would add Two-Spirit people, who have also played important roles in Anishinaabeg societies and have traditionally been honoured and sought for their unique wisdom and gifts. In Anishinaabe and Cree thinking, principles of self-determination and fluidity are highly valued, and non-colonial genders and sexualities have been practiced for generations (Highway 2008; Lamouche 2021; L. Simpson 2017). As Two-Spirit literary scholar Daniel Heath Justice articulates, "taking joy in our bodies—and those bodies in relation to others—is to strike out against five-hundred-plus years of disregard, disrespect, and dismissal" (2008, 104).

Multiple Knowledges, Many Teachers

One day, I brought my child to school. He had an earache. I set up blankets, crayons, paper, playdough, and a tablet with headphones in the corner. In that particular class, we had read Kim Anderson's (2011) chapter in *Life Stages and Native Women* about babies and the gifts they bring from the star world. Some Mi'kmaq and Anishinaabe students reflected on the second chance babies might offer some parents a chance to love and parent respectfully in a way that reclaims and heals. My five-year-old lectured for one minute in that class, suddenly, about working for the water, recycling initiatives, and how waters that flood are not angry but seeking homes. He gave each of the forty students a sticky note with an *A* on it and took those who wished to join on a field trip during our break. We travelled the halls and wrote positive affirmation notes to strangers and dropped them over the balcony. I felt my child's strong giftings and how lucky we were to have them in class that day, showing us what babies are made of.

Expanding our idea of who a teacher is, is part of learning in circle. We have had Elders in class and have met with elderly knowledge holders on fieldtrips. One class' first assignment is to introduce me to a grandparent figure in their lives, focusing on connection to place and intergenerational knowledge sharing. Course texts amplify the voices of Elders, youth, and diverse bodies and minds across nations Indigenous to Turtle Island. Indigenous learning is intergenerational and interdependent on a diversity of giftings and ways of being in the world. Indigenous knowledge also acknowledges dependence upon the intelligences of many beings. When Leanne Betasamosake Simpson (Michi Saagiig Nishnaabeg) (2020) discusses learning from amik, the beaver, she addresses land as a teacher who emphasizes relationality and interdependence: "This land has taught me that Anishinaabe life is continual, reciprocal and reflective. It is a sometimes critical engagement with my ancestors, those yet to be born, and the nations of beings with whom I share land. It is a living constellation of co-resistance with all of the anti-colonial peoples and the worlds they build. This land has taught me that Anishnaabe life is a persistent world-building process. Despite and in spite of, the constant imposition of the colonial machinery of elimination." Similarly, Lynn Gehl (Algonquin Anishinaabe) emphasizes that in Anishinaabe creation stories human beings are the last to be created. When humans arrive, they depend upon the plants, animals, and birds to teach them how to survive through intelligent relationship with their surroundings (Gehl 2017, 93). We are children on the land, not stewards, as Michi Saagiig Elder Dorothy Taylor (2020) has expressed. This conceptual move positions us as interdependent learners. Anishinaabe thought consistently draws upon the intelligences of children, babies, grandparents, animals, plants, water bodies, and the cosmos. We are learning and we can learn from many inspirited beings.

During our first meeting, I often invite the class to introduce ourselves by sharing a water body to which we are connected. This can be a lake, ocean, river, or creek from our childhood homes, our ancestral lands, our current backyard. We begin to connect with one another as we vocalize these relationships to water, to place, to the sensations that arise when we are with these waters that have supported us, as we express memories of fishing, swimming, getting in trouble for getting muddy, walking with wave sounds, and of the people speckling these waterscapes. We begin to practice holding one another's stories with care. We begin to build and tune into our networked interdependence across place and time. We begin to collectively honour our relations.

I feel the power of one another in circle. When we centre Indigenous Peoples' voices, those voices bring millennia of interconnected, reciprocal relationships with them: to place, to plants and medicines, to cultural practices and the many beings part of our ceremonies and technologies, to clan responsibilities and star beings, to ancestors and generations to come. The circle is much bigger than we can imagine, bigger than the classroom, and the scope of networks of interspecies care is magnificent. When I am in circle with students, older and living Anishinaabe concepts of care come into our shared pedagogical practice. We open space for our many relationships, forms of knowledge, and fluid and generous understandings of gender and sexuality. We lean into this shape and it supports us. Circle practice is kanawenjigewin practice. When students and I activate the part of ourselves that cares, we learn with depth and keen intelligence. While our circle practice is rooted in Anishinaabe connections and understandings, the circle is available to anyone who steps in with good intention. What emerges in each circle is specific to the people in it, the gifts they bring, the moment in time. I am learning to trust this.

References

Absolon, Kathleen E. (Minogiizhigokwe). 2011. *Kaandossiwin: How We Come to Know*. Halifax: Fernwood Publishing.

Ahmed, Sara. 2017. *Living a Feminist Life*. Durham, NC: Duke University Press.

Allen, Paula Gunn. 1984. "Who Is Your Mother? Red Roots of White Feminism." *Sinister Wisdom* 25 (Winter): 34–46. http://www.sinisterwisdom.org/sites/default/files/Sinister%20Wisdom%2025.pdf.

Anderson, Kim. 2011. *Life Stages and Native Women: Memory, Teachings and Story Medicine*. Winnipeg: University of Manitoba Press.

Bell, Nicole. 2013. "Anishinaabe Bimaadiziwin: Living Spiritually with Respect, Relationship, Reciprocity, and Responsibility." In *Contemporary Studies in Environment and Indigenous Pedagogies: A Cirricula of Stories and Place*, edited by Andrejs Kulnieks, Dan Roronhiakewen Longboat, and Kelly Young, 89–107. Rotterdam: Sense Publishers.

Carter, Sarah. 2008. *The Importance of Being Monogamous: Marriage and Nation Building in Western Canada in 1915*. Athabasca, AB: Athabasca University Press.

Dewar, Jonathan, David Gaertner, Ayumi Goto, Ashok Mathur, and Sophie McCall. 2013. *Practicing Reconciliation: A Collaborative Study of Aboriginal Art, Resistance and Cultural Politics. A Report Commissioned by the Truth and Reconciliation Commission on Indian Residential Schools*. Kamloops, BC: CiCAC; Sault Ste. Marie, ON: Shingwauk Residential Schools Centre.

Gehl, Lynn. 2017. *Claiming Anishinaabe: Decolonizing the Human Spirit*. Regina: University of Regina Press.

Green, Joyce, ed. 2017. *Making Space for Indigenous Feminism*. 2nd ed. Halifax: Fernwood Publishing.

Greyeyes, Carol. 2019. "Making Our Own Bundle: Philosophical Reflections on Indigenous Performance Education." In *Performing Turtle Island: Indigenous Theatre on the World Stage*, edited by Jesse Rae Archibald-Barber, Kathleen Irwin, and Moira J. Day, 51–71. Regina: University of Regina Press.

Halluci Nation. 2014. "Sisters." YouTube, video, 3:31, https://www.youtube.com/watch?v=QbrvwaVXJ48.

Highway, Tomson. 2008. "Why Cree Is the Sexiest of All Languages." In *Me Sexy*, edited by Drew Hayden Taylor, 33–40. Vancouver: Douglas & McIntyre.

Justice, Daniel Heath. 2008. "Under a Changeling Moon." In *Me Sexy*, edited by Drew Hayden Taylor, 87–108. Vancouver: Douglas & McIntyre.

Kimmerer, Robin Wall. 2013. *Braiding Sweetgrass: Indigenous Wisdom, Scientific Knowledge, and the Teachings of Plants*. Minneapolis: Milkweed Editions.

Kovach, Margaret. 2009. *Indigenous Methodologies: Characteristics, Conversations and Contexts*. Toronto: University of Toronto Press.

Lamouche, Sandra. 2021. "*Ê-nitonahk Miyo-Pimâtisiwin* (Seeking the Good Life) through Indigenous Dance." MA thesis, Trent University. https://digitalcollections.trentu.ca/objects/etd-1045.

Makokis, James. 2020. "The Indigenous Doctor Helping Trans Youth." YouTube video, 12:13. https://www.youtube.com/watch?v=4Hj-a5AE-VM.

McCue, Duncan. 2014. "What It Takes for Aboriginal People to Make the News." *CBC*, January 29, 2014. https://www.cbc.ca/news/indigenous/what-it-takes-for-aboriginal-people-to-make-the-news-1.2514466.

McKegney, Sam. 2016. "'pain, pleasure, shame. Shame': Masculine Embodiment, Kinship, and Indigenous Reterritorialization." In *Arts of Engagement: Taking Aesthetic Action in and beyond the Truth and Reconciliation Commission of Canada*, edited by Dylan Robinson and Keavy Martin, 193–214. Waterloo, ON: Wilfrid Laurier University Press.

Morrison, Danielle. 2021. "Coming for Everything Our Ancestors Were Denied: Indigenous Lawmakers Forging Pathways Ahead." *Niiyobinaasiik* (blog). October 27, 2021. https://www.niiyobinaasiik.com/blog/coming-for-everything-our-ancestors-were-denied?fbclid=IwAR0FkxbhAAk0Jcl38iJLuEVVRT213SWZBrnyG3MoRoyFISAwOuxpnxHbwmo.

Mumford, Cara. 2016. "Le(e/a)Ks: Being Anishinaabekwe on the Land Is Political." *The English Journal* 106 (1): 31–37. https://www.jstor.org/stable/26359313.

Mumford, Marrie. 2018–21. Personal conversations with the author.

Robinson, Dylan, and Keavy Martin, eds. 2016. *Arts of Engagement: Taking Aesthetic Action in and beyond the Truth and Reconciliation Commission of Canada*. Waterloo, ON: Wilfrid Laurier University Press.

Simpson, Audra. 2014. "The Chiefs Two Bodies: Theresa Spence and the Gender of Settler Sovereignty: Unsettling Conversations." R.A.C.E. 2014: Keynote 1, November 4, 2014. https://vimeo.com/110948627.

—2016. "The State Is a Man: Theresa Spence, Loretta Saunders and the Gender of Settler Sovereignty." *Theory & Event* 19 (4). https://muse.jhu.edu/article/633280.

Simpson, Leanne Betasamosake. 2011. *Dancing on Our Turtle's Back: Stories of Nishnaabeg Re-Creation, Resurgence, and a New Emergence.* Winnipeg: Arbeiter Ring Publishing.

—2017. *As We Have Always Done: Indigenous Freedom through Radical Resistance.* Minneapolis: University of Minnesota Press.

—2020. "The Brilliance of the Beaver: Learning from an Anishinaabe World." *Ideas, CBC Radio*, April 16, 2020. https://www.cbc.ca/radio/ideas/the-brilliance-of-the-beaver-learning-from-an-anishnaabe-world-1.5534706.

Smith, Linda Tuhiwai. 2012. *Decolonizing Methodologies: Research and Indigenous Peoples.* London: Zed Books.

TallBear, Kim. 2016. "Making Love and Relations Beyond Settler Sexualities." Social Justice Institute Noted Scholars Lecture Series, University of British Colombia, filmed February 24, 2016. YouTube video, 55:39. https://www.youtube.com/watch?v=zfdo2ujRUv8&t=2869s.

Taylor, Anne. 2021. *Nibi: Elder's Gathering Film Panel*. Peterborough, ON: Nozhem First People Performance Space.

Taylor, Dorothy. 2020. "Let's Talk about Kindness with Dorothy Taylor." Native Child and Family Services of Toronto. Facebook, November 30, 2020. https://www.facebook.com/nativechildandfamily/videos/204035988063966.

Williams, Alice. 2019. Personal communication (email). June 11, 2019.

17

Collaboration Pedagogy

Co-creating a Handbook and Toolkit for Teaching the Intro Course

SABINA CHATTERJEE AND KRISTINE KLEMENT

Sabina: I was born in the traditional lands of the Anishinaabe, Haudenosaunee, and Huron-Wendat peoples. As the daughter of immigrants, and as a racialized settler, I believe it is my responsibility to centre decolonization in my work as an activist, community member, and scholar. Troubling the isolation and competition of the academy has led to the creation of amazing collaborative partnerships, including the one I have with Kristine.

I believe that honouring people's lived experiences and the many ways in which people hold, produce, and share knowledge is

Kristine: I was born in Tkaronto, covered by Treaty 13, the Toronto Purchase, and the Dish with One Spoon Wampum Belt Covenant. As a white settler, growing up I only knew this place as Toronto, Canada. The work of decentring whiteness in my own life, my writing, and my teaching is ongoing. The collaborative relationship that I have built with Sabina and foster on teaching teams and in classrooms is a significant part of that work.

I believe that teaching and learning are deeply personal endeavours. What my work as a psychotherapist and psychoanalyst shares with my

| integral to the way we teach and learn. I have built my feminist pedagogical praxis through activism and social service provision. The importance of critical thinking and intersectionality, and the necessity of challenging colonization as well as anti-Black and anti-Indigenous racism, has informed my work with survivors of domestic abuse and street-involved youth and has been woven into developing and facilitating human rights workshops and creating training programs for staffing teams and community service providers. | teaching is a belief in the transformative potential of thinking when it is not divorced from feeling and experience. This is why critical pedagogy is so exciting, because it is about teaching and learning with our whole selves. All of us who are involved in the education system in Canada have a responsibility to actively work towards decolonizing education and countering the anti-Black racism that is historically and institutionally embedded in the ways that we think and work. |

At the time of writing, we are a PhD candidate (Sabina) and contract faculty (Kristine) at the School of Gender, Sexuality, & Women's Studies at York University. We met while teaching Introduction to Gender and Women's Studies, where Kristine was the course director (CD) and Sabina was a teaching assistant (TA). Our relationship has evolved from instructor-TA to co-authors of a handbook and toolkit for teaching the intro course called *Critical Thinking Skills for a Feminist Classroom: Teaching and Learning for Critical Consciousness, Handbook and Toolkit*.[1] At the heart of the handbook and toolkit is a pedagogical approach that we are calling "collaboration pedagogy," inspired by

---

1. Our third co-author is fellow Gender, Feminist, & Women's Studies graduate student Jenna Danchuk.

intersectional feminist and critical pedagogies that upend the traditional instructor-TA-student hierarchy.

The handbook and toolkit is structured around a series of skills for critical consciousness, which are introduced during the lecture, explored through activities and discussion in tutorials, and practiced/assessed through the assignments. They are also practised by the CD and TAs through the collaborative teaching team approach, which makes space for honouring the different experiences and expertise held by all participants, CD, TAs, and students alike. The collaborative environment creates the scaffolding necessary so that we can learn from one another and take risks that help us engage in anti-racist, anti-colonial, and feminist teaching practices that make social justice and critical pedagogies possible within higher education. Despite the constraints created by institutional structures, we centre an understanding of how power structures both our institutional locations and the relations of power, privilege, and oppression that come with our diverse social locations across race, class, gender, nationality, sexuality, and so on. Because of these inherent power dynamics in the classroom, rethinking the ways that instructors engage with students and collaborate with colleagues can be a transformative way of reframing education. By disrupting traditional understandings of "critical" thinking by making pedagogy more central in the training of graduate students and the intellectual life of our departments, we believe collaboration pedagogy can be a transformative tool for teachers and students alike. We organize this chapter across six skills for critical thinking outlined in our handbook and toolkit. Across these skills, we introduce the pedagogical practices and strategies for collaboration that we have developed and tested in the classroom, which can serve as a model or examples for how you might consider using collaboration pedagogy in your own teaching. We have included each author's personal reflections throughout the chapter in order to transmit something of that collaborative spirit and demonstrate the nuances of how we work together.

Skill 1: Setting the Tone and Creating a Collaborative Learning Environment

We begin each semester by foregrounding collaboration with our teaching team, which sets the stage for how we work with students. Collaboration requires honouring each participant's voice and the set of experiences that they bring to the classroom, with the goal of empowering both students and teaching staff from minoritized communities who are often silenced in institutional settings.

Sabina: As with many PhD students, I have been a TA throughout my doctoral studies. Having a background in community education, I was surprised by the assumptions made about TAs—that either we would have no idea what to do and would therefore need excessively strict management by CD, or that we would have the academic and life learning to teach with a great deal of autonomy. The latter appealed to me, and I was really grateful that Kristine was very open to not only having TAs shape the learning environment in our classrooms, but also seemed open to thoughtful suggestions about the course, the syllabus, and the content she was covering. Having had some really great conversations with Kristine during teaching team meetings, it felt important to

Kristine: When I first started teaching the intro course, I tried to convey an openness to feedback and input from the TAs assigned to the tutorials. I was not far removed from being a TA myself and was keenly aware of the power that CD have to bolster or undermine a TA's autonomy and their authority with their students. I also felt my own limitations in terms of my familiarity with certain topics and approaches and knew that it was quite possible that sometimes TAs would know more about these topics than I did. Little did I know that Sabina and Harshita would take me up on my invitation and generously (perhaps bravely) shared with me some of their feedback on the way that I approached topics concerning racism and colonization. It was hard to hear that I was reinforcing Euro-colonial

Harshita[2] and me to share with her some suggestions for resources and other possible approaches she might consider when talking about key issues within the course, including colonization and anti-Black racism. I appreciated the openness that Kristine demonstrated, hearing our concerns and suggestions. Since then, we have been able to build trust, strengthening our work together from very different spaces and perspectives. The care, thoughtfulness, and intentionality that has gone into building this collaborative partnership is something I value deeply.	narratives of colonization, and hard to see the ways that I was uncomfortable talking about anti-Blackness. I imagine that it was harder for them to be in yet another classroom with a white teacher reinforcing whiteness and to take the risk of speaking with me about it. I had no idea that those difficult conversations were the beginning of a deepening and productive academic collaboration and that the discomfort that we all felt from our different positions in the hierarchies of the classroom and university could be transformative.

The focus on competition and individual success in higher education makes collaborative spaces seem all too rare. In a collaborative teaching team, we cannot assume that all members will be bringing the same or similar knowledge to the classroom; instead our goal is to make space for members to be open to learning and sharing knowledge with each other. In courses dealing with topics that can be personally and politically charged, it is crucial to build intentional support and resources for TAs who may not share the same kinds of critical understanding or experience with social justice paradigms. For example, in a course that teaches about anti-colonialism and material that challenges anti-Black, anti-Indigenous, and other forms

2. Harshita Yalamarty is a graduate from the Gender, Sexuality, & Women's Studies program who also worked as a TA in the class.

of racism, we cannot assume that all members of our teaching team will have learned about the history and contemporary forms of colonization at the core of this curriculum. International students, for instance, may not have had the opportunity to learn about histories of violence and oppression that are part of Canadian history. Contextualizing classroom learning by onboarding TAs into the geopolitically specific histories of genocidal policies, enslavement, and other forms of state violence can help establish a better common foundation for the teaching team.

Collaboration pedagogy relies on reflexivity and accountability from all members of a teaching team, including learning about our reactions and responsiveness to the material. Despite the limited institutional support for learning anti-racist, intersectional, and anti-colonial pedagogies, teaching teams can become sites for this type of training. One model for doing this is to use regular teaching team meetings to invite team members to lead workshops or discussions on approaches to upcoming topics that may not be shared areas of knowledge within the team. These workshops allow each of us the opportunity to learn from one another throughout the course, and this approach translates into our classrooms as teachers also become comfortable learning from students with diverse lived experiences and knowledge. This approach also allows the classroom to be a space where knowledge, expertise, and leadership are achieved through class activities and discussions that build trust with transparency and thoughtfulness, rather than through the authority of the figure of the teacher.

Skill 2: Developing an Intersectional Analysis

Patricia Hill Collins and Sirma Bilge (2016) emphasize that intersectionality is a tool for thinking critically about social inequality and human experience that considers various axes of power and identity. Defining intersectionality, they write, "when it comes to social inequality, people's lives and the organization of power in a given society are better understood as being shaped not by a single axis of social division, be it race or gender or class, but by many axes that work together and influence each other" (2). Taking an intersectional approach to pedagogy means considering diversity and difference in various facets of course design, beginning with topics/themes, critical approaches, readings, and assessment. However, to really integrate an intersectional feminist, anti-racist, and anti-colonial approach, we must think beyond the syllabus, to consider all aspects of our teaching and learning, including rethinking the foundations of critical thinking and the very relationships of power that shape the classroom.

Although education can be empowering, research has also illustrated how education can be a scene of violence for Black, Indigenous, people of colour, queer, trans, and other marginalized students (Ahmed 2012). Experiences of disempowerment, being delegitimized, and dehumanized are part of our education system, especially given the role of education and the residential school system in settler colonization and the genocide of Indigenous Peoples (Smith 2012). As the Truth and Reconciliation Commission (2015) on residential schools has concluded, education is one of the key areas of public life in Canada that needs decolonizing.

Skill 3: Finding and Developing Your Voice

Potawatomi-Lenapé teacher educator Susan Dion points out that fears often lead to silence from teachers who know that they should be addressing "difference" in their classrooms but don't know how (2007, 331). Dion has observed that this combination of fear and silence leads many teachers to repeat the dominant discourses "as a way of protecting themselves from having to recognize their own attachment to and implication in knowledge of the history of the relationship between Aboriginal people and Canadians" (331).

> **Kristine:** I have felt this fear and silence myself, caught between wanting to do justice to important topics while lacking the tools and knowledge through which to do so. I can also feel the pull towards taking up an autocratic position in the classroom in order to steel myself from imagined criticism. And this may be how many educators repeat the violence of institutional racism, sexism, homophobia, transphobia, and ableism.

How do we create the conditions in which teachers' good intentions can lead to transformative experiences of teaching and learning, rather than defensiveness and the status quo? Through her work with teachers in training, Dion has developed an approach that supports teachers in investigating their own internalized belief systems in order to ultimately move beyond what she calls "molded images." She writes, "Recognizing the labour of self-understanding...and the significance of dialogue, I work at co-creating with students a space in which to engage in sustained dialogue" (2007, 332). We believe that this spirit of dialogue, co-creation, and space holding is key to the practices of collaboration and coalition that we foster on the teaching team and in our classrooms. As Dion describes it, learning to teach in ways that really transform us requires making ourselves present in our teaching and learning and fostering an ongoing practice of self-reflection. This is only possible when we have spaces that can hold and contain the anxieties that come up when we challenge cherished, but ultimately damaging, ideas about ourselves and our world. The teaching team and classroom as collaborative spaces work towards this space-holding by providing a kind of scaffolding for teachers and students alike to learn from one another.

One of the assignments that we use is called "The Personal History Project." The project consists of six short journals where students are invited to reflect on the ways that their personal histories (including histories of school and education, of migration and displacement, of elder women in their families of origin or choice, of connections to the land we now call Canada) intersect with the histories of feminist resistance, colonization, and enslavement that we explore throughout the course. This assignment is a turning point for many students in "making themselves present" in the course and seeing their lives as important parts of history.

Skill 4: Pedagogies of Discomfort

One of the amazing things about teaching within gender studies is that there is often (although not always) an openness to creating responsive, respectful, and reflective spaces within and outside of the classroom. Teaching first-year students in our program holds many opportunities to support students in finding out how *they* feel about issues. For some, this may also be the first time they have been given space and encouragement to think about whose voice(s) are amplified in mainstream classrooms, and why. At our institution, the majority of students in undergraduate courses are people of colour, so within our tutorials it feels natural to centre the class in ways that disrupt colonial narratives and to support students in developing their own analyses and critical thinking. Megan Boler and Michalinos Zembylas (2003) and Delores van der Wey (2011) suggest that a pedagogy of discomfort is also necessary to create opportunities for deeper learning and accountability. Paulette Regan (2010) posits that a pedagogy of discomfort is a necessary intervention within the classroom that aims to confront systemic violence in education. By creating space in the classroom for *discomfort* through decentring white settler narratives and critically examining the complexities and complicities in students' relationships to/with colonization, we also create space(s) to learn, heal, and take action in response to legacies of violence. Jeff Corntassel and Adam Gaudry (2014) suggest that pedagogies of discomfort, combined with what they call "insurgent education," can offer insights to counteract the violence of extractive research, including troubling the superficial engagement with Indigenous people that are so often a part of extractive research.

> **Sabina:** I am deeply aware of my own position at the front of the class as a light-skinned mixed-race queer woman with disabilities who grew up in Canada—and I often choose to share my own connections, processes, and reflections with my students, while also encouraging them to share theirs. I know that is not unusual, perhaps, but most of my students have never had a racialized instructor. Most of them have never had a chance to talk about their own experiences and connections to colonization. We discuss the importance of learning relationships—that each of us has knowledge that we bring into the classroom, and that we can learn so much from sharing both the exciting and the "messy" parts of our explorations of the course material and how it connects to "real" life. While this is not generally a space of conflict, it is important to be attentive to the tensions held between the students' range of beliefs about hegemonic narratives and societal norms, and how they have been impacted by those norms and narratives. I am cognizant that having a space that is occupied by "othered" people, being taught by an "othered" person brings possibility and risk into the ways in which my teaching is understood—not only by my students, but especially by TAs and CDs who are more closely aligned with hegemonic narratives.

One of the key strengths of having a teaching team is the potential for exploring difficult issues together. Using discomfort as part of the framework of teaching necessitates the navigation of very different kinds of privilege/connection with hegemonic Western narratives. While anti-oppressive teaching and research may encourage people to understand their social location and how it connects with the work they are doing, having instructors actively engage in pedagogies of discomfort means that we also need to take some accountability for the ways that the discomfort of disrupting hegemonic narratives operates within our classrooms.

Tutorials provide amazing opportunities to create communities of learning that embrace the tensions held between students' social locations, the worldviews with which they have been raised, colonial/

colonizing narratives, and critical intersectional, anti-colonial, and anti-oppressive course curricula. Whether online or in-person, students can be encouraged to embrace the discomfort involved with learning "against the (hegemonic) grain" by building self-reflexive skills, making connections between the course readings and issues in their own lives or communities, and (perhaps most importantly) using critical thinking skills to trouble whose stories get told, whose knowledge is prioritized, and to examine narrative silences to see what is at stake in laying the hardest stories bare.

Skill 5: Asking Good Questions and Questioning Everything as a Critical Thinking Skill

Writing about education, bell hooks distinguishes "the difference between education as the practice of freedom and education that merely strives to reinforce domination" ([1994] 2017, 4). The traditional model of education, which Paulo Freire ([1970] 2020) has famously called the "banking model," positions teachers as the holders of skill and information and students as empty vessels ready to absorb our teaching. Freire critiques the banking model as alienating to students and dehumanizing to teachers, who have to hide the ways we are ourselves always learning and may have conflicting ideas and feelings about the materials we teach (44). hooks reminds us that part of the excitement of teaching and learning is that it involves taking risks and allowing oneself to be transformed by ideas and one another ([1994] 2017, 21). Students lose interest in the classroom when they find themselves with no entry point into material that may seem distant from their own experiences, or worse, feel silenced by the power relations that are inherent in the classroom environment.

Traditionally, critical thinking skills are understood as combining aspects of rhetoric and logic, argument and reasoning. Critical thinking textbooks largely demonstrate the Western cultural bias of "critical thinking": arguments are evaluated for the logic of their reasoning and the veracity of their claims; students learn research skills; how to develop a thesis, outline, and finally, the traditional essay. This form of critical skills instruction is not without merit. In an age of "fake news," the ability to assess and evaluate arguments is an important skill to have. However, the problem arises when these are the only skills that are recognized, taught, assessed, and modelled as "critical thinking" in the classroom. In intersectional feminist classrooms, these skills may be useful, but they do not go very far in providing minoritized students language to make sense of their experiences, connect to course materials, or feel represented and valued in their education. One way of reframing critical thinking skills is to invite students to draw on argument structures, knowledge systems, and their own experiences to interrogate ideas. In this way, critical thinking is not a set method, but an approach to thinking from multiple standpoints and perspectives.

> **Kristine:** When we centre the knowledge that is already held by our students and choose materials and ideas that are near enough to their experiences, they are excited to participate because they are actually included. When I have begun a course by putting my own position of authority, my own knowledge, and the traditional ways of thinking that are practised in the university in question, I can see the difference in the way that BIPOC students relate to me and to the course. We ask our students to ask questions about the materials, topics, and issues as a way to draw them in and stoke their interest. When we also invite them to question the historical foundations of the institution, the epistemological foundations of the discipline, and the structures of power and authority that permeate both, we are enacting the critique that otherwise is only performative. To really invite this inquiry, teachers have to be open to being questioned without defensiveness and need to respect students' perspectives and welcome their voices, even when they sound different from our own.

Skill 6: Developing Your Critical Consciousness through Desire-Based Research

> **Sabina:** Standing at the front of my own classroom, I watch my students' faces as I tell them story after story about how many Indigenous women are missing and presumed murdered. Watch their faces as we talk about anti-Black racism and colonization. Watch their faces as we talk about tragedy after tragedy. And I reach, yet again, for ways to disrupt the academy's (and society's) love of learning through focusing only on pain, tragedy, and despair.

One of the risks of intersectional and decolonial education is that teachers and students alike will only focus on what Eve Tuck and K. Wayne Yang (2014) call "pain narratives." Pain narratives position people (often minoritized) as wounded, where the only stories told are of pain and struggle. In "R-Words: Refusing Research," Tuck and Yang write, "settler colonial ideology, constituted by its conscription of others, holds the wounded body as more engrossing than the body that is not wounded (though the person with a wounded body does not politically or materially benefit for being more engrossing)... Emerging and established social science researchers set out to document the problems faced by communities, and often in doing so, recirculate common tropes of dysfunction, abuse, and neglect" (2014, 229). Resisting the impulse of education to gather knowledge from others and instrumentalize stories of pain, teachers and students alike need to develop critical consciousness around sharing experiences of pain, oppression, and trauma. One way to do this is by asking whether sharing these stories helps empower and respect someone's self-determination and autonomy, or does it replicate the objectifying and fetishizing relationship between education and colonial extraction through knowledge?

Because minoritized people are at risk of being positioned and talked about exclusively through trauma, loss, and struggle, educators must ask themselves, How else could students learn about these histories and conditions of violence? Thinking alongside bell hooks, Tuck and Yang (2014) interrogate the way the voices of the people whose lives and stories we are teaching about become a spectacle for victimhood. They challenge the academic impulse to identifying oppression over affecting social change by "reproduce[ing] stories of oppression in its own voice" (225). Developing a critical consciousness as teachers around how we tell stories of suffering and violence can help us confront how education risks upholding colonial ideologies, especially in narratives that position oppressed peoples as in need of being saved or pitied.

Instead of focusing on narratives of struggle and trauma, teachers draw on what Tuck calls "desire-based research," which can be seen as an antidote for pain narratives as it "does not deny the experience of tragedy, trauma, and pain, but positions the knowing derived from such experiences as wise…Utilizing a desire-based framework is about working inside a more complex and dynamic understanding of what one, or a community, comes to know in (a) lived life" (Tuck and Yang 2014, 231). In this way, a collaborative learning environment can help us seek out knowledge and wisdom from community, survival, and struggle beyond suffering and pain. One way of accomplishing this in the classroom is to collaboratively develop assignments that provide opportunities for students to engage with an issue creatively, such as reflecting on the importance of honouring activism and the hopefulness and celebration that is a necessary part of change. In an assignment that we have used, called "Art, Activism, and Social Change," students are invited to research an example of feminist, anti-racist, queer, anti-colonial, and/or trans activism and to tell the story of this activism by representing it artistically. This example of desire-based research develops student critical consciousness by allowing them to connect to learning through narratives that honour and celebrate the experiences of communities that have struggled. The process of researching examples of activism counters the pain narratives that are also included in the course. This project serves as an antidote to the stories of oppression and inequality that may disempower students.

Conclusion

Sabina: There is so much at stake in how we choose to teach and work together within the academy and the community. I truly believe that working in collaboration enhances the work we do—by creating space to share and mobilize knowledge within the teaching team, we create space for vulnerability, for solidarity, and for deeper intersectional and anti-colonial praxis. By troubling our own "expertise" we also open critical spaces for our students to understand the value of their own lived and learned knowledge, another key aspect of pedagogies of disruption and collaborative intersectional feminist pedagogical praxis. I am so excited about what we can build— and challenge—together.	**Kristine:** For me, collaboration pedagogy is an antidote to the challenges of working within a large institution like York University. Teaching and research can often be lonely endeavours, and teaching on contract can be even more alienating. Teaching in collaboration with a team of fellow teachers and students creates a community where we can receive the support we need to teach and learn. I am inspired everyday by my students and colleagues and feel privileged to learn from them and with them.

We practice collaboration pedagogy as a methodology for transforming hierarchical relationships of power within our classrooms. Collaboration on the teaching team supports a collaborative environment in the classroom that honours relational and reflective practices, providing the scaffolding for an integrative skills-based approach to teaching the intro course. By focusing on skills for critical consciousness, we work towards making our classrooms spaces of freedom and empowerment through thinking, risking both discomfort and desire. Perhaps above all, collaboration pedagogy is a form of praxis, wherein we live by the feminist, anti-colonial, and anti-racist theories, arguments, and perspectives that we study and teach.

References

Ahmed, Sara. 2012. *On Being Included: Racism and Diversity in Institutional Life.* Durham, NC: Duke University Press.

Boler, Megan, and Michalinos Zembylas. 2003. "Discomforting Truths: The Emotional Terrain of Understanding Difference." In *Pedagogies of Difference: Rethinking Education for Social Change,* edited by Peter Pericles Trifonas, 110–36. New York: Routledge Falmer.

Collins, Patricia Hill, and Sirma Bilge. 2016. *Intersectionality.* Cambridge, UK: Polity Press.

Corntassel, Jeff, and Adam Gaudry. 2014. "Insurgent Education and Indigenous-Centred Research: Opening New Pathways to Community Resurgence." In *Learning and Teaching Community-Based Research: Linking Pedagogy to Practice,* edited by Catherine Etmanski, Budd L. Hall, and Teresa Dawson, 167–85. Toronto: University of Toronto Press.

Dion, Susan D. 2007. "Disrupting Molded Images: Identities, Responsibilities and Relationships—Teachers and Indigenous Subject Material." *Teaching Education* 18 (4): 329–42. https://doi.org/10.1080/10476210701687625.

Freire, Paolo. (1970) 2020. *Pedagogy of the Oppressed.* 50th anniversary ed. New York: Bloomsbury Academic.

hooks, bell. (1994) 2017. *Teaching to Transgress: Education as the Practice of Freedom.* New York: Routledge.

Klement, Kristine, Sabina Chatterjee, and Jenna Danchuk. 2019. *Critical Thinking Skills for a Feminist Classroom: Teaching and Learning for Critical Consciousness, Handbook and Toolkit.* Unpublished.

Regan, Paulette. 2010. *Unsettling the Settler Within: Indian Residential Schools, Truth Telling, and Reconciliation in Canada.* Vancouver: UBC Press.

Smith, Linda Tuhiwai. 2012. *Decolonizing Methodologies: Research and Indigenous Peoples.* London: Zed Books.

Tuck, Eve, and K. Wayne Yang. 2014. "R-Words: Refusing Research." In *Humanizing Research: Decolonizing Qualitative Inquiry with Youth and Communities,* edited by Django Paris and Maisha T. Winn, 223–48. Thousand Oakes, CA: Sage Publications.

Truth and Reconciliation Commission of Canada. 2015. *Calls to Action*. https://www2.gov.bc.ca/assets/gov/british-columbians-our-governments/Indigenous-people/aboriginal-peoples-documents/calls_to_action_english2.pdf.

Van der Wey, Delores. 2011. "Explicating a Shared Truth about a Colonial Past: Knowledge Mobilization, Coalition-Building, Aboriginal Literature, and Pedagogy." In *Knowledge Mobilization and Educational Research: Politics, Languages and Responsibilities*, edited by Tara Fenwick and Lesley Farrell, 198–210. New York: Routledge.

18

Pedagogies of Abolition

Community-Engaged Learning and Struggles for Change from the Prison to the Classroom

CHANDNI DESAI

In recent years, abolitionist politics—which includes the defunding of police, no-borders activism, decriminalization movements, and the abolition of prisons and other forms of incarceration—have become central to the theoretical and political work of gender and sexuality studies. Both feminist and sexuality scholarship and activism have developed a robust analysis of the gender, race, and sexual politics of policing, prisons, detention centres, and related institutions (Davis 2003; Gilmore 2017, 2022; Maynard 2017; Walia 2021). Yet, despite a growing popularity, the prison abolitionist movement has been largely discussed in abstract terms in the university, without many models for applied abolition in the classroom. Educational institutions have either enforced carceral logics (e.g., the school-to-prison pipeline), or, in other instances, education has been conceptualized as a solution to societal oppression. While some students may have direct or indirect experiences with police, racial profiling, carding, arrest, detention, or incarceration, there is a general sense that the university is not a space for abolition beyond its theoretical engagement, particularly in the context of Canada. Using an applied approach to abolition as a pedagogical tool for my teaching, this chapter investigates how a classroom experiential community-engaged learning project can illustrate the transformative potential of abolition pedagogy for student learning and working across the classroom and community groups.

I first began teaching about abolition in 2016. Informed by the praxis of abolition feminists and anti-colonial, anti-imperialist thinkers, my teaching preceded the momentum for abolition that widely gained prominence in recent years. My first encounter with abolitionism was at the age of seven. While growing up in Southern Africa (Zambia) during the height of the anti-apartheid movement in South Africa, many of my formative experiences were shaped by the context of a frontline state that served as the main headquarters of the African National Congress because of its strategic geopolitical location.[1] The partial abolition of apartheid and racial capitalism shaped my consciousness early on, and it was during this time that I learned about global liberation struggles, from South Africa, to other African liberation movements, to Palestine. From the outset, my approach to abolition has been international(ist), connected to transnational social movements. Despite this formative experience, developing my course Abolition in the Global Context: Theorizing Uprisings and Youth Activism against Prisons and Policing introduced a challenge, as abolition in the classroom appears to be more theoretical than grounded in praxis. As I experimented with various assignments, readings, discussions, and community-engaged learning collaborations between students and grassroots groups, I grappled with what it would look like to centre my course on an experiential community-engaged learning project connected to a local social justice movement. I drew on Dylan Rodríguez's conceptualization of abolition as a praxis of creativity, which he defines as "a fundamental critique of existing systems of oppression while attempting to actively imagine as it practices forms

---

1. Zambia was home to major liberation movements (ZAPU, ZANU, MPLA, FRELIMO, and SWAPO) in Africa.

of collective power that are liberated from hegemonic paradigms, including but not limited to forms of power constituted by the logic of carcerality, patriarchy, coloniality, racial chattel, racial capitalism, and heteronormativity" (2019, 1612).

I wanted my teaching on abolition to centre a revolutionary praxis that connected student learning to the practices of political projects for change both locally and globally, unlike most courses on policing, prisons, and/or the criminal justice system. In this chapter, I reflect on teaching revolutionary and political material on abolition. I argue that an abolition approach can illustrate how the classroom can be a space that helps students understand their potential to be active participants in the world around them. I start by discussing the origins of abolition and its connection to education. Given the global uprisings against carceral violence and the intensification of carceral institutions that disproportionately lock up Black, Indigenous, and people of colour, the chapter reflects on how undergraduate students and myself (their professor) developed a praxis of abolition through course readings, discussions, and community-engaged learning.[2] Literature on abolition pedagogy is sparse at this time, though burgeoning, and the limited existing literature focuses on either teaching in K–12 classrooms or on education within US prisons (Love 2019; Meiners 2011, 2016; Stovall 2018). Additionally, the existing literature on abolition pedagogy primarily focuses on the US context. This chapter focuses on a student campaign that we developed in the classroom in connection to #JusticeforMoka, a social movement campaign to free a Black trans-identified sex worker, who was wrongfully incarcerated by the Canadian settler-colonial state. The chapter concludes with discussion on abolition pedagogy and the usefulness of a pedagogical approach that engages students in liberatory, rather than punitive,

---

2. Carceral violence and institutions are those relating to the prison system, immigrant detention system, policing, law, and other facets of a social system that uses incarceration to punish.

methods of teaching and learning. The chapter contributes to the literature on abolition pedagogy and specifically provides insights on teaching and learning from the Canadian context.

Abolition

In recent years the police killings of Trayvon Martin, Michael Brown, Rekia Boyd, Freddie Gray, Philando Castile, Ramarley Graham, Ahmaud Arbery, Marlon Brown, Breonna Taylor, Tony McDade, Kendrick Johnson, Amadou Diallo, Jordan Davis, Eric Garner, Sean Bell, Tamir Rice, Oscar Grant, Priscilla Slater, Atatiana Jefferson, Crystal Ragland, Sandra Bland, and many others, led to mass mobilizations and uprisings led by the Movement for Black Lives, including Black Lives Matter. In 2020, during the global COVID-19 pandemic, the police killing of George Floyd, a forty-six-year-old African American man who was murdered by Derek Chauvin, a Minneapolis police officer, led to an extraordinary mass uprising against police brutality, racism, and state violence that spread from the United States to streets around the globe. Floyd's death inspired a groundbreaking call for abolition among the masses and growing momentum in the United States and Canada for the disarming and defunding of police, prisons, and the judicial system.

Although connected to the abolition of slavery and the history of segregation in the United States, contemporary abolition politics took hold in the 1970s when Black, Brown, and Asian activists in the United States opposed the Vietnam War and the imprisonment of conscientious objectors (Felber 2020). The emergence of international abolition gatherings began to take place in the 1980s and '90s, first at the International Conference on Penal Abolition, and later in the formation of Critical Resistance (in the Bay Area) (Felber 2020).[3] In addition

---

3. Other groups that also adopted abolition into their praxis for liberation included Incite!, Survived and Punished, Dream Defenders, the California Coalition

to parallel movements on restorative and transformative justice, the prison abolition movement gained both an intellectual and political base through the work of Black feminist thinkers, such as Angela Davis (2003), Ruth Wilson Gilmore (2022), Beth Richie (2012), Mariame Kaba (2021),[4] and others who have advocated for non-punitive, transformative, and community-based approaches and responses to violence. In her groundbreaking book *Are Prisons Obsolete?* Davis (2003) draws on her decades of experience working on prison activism to advance an anti-racist, anti-capitalist, feminist critique of carceral feminism.[5] She argues for an abolitionist approach to gendered violence that focuses on how the state mirrors intimate violence.

Because prison is a gendered structure (Davis 2003), by challenging patriarchal and racialized violence, abolition feminists, like Davis, connect the work of gender liberation to racial oppression and draw on a long and diverse tradition of organizing and thinking from the Black radical tradition, Marxist, anarchist, queer, and feminist analysis, as well as anti-colonial thought. For Gilmore (2015) prisons and policing aren't solutions to social problems; therefore, abolition can also serve as a set of practices and policies that call for government investment in education, housing, employment, and health care. For her, abolition is about investing and creating vital systems of support that resolve inequities and get people the resources they need. This investment and creation is necessary because of what Gilmore calls "organized abandonment," abandonment by the state and capital that

---

for Women's Prisoners, the National Council for Incarcerated and Formerly Incarcerated Women and Girls, Movement 4 Black Lives, and several other organizations based primarily in the United States.

4. In Canada, this work has further been developed by thinkers such as Beverly Bain, Lynn Jones, Patricia Monture-Angus, Kim Pate, Julia Chinyere Oparah (formerly Sudbury), Emily Aspinwall, Filis Iverson, Sonia Marino, Rinaldo Walcott, Robyn Maynard, and many others.

5. Carceral feminism is a feminist approach to ending violence against women that relies on punitive state power and criminalization.

makes people, households, communities, and neighbourhoods (particularly poor and racialized communities) susceptible to unequal levels of support and protection for survival, and consequently vulnerable to various forms of state violence. Critical Resistance (n.d.), a US-based prison abolition organization founded in 1997, explains that "abolition is both a practical organizing tool and a long-term goal... Abolition isn't just about getting rid of buildings full of cages. It's also about undoing the society we live in because the prison industrial complex both feeds on and maintains oppression and inequalities through punishment, violence, and controls millions of people." Abolition is thus a vision to eliminate incarceration, policing, surveillance, and criminalization and pushes for a reinvestment in social services and infrastructure in order to create long-lasting alternatives to punishment and imprisonment.

In the classroom, teaching abolition can play a part in the unfinished work of transforming the afterlives of slavery, capitalist imperialism, and the various political, economic, and social systems that persist today. I begin my course with the conceptual aspects of colonial, capitalist-imperialist, and patriarchal social relations that produce and reproduce the prison-industrial complex, military-industrial complex, border-industrial complex, and policing. Once students have a theoretical understanding of the social relations that structures violence globally, we then learn about social movement opposition to carceral regimes, linking the Canadian contexts to other geopolitical contexts. I invite guest speakers who are part of social movements involved in abolition work to share their organizing experiences, which enables students to hear from those who are on the frontlines working on campaigns to oppose prisons and policing. I also invite formally incarcerated people (e.g., the Toronto Prisoners' Rights Project, Palestinian political detainees, racialized people on Canadian security certificates, deportation orders, and extradition orders) to come and share their experiences with students. Hearing firsthand experiences of the carceral system, including immigration and the border regime, provides students an opportunity to understand and apply theory outside of the classroom and builds the foundational relationships that are necessary for doing community-engaged learning with grassroots groups locally and internationally.

Experiential Learning in the #JusticeforMoka Campaign

Moka Dawkins, a Black and Indigenous transgender sex worker, was convicted of manslaughter for the death of Jamie Foster, her client. In her account of the events on August 3, 2015, Moka shared in public documents that she visited her client's apartment, but when she attempted to leave, Foster became aggressive and demanded she stay, yelling, "I told you you're not going anywhere," before stabbing her in the face (Lourenco 2018). Moka testified that she screamed for help on the balcony and fought back. After stabbing Foster in self-defence, she called 911. Foster fled the apartment and Moka followed, where she was met in the hallway by police.

Foster bled to death and Moka was charged with second-degree murder. The judge in her trial said that Moka was provoked but ruled that her actions went "beyond legitimate self-defence" (Powell 2018) because she took too long to call 911. Moka was found guilty of manslaughter, despite evidence of the deceased client's violent past and a larger social context where trans sex workers face disproportionately high rates of violent homicide and assault (D'Amore 2020).[6]

Moka shared publicly that she was misgendered and mocked throughout the legal process (D'Amore 2020). Given the option to be housed in solitary confinement in a women's prison or placed in a men's prison, she chose the men's prison because of the mental health

---

6. Since 2013 more than four trans sex workers have been killed in Canada, including Rosa Ribut (beaten to death in Edmonton in 2013); Sumaya Dalmar (murdered in Toronto's east end in 2015); Alloura Wells (found dead in a ravine in Rosedale in 2017); and Sisi Thibert (stabbed to death in Montreal in 2017).

consequences solitary confinement is said to have on prisoners. Moka spent four years in a men's prison in Toronto and experienced sexual violence. She was denied gender-affirming medications, clothing, and make-up, and was placed in solitary confinement; her advocates shared that she was routinely harassed by prison guards who would push her, spit in her face, take away her mattress and replace it with a dog mat (D'Amore 2020). She was also harassed and assaulted by prison inmates. In response to her conviction and the gender-based violence she experienced in prison, the #JusticeforMoka campaign was launched by community organizations, such as Prisoners with HIV/AIDS Support Action Network and Maggie's (a sex worker advocacy agency based in Toronto), to call for her release.

In 2019 students from my course collaborated with a local organization and worked to support the #JusticeforMoka campaign. First, the students in the course wrote letters to Moka while she was incarcerated. Prison abolitionists have asserted that letter writing provides emotional support for incarcerated people through a safe medium, particularly as isolation is a central part of the prison experience. Sometimes prisoners are also prohibited from making or have limited access to phone calls. As such, letters become a lifeline and help build solidarity across the prison walls. Letter writing can also help build community, as like-minded people come together to discuss the plight of incarcerated people and ways they can organize for abolition. In addition to writing letters, my students participated in awareness-raising activities on campus and in the city as part of a broader strategy to mobilize support for the campaign.

The students attended Moka's court hearing on October 21, 2019, and advocated that people "pack the court" to show their support at her bail hearing to pressure the courts for her early release. They participated in a fundraiser that raised money for her support fund, and they made calls to various offices to advocate for her release. An integral part of my praxis was working directly with the students to discuss solidarity and how to engage in this campaign work in responsible and ethical ways, while centring an abolitionist framework. Movement organizations are largely under-resourced and their staff and volunteers are overworked. Rather than burdening the organization, I ensured that students had guidance to organize in ways that uplifted the work of Moka's advocates and the #JusticeforMoka campaign. As I facilitated this process, I drew on my community organizing experiences and principles, transforming the classroom into a space of study and struggle.

As an educator I draw on Robin D.G. Kelley's (2016) radical conceptualization of "love, study and struggle," inspired by the works of radical thinkers such as James Baldwin, Walter Rodney, Fred Moten, and Stefano Harney. Kelley argues, "Limiting our ambit to suffering, resistance, and achievement is not enough. We must go to the root—the historical, political, social, cultural, ideological, material, economic root—of oppression in order to understand its negation, the prospect of our liberation. Going to the root illuminates what is hidden from us, largely because most structures of oppression and all of their various entanglements are simply not visible and not felt." Going to the root of oppression, I encourage my students to study deeply, to engage in historical analysis, embrace theory, and partake in critique that helps illuminate that which is hidden. During in-class discussions we read about abolition and discussed the importance of non-reformist reforms. Since abolition is a long-term process, some abolitionist thinkers call for non-reformist reforms, which are "measures that reduce the power of an oppressive system while illuminating the system's inability to solve the crisis it creates" (Berger, Kaba, and Stein 2017). Non-reformist reforms can be used in the interim through a broader transformative vision, such as by ending solitary confinement and the death penalty, opposing prison expansion, eradicating cash bail, stopping the expansion of prisons and police infrastructure, and developing conflict resolution and safety mechanisms that do not rely on a system of punishment. Examining non-reforming reforms in Moka's case enabled the students to understand that although the

#JusticeforMoka campaign was based on an individual case and not entirely framed around an abolitionist lens, the organizations working to support her were part of a wider network of groups providing life-affirming resources that would support Moka, and others like her, upon her release, including housing and health care services. Through this process, the class made connections between support for individual cases and an abolitionist lens that included calls to eradicate bail and solitary confinement, and develop safety mechanisms for sex workers, particularly racialized trans sex workers.

The readings also enabled an analysis of the gender-based disposability that Moka experienced.[7] We read the work of queer and trans abolitionists and disability justice activists, including scholars such as Morgan Bassichis, Alexander Lee, and Dean Spade (2015), Liat Ben-Moshe (2018), and Erica Meiners (2016). We drew inspiration from Davis's (2020) feminist refusal of the binary structure of gender, where she argues "that women, queer people, and particularly the trans community have shown us that because they show that the normalcy of cisheteronormativity and patriarchy can be challenged, the normalcy of police, jails, and prisons can also be challenged." Trans communities in particular are constant targets of violence, including state violence, individual violence, stranger violence, and intimate violence—all forms of violence Moka Dawkins experienced. Davis (2020) asserts that the "trans community has taught us how to challenge that which is totally accepted as normal. And I don't think we would be where we are today—encouraging ever large numbers of people to think within an abolitionist frame—had not the trans community taught us that it is possible to effectively challenge that which is considered the very foundation of our sense of normalcy."

---

7. Gendered disposability refers to the ways women, queer, and trans people are expendable in settler colonialism and to the state. Sherene Razack argues that "sexualized violence is key to disposability, and flesh is the site at which racial and sexual power are both inscribed" (2015, 285).

Davis thus illustrates how a feminist abolitionist framework can help us challenge capitalist patriarchal social relations and alludes to the pedagogical ways that trans people's experiences can expand our epistemological and ontological understandings of how to live in this world beyond the limits of the current system.

After being released from prison, Moka visited my classroom at the University of Toronto and talked to the students about their support and participation in the #JusticeForMoka campaign. Through dialogue with my students about their final presentations for their community-engaged learning project, abolition took on a deeper meaning than an academic exercise. This meeting became an opportunity for collaborative learning about the everyday practices of abolition across the theoretical, activist, and lived experience of encountering and resisting the carceral system. While the course readings facilitated students to envision a wider array of supports for Moka beyond her release, such as health care, affordable housing, food, and mental health services, students were able to combine a critique of the punitive approaches practised by the state to abolitionist arguments for resource redistribution and community support. The abolitionist framework taught my students to understand Moka's case outside of a law-and-order or punishment lens, which helped students critique a crime-centred approach, whereby the state pushes for legal enforcement (police brutality, arrests, detention, racial profiling), penalties (sentencing, mass incarceration, prison overcrowding), and surveillance in racialized and poor communities. They developed complex analytical skills that allowed them to interrogate the social and material conditions that led to the violent encounter that resulted in Foster's death and Moka's experiences in the carceral system. They also developed a clear understanding of their capacity and power to act as agents of change, following a campaign and witnessing the positive results of collective organizing. This form of community-engaged learning helped students translate concepts into real-world settings and equipped them with tools they can take beyond the classroom.

Abolition Pedagogy

Through the experiential learning component of my class, students came into dialogue with the courts, the carceral system, and community groups to think through possibilities for survival within systems designed to punish, confine, and let die. This way of organizing with my class enabled me to build community with my students, where we became co-learners in the process of advocacy and solidarity, shifting the power dynamics of the classroom. These outcomes illustrate the power of abolition pedagogy. Abolition pedagogy "pursues a transformative orientation to histories of violence, asking how to sustain strategies for their unmaking" (Gillespie and Naidoo 2021, 284). Rather than accepting dominant approaches to justice in the form of policing and punishment as a mode for responding to social antagonism and conflict, abolition introduces reparative approaches to violence and harm. Abolition pedagogy, as a theoretical field and approach to community-engaged learning, enables students to deepen their understanding of harm, including its social, systemic, and interpersonal causes, and envision responses in conjunction with restorative justice practices, which provide models for accountability and healing from violence. To illustrate these differences, we can look at Moka's case once again.

The carceral justice approach taken by the police and the courts placed Moka in a men's prison, where she suffered gender-based violence; a restorative justice approach would aim to understand the causes of how and why Moka killed someone in self-defence and understand justice beyond the act that led to Foster's death—the wider conditions of economic, social, and structural relations that shaped her experiences. In the carceral model, the prison became another scene of gender-based violence, where Moka was doubly punished when she was placed in solitary confinement as a response to her victimization by homophobic, misogynistic, and racist violence. A restorative justice approach would prioritize breaking the cycle of violence by ensuring support for Moka over the logistic management of her imprisonment through solitary confinement. Abolition pedagogy, as a framework for both teaching and learning, enabled me to provide students with important conceptual and analytic tools "to stage a query about how to live amidst the repertoires of violence that we have inherited" (Gillespie and Naidoo 2021, 288).

Abolition pedagogy requires students to pursue lines of inquiry that push them to think critically about histories of violence. Creating opportunities for students to partake in community-engaged learning by working alongside a community organization opened up new modes of study that do not restrict learning to the classroom. By having to think and work with an incarcerated person during an ongoing criminal case, students were provided a rich learning opportunity that connected classroom readings and discussion to local community groups organizing and to the broader world that shapes people's experiences of violence in material ways. Violence was not just an abstract concept to connect to course readings and theories, and the experiences of prisoners, like Moka, were not simply "learning opportunities." Rather, these became moments of collaboration, solidarity, and empowerment for everyone involved. Providing students with the analytical tools and training to work with a community organization can be a radical act by reframing experiential learning from the workplace into the social and political world outside of school. As Kelly Gillespie and Leigh-Ann Naidoo suggest, "abolition pedagogy requires a radical re-envisioning of education—as institution, as curriculum, as critical disposition, and as pedagogy—to meet the historical demands of an exit from colonial and apartheid histories and their long legacies of violence" (2021, 288). Starting with the class structure and assignments is one way to re-envision the role of education: to not simply learn about injustice but to learn how to collaborate with others to help effect change. Collective praxis disrupts the colonial model of education, which aims to discipline students through the passive accumulation of knowledge, and instead shows students how the practice of working collectively and in collaboration can be itself a method for learning. As Gillespie and Naidoo remind us,

> Abolition pedagogy means, in our multiple modes and spaces of study, the building of force fields through which to reckon with that history [of violence] and its mess in the present; it means holding space for intensity, allowing intensity to build without fear—or understanding our fears readying our own subjectivities for different worlds, and surely for the many scary moments in the coming time. The best we can do is to sit with the mess, knowing that our own understandings and subjectivities have been created by it, making them inadequate but nonetheless all we have to work with in crafting alternatives together. (307)

For critical educators wanting to transform the classroom, an abolitionist pedagogical framework begins with building "on the creativity, imagination, boldness, ingenuity, and rebellious spirit and methods of abolitionists to demand and fight for an educational system where all students are thriving, not simply surviving" (Love and Muhammad 2020, 695). An abolitionist framework requires educators to resist punitive practices, such as calling campus police/security or kicking students out from a classroom space when misconduct takes place. Abolition pedagogy also requires educators to resist punitive measures of assessment, such as punishing students for late work when they have reasonable reasons for requesting extensions; reporting improper citational practices as plagiarism, rather than working with students to learn citation conventions; or disciplining students for discussing non-dominant perspectives in the classroom (e.g., when students are called anti-Semitic for discussing Palestine). Those who want to practice abolition pedagogy need to consider what others ways they can address harm or misconduct enacted in the classroom. For instance, are there accountability approaches that can be adopted in the classroom, rather than punitive disciplinary tactics that punish students? Moreover, abolitionist pedagogy invites faculty to be in dialogue with students about the curriculum, assignments, and feedback on the course structure, which makes room for greater access and adaptation to the needs of the students in the class. Abolition pedagogy also invites educators to get to know student experiences of racism, sexism, ableism, and other oppressions, to help create classroom spaces where marginalized students can share their perspectives. Across disciplines, educators can commit to "teach to transgress" racial and class boundaries, as bell hooks (1994) advised, in order to pursue education that is life-sustaining, joyful, and imaginative. Abolition pedagogy is ultimately about awakening what Paulo Freire ([1970] 2005) called critical consciousness (*conscientização*) and liberation. For this, educators must create radical spaces for rigorous study linked to struggle from a place of love, which can empower students to make social change and restore their and our collective humanity.

References

Bassichis, Morgan, Alexander Lee, and Dean Spade. 2015. "Building an Abolitionist Trans and Queer Movement with Everything We've Got." In *Captive Genders: Trans Embodiment and the Prison Industrial Complex*, rev. ed., edited by Eric A. Stanley and Nat Smith, 21–46. Oakland, CA: AK Press.

Ben-Moshe, Liat. 2018. "Dis-epistemologies of Abolition." *Critical Criminology* 26 (3): 341–55. https://doi.org/10.1007/s10612-018-9403-1.

Berger, Dan, Mariame Kaba, and David Stein. 2017. "What Abolitionists Do." *Jacobin*, August 24, 2017. https://jacobin.com/2017/08/prison-abolition-reform-mass-incarceration.

Critical Resistance. n.d. "The Prison Industrial Complex." Accessed April 14, 2024. https://criticalresistance.org/mission-vision/not-so-common-language/.

D'Amore, Rachel. 2020. "She Spent 4 Years in a Men's Prison – How Canada Often Ignores Complexities in Trans Violence." *Global News*, February 17, 2020. https://globalnews.ca/news/6272571/gender-based-violence-trans/.

Davis, Angela Y. 2003. *Are Prisons Obsolete?* New York: Seven Stories Press.

—— 2020. "On the Role of the Trans and Non-binary Communities." Facebook, video, July 17, 2020. https://www.facebook.com/DarkEntriesRecords/videos/dr-angela-davis-on-the-non-binary-community/4049025058500829/.

Felber, Garrett. 2020. "The Struggle to Abolish the Police Is Not New." *Boston Review*, June 9, 2020. https://bostonreview.net/articles/garrett-felber-police-abolition-not-new/.

Freire, Paulo. (1970) 2005. *Pedagogy of the Oppressed*. New York: Continuum Press.

Gilmore, Ruth Wilson. 2015. "Organized Abandonment and Organized Violence: Devolution and the Police." Humanities Institute at UCSD. Vimeo, video, November 11, 2015. https://vimeo.com/146450686.

—— 2017. "Abolition Geography and the Problem of Innocence." In *Futures of Black Radicalism*, edited by Gaye Theresa Johnson and Alex Lubin, 225–40. London: Verso Books.

—— 2022. *Change Everything: Racial Capitalism and the Case for Abolition*. Chicago: Haymarket Books.

Gillespie, Kelly, and Leigh-Ann Naidoo. 2021. "Abolition Pedagogy: Force Fields of Critique." *Critical Times* 4 (2): 284–312. https://doi.org/10.1215/26410478-9093094.

Harney, Stefano, and Fred Moten. 2013. *The Undercommons: Fugitive Planning and Black Study*. Brooklyn, NY: Minor Compositions.

hooks, bell. 1994. *Teaching to Transgress: Education as the Practice of Freedom*. New York: Routledge.

Kaba, Mariame. 2021. *We Do This 'til We Free Us: Abolitionist Organizing and Transforming Justice*. Chicago: Haymarket Books.

Kelley, Robin. D.G. 2016. "Black Study, Black Struggle." *Boston Review*, March 1, 2016. https://www.bostonreview.net/forum/robin-kelley-black-struggle-campus-protest/.

Lourenco, Denio. 2018. "Trans Sex Worker on Trial for Murder: 'I Thought He Was Going to Kill Me.'" *Toronto Star*, October 16, 2018. https://www.vice.com/en/article/wj9kyy/trans-sex-worker-on-trial-for-murder-i-thought-he-was-going-to-kill-me.

Love, Bettina. 2019. *We Want to Do More Than Survive: Abolitionist Teaching and the Pursuit of Educational Freedom*. Boston: Beacon Press.

Love, Bettina L., and Gholnecsar E. Muhammad. 2020. "What Do We Have to Lose: Toward Disruption, Agitation, and Abolition in Black Education." *International Journal of Qualitative Studies in Education* 33 (7): 695–97. https://doi.org/10.1080/09518398.2020.1753257.

Maynard, Robyn. 2017. *Policing Black Lives: State Violence in Canada From Slavery to the Present*. Halifax: Fernwood Publishing.

Meiners, Erica R. 2011. "Ending the School-to-Prison Pipeline / Building Abolition Futures." *The Urban Review* 43 (4): 547–65. https://doi.org/10.1007/s11256-011-0187-9.

———. 2016. *For the Children? Protecting Innocence in a Carceral State*. Minneapolis: University of Minnesota Press.

Powell, Betsy. 2018. "Judge Grants Killer Enhanced Credit for Time Served as Transgender Women in All-Male Toronto Jail." *Toronto Star*, November 7, 2018. https://www.thestar.com/news/gta/2018/11/06/judge-grants-convicted-killer-credit-for-time-served-as-transgender-women-in-all-male-toronto-jail.html.

Razack, Sherene H. 2015. *Dying from Improvement: Inquests and Inquiries into Indigenous Deaths in Custody*. Toronto: University of Toronto Press.

Richie, Beth. 2012. *Arrested Justice: Black Women, Violence, and America's Prison Nation*. New York: NYU Press.

Rodríguez, Dylan. 2019. "Abolition as Praxis of Human Being: A Foreword." *Harvard Law Review* 132 (6): 1575–1613. https://harvardlawreview.org/print/vol-132/abolition-as-praxis-of-human-being-a-foreword/.

Stovall, David. 2018. "Are We Ready for 'School' Abolition?: Thoughts and Practices of Radical Imaginary in Education." *Taboo: The Journal of Culture and Education* 17 (1): 51–61. https://doi.org/10.31390/taboo.17.1.06.

Sudbury, Julia. 2009. "Maroon Abolitionists: Black Gender-Oppressed Activists in the Anti-Prison Movement in the U.S. and Canada." *Meridians* 9 (1): 1–29. https://www.jstor.org/stable/40338764.

Walia, Harsha. 2021. *Border and Rule: Global Migration, Capitalism, and the Rise of Racist Nationalism*. Chicago: Haymarket Books.

19

Regional Perspectives on Gender and Sexuality in the Classroom

A Roundtable

CAROL LYNNE D'ARCANGELIS, MYLÈNE YANNICK GAMACHE, NICHOLAS HRYNYK, AND SUZANNE LENON

Natalie Kouri-Towe: As faculty teaching in institutions based in British Columbia, Alberta, Manitoba, and Newfoundland, many of you have thought carefully about your roles as teachers, not only in relation to gender and sexuality studies but also as a political relationship between embodiment, politics, and education. The regional contexts shaped by local communities, including Indigenous communities that some of you belong to or are in solidarity with, anchor many of your approaches to teaching. Can you share some of your thoughts about your current role, relationship to communities, and how you're situated? What got you to this point, what drove you to the work you're doing, and why is this work important where you are?

Mylène Yannick Gamache: As an urban Franco-Métis assistant professor based in Winnipeg, I am home, teaching in the same classrooms I sat in as an undergrad. I like to imagine this was somehow willed into actuality by my revered mother and made possible by the loving guidance of adored relatives, friends, peers, colleagues, teachers. I've been preoccupied lately with the idea that subtle everyday acts of disobedience (Anderson 2021; Voth 2020a), which animate(d) our ancestors' livelihoods, live on in us; a trans-temporal procession which continues to ignite our perspectives, our values, even our (in)actions. Since January 2023, I have been slowly reading journals written by my maternal grandmother, Lucile, at ages fourteen to twenty-one while living on the Beauchemin family farm in Île-des-Chênes (a township located south of Winnipeg), and later, at ages thirty-two to thirty-five, while married to Oswald Carrière and raising a family in the historic Rat River settlement near the perimeter of St-Pierre-Jolys, Manitoba. Throughout my grandmother's journals, glimmers of her fiery indignation can be felt. In my contribution to editors Aubrey Hanson and Celiese Lypka's forthcoming *Métis Voices* anthology (University of Manitoba Press), I write, near the end, with immense caution and care, about her hardened refusal to adapt to heteropatriarchal authority in her own marriage. I mention this briefly here in an effort to retrace the tenor of certain felt immediacies and tendencies shared by cousins and aunts, which my mother, Paulette, refracted and reflected in her own lived engagements, and which my sister and I now also mirror in ours; not simply in our work (as a midwife, in my sister's case, living and working on Mi'kma'ki lands, or in the pedagogical approaches I assume living and working on shared Saulteaux, Cree, Nakoda, Dakota, and Métis homescapes) but in our everyday inclinations and commitments. My fiery interest in gender and sexuality studies is informed by my grandmother and mother and the constellated beings who informed them both.

Suzanne Lenon: I am currently Professor cross-listed between the departments of Women and Gender Studies and Sociology at the University of Lethbridge, Alberta. My research is in the field of law, gender, and sexuality, and is theoretically informed by queer theory and critical race feminisms. I teach women and gender studies undergraduate courses as well as a graduate queer theory course in my university's interdisciplinary social sciences and humanities graduate program. I came to graduate education and particularly my doctoral studies somewhat later than many of my peers and colleagues. I took many years off in between completion of my undergraduate degree and my master's, and between my MA and doctoral studies. In these intervals, I worked in various non-profit organizations doing anti-poverty/economic justice research, public education for a women's addiction centre, and public education and crisis counselling at a rape crisis centre. These were tremendously formative periods in my life and to my commitments to the study of law, gender, and sexuality. Three key moments in the early 2000s stand out in particular: the legalization of same-sex marriage in Ontario and wondering what was at stake in such a significant legal victory; Kimberly Nixon's human rights complaint filed against Vancouver Rape Relief, the difficult discussions about gender at the rape crisis centre at which I was working, and what struck me as a doubling-down on biological essentialism; and reading Sherene Razack's (1998) *Looking White People in the Eye: Gender, Race, and Culture in Courtrooms and Classrooms*. This book's theorization of complicity and accountability provided me with language to begin to grapple with the gender, sexual, and racial politics of these two human rights cases. These three moments were part and parcel of the decision to pursue more formalized (doctoral) studies. My teaching and research are underpinned by commitments to racial and social justice, to what Katherine McKittrick names as "the difficult labor of thinking the world anew" (2015, 6–7).

Nicholas Hrynyk: I am an assistant teaching professor in history. I specialize in Canadian history, specifically histories of gender and sexuality. My interest in Canadian histories of gender and sexuality were largely shaped by my own position as a white, cis-gay man. Being cognizant of the sexual politics in queer communities, I sought to understand how contemporary issues of inclusion, diversity, acceptance, and desire came to be, and how they were (re)shaped over the twentieth century. In many ways, my research is an effort to understand the history behind my own experiences of navigating the racial, sexual, gendered, and ableist politics of representation and desire in queer communities. Teaching gender and sexuality in British Columbia's interior is, first and foremost, a rewarding experience because I am providing students with the opportunity to better explore and understand the complexities of the world around them. Most of my students grew up in smaller communities in British Columbia or the western provinces, many of which lack resources, information, and support systems related to gender and/or sexual identity. The challenge is that students may not possess the familiarity with or exposure to non-heteronormative, cisgender ideas of gender or sexuality compared to those who were raised in larger cities. However, this same lack of information has made my students particularly curious and hungry for knowledges in the fields of gender and sexuality studies. Their lack of exposure to theories and concepts in gender and sexuality scholarship is by no means a reflection of academic prowess but rather reflects a marked urban/rural divide that is seemingly bridged at smaller academic institutions (Ardoin 2018). Thus, my teaching of gender and sexuality content becomes part of a broader personal and institutional effort to offer students the opportunity to engage in the same conversations and debates as students who are served in larger cities with more universities that have larger faculty complements.

Carol Lynne D'Arcangelis: After over twenty years of teaching—first in Toronto and now in St. John's—I am interested in those "ah-ha" moments when a sudden clarity punctures my taken-for-granted assumptions about the world, or the assumptions of my students. These moments are rare, and cultivating them, a fine art. I'd like to reflect on some of my ah-ha experiences as a white settler feminist woman teaching Indigenous feminisms to a primarily white classroom in the province of Newfoundland and Labrador. In short, I explore how these place-based experiences have precipitated (and continue to precipitate) changes in my pedagogy. Several theoretical framings have guided my process, in particular, Eve Tuck (Unangax̂) and K. Wayne Yang's (2014) insights into "pedagogies of refusal" and "colonial inquiry as invasion," and Katherine Morton's (2022) use of Jack Halberstam's (2011) concept of failure in relation to settler scholar decision-making. The latter I apply while mindful of the need to problematize any such public "admissions of failure" (D'Arcangelis, 2018, 2022).

While I suspect there is some universality to the challenges noted below, there are also particularities related to the Newfoundland and Labrador context illustrated by the sedimentation of a general lack of knowledge on the part of the non-Indigenous population about the Inuit, Innu, and Mi'kmaq nations of the province. Of course, Indigenous-led organizations such as First Light: St. John's Friendship Centre, Labrador Friendship Centre, Aboriginal Women's Action Network, and Mokami Status of Women Council have pushed back against state-sanctioned invisibility. Moreover, as the sole university in the province, Memorial University has recently adopted an Indigenization strategy that included hiring a slate of Indigenous scholars. Nonetheless, the Office of Indigenous Affairs, the entity mandated with implementing the strategy, remains understaffed and overworked. Enter yours truly, a gender studies professor committed to dismantling settler colonialism, decentring whiteness, and centring Indigenous resistance and resurgence in and beyond the classroom. What has it meant to teach Indigenous feminist theory and practice as a white woman in this setting? In my experience, the most profound challenge has been to mitigate the non-Indigenous tendency—my own included—to reproduce notions of Indigenous dysfunction or trauma that saturate Canadian settler-colonial society writ large.

SL: Many of the undergraduate students at the University of Lethbridge come from small, rural communities in the area—Lethbridge *is* the "big city," even with a population of just over 106,000. Situated on the homeland of the Kainai (Blackfoot Confederacy) and in Treaty 7, Lethbridge is the region's commercial and health care hub, a region known for its fierce winds and social and religious conservatism. The most obvious challenge to teaching gender and sexuality in my region is this: the province of Alberta, as a settler-state form, has long worked to implement punitive laws explicitly targeting LGBTQ+ people, to resist the inclusion of queer citizenship claims, and to imagine Alberta—in the words of former premier Ralph Klein—"as the province of the severely normal." Indeed, at the United Conservative Party's policy convention in October 2022, party members overwhelmingly passed an anti-trans resolution that upholds parental rights to not "require them to affirm or socially condition a child in gender identity that is incongruent with the child's birth sex" (2022, 8). In the 2023 provincial election, an initial United Conservative Party nominee for the riding of Lethbridge-West posted a video claiming teachers are exposing children to pornography and gender reassignment with no parental consent or knowledge. In July 2023 at the Calgary Stampede, Premier Danielle Smith posed for a photograph with a man in a "Straight Pride" t-shirt. Things have not and do not bode well for racialized/trans/queer folks in this province. The interconnected "atmospheres" (Sharpe 2016; Stanley 2021) of white supremacy, heteronormativity, and trans-antagonism in this province are palpable. These bear upon the gender and sexuality classroom in a myriad of ways. This includes (but is certainly not limited to) resistance to material being taught through to the disclosures by students who have been kicked out of their (often Mormon) faith and/or family because they are queer through to the chronic under-resourcing of women and gender studies as a department. And yet, there have long been queer counter-publics in the province. Queer life, queer love, queer kinship, queer communities, queer resistances are *also* palpable, including in Lethbridge as a city and on campus. At the risk of sounding cliché, teaching gender and sexuality in southern Alberta is as much a political act and commitment to socialities queerly lived, queerly felt, queerly desired here in this place as it is an intellectual commitment (yet in the aftermath of the 2023 stabbing at the University of Waterloo, I will admit both a deepened resolve and a heightened anxiety about this claim). In other words, what is important to me in the teaching of gender and sexuality here, in this time and place, is the urgency to "tackle the conditions and the terms under which we might come to live differently, together" (Walcott 2019, 394).

NKT: You all speak so thoughtfully about your relationship to teaching. Can you share more about what gives meaning or value to your pedagogical approaches? Have there been emergences or encounters in the classroom that have shaped how you view teaching? Have you changed something about your teaching over time?

NH: My pedagogical approach is entirely student-centred and informed by my own personal activism. I seek to upset neocolonial, neoliberal ideas of excellence and classroom structure. Teaching means providing students with the opportunity to understand, challenge, and forge new intellectual pathways that might contribute to a more equitable and just future. I place the greatest value in having students apply their education to the world around them and bring the classroom to the community. In some of my classes, I have students engage with community organizations and apply many of the core principles and ideas they learn in class. This not only destabilizes the meaning of what a "classroom" is but provides students with the opportunity to turn praxis into action and directly benefit their communities. With respect to teaching in history, I heed the directive of Christopher Martell and Kaylene Stevens (2021) to have students connect historical notions of gender and sexuality with contemporary issues.

Teaching in Kamloops has taught me that courses in gender and sexuality studies are arguably more important than ever because they expose students to important ideas and concepts. Many students have not had the opportunity to encounter concepts or ideas presented in gender and/or sexuality courses, thereby marking their importance moreover. These courses provide students with feminist, queer, critical race, and disability/crip tools to help them navigate the world around them. Additionally, teaching these courses has taught me that gender and sexuality pedagogy begins with an activist mindset.

SL: There have been two teaching encounters, broadly defined, that have significantly shaped my teaching over the last decade and a half. First, there are an increasing number of under/graduate students enrolled in my classes who self-identify as trans, non-binary, and/or genderqueer. As I mentioned in my previous answer, many of these students disclose experiences of trans-antagonism by family and kin, and on my university campus. However, they have also generously, if not fiercely, pushed me to think in much more nuanced ways about gender as a social category that distributes vulnerability and security (Spade 2015). Many of these students bring a sharp critique to the biological determinism that continues to underpin women's and gender studies, and sociology. They have brought a sharp critique to assigned readings. They pose meaningful provocations in the classroom often from their lived experiences in an often-times hostile prairie city. I am trying to be accountable to these critiques by reworking course content and classroom practices, and by developing an educational resource for "teaching beyond the gender binary" for my colleagues across campus. The second teaching encounter is perhaps more regionally specific in that the Blackfoot students I have taught (and teach) call me to be accountable to the quality of materials about Indigenous women's lives and struggles I include on course syllabi. In the first few years of teaching here, Indigenous women only showed up in a course syllabus as either victims of violence or as dead, through emphasis on the issue of Missing and Murdered Indigenous Women and Girls. One student said to me, "Suzanne, I came to these readings with a broken heart"; another said, "but, Suzanne, I am here, I am healthy, I am alive, my family is alive!" My pedagogy now foregrounds issues of land, resource extraction, activisms, and settler complicity as frames to think through gendered racial violence. In short, it is precisely these encounters with and challenges by students in the specificity of this place that imbue meaning into my teaching.

CLDA: I am indebted to an Indigenous student for jolting me into awareness—the very first time I taught a course on Indigenous feminisms—of the tendency to reproduce certain stereotypical depictions of Indigenous Peoples in the classroom. This student experienced the course as relying too heavily on portrayals of Indigenous people in despair and as defeated by settler colonialism. Taking her point to heart, I have become better, though imperfect, at conveying the severity of settler-colonial impacts without completing capitulating to "damage-centered studies, rescue research, and pain tourism" (Tuck and Yang 2014, 812). More recently, I have taken cues from the National Inquiry into Missing and Murdered Indigenous Women and Girls (2019) to encourage Indigenous and non-Indigenous students alike to focus on a structural analysis of settler-colonial power, including how they are located vis-à-vis this power. The second biggest challenge I have faced has been to avoid facilitating white saviourism—another work in progress made urgent given the recent hearings in Newfoundland and Labrador about Innu children in the child welfare system. Here I nudge students to think through Leanne Betasamosake Simpson's (Michi Saagiig Nishnaabeg) (2017) critique of the helping imperative, by asking several questions in succession: Why does Simpson insist that Indigenous Peoples "do not need the help of Canadians. We need Canadians to help themselves" (101)? How does Simpson clarify Tuck and Yang's (2014) appraisal of damage narratives?

Relatedly, I like to complicate solidarity, which requires transparency about my own mistakes and limitations in allyship. While eager to invite Indigenous feminists and other local Indigenous community members into the classroom, I learned the hard way that assisting *me* is not and should not be their priority, especially when this labour is uncompensated. One approach I have taken instead is to bring students to events in the broader community. Perhaps the most memorable class trip was to the 2018 hearing in St. John's of the above-mentioned National Inquiry. When funds are available, I organize guest lectures and public talks with Indigenous scholars, activists, and artists from Newfoundland and Labrador and elsewhere, including Barbara Barker (Mi'kmaw), Michelle Sylliboy (Mi'kmaw), Kim TallBear (Sisseton-Wahpeton Oyate), and Alex Wilson (Cree), to name a few. These speakers have helped my students understand different Indigenous experiences and realities beyond the classroom material, as well as helped raise the profile of these scholars, activists, and artists in the province more broadly.

NKT: Many of you have shared your reflections on the role of the relationships you build with your students and local communities. This orientation towards bridging the classroom and the world, bridging students as learners and as teachers themselves, is perhaps one of the most common themes in gender and sexuality pedagogy. That what happens in the classroom is about more than just classroom learning. What are some lessons you've taken away from your teaching, and what would you want colleagues outside of gender and sexuality studies to know about the perspectives and approaches you use?

MYG: While I teach primarily courses in Indigenous women's literatures and Indigenous feminisms, I wish to share a few notes about the anticipatory challenge of teaching a survey course on Indigenous Peoples "within" Canada (Gaudry 2016, 48) with two hundred registered students. My pedagogical approach in this course is partly informed by Gina Starblanket and Heidi Kiiwetinepinesiik Stark's relational approach to gender, with their emphasis on its "social and cultural productions [as] shaped in relation to colonial and decolonial projects" (2018, 188), and by Nicki Ferland's work on land-based education, which works to uncover and elevate Métis women and Two-Spirit people's embodied relations to Winnipeg (2022, 35). As Starblanket and Stark explain, "Discourses of land that essentialize our relationships as fixed in some pre-contact context risk eliding the ways in which grammars of race, class, gender, sexuality, and sovereignty operate at the local, regional, and global levels to produce the settler state. One way we can combat this is by being attentive to how place matters" (2018, 190). For Starblanket and Stark, such critical reflexivity requires "understanding ourselves in relationship to the place we are" in ways that story our relations to one another, including more-than-human kin and our movements across territories (190).

Early encounters with local and non-local Indigenous Creation stories in the course are situated in relation to Vanessa Watts's Haudenosaunee and Anishinaabe analysis of Indigenous Place-Thought, where Land is embodied as "alive and thinking and [where] humans and non-humans derive agency through the extensions of these thoughts" (2013, 21). Place-Thought "rises," according to Dian Million's reading, "from ancient knowledge that rarely agrees with Western assumptions about the world, whether about sex, gender, or what matter is" (2017, 96), thus reflecting an understanding of matter as susceptible to change and a consideration of gender as relational rather than fixed (100). While this course involves engaging thematically and historically with Indigenous places, agents, and communities in ways that emphasize complexity, relationality, and plurality, part of the work also involves presencing urban cities as Indigenous Lands, and more specifically, Winnipeg, then, as "an enduring Indigenous population centre" (Voth 2020b, 95) "that has and still does exist first and foremost in relationship to Indigenous people" (Styres 2019, 28). While this work requires nuancing both the overlapping and discerning ways in which the study of gender and sexuality is lived and conceptualized from place-specific Indigenous perspectives, another challenge involves presencing women, trans, queer, and non-binary community members in ways that importantly refuse "The Great [Indigenous] Men of History" narratives that dominate the nineteenth-

and twentieth-century historiographic record (Parent quoted in Swain 2018, 3, 8).

To colleagues interested in regional gender and sexuality studies, I invite them first to seek out "an understanding of the [local Indigenous] stories and knowledges embedded in those lands…not the least of which is an acknowledgment of the ways [they themselves are] implicated in the networks and relations of power that comprise the tangled colonial history of the lands [they are] upon" (Styres 2019, 29). I recommend heeding the shared cautionary note, as issued by many Indigenous gender and sexuality studies scholars, against generalized references to Indigenous "culture" or "tradition," given that both terms are all too often deployed in ways which sustain homogeneity, systemic hierarchy, and gendered harm (Coburn and LaRocque 2020, 108; Pyle 2020, 112–16; Snyder, Napoleon, and Borrows 2015, 595; Starblanket 2017, 27–28). I invite colleagues to grapple with Emily Snyder, Val Napoleon, and John Borrows's Indigenous feminist legal methodology, their analyses of stories as conveyors of Indigenous legal principles (2015, 595–600), their important warnings against any tendency to generalize the pre-colonial past (607), nor to necessarily romanticize Indigenous Peoples as non-sexist (594) or "gender fluid" (Coburn and LaRocque 2020, 112; Towle and Morgan 2002), and their insistence on challenging the idea that gendered violence within Indigenous communities simply did not exist pre-contact (Snyder, Napoleon, and Borrows 2015, 596). While Million writes that Indigenous Creation stories "center on relations among different entities and their responsibilities rather than on their identities, such as gender identities" (2017, 99), Snyder, Napoleon, and Borrows conversely insist that "while there are some limited oral traditions and written accounts that describe how historic Indigenous societies did not deploy power in ways that were damaging to gendered relations, there are also extensive contrary oral and written sources" (2015, 609).

Lastly, I invite colleagues to "see the global within the local" (Blackhawk 2013, 31)—that is, to understand the structural and individual dimensions of racial capitalism, imperialism, and settler colonialism and its cascading effects on Indigenous political formations, and to strive to understand Indigenous Peoples as themselves actors who, at once, "adapted to the challenges of colonialism's onslaught by drawing upon familiar as well as new logics" and who "powerfully shaped the emergent colonial sphere as well as maintained forms of authority, knowledge, and sociality throughout the colonial era" (34).

CLDA: I grapple with the ever-present challenge of how to avert promoting what Emma LaRocque (2010) refers to as the "lumping effect" or the homogenization of diverse Indigenous nations. In hindsight, this risk should have been obvious from the start, but eight years later, I still search for strategies that might disrupt this phenomenon—reinforced by the very settler–Indigenous dichotomy that is at once necessary and problematic. What I have decided on for the next version of the Indigenous feminisms course that I teach is to pointedly identify the specific provenance of every author we read, be they Indigenous or non-Indigenous. Similarly, I have belatedly come to understand the critical importance of incorporating local scholars, who are Inuk, Innu, or Mi'kmaw, into the syllabus. Foregrounding how the syllabus can be a way of building accountability at the local level into my teaching, I see this as a viable alternative to relying on the labour of over-solicited Indigenous community members.

I tell my students, if I were an Indigenous professor, Indigenous Feminisms in Theory and Practice would be a very different course. As a white settler woman, I often ask myself, should I even be teaching this course? My goal as a teacher is not to be the gatekeeper or bearer of knowledge of Indigenous feminisms for my students, but to invite them to join me in centring Indigenous knowledge, history, theories, culture, activism, stories, and voices in a context where Indigenous Peoples have been historically excluded. Doing this work in a predominantly white classroom is part of my approach to being accountable to the work of Indigenous feminists.

NH: I would like my colleagues to understand that gender and sexuality studies plays an integral role in providing students with a holistic post-secondary education. The world is a complex place, and many students growing up or studying at institutions outside of major cities must be provided with the same type of comprehensive education as those who study in cities such as Toronto, Vancouver, or Montréal. Gender and sexuality studies at regional schools also serves a secondary purpose of community building and fostering activism among the student body. Part of what makes teaching gender and sexuality studies outside of major metropolitan areas so exciting is that students come to these courses with unique perspectives that enable them to understand, apply, and disseminate core ideas and concepts learned in class back in their home communities. In doing so, students become leaders for equity and justice in towns and cities, big and small.

References

Anderson, Kim. 2021. "Multi-Generational Indigenous Feminisms: From F Word to What IFs." In *Routledge Handbook of Critical Indigenous Studies*, edited by Brendan Hokowhitu, Aileen Moreton-Robinson, Linda Tuhiwai-Smith, Chris Andersen, and Steve Larkin, 37–51. New York: Routledge.

Ardoin, Sonja. 2018. *College Aspirations and Access in Working-Class Rural Communities: The Mixed Signals, Challenges, and New Language First-Generation Students Encounter*. Lanham, MD: Lexington Books.

Blackhawk, Ned. 2013. "Teaching the Columbian Exchange." *OAH Magazine of History* 27 (4): 31–34. https://doi.org/10.1093/oahmag/oat033.

Coburn, Elaine, and Emma LaRocque. 2020. "Gender and Sexuality: Indigenous Feminist Perspectives." In *The Palgrave Handbook of Gender, Sexuality and Canadian Politics,* edited by Manon Tremblay and Joanna Everitt, 101–19. Cham: Palgrave Macmillan.

D'Arcangelis, Carol Lynne. 2018. "Revelations of a White Woman Settler-Activist: The Fraught Promise of Solidarity." *Cultural Studies ↔ Critical Methodologies* 18 (5): 339–53. https://doi.org/10.1177/1532708617750675.

—2022. *The Solidarity Encounter: Women, Activism, and Creating Non-colonizing Relations*. Vancouver: UBC Press.

Ferland, Nicki. 2022. "'We're Still Here': Teaching and Learning about Métis Women's Two-Spirit People's Relationships with Land in Winnipeg." MEd thesis, University of Saskatchewan.

Filax, Gloria. 2006. *Queer Youth in the Province of the "Severely Normal."* Vancouver: UBC Press.

Gaudry, Adam. 2016. "Fantasies of Sovereignty: Deconstructing British and Canadian Claims to Ownership of the Historic North-West." *Native American and Indigenous Studies* 3 (1): 46–74. https://doi.org/10.1353/nai.2016.a635763.

Halberstam, Jack. 2011. *The Queer Art of Failure.* Durham, NC: Duke University Press.

LaRocque, Emma. 2010. *When the Other Is Me: Native Resistance Discourse, 1850–1990.* Winnipeg: University of Manitoba Press.

Martell, Christopher C., and Kaylene M. Stevens. 2021. *Teaching History for Justice: Centering Activism in Students' Study of the Past.* New York: Teachers College Press.

McKittrick, Katherine. 2015. "Axis, Bold as Love: On Sylvia Wynter, Jimi Hendrix, and the Promise of Science." In *Sylvia Wynter: On Being Human as Praxis,* edited by Katherine McKittrick, 142–63. Durham, NC: Duke University Press. https://doi.org/10.2307/j.ctv11cworj.9.

Million, Dian. 2017. "Indigenous Matters." In *Gender: Matter,* edited by Stacey Alaimo, 95–110. New York: Macmillan.

Morton, Katherine. 2022. "Unsettled Grounds: Settler Colonialism, Discourses of Violence, and the Limitations of Settler Research." PhD diss., Memorial University of Newfoundland.

National Inquiry into Missing and Murdered Indigenous Women and Girls. 2019. *Reclaiming Power and Place: Executive Summary of the Final Report.* Ottawa: National Inquiry into Missing and Murdered Indigenous Women and Girls. https://www.mmiwg-ffada.ca/wp-content/uploads/2019/06/Executive_Summary.pdf.

Pyle, Kai. 2020. "Reclaiming Traditional Gender Roles: A Two-Spirit Critique." In *In Good Relation: History, Gender, and Kinship in Indigenous Feminisms,* edited by Sarah Nickel and Amanda Fehr, 109–22. Winnipeg: University of Manitoba Press.

Razack, Sherene. 1998. *Looking White People in the Eye: Gender, Race, and Culture in Courtrooms and Classrooms.* Toronto: University of Toronto Press.

Sharpe, Christina. 2016. *In the Wake: On Blackness and Being.* Durham, NC: Duke University Press.

Simpson, Leanne Betasamosake. 2017. *As We Have Always Done: Indigenous Freedom through Radical Resistance.* Minneapolis: University of Minnesota Press.

Snyder, Emily, Val Napoleon, and John Borrows. 2015. "Gender and Violence: Drawing on Indigenous Legal Resources." *UBC Law Review* 48 (2): 593–654. https://commons.allard.ubc.ca/ubclawreview/vol48/iss2/9.

Spade, Dean. 2015. *Normal Life: Administrative Violence, Critical Trans Politics and the Limits of Law.* Durham, NC: Duke University Press.

Stanley, Eric A. 2021. *Atmospheres of Violence: Structuring Antagonism and the Trans/Queer Ungovernable.* Durham, NC: Duke University Press.

Starblanket, Gina. 2017. "Being Indigenous Feminists: Resurgences against Contemporary Patriarchy." In *Making Space for Indigenous Feminism*, edited by Joyce Green, 22–41. Halifax: Fernwood Press.

Starblanket, Gina, and Heidi Kiiwetinepinesiik Stark. 2018. "Towards a Relational Paradigm – Four Points for Consideration: Knowledge, Gender, Land, and Modernity." In *Resurgence and Reconciliation: Indigenous-Settler Relations and Earth Teachings,* edited by Michael Asch, James Tully, and John Borrows, 175–207. Toronto: University of Toronto Press.

Styres, Sandra. 2019. "Literacies of the Land: Decolonizing Narratives, Storying, Literature." In *Indigenous and Decolonizing Studies in Education: Mapping the Long View*, edited by Linda Tuhiwai Smith, Eve Tuck, and K. Wayne Yang, 24–37. New York: Routledge.

Swain, Molly Suzanne. 2018. "Victim of Deceit and Self-Decent: The Role of the State in Undermining Jim Brady's Radical Métis Socialist Politics." MA thesis, University of Alberta.

Towle, Evan B., and Lynn Marie Morgan. 2002. "Romancing the Transgender Native: Rethinking the Use of the 'Third Gender' Concept." *GLQ: A Journal of Lesbian and Gay Studies* 8 (4): 469–97. https://www.muse.jhu.edu/article/12222.

Tuck, Eve, and K. Wayne Yang. 2014. "Unbecoming Claims: Pedagogies of Refusal in Qualitative Research." *Qualitative Inquiry* 20 (6): 811–18. https://doi.org/10.1177/1077800414530265.

United Conservative Party. 2022. *United Conservatives: Alberta Strong & Free.* https://www.unitedconservative.ca/wp-content/uploads/Member-Policy-Declaration-Approved-October-2022.pdf.

Voth, Daniel. 2020a. "'Descendants of the Original Lords of the Soil': Indignation, Disobedience, and Women Who Jig on Sundays." *Native American and Indigenous Studies* 7 (2): 87–113.

——— 2020b. "Invitations from the Land and Waters: Lessons from the Peace of Fort Garry." *Canadian Journal of Urban Research* 29 (1): 87–97. https://www.jstor.org/stable/26929899.

Walcott, Rinaldo. 2019. "The End of Diversity." *Public Culture* 31 (2): 393–408. https://doi.org/10.1215/08992363-7286885.

Watts, Vanessa. 2013. "Indigenous Place-Thought and Agency amongst Humans and Non Humans (First Woman and Sky Woman Go on a European World Tour!)." *Decolonization: Indigeneity, Education and Society* 2 (1): 20–34. https://jps.library.utoronto.ca/index.php/des/article/view/19145.

20

Education for All

Open Access and Community-Based Pedagogy through the Toronto Queer Film Festival

KAMI CHISHOLM

Editor's Note: I was invited to be a keynote speaker at the Toronto Queer Film Festival (TQFF) symposium in 2019. I was already familiar with the festival since my partner had worked there for several years. When I began thinking about contributing authors, I was interested in the important role that community-based and popular education plays in bringing gender and sexuality pedagogies to spaces outside of institutions. I was inspired by the model Kami developed along with the other collective members at the TQFF, so I approached them to contribute to the book. We decided to audio record a conversation between us and then edit the transcript together. The result is a conversation on the importance of democratizing education.

Natalie Kouri-Towe: The Toronto Queer Film Festival (TQFF) is a collective run organization that you launched in 2016 along with a group of other queer artists, activists, and organizers. One of the things that has struck me about TQFF is that it functions beyond a film festival: bridging academic and activist engagement through your annual symposium; providing workshops and training for emerging artists; and even serving as a mutual aid organization. How did the idea for the TQFF come about and develop, and what helped shape your vision of the organization as something more than just a film festival?

Kami Chisholm: TQFF came out of a desire to democratize and collectivize the queer film festival scene, to centre community work, community organizing, and community building. Our first festival was small—just three screenings over three nights at a small space in downtown Toronto. Two nights of short film screenings and then the third night was a feature screening accompanied by shorts along with a panel. And the first feature screening was actually a film that I directed called *Pride Denied: Homonationalism and the Future of Queer Politics*. My desire to start TQFF really came out of two contexts: a response to the digital revolution and a need to be part of a queer filmmaking community that doesn't require high budgets or access to expensive technology. When I first went to film school, the tools for filmmaking weren't widely accessible or available. Digital film and video making comes out of a long and important history of lesbian film and video makers who shot on video because of lack of access to the funds, means, and technology of film production. DIY and underground activist filmmaking went through major changes with the availability and affordability of cell phone cameras and other technologies that became more accessible to the public.

The democratization of technology has happened through access to a cell phone and a computer. Even if people don't have their own smart phones or computers, these technologies are widely available throughout the world through many libraries, community centres, and organizations, like TQFF. It was also important for me to be part of a festival that features and foregrounds the stories that are being told by people in our communities—not just those who have access to wealth and privilege to make high budget films. Art industry professionals and art institutions tend to think of high-budget work versus low-budget work as a matter of quality. The presumption being that having access to a big budget necessarily produces better quality work. This is something that I just flat out disagree with and wish to challenge. TQFF doesn't program low budget just to be more accessible. We program work that we find to be the most interesting: real stories, stories that actually touch on and reflect the experiences of our communities, of the people who are the least powerful, who have the least access to resources, and who are extorted and extracted from on a daily basis. These are the most interesting stories to tell, not because we're trying to paternalistically give voice to the voiceless but because these stories reflect the reality of how queer and trans people live. I'm not interested in the stories we see represented all the time in mainstream festivals, that focus on people with the most privilege and access to resources.

Our organization also comes out of queer traditions and narratives of DIY art making, organizing, and community building. The work we do follows in the traditions of queer activism in the United States, like Queer Nation and the Lesbian Avengers; and globally through queer counter festivals, like Queeruption—a queer DIY series of gatherings that were organized in response to World Pride festivals—and Pervers/cite—a queer counter-Pride festival that happens annually in Montréal. These are all sites of resistance to homonationalism and homonormativity, which have come to shape the cultural spaces of gay and lesbian festivals into neoliberal projects. Coming out of traditions that challenge capitalist, neoliberal, and colonial modes of storytelling and media production, we wanted to create space for the stories in our community that are excluded in mainstream media.

We intentionally built TQFF as a collective: a structure where we each have our own jobs and positions, but all major decisions are made collectively by the entire staff and board, by the entire organization. There's no top-down decision-making regarding our programming, our schedules, even who we invite to join our collective. It is all decided collaboratively. The first TQFF was run with three hundred dollars. Those material conditions affect our communities in terms of who can volunteer, who can participate in organizing, who has the capacity to do organizing work. My priority from the beginning with TQFF was to scale-up the organization and stabilize funding, so that everyone who works with TQFF would be paid a living wage. So, modelling an organization where the labour of people is not dependent on their educational background, or on their professional networks, or their access to opportunities to advance their careers, is important for our collective work. Everyone is being paid fairly, including everyone we work with on contract, every artist whose works we show, and all our collaborations. Our staff are better paid than most film festivals or arts organizations; we pay artists to show their work instead of charging them submission fees. All of that is crucial to TQFF's success, both in terms of the work that we produce as an organization and the work we support through the festival. When your staff is taken care of, when they aren't worried about having to feed themselves, when they're not working five jobs to make ends meet, we can see this in the quality of the curation and production at TQFF. It also matters in terms of inspiring artists and encouraging artists to see their work as having value, and hopefully normalizing and changing industry norms that extract from artists rather than pay them. Across festivals and curatorial and artistic and educational work, everyone needs to be paid well.

Our collective, our staff, and our board are majority artists, which signals how important it is for us to position ourselves as part of the practices around artist-run centres and collectives. TQFF has a double mandate: in addition to our obligation to artists, we also have a deep obligation to our audiences and our community. Given the geopolitical death drive toward ecological devastation and climate destruction, we believe that community power and focus on building local connections to help mutually sustain each other is an essential part of our work. This includes things like supporting local artists by ensuring people have enough food to eat. Even as our festival builds more connections between the local and the global, we try to bring those connections back into our local communities. For us, that means addressing poverty in our queer communities, which is at the centre of how we understand access to our festival. It also means confronting white supremacy and centring the stories of Indigenous people, of people of colour, and disabled people in our programming. We are most interested in the stories created by and for people who have the least access to resources. It's well documented by the social sciences that health, economic, and other outcomes for queer and trans people are disproportionately low.

NKT: What TQFF is doing is not only programming compelling stories from queer and trans filmmakers, but also as you put it, democratizing filmmaking by creating workshop opportunities and spaces for people who don't have backgrounds in filmmaking to develop skills. Can you talk more about the kinds of pedagogical work that TQFF has been building? I'm thinking here about the workshops you run, and the focus on providing resources and skills building for emerging queer filmmakers and members of the community, as well as the role of collective queer DIY structures you talked about above. I'm interested in how pedagogy is not just about official and formal educational institutions, but about knowledge sharing, skill sharing, and providing spaces and opportunities for people to learn.

KC: Helping to provide access to the means of production, and knowledge and skill sharing outside of formal academic context, to me, is vital. As soon as we were able to, we started offering workshops. The first workshops we did were one-day or one-afternoon workshops. But eventually we started applying for grants to help us run our first Indigiqueer filmmaking workshop, which was organized by two Indigenous filmmakers, TJ Cuthand and Fallon Simard, who ran several workshops with us over a three-year period. Those first workshops were exclusively for Indigenous, Indigiqueer, and Two-Spirit identified people. Our goal has always been to help familiarize emerging filmmakers, people who don't have much experience with film but who are interested in learning how to make films and tell their stories. This includes learning the most basic strategies, like when you're shooting on a cell phone, you always want to hold your device to capture the picture in landscape, as well as more advanced techniques. If you're trying to capture anything and you want to be able to use it later, shooting portrait style with your camera positioned vertically does not create very workable images, unless you have a specific artistic vision for deciding to frame it that way. So, it's about teaching people how to use the technology in their pocket, and how to use affordable and easily accessible editing software and apps.

One approach that we take to workshops is that we partner with other organizations. We've partnered with several organizations, including local groups and film and video organizations, like Trinity Square Video, which does workshops, classes, and provides equipment rentals, editing suites, and post-production rentals to the Toronto community. When we partner with them, they provide free access to all their equipment and to their editing suites, both in their offices downtown and remotely through cloud licensing, so if people have access to computers at their home, they can access professional software for free.

Part of the point of our workshops is to teach people the fundamentals of how to plan, how to script, how to edit, how to make use of these technologies, so that even if they don't have access to professional facilities and professional equipment, they can still make use of whatever they have on hand. Empowering people to understand the resources that they have around them is absolutely vital to TQFF's mission. We've also developed more intensive workshops that run over a few weeks and walk participants through the creation of a short film. Then, we screen their works, either at our festival or at special screenings. This is important not only for encouraging artists and getting them comfortable working in a new medium, but also to experience going through the entire process of making a film, having it screened at a festival, and getting paid for it. So, part of our mission is normalizing getting paid for your work, even as a beginner. Unlike most mainstream festivals that charge artists a submission fee, we want to normalize paying artists for their work, to expect payment, and demand more of people who would try to exploit them.

Another big part of the educational work that we're doing, in terms of public pedagogy, is hosting an annual symposium. We've done this now twice, but plan to run the symposium for another two years. We've organized the festival around two components every year. There's the actual film festival itself, which is primarily about the curation of artworks. Then, we hold the symposium, which is a space for academics, media activists, and artists to all come together and talk about the issues that are relevant to queer media production and queer communities today. Our lens is through the media landscape, but we're trying to get at larger issues of activism, community building, and organizing as well. This kind of interdisciplinary work is extremely vital to actually doing the work that our communities and audiences need.

NKT: The way you articulate the transformative role of the work TQFF does, not only for how people learn to make films but also changing the economic and political landscape around festivals, is really interesting. Does the practice of running an artist-run collective festival like TQFF transform and change how you think about queer organizing? What place does this have within the history of queer activism and queer organizing more broadly?

KC: I come from a generation when queer film festivals first emerged. Because of this, I'm very attached to the experiences I had at queer film festivals when I was younger. When I was in grad school, the Frameline Film Festival in San Francisco was everything to me. Every year, all my friends and I would go to the festival. We would sit in the theatre almost all day. It was where we met other artists, it was where we hung out as critics and scholars, it was where we met up with and hung out with friends in our community. It was a community event. Queer film festivals emerged not just as sites for professional networking, not just for screening works, not just for industry professionals, but as spaces to see work being made by independent artists, and queer artists at that. There was nothing on TV, there was no internet, so that was where we went. Those festivals were not primarily screening mainstream works. They were screening the works of all the artists who were not getting featured in major film festivals, and who were not getting access to theatrical distribution or TV. That communal experience was formative for me as an artist, as a scholar, but also as a queer person and as a queer activist. That was where so many connections were made, and for me that's what's missing from so many film festivals today, including the LGBTQ+ film festivals that have had the most longevity. Many of these festivals have now become mainstream, and have become industry focused.

TQFF is more than just a film festival; it connects to the history of queer film festivals as spaces where queer culture is being made and shared, not just a venue for capitalist money-making schemes. Telling queer stories through film has always been a lifeblood, especially for communities that have disproportionate mental and physical health struggles, who are economically depressed, who are victims of family, social, and state violence. Having access to stories that reflect your reality, to see your stories reflected on screen, to see people thinking about and imagining alternative realities to the violence that we live in today, that to me is the work of the queer film festival. I view this work as far more than mere curation. This is vital community engagement and organizing work. By creating actual physical and online spaces for people to connect, find communities, and find people sharing the same circumstances, we're writing our own narratives outside of media narratives that don't reflect our experience at all, or worse, that cause great harm through the norms that they depict that just simply aren't possible for most people.

Process is more important to me than the end result, process is more important than curation, process is more important than the production itself when we're making films. The process of how the film festival is put together and organized, in terms of how people access it, is just as important as what is curated and what is being presented. Eschewing the notion of product altogether and centring the process is actually what makes our curation and the work that we do transformative. As a disabled and mostly poor and precarious filmmaker, for most of my life, TQFF has been an exercise in how to live and survive in a world that discards the lives of people like us. I'm currently finishing up production on a feature documentary that is one of few films that is entirely produced and made by disabled people. The process of making that film in this different way, of not having a long day shooting, of not engineering shots that are physically impossible for me to do, that centres resting and sitting, comes out in the aesthetics and in the final construction of the work itself. It's the same for our centring of process and accessibility for our staff, our artists, as well as making sure that there is robust involvement with people representing all aspects of our community involved in the curatorial process, and not just the curatorial process but in the actual production of the festival itself and in all the work that we do. All of that impacts the final "product" that people see, and it's not incidental to it, it's central to the uniqueness of the work that we produce.

NKT: One of the things I'm thinking through with this collection is how classroom strategies and wider political strategies are connected to one another. I think about students who come to gender and sexuality classrooms with familiarity around concepts like intersectionality, abolition, normativity, the gender binary, all concepts that only a few decades ago were isolated in academic or particular kinds of political or activist spaces. What is interesting about TQFF is that the festival's pedagogical role seems to function in a similar way; you're drawing on the knowledge and skills people already bring to the table, but then introduce educational approaches into the organization. Added to this is the wider political work TQFF is doing around changing how queer and trans culture is produced and circulated through the film festival world. To my mind, this is the work of popular education as much as it is about building an organization. Can you talk more about the larger vision of popular education at TQFF?

KC: Maybe it's because I come from the humanities and also specifically studying film, but my experience of the history of queer theory as it emerged in the 1980s and '90s has always been very much centred around representational politics more broadly, and that makes complete sense considering that a big part of queer activist work historically has been to challenge mainstream narratives and representations of queer people as perverse, deviant, other, less than, abject, etc. A lot of work has challenged those narratives, which in turn has been lost in the mainstream assimilation and appropriation of queer activism and media in the last few decades. The skills and tools of media analysis, representational analysis, and discourse analysis are probably even more vital today than they were even twenty, thirty, forty years ago. We are living in an unprecedented era of media consolidation, where the ultra-rich control almost all aspects of the media. Billionaires literally own their own media empires. Network television, giant media conglomerates, and streaming platforms are collapsed. The impact of this is non-stop propaganda, an absence of diverse and factual information that challenges power, and the obscuring of atrocities the powerful commit. We don't get to see stories about resistance and there are fewer and fewer spaces for independent artists, filmmakers, and narratives to be showcased when our lives are saturated with mainstream media and independent distribution networks are disappearing. Even when independent platforms exist, we face the problem of visibility, and independent work is often left unseen because alternative platforms are so marginalized and so dispersed. Because of all this, we need better media literacy. Now more than ever. Our queer and trans communities need access to discourse analysis and critical media education, as much as we need access to technology and skills for making art.

Within the university, the humanities have been under attack for decades and that's deliberate because these fields teach vital critical literacy skills. The decimation of education more broadly is part of this process, and the barriers to access to alternative media, to alternative reporting, to alternative documentaries, to alternative narratives, are connected. Being able to parse what is being fed to us by mainstream narratives is important for our communities. With the corporatization of the university, we need education that is accessible to everyone. Assuming that critical thinking work can and should only happen in academia is just devastating to marginalized communities, especially for queer and trans people who are multiply marginalized. People are turning elsewhere to educate themselves. I see alternative forms of education happening on video streaming sites, on social media, on platforms run by the mega conglomerates. People have found ways of using these platforms to democratize education. At the same time, we need to prepare for the censorship and restriction of these platforms, since platforms and algorithms aren't neutral, they're in service of profits for corporations. This is definitely impacting queer independent content creation and sharing, since restrictions on nudity, politics, sex, like especially sex, and especially explicit depictions of sex, are already under attack on most platforms through either direct censorship for violating company terms and conditions, sometimes called "community guidelines," or being shadow banned by algorithms, which is when a user is muted or stops showing up on feeds without being notified by the platform. This is why we organize an annual symposium, and why we're trying to bring people across disparate fields and industries into conversation. We need to be learning from each other, we need to be building from the work that we're doing across sectors, and to resist the silos of academic work, filmmaking, media making, and activism.

Assuming that we're going to have access to these platforms forever is probably a mistake. What we need are alternative and community-based sites for education. This is where film festivals and other non-profits organizations and collectives can come in. Models for education that people can organize for themselves. How many people run their own workshop series independently, just do it for themselves? People want to learn, they want to learn from people who are working on ideas that they care about, and it's getting harder to find this in academia, or it's inaccessible to them through academia. I've always had a fantasy of a TQFF University, or whatever we would want to call it, that basically offers much of the same things that a film school might, but goes even further: educating our communities on queer history, queer theory, media analysis, discourse analysis, cultural studies, all the humanistic traditions of theories of race and ethnicity, of colonization and decolonization. Community-based education would be immensely transformative if we could make it more readily available and accessible. I say this to academics, because I think academics feel trapped: you spent all this time studying, you spent all this time being trained to be an educator, being trained to be a scholar, and then you're thrown into this neoliberal world where your skills are not valued at all. Seventy percent of people with PhDs can't get more than adjunct contracts. So many people feel trapped and like there's no alternative for them to put these skills to use outside of an abusive academic system. But we can create alternative spaces for education if we create alternative schools, classes, workshops, frameworks, and co-ops to provide education that people really want and need.

NKT: Thank you for sharing this work and your thinking on education and the festival for this collection. I know it can be strange to see a piece on a film festival in a book on higher education, but I think you've really illustrated the stakes around education beyond the university classroom, and that thinking past our institutions can help us envision ways of co-creating the kinds of spaces for learning that we want and need.

CONCLUSION

The Classroom as a Coalition
A Pedagogical Manifesto

NATALIE KOURI-TOWE

> The question here is whether we, as teachers and students, aspire to reproducing even the best versions of those scenes of identity and domination, or whether, in our pedagogy and our sense of the public conditions of self-definition and practice, we want to focus on more broadly imagining and creating the conditions for the yet unformed coalitions and unlived worlds into which we might want to translate ourselves.
>
> —Laurent Berlant, "Feminism and the Institutions of Intimacy" (1997)

> It is easy to mock the language of harm and violence, or to dismiss it as "woke." What is more difficult is to craft an alternative language—a language that refuses to negate the real feelings of dismay that arise when authority figures fail to live up to the fantasies or expectations projected onto them, but that also refuses to describe this failure as an act of violence, or to treat it as a punishable offense.
>
> —Merve Emre, "Are You My Mother? Transference and the Contemporary Classroom" (2023)

I write the conclusion to this book at a time of increasing attacks on the education sector that seek to delegitimize the expertise of scholars of gender and sexuality as holding "opinions" or "perspectives." This is a political terrain that triangulates far-right discourses that deny basic human rights in opposition to gender-inclusive policies and practices as if these were two comparable sides of the same debate (see Duggan 2002 on the effects of neoliberal triangulation). As educators, we are well positioned to both identify and denounce the fallacy of this triangulation. Gender and sexuality are not simply matters of opinion but shifting parameters through which all people must navigate across their lifespan and across sectors of society, including the family, civil society, governmental policies and bureaucracies, employment, health care, consumerism, aesthetics, and education. As this book illustrates, the debates that shape gender and sexuality in education are more nuanced than what is given a platform in public debate. Scholars of gender and sexuality are thinking carefully about how we teach and learn as gendered subjects, what barriers are in place that prevent the transformative effects of learning from taking shape in our classrooms, and how to build practices in our roles as educators that encourage difficult conversations both in the classroom and in society more broadly. Indeed, many of this book's contributors share techniques, strategies, or experiences in the classroom that illustrate a willingness to risk their own careers by standing up for justice within their institutions, to experiment with unconventional techniques in their classes, and to push back against institutional policies and procedures in the hopes of building better practices for teaching and learning. Although more than what any one person can accomplish in their career as a teacher, these works offer insight into how we might slowly, and with generosity to both ourselves and our students, rework our relationship to education. While each text speaks from the lens of gender and sexuality, my hope is that our works collectively invite a wide array of readers into conversation with us, perhaps even towards coalition.

While this book looks at higher education, the lessons learned are transferrable across educational contexts. Taking risks, developing tools of accountability, understanding power, and building capacity to withstand uncertainty are all essential for both the classroom and for surviving a world of increasing disparity. Classrooms today demand the teaching and learning of critical thinking skills; at the same time, teachers must be attuned to the effects of larger systemic and structural forms of violence that frame education. This means that teachers today need skills not just in their areas of expertise but also in facilitating difficult discussions, navigating conflicts, recognizing intersecting oppressions, responding to harm, grappling with precarity (both among students and contingent faculty), and inspiring new pathways into learning.

Despite the structural asymmetries that shape the teacher-student relationship in education—in addition to the asymmetries between tenure-track/tenured and non-tenure-stream instructors—the oppositional formulation of the classroom as a space where students sit on one side and the teacher on the other presumes a natural order that obscures and restricts our capacity to rethink power, learning, and education. In addition to the countless strategies educators use to rework the classroom, such as ungrading, student-centred learning approaches, student-led discussions and assignments, and community engagement, the structure of education makes it difficult to see the classroom as anything but a space of institutional authority and resistance to that exercise of power.

As many of the chapters in this book demonstrate, the power dynamics of the classroom are complicated by the desires of teachers and students alike, what Deborah Britzman (1998) identifies as the entanglement of the teacher's emotional ties and the student's navigation of their psychic defences. Likewise, for Megan Boler emotions are central to education as a feature of power through social control and resistance (1999, xiv, xv). For Britzman, the task is not to turn away from difficult knowledge or encounters, but to consider "the repressed psychic events of teaching and learning, which return to haunt education in the form of its contested objects: as conflicts, as disruptions, as mistakes, and as controversies" (1998, 19). Thinking about power and resistance, such as institutional power and psychic resistance, can add to our capacity to think differently about our roles and relationships in education. If the challenge of difference in education is not to overcome difference, but to recognize the points of friction, tension, conflict, and anticipation in our encounters across differences in the classroom, then we need approaches that help facilitate our working alongside these "contested objects."

The work of navigating difficult knowledge and difference in education requires a degree of self-reflection and self-reflexivity on the part of the teacher if we hope to also amplify these skills within our students. Pedagogical reflectivity and reflexivity entails understanding how one "is implicated in the dynamics of oppression" and "brings this knowledge to bear on [one's]...own sense of self" (Kumashiro 2000, 45), which can be accomplished by interrogating the assumptions that we bring into the classroom and the role of power and hegemony within the context of education (Brookfield 2017, 9). This pedagogical approach requires a degree of self-awareness alongside a willingness to engage with our own discomforts in our roles as teachers. Britzman argues it "behooves educators to engage in the making of reparation that begins in the acknowledgement of their own psychic conflict in learning and how this conflict is transferred to pedagogy" (1998, 134). To do what Britzman proposes involves an orientation to teaching and learning that leans heavily on the teacher's willingness to enter the work of repair, rather than envisioning an ideal set of pedagogical practices. But what characteristics make such reparative work possible? If we take lessons from our contributors, at the heart of this challenge is a capacity to soften in the face of defensiveness and resistance,[2] to make apparent the choices we grapple with, and show our vulnerability,[3] to enter meaningful dialogue with our students as collaborators in learning,[4] and to risk something

2. See Dyer, Kouri-Towe, and Miller; Georgis; Irving; and Trimble in this collection.
3. See Batraville; Luhmann; Poirier-Saumure; and Sinclair-Palm in this collection.
4. See Cole; D'Arcangelis, Gamache, Hrynyk, and Lenon; Fritsch; Gagliardi; and Yang, Joachim, and Manning in this collection.

different through our pedagogical practices.[5] When we move outside of an oppositional framework between students and teachers, these roles and subject positions can be reinterpreted through a model of education wherein we pay attention to the interconnected threads that introduce friction or contestation, at the same time that they offer points of entanglement, resonance, and engagement across differences. While Boler is critical of the self-reflexive turn in education, what she calls the liberal individualism of critical inquiry (1999, 176), her concern over the impact of pedagogical moves that evacuate the political possibilities of education through a turn to the self are worth considering if we take seriously the need for more reflection and reflexion in education. Boler proposes an approach to self-reflexivity rooted in collectivity and flexibility through a pedagogy of discomfort (178). This means that, rather than calling on students and teachers to perform confessional, self-effacing, or empathizing roles in the classroom, we are better served by rethinking the role of the classroom as a space for collectivity and collaboration rather than opposition. This is a coalitional vision of the classroom.

Seeing the Classroom as a Coalition

What does the classroom as a coalition look like? Unlike assemblages emergent out of collective-identity experiences or shared identifications, coalitions are forms of affiliation, collaboration, and cooperation that do not rely on a stable basis of shared experience, shared standpoints, or shared vision. Coalition is, by definition, an assembly across differences, one that is temporary, limited rather than encompassing, and requires working for a shared goal, even if such collaboration is framed by discomfort, risk, and uncertainty. Unlike solidarity, where the orientation across differences implies

---

5. See Charania; Chatterjee and Klement; Chisholm; Desai; Georgis; Mahrouse; and Rambukanna in this collection.

a sustained attachment of interconnection and investment in the other, coalitions do not require identification across differences and may even require working with those one might be otherwise in opposition to (Reagon 1983). Despite this possible challenge, coalitional work holds impressive potential to transform structures, systems, and institutions through strategic alliances developed out of an understanding of shared marginalization vis-à-vis structures and systems of power (Cohen 1997, 458). Coalitions also hold the potential to address the problem of power in the turn towards care (Hobart and Kneese 2020) and can introduce unexpected encounters that might lead to self-transformation through working across differences. A coalitional model of the classroom attends to the way students and teachers will be in opposition to one another in the context of education. At the same time, a coalitional model captures how students and teachers can be allies or share standpoints, and how students can be in opposition to one another (and often are). The classroom as a coalition can also illustrate the way teachers are often in opposition to their institutions and administrations, emphasizing the shared relationship to structures of power that can shape the student-teacher roles. Rather than try to achieve a kind of homogeneity in education, rethinking the relationship between teachers and students based on coalition opens the possibility of what Roderick Ferguson calls the informalizing potential of coalition (2015, 51), such as within interdisciplinary fields,[6] as an antidote to institutionalization (53).

I write this conclusion as a coalitional manifesto for the contemporary classroom to introduce a set of strategies, orientations, and approaches to education that can be used to open pathways into shifting the dynamics of the classroom and the outcomes of education.

---

6. Ferguson is interested in how interdisciplinary subjects, as formalized in institutional programs such as ethnic studies and women's studies, along with minority subjects, such as "people of color, queers, women, disabled folks" (2015, 53) continue to hold potential for revolutionary politics in the interplay between institutionalization/formalization and informalization.

Because this book speaks not only to the self-reflexive, self-reflective, and theoretical approaches to the classroom but also the very practice of teaching, including the strategies and orientations gender and sexuality scholars bring to their teaching, I end the book with a series of prompts for thinking about how to build the classroom as a coalitional space, drawing on the pedagogical insights discussed by the contributors across their chapters in this book. These prompts are anchored in five approaches to pedagogy emergent across various frameworks throughout the book, namely: 1) embodied pedagogies; 2) pedagogies of complicity, implication, and accountability; 3) collaborative pedagogies; 4) transformative pedagogies; and 5) pedagogies of contradiction. What comes next are not instructions for how to be the "right" kind of teacher; instead, these prompts, reflections, orientations, and provocations are invitations to accompany your own thinking and practices when it comes to the classroom.

Five Approaches for a Coalitional Classroom

1) Embodied pedagogies: How to address power, erasure, and exclusion in education

Centring embodiment in the classroom entails acknowledging the embodiment of both the teacher and students, a theme that emerged across many of the contributions in this collection.[7] Drawing our attention to embodiment raises two considerations informed by gender and sexuality approaches to pedagogy. First, it is necessary to understand the role and impact of embodied histories of violence and oppression in shaping one's entry into the classroom to make sense of how power functions within education. This approach is informed by feminist standpoint theory (Haraway 1997; Harding 1993; Hartsock 1983) and Black feminist thought (Collins 1998; Crenshaw

---

7. See Charania; Fritsch; Irving; Luhmann; Poirier-Saumure; and Trimble in this collection.

1991; hooks [1984] 2000), two fields of feminist thinking that illustrate how gendered and racialized subject positions yield epistemic privilege, a form of knowledge available to those who experience forms of subjugation and who gain an understanding of how power functions through exclusion, expulsion, and marginalization. Embodied experiences of gendered, racialized, classed, disabled, and other positionalities lend a material, rather than purely theoretical, understanding of power,[8] which helps develop an understanding of privilege and oppression in the classroom. However, beyond an understanding of how identity shapes knowledge, the role of embodiment in embodied pedagogies invites us to consider the interplay between subject positions and structural violence, interpersonal violence, and legacies of trauma in classroom experiences that manifest across differences in unconscious and affective ways. Attending to embodied pedagogies involves taking seriously who is in the classroom, and why certain kinds of subject positions may be absent, missing, excluded, seen as difficult or unruly, or unintelligible to us as teachers.[9]

Second, understanding embodiment involves recognizing the way learning is felt in the body through classroom dynamics, which may give rise to feelings of safety and uncertainty, anxiety and fear, or excitement and anticipation. Recognizing our own discomforts, the space we take up or shy away from, our affective orientations in the classroom, and our embodiment of authority or epistemic expertise can inflect our relationship to ourselves and our students. This kind of self-awareness requires attending to the impacts of affective unsettling, discomfort, disruptions, silences, and outbursts as part of the embodied dynamics of the classroom, rather than antithetical to teaching and learning. Thus, an embodied pedagogy requires thinking both about the body as a site and scene of politics *and* a relationship

---

8. See Gagliardi in this collection for a detailed discussion on how this dynamic plays out in universities with racialized students.
9. See Yang et al. and Rivers-Moore in this collection.

to self that can facilitate or foreclose learning. Instead of shying away from embodied events in the classroom, an embodied pedagogy seeks to find ways to create what Dina Georgis calls the "balance between safety and risk" (this volume, 272) to make room for learning. Contending with this balance can entail creative forms of pedagogy, but also acknowledging and responding to the embodied experiences of violence that we carry with us in learning and developing strategies for contending with that violence in ways that open space for exploration amidst uncertainty and risk.

2) Pedagogies of complicity, implication, and accountability:
How to manage and work through conflicts, rather than
avoid discomfort

It is impossible to avoid all conflict in education, especially if we take seriously Britzman's (1998) insights into the fundamental challenge of education that emerges in the scene of resistance to knowledge. Building our capacity to work through conflict, friction, discomfort, and failure holds the possibility of transforming those encounters as pathways to learning, both for students and the teacher.[10] At the same time, Susanne Luhmann (this volume) reminds us that complicity and implication are pathways to learning about violence that risk locking us in feelings of shame and guilt. To address this risk, she proposes that we pair learning about implication within systems and histories of violence with building our capacity to hold responsibility and accountability, both individually and collectively. Drawing on critical thinking techniques alongside self-reflexive strategies in the classroom to understand the difference between personal and collective responsibility, a pedagogy of complicity, implication, and accountability builds classroom capacities for holding difficult knowledge *and* requires us to work through the resistance to difficult knowledge in

---

[10]. See Charania; Chatterjee and Klement; Dyer et al.; Gagliardi; Georgis; Luhmann; Poirier-Saumure; and Yang et al. in this collection.

ways that allow teachers and students alike to identify our roles in structures of power. By working through challenging classroom (or campus) dynamics, rather than trying to avoid them, this pedagogical approach opens the possibility of building actionable outcomes of holding and being held accountable from our locations within systems of power.

While calls for accountability are common in educational settings, such as when students request trigger warnings or when institutional complaints processes are used to address conflicts or harm, contending with accountability as a relational process is more elusive. In the context of education this is made more difficult by how emotions emerge in the classroom, and beyond, whereby feelings of discomfort around difficult encounters can resonate with discourses around harm. To unpack the difference between discomfort and harm requires us to be able to identify how power is functioning within a given circumstance—both institutional power and interpersonal power dynamics, including epistemic power—to make sense of where feelings and violence converge. Because our feelings do not evenly map onto power—for instance, it can feel threatening to have power taken away from us, or unsafe to be called out—we cannot rely on discomfort as a vector for making sense of injustice in education (Applebaum 2017). This means we need critical analytic skills in understanding power and violence, along with attentiveness to the circulation of emotions in education, which can be achieved by reflecting on how complicity and implication position us.

Complicity, which involves more than simply being a willing party to systems and structures of violence, is a concept that asks us to contend with the ways we are conscribed into power, regardless of our intentions. Anti-racism, anti-imperial, and anti-colonial scholarship and activism have long drawn on the concept of complicity to make sense of how ordinary people benefit from and participate in structures of racial violence, white supremacy, settler colonialism, and imperialism through the normalization of these structures of violence in everyday life (Applebaum 2017; Choudry and Kapoor 2013; Zembylas 2020). In the classroom, Luhmann (this volume) argues, a "pedagogy of implication challenges our deeply rooted desire for innocence, which can be especially pronounced in students and faculty with firm commitments to social justice" (120). This means that we are implicated within systems and structures of violence, regardless of our desires. Developing a capacity to contend with complicity and implication, beyond individual guilt or shame, can empower us in the educational context to confront and grapple with power and injustice in material ways, such as through changes in hiring and evaluation/promotion policies, developing inclusive pedagogical approaches in our classrooms, and holding our departments and institutions accountable for forms of harm that emerge in interpersonal, administrative, and institutional contexts.

In her book *Feminist Accountability*, Ann Russo argues that the "process of taking individual and collective accountability is an ongoing one, and it requires a willingness not only to name oppression but to understand our relationship to its perpetuation. In other words, rather than a practice of locating the problem outside of ourselves and the movements with which we affiliate, it is a practice of awareness about how our ideas, organizations, policies, and activism are often embedded in the logics and structures of power. This awareness creates the potential for taking active accountability in ways that lead to change and transformation" (2018, 11). At its core, accountability can only occur when we understand complicity and implication (164), which means attending to our role (even if indirect) in upholding forms of violence and harm within our institutions. This task requires a relational process of holding accountability that involves a mutual commitment to consider one's own actions/behaviours/roles alongside a willingness to remain present and in relation to someone who is being held accountable. To achieve accountability requires a shift in our thinking away from punitive models towards more transformative approaches (not without consequence), which include understanding our own role in shaping and upholding behaviours and structures that harm (157). The work of accountability is uncomfortable work because it requires confronting both the other and our own selves. A model of accountability that exalts one subject position while denouncing another serves only to evade our complicity and implication within structures of violence. Instead, we must contend with how the alleviation and transformation of harm can be achieved through our sustained commitment to addressing harm within our own actions and those of others (162).

3) Collaborative pedagogies: Building skills, relationships, and capacities to work across our differences

The legacy of education's role in colonialism, imperialism, domination, and normalization cannot be understated. Yet, as Ferguson (2012) has illustrated, since the emergence of minority differences as interdisciplinary fields in higher education in the mid- to late twentieth century, education has also provided a space for critical, political, and transformative thinking to develop in ways that both resist and have brought about change at the institutional level. The impact of women's, gender, and sexuality studies as fields, along with Black studies, disability studies, ethnic studies, and Indigenous studies, have changed institutional hiring practices, curriculum, university policies, publishing, and governance systems. Alongside these institutional changes, these fields have also been co-implicated in social movements and wider practices of social change. As the contributors in this book have illustrated, much of this work has been (and continues to be) accomplished through collaboration.[11] Developing our own capacities, and those of our students, to collaborate is essential for coalition building. At the same time, these skills can be antithetical to the skills that are usually cultivated and celebrated in education,

---

11. See Chatterjee and Klement; Chisholm; Cole; D'Arcangelis et al.; Desai; Fritsch; Gagliardi; and Yang et al. in this collection.

where competition and individual exceptionalism are rewarded through the tenure and promotion process, grants and funding, and awards and accolades. Although in Canada most funders encourage research collaboration, this form of collaboration is still anchored in competition and exceptionalism under the rubrics of excellence, innovation, and impact. Similarly, grading systems lead many students to see group work (one of the few opportunities for classroom collaboration) as disadvantageous. Finding ways of both encouraging and fostering collaboration in our classrooms will build the potential for coalition-building outside of our classrooms. To accomplish this, we need skills for not only communicating and working together but also for working across differences, especially when difficult and uncomfortable feelings emerge when confronted with systemic violence and harm. Collaborative pedagogies must be connected to pedagogies of complicity, implication, and accountability to help us move from guilt, shame, and defensiveness to build our capacities to bear witness, hold responsibility, and take accountability in our actions (Russo 2018, 166). Collaboration involves not simply holding ourselves and our peers accountable as individuals but working together to bring about the changes we hope to achieve and participating in that process through capacity building at the collective level.

4) Transformative pedagogies: Techniques to help move through difficult learning by cultivating pleasure, hope, anticipation, and possibility in the classroom

Pain, harm, injury, and anxiety can frame many people's entry into the classroom. Whether as students or teachers, we bring our histories of violence with us as we enter into learning. Additionally, classroom encounters can introduce new scenes of violence or even revictimize those who come with existing trauma (Bedera 2021). While attending to the legacies of violence in the classroom can be an important intervention into the context of the classroom, many of the contributors in this book have illustrated the pedagogical importance of play, desire, pleasure, hope, and excitement alongside justice, accountability, and critique.[12] In her popular writing on transformative justice, Mariame Kaba writes, "collective action is not the only ingredient to make transformative change. We also need sound strategy and resources. And we need radical imagination" (Hayes and Kaba 2023, 230). Transformative pedagogies are those practices that take us beyond critique and analysis alone and open space for exploration, experimentation, and the unexpected as techniques for changing our own relationships and attachments to what we think we already know and building our capacity to think and act beyond ourselves with others. According to Britzman, "learning, it turns out, is crafted from a curious set of relations: the self's relation to its own otherness and the self's relation to the other's otherness" (1998, 134). To move through these relations, Britzman proposes a psychoanalytic inquiry into the teacher's psychic conflicts emergent in pedagogy; however, one need not be versed in psychoanalysis to adopt these techniques or insights. Transformative pedagogies offer a set of tools for doing this kind of relational work outside of the scope of psychoanalysis by focusing on strategies that connect the relationship between trauma, healing, violence, oppression, and the political to connection, collaboration, and interdependency. Gaztambide-Fernández, Brant, and Desai call this a pedagogy of solidarity that involves "an ethical project committed to transformation and to negotiating difference. This requires an ethic of consent and reciprocity, including a commitment to mutual transformation" (2022, 259). This approach to pedagogy can involve attending to how we understand our roles in transforming systemic oppression in classroom and institutional dynamics, softening in scenes of conflict, sharing in vulnerability across power asymmetries, creating spaces for play and experimentation in the classroom, holding ourselves and our peers accountable and responsible for harm through action, and

---

12. See Batraville; Chisholm; Cole; Desai; Fritsch; Irving; and Mahrouse in this collection.

developing capacity and aptitude for failure, uncertainty, and repair when things go wrong.

5) Pedagogies of contradiction: How to hold contradictions and act ethically in education

In her work on feminism and institutionality, Robyn Weigman argues that the domestication of "radicality and political transgression" (2016, 89) in feminist scholarship within the university relies on a false presumption that disciplinarity is antithetical to the political. Weigman explains, "as I understand it, discipline is neither a contraction of the political nor its subordination. On the contrary, it is the force that extends, proliferates, excites, and renews" (89). Drawing on Weigman's insights into the structure of power that shapes disciplinarity, I propose that pedagogies of contradiction can offer us tools for making sense of the way education can serve as a space of both coercion and transformation. Pedagogies of contradiction allow us to hold oppositional perspectives and find room for alternative entry points into confounding problems. The goal of this pedagogical approach is not to seek out a neutral, innocent, or righteous position; rather, pedagogies of contradiction try to understand how to navigate the ethical challenges and dynamics of working within systems in which we are complicit and implicated. Pedagogies of contradiction equip us with tools for accountability and flexibility for acting without having all the answers, which allows us to hold utopian visions alongside pragmatic considerations over how to manoeuvre, survive, and change the things most immediately available to us. This last pedagogical approach is the bridge between pedagogies of complicity, implication, and accountability, and that of transformation. Holding contradiction allows us to suspend the impulse to resolve every conflict and fix every problem, and instead take stock of what can and can't be done, why this may be the case, and equip us with the tools to be able to determine what kinds of strategic alliances to build, where to introduce flexibility into our ideals, and how to live with the reality of where we do and do not have power to change the systems and structures of violence that shape our world.

If the function of a feminist Foucauldian understanding of power and resistance is not simply to recognize the repressive force of institutionalization, but also the productive force of transforming institutions, this book offers the reader a set of strategies for how to navigate the contradiction between these two features of educational life. Despite the institutionalized forms of equity, diversity, and inclusion that co-opt the transformative demands for institutional change coming from gender and sexuality studies and related fields, this form of cooptation cannot be resisted through critique alone. Because education introduces a scene where teachers serve administrative roles, many of us occupy an often-contradictory position by bridging the demands of institutionalization and the desire to critique and transform these institutions (as well as the world outside of the classroom). Rather than refuse this contradictory standpoint, I suggest that harnessing contradiction in the service of accountability can help educators bridge the divide between holding power within institutional settings and being subjected to these same structures of power. Similarly, working with students to help them amplify their collective locations within higher education settings can build coalitional possibilities and allyship between teachers and students in ways that benefit everyone within our institutions. For example, in a climate where physical threats to gender and sexuality classrooms emerge alongside wider public debate over discrediting gender and sexuality expertise as "gender ideology," faculty and students hold the possibility for developing strategies for institutional transformation of gender-based violence by working in coalition to call for institutional change. Likewise, faculty can play an important role in supporting and mobilizing around student demands, such as gender-inclusive washrooms, access to better mental health services on campus, access to affordable education, and calls for reparations and diversification of our faculty and administrators.

Although many of the above pedagogical approaches will be familiar to some readers, especially those already working with popular education techniques in their teaching, the interplay of each of these approaches can facilitate coalitional work in the classroom. Because coalitions are forms of assembly that invite different subject positions and groups into collaboration in finite contexts, the classroom can be a hospitable space for them. To accomplish this shift, teachers can adapt their classrooms by mobilizing pedagogical approaches that facilitate, cultivate, and develop capacities for this kind of work. The classroom as a coalition entails developing pedagogies that build coalitional competencies among students, but also adopting reflective and reflexive approaches to teaching that contend with power, hierarchies, and the legacies of violence in material ways beyond acknowledgement alone.

Coalitional work in the classroom is already underway—even if it is not articulated as such—when teachers use anti-oppressive techniques or incorporate peer-based learning into their courses. However, developing a coalitional orientation can help coalesce these strategies in directed ways that build capacity for working across our differences. If we think of learning as a space for coalition—finding common goals despite our differences and being open to being changed by our encounters with learning from and through difference—the classroom can unlock new capacities in our own relationship to educational and institutional life.

References

Applebaum, Barbara. 2017. "Comforting Discomfort as Complicity: White Fragility and the Pursuit of Invulnerability." *Hypatia* 32 (4): 862–75. https://doi.org/10.1111/hypa.12352.

Bedera, Nicole. 2021. "Beyond Trigger Warnings: A Survivor-Centered Approach to Teaching on Sexual Violence and Avoiding Institutional Betrayal." *Teaching Sociology* 49 (3): 267–77. https://doi.org/10.1177/0092055X211022471.

Berlant, Lauren. 1997. "Feminism and the Institutions of Intimacy." In *The Politics of Research*, edited by E. Ann Kaplan and George Levine, 143–61. New Brunswick, NJ: Rutgers University Press.

Boler, Megan. 1999. *Feeling Power: Emotions and Education*. New York: Routledge.

Britzman, Deborah. 1998. *Lost Subjects, Contested Objects: Toward a Psychoanalytic Inquiry of Learning*. Albany: SUNY Press.

Brookfield, Stephen. 2017. *Becoming a Critically Reflective Teacher*. 2nd ed. San Francisco, CA: Wiley.

Choudry, Aziz, and Dip Kapoor. 2013. *NGOization: Complicity, Contradictions and Prospects*. London: Zed Books.

Cohen, Cathy J. 1997. "Punks, Bulldaggers, and Welfare Queens: The Radical Potential of Queer Politics?" *GLQ: A Journal of Lesbian and Gay Studies* 3 (4): 437–65. https://doi.org/10.1215/10642684-3-4-437.

Collins, Patricia Hill. 1998. *Fighting Words: Black Women and the Search for Justice*. Minneapolis: University of Minneapolis Press.

Crenshaw, Kimberle. 1991. "Mapping the Margins: Intersectionality, Identity Politics, and Violence against Women of Color." *Stanford Law Review* 43 (6): 1241–99. https://www.jstor.org/stable/1229039.

Duggan, Lisa. 2002. "The New Homonormativity: The Sexual Politics of Neoliberalism." In *Materializing Democracy: Toward a Revitalized Cultural Politics*, edited by Russ Castronovo and Dana D. Nelson. Durham, NC: Duke University Press.

Emre, Merve. 2023. "Are You My Mother? Transference and the Contemporary Classroom." *The New Yorker*, July 11, 2023. https://www.newyorker.com/culture/cultural-comment/are-you-my-mother.

Ferguson, Roderick. 2012. *The Reorder of Things: The University and its Pedagogies of Minority Difference*. Minneapolis: University of Minnesota Press.

—— 2015. "University." *Critical Ethnic Studies* 1 (1): 43–55.

Gaztambide-Fernández, Rubén, Jennifer Brant, and Chandni Desai. 2022. "Toward a Pedagogy of Solidarity." *Curriculum Inquiry* 52 (3): 251–65. https://doi.org/10.1080/03626784.2022.2082733.

Haraway, Donna. 1997. "The Persistence of Vision." In *Writing on the Body: Female Embodiment and Feminist Theory*, edited by Katie Conboy, Nadia Medina, and Sarah Stanbury, 292–304. New York: Columbia University Press.

Harding, Sandra. 1993. "Rethinking Standpoint Epistemology: What is 'Strong Objectivity?'" In *Feminist Epistemologies*, edited by Linda Alcoff and Elizabeth Porter, 49–82. New York: Routledge.

Hartsock, Nancy. 1983. *Money, Sex, and Power: Toward a Feminist Historical Materialism*. New York: Longman.

Hayes, Kelly E., and Mariame Kaba. 2023. *Let This Radicalize You: Organizing and the Revolution of Reciprocal Care*. Chicago: Haymarket Books.

Hobart, Hiʻilei Julia Kawehipuaakahaopulani, and Tamara Kneese. 2020. "Radical Care: Survival Strategies for Uncertain Times." *Social Text* 38.1 (142): 1–16. https://doi.org/10.1215/01642472-7971067.

hooks, bell. (1984) 2000. *Feminist Theory: From Margin to Center*. 2nd ed. London: Pluto Press.

Kumashiro, Kevin. 2000. "Toward a Theory of Anti-Oppressive Education." *Review of Educational Research* 70 (1): 25–53. https://www.jstor.org/stable/1170593.

Reagon, Bernice Johnson. 1983. "Coalition Politics: Turning the Century." In *Home Girls: A Black Feminist Anthology*, edited by Barbara Smith, 343–55. New Brunswick, NJ: Rutgers University Press.

Russo, Ann. 2018. *Feminist Accountability: Disrupting Violence and Transforming Power*. New York: NYU Press.

Weigman, Robyn. 2016. "No Guarantee: Feminism's Academic Affect and Political Fantasy." *Atlantis: Critical Studies in Gender, Culture and Social Justice* 37.2 (2): 83–95. https://journals.msvu.ca/index.php/atlantis/article/view/83-95%20PDF.

Zembylas, Michalinos. 2020. "Re-conceptualizing Complicity in the Social Justice Classroom: Affect, Politics and Anti-Complicity Pedagogy." *Pedagogy, Culture & Society* 28 (2): 317–31. https://doi.org/10.1080/14681366.2019.1639792.

CONTRIBUTORS

Nathalie Batraville is an associate professor at Concordia University's Simone de Beauvoir Institute, where she teaches and conducts research in the areas of Black feminisms, queer theory, Haitian studies, and prison abolition. She seeks to generate and illuminate frameworks that challenge both state violence and interpersonal violence. Her scholarship has appeared in scholarly publications such as *Small Axe*, the *Journal of Haitian Studies*, the *CLR James Journal*, and *Tangence*, in addition to other media sources such as *Canadian Art*, *Spirale*, and *Ricochet*. She is completing her first book, *Disruptive Agency: Towards a Black Feminist Anarchism*, forthcoming with Duke University Press, in which she rethinks notions of agency from a Black feminist perspective. Whenever she can, she also makes pottery, collages, prints, and other forms of art.

Gulzar R. Charania is an associate professor at the Institute of Feminist and Gender Studies, University of Ottawa. Her interdisciplinary research and teaching commitments are shaped by feminist, critical race, and queer theories, and qualitative methodologies. She studies the impacts of racial violence and, in particular, how racism and memories of it shape the educational experiences, trajectories, and political formation of racialized people. Dr. Charania is committed to the classroom as a space of pedagogical and political possibility. Her book *Fighting Feelings: Lessons in Gendered Racism and Queer Life* (2023) is available from UBC Press.

Sabina Chatterjee is a long-time activist, community educator, and advocate for social justice, equity, and belonging. Sabina has an extensive background in social service provision and organizational management, having created and directed support services for street-involved youth in southwestern Ontario, as well as anti-violence programs for multiracial and Indigenous youth in British Columbia. As a community consultant, her work has focused on developing trauma- and disability justice–informed programs, curricula, and evaluation frameworks that intentionally challenge anti-Indigenous and anti-Black racism. Sabina is a PhD candidate at York University in the Graduate Program in Gender, Feminist & Women's Studies, and she is the equity and community inclusion education and strategy consultant at the Centre for Excellence in Learning and Teaching at Toronto Metropolitan University.

Kami Chisholm is an independent filmmaker and the artistic director and co-founder of the Toronto Queer Film Festival. They hold a PhD in history of consciousness and feminist studies from UC Santa Cruz, and an MFA in film production from York University.

Jenn Cole is mixed-ancestry Algonquin Anishinaabe from Kiji Sibi watershed territory. She is Assistant Professor of Indigenous performance and gender at Trent University and artistic director for Nozhem First Peoples Performance Space in Michi Saagig territory. She is editor for *Canadian Theatre Review*'s "Views and Reviews." Her 2021 special issue, "Performing (in) Place: Moving on/with the Land," co-edited with Melissa Poll, appears online in *Performance Matters*.

Carol Lynne D'Arcangelis is an associate professor of gender studies at Memorial University, where she received a 2019 Dean's Award for Teaching Excellence in the Faculty of Humanities and Social Sciences. Since 2005 she has been a white settler member of No More Silence, a Toronto-based grassroots network dedicated to raising awareness about Missing and Murdered Indigenous Women, Girls, and Two-Spirit people. She has published on Indigenous–non-Indigenous solidarity, white settler feminism, and decolonial feminism in journals that include *Cultural Studies ↔ Critical Methodologies*, *Atlantis: A Women's Studies Journal*, *Canadian Woman Studies*, the German journal *Peripherie*, and the Brazilian journal *Revista ANPHLAC*. She is the recipient of the 2023 Atlantic Book Award for Scholarly Publishing for her book *The Solidarity Encounter: Women, Activism, and Creating Non-Colonizing Relations* (UBC Press, 2022).

Chandni Desai is an assistant professor at the University of Toronto. She has published in the *Journal of Palestine Studies*; *Race and Class*; *Curriculum Inquiry*; *Decolonization: Indigeneity, Education and Society*, and several anthologies. She is working on her first book tentatively titled *Revolutionary Circuits of Liberation: The Radical Tradition of Palestinian Resistance Culture and Internationalism*. Desai is the host of the *Liberation Pedagogy Podcast* and a seasoned transnational organizer.

Hannah Dyer is an associate professor in the Department of Child and Youth Studies at Brock University. She is a cultural theorist of childhood with concentration in art/aesthetics, social conflict, queer theory, and psychoanalysis. Her first book, *The Queer Aesthetics of Childhood: Asymmetries of Innocence and the Cultural Politics of Child Development* (Rutgers University Press, 2020), explores how children's art and art about childhood can imagine new models of social life that redistribute care, belonging, and political value.

Kelly Fritsch is an associate professor in the Department of Sociology and Anthropology at Carleton University. She is cross-appointed to the Feminist Institute of Social Transformation and the Institute of Political Economy and is co-director of the Disability Justice and Crip Culture Collaboratory. As a crip theorist and critical disability studies scholar, her research probes the workings of ableist social relations, the neoliberal biopolitics of disability, and anti-assimilationist crip culture and politics. She is co-author of *We Move Together* (AK Press, 2021), a children's book about ableism, accessibility, and disability culture; and co-editor of *Disability Injustice: Confronting Criminalization in Canada* (UBC Press, 2022) and *Keywords for Radicals: The Contested Vocabulary of Late-Capitalist Struggle* (AK Press, 2016).

Meghan Gagliardi is a PhD candidate in human geography at the University of Toronto. Her doctoral research explores how multi-scalar white-settler activity in small-town Canada projects, materializes, and fortifies the settler-colonial imaginary by restricting and constraining racialized communities' right to access the city and to produce urban space.

Mylène Yannick Gamache is a Franco-Métis assistant professor cross-appointed in Indigenous Studies and Women's and Gender Studies at the University of Manitoba. Red River Métis by her mother line with Carrière relations in St-Pierre-Jolys, Manitoba, and Beauchemin relations in Îles-des-Chênes via Grande Pointe, St. Vital, and St. Boniface, she is a member of l'Union Nationale Métisse Saint-Joseph du Manitoba and a Manitoba Métis Federation citizen. Her recent research engages Indigenous literacies of the unknown, Freudian psychoanalysis, and critical borderland studies through collaborative engagement with Iron Alliance historiographies as one of five Indigenous researchers and co-founders of *Iapi debwewin aansaamb*. Her work is published in *Feminist Review*, *The Oxford Literary Review*, *English Studies in Canada*, *Living and Learning with Feminist Ethics, Art, and Literature* (University of Alberta Press, 2024) and *Métis Coming Together: Sharing Our Stories and Knowledges* (Peter Lang Publishing, 2024).

Dina Georgis is an associate professor and graduate program director at the Women and Gender Studies Institute at the University of Toronto. Her work is situated in the fields of postcolonial and sexuality studies. She draws on psychoanalytic concepts to think through how expressive and political cultures are responses to difficult experience. Her book *The Better Story: Queer Affects from the Middle East* (SUNY Press, 2013) considers the emotional dynamics of colonial traumas and the stories and cultures they produce. She has published essays on war and memory, aesthetics and queer hope, and on Arab sexualities. Her work can be found in *Psychoanalysis, Culture and Society*, *Studies in Gender and Sexuality*, and *International Journal of Middle East Studies*.

Nicholas Hrynyk is an assistant professor of history at Thompson Rivers University in Kamloops, British Columbia. He is an interdisciplinary historian whose research and teaching spans the disciplines of history, women's and gender studies, queer studies, disability studies, and critical race studies. His research has explored the aesthetics of gay male masculinity in Canada during the gay liberationist years of the 1970s and 1980s, as well as the overlapping discourses of disability and disease in narratives of HIV/AIDS. He is currently researching anticipations of violence among queer people and how violence literally and figuratively haunts individuals, shaping queer people's relationship with the state, cis-heterosexual society, and even one another. His work has appeared in the *Journal of Canadian Studies*, *Disability Studies Quarterly*, *Canadian Journal of Anesthesia*, and is forthcoming in *Monumental Memories: A Critical Reading of Memorials, Monuments, and Statues in Canada's Capital Region* (McGill-Queen's University Press).

Dan Irving is an associate professor cross-appointed to the Feminist Institute of Social Transformation and the Human Rights and Social Justice programs at Carleton University. His research focuses on under- and unemployment amongst Two-Spirit, trans, and non-binary people in Canada.

Rebecca Gaëlle Joachim (a.k.a. Beck) is a Black feminist, book lover, fashion enthusiast, and co-host of the podcast *Woke or Whateva*, a

Black women-led podcast based out of Montreal. Beck is also a graduate from the Simone de Beauvoir Institute with a major in women's studies.

Kristine Klement (PhD, RP, FIPA) teaches in the School of Gender, Sexuality & Women's Studies at York University and the Toronto Institute of Psychoanalysis. Her interest in critical feminist and antiracist pedagogy has grown out of her experiences in the classroom, teaching Introduction to Gender and Women's Studies at York University. She is also a psychoanalyst and psychotherapist in private practice and is currently working on a book on whiteness, hysteria, and trauma in feminist and mental health discourses.

Natalie Kouri-Towe is an associate professor of feminism and sexuality at the Simone de Beauvoir Institute at Concordia University, where she serves as the program and practicum director for the Interdisciplinary Studies in Sexuality program. Her research investigates the politics of solidarity under neoliberalism, with areas of focus ranging across responses to war in the Middle East, refugee crises, queer activism, and gender and sexuality pedagogies. She has also published on topics relating to affect theory, masculinity, queer kinship, and transnational solidarity.

Suzanne Lenon is an associate professor in the departments of Sociology and Women and Gender Studies at the University of Lethbridge. She teaches and researches in the areas of critical race feminisms, queer theory, and law, gender, and sexuality, with a particular interest in marriage and inheritance laws as regimes of state-led social reproduction that sustain racial, gendered, and classed relations of domination. Her work has been published in *Canadian Journal of Women and the Law*, *Feminist Legal Studies*, *Social Identities*, and *Studies in Social Justice*, among others. With OmiSoore H. Dryden, she is co-editor of the book *Disrupting Queer Inclusion: Canadian Homonationalisms and the*

Politics of Belonging (UBC Press, 2016); and with Daniel Monk, she is co-editor of the book *Inheritance Matters: Kinship, Property, Law* (Hart Bloomsbury, 2023).

Susanne Luhmann is a professor in the Department of Women's and Gender Studies at the University of Alberta, where she served from 2018 to 2020 as the inaugural director of Intersections of Gender, a Signature Area of Research and Teaching in the Office of the Vice-President, Research and Innovation. Her teaching and research interests include the institutionalization of intersectional gender studies and research; feminist and queer pedagogies; trauma and cultural memory; and sexuality studies. Luhmann co-edited *Feminist Praxis Revisited: Critical Reflections on University-Community Engagement* (Wilfrid Laurier University Press, 2019) and co-authored *Troubling Women's Studies: Pasts, Presents, Possibilities* (Canadian Scholars, 2004). She is currently working on the monograph *Domesticating the Nazi Past: Gender and Generation in Recent German Cultural Memory*.

Gada Mahrouse is an associate professor at the Simone de Beauvoir Institute at Concordia University in Montreal. Her interdisciplinary work is informed by critical race studies, cultural studies, transnational feminist frameworks, and post/anti-colonial theories.

Kimberley Ens Manning studies Chinese politics and gender and politics. The author of *The Party Family: Revolutionary Attachments and the Origins of State Power in China* (Cornell University Press, 2023), Kimberley's current research, writing, and advocacy focuses on the well-being of transgender youth and their families. She is a professor of political science and principal of the Simone de Beauvoir Institute at Concordia University, Montreal.

Michelle Miller is an assistant professor, Teaching Stream, in the Faculty of Arts and Science at the Ontario College of Art and Design

University in Toronto. A scholar of both English literature and teaching and learning, Michelle divides her research focus into representations of queer adolescence in comic books and into principles of care and the emotional life of teaching and learning. Her work has been published in *Girlhood Studies, English Studies in Canada, Changing English*, and is forthcoming in the *Journal of Curriculum Theorizing*.

Alexis Poirier-Saumure is a PhD candidate and instructor in the Department of Communication Studies at Concordia University. His thesis interrogates the educational practice of sexual education teachers in the context of critical, anti-oppressive, and queer approaches to pedagogy. His research practice also touches upon various contemporary discourses around pedagogy, such as classroom climate, sensitive topics, and debates around academic freedom.

Nathan Rambukkana is an associate professor in Communication Studies at Wilfrid Laurier University, in Waterloo, Canada. His work centres the study of discourse, politics, and identities, and his research addresses topics such as digital and platform intimacies, AI and robotics, hashtag publics, intimate privilege, and non/monogamy in the public sphere. He is the author of *Fraught Intimacies: Non/Monogamy in the Public Sphere* (UBC Press, 2015) and the editor of *Hashtag Publics: The Power and Politics of Discursive Networks* (Peter Lang, 2015) and of *Intersectional Automations: Robots, AI, Algorithms, and Equity* (Rowman & Littlefield, 2021).

Megan Rivers-Moore is a settler on the unceded and unsurrendered territories of the Algonquin-Anishinabeg Nation, where she is an associate professor at the Feminist Institute of Social Transformation at Carleton University. Megan is an interdisciplinary scholar whose work is located at the intersection of sociology, gender studies, and Latin American and Caribbean studies. Her research focuses on how gender and sexuality operate transnationally, including projects on sex tourism in Costa Rica, sex worker organizing across Latin America, and clandestine abortion. Her book *Gringo Gulch: Sex, Tourism, and Social Mobility* was published in English by the University of Chicago Press (2016) and in Spanish by the University of Costa Rica Press (2019).

Julia Sinclair-Palm is an associate professor in Childhood and Youth Studies in the Institute of Interdisciplinary Studies at Carleton University. They completed their doctorate in education in the Faculty of Education at York University. Her research with young people considers how conceptualizations of children and youth are tied to concerns about violence, risk, and mental health often at the exclusion of other, more complex narratives of identity, gender, and belonging.

S. Trimble is an assistant professor, Teaching Stream at the Women and Gender Studies Institute at the University of Toronto. She has written cultural criticism for both scholarly and mainstream publications, and her book *Undead Ends: Stories of Apocalypse* (2019) is available through Rutgers University Press. Trimble's latest project is organized around conducting life-history interviews with scholars working in and around feminist cultural studies.

Mitchell Rae Yang is a graduate from the Simone de Beauvoir Institute with a double major in women's studies and interdisciplinary studies in sexuality. His current master's work in sociology focuses on the role that commercially available genetic DNA tests play in the formation of white racial identity and the rising trend of race-shifting amongst ostensibly white Canadians. He is also a steering member of the Access in the Making (AIM) Lab, which researches what disability and accessibility look like in practice.

INDEX

ableism: about, 23, 45–46, 49–50; collective access, 23, 46, 55–57; equality as sameness, 52; financial costs, 50; forced intimacy and disabled people, 46, 48, 56–57; neoliberal culture, 57–58; self-advocacy by disabled people, 51–53; stigma, 50–51; structural ableism, 45–46. *See also* disabilities

abolition: about, 316–19, 321–23; abolition feminists, 314, 317, 322–23; abolition movements, 314–19, 321–23; accountability, 326–27; community experiences (#JusticeforMoka), 277, 314–15, 319–25; course design, 277, 314–15, 318, 320–21, 325–27; guest speakers, 137–38, 318–19, 323; "love, study and struggle," 321–22; pedagogies, 276–77, 313–16, 318, 324–27; power dynamics, 276–77, 324, 326; as praxis of creativity, 314–15; resistance to punitive approaches, 326–27; resource distribution, 323; restorative justice, 323–25; scholarly literature, 315, 317, 322–23, 325–26

Absolon, Kathleen E., 280

academy. *See* higher education

accountability: about, 10, 21–25, 370–72; community-engaged learning, 277; complicity and implication pedagogies, 25, 113, 119–21, 369–73; cultural shifts, 8–9, 14–15; guest speakers, 67–68, 137–38; in labour of care, 222–23; pedagogies of contradiction, 375–76; peer teaching, 212, 223–28; safe spaces in classrooms, 174–76; teacher's responsiveness, 100–101; trigger warnings as, 370. *See also* complicity and implication

activism: abolition pedagogies overview, 276–77, 313–16, 326–27; allyship overview, 134–38; celebrations of, 308–309; evaluation and assessment, 104; film festivals (TQFF), 349, 353–54; non-reformist prison reforms, 321–22; solidarity activism, 276–77. *See also* abolition; social justice

advocacy for self. *See* self-advocacy

affect. *See* emotions

Ahmed, Sara: on citing white men, 157; on diversity work, 163, 176; on embodiment, 283; on eye rolling, 170; on fragility, 185; on histories of arrival, 77; on killjoys, 175, 190; on lifelines, 85; on racialized dynamics, 172; on transforming universities, 165–66, 169; on trigger warnings, 190

Alberta. *See* Lethbridge, Alberta, region

Alexander, M. Jacqui, 153

Allen, Louisa, 135–36, 141

Allen, Paula Gunn, 289
allyship: about, 134–38; in the classroom, 376; coalitions, 15–16, 365–66, 377; critiques of, 137; guest speakers, 67, 137–38, 339–40; Indigenous activism, 136–37, 339–40; power dynamics, 136–37, 366
Anderson, Kim, 289
Anishinaabe people, 279–83, 286–291. *See also* Indigenous pedagogies, circle of care
anti-racism: about, 22–23, 27–42, 370; assignment of responsibilities, 27–30, 34–42; complicity, 22–23; "empowered student" narrative, 30–31; funding, 29, 31–33; institutional racism, 22–23, 39–43, 169; intersectional, 114; key questions, 22, 41–42; neoliberal context, 28–33, 40–42; pedagogical framework, xiiin1, 6, 12, 147, 166, 175–76, 240–41, 297, 300; power hierarchies, 31, 34–37, 41–42, 164; racialized and white responsibilities, 22–23, 34–42, 167–68; redistribution proposal, 29, 39–42; research project, 22–23, 28–30; responsibilities of white actors, 22–23, 37–42, 170–74; risk of harms to students, 35–36, 40–41, 171–72; self-advocacy, 34–37; workloads, 33–37, 40
anti-Semitism, 112, 326
anxiety. *See* emotions
Anzaldúa, Gloria, 149
areas of study. *See* fields of study; fields of study, interdisciplinary
Arluke, Arnold, 130–31
artificial intelligence (AI), 247–48, 255–57. *See also* digital intimacies
arts. *See* cultural studies; film and video; literature

Arvin, Maile, 147, 154–55
Asian people, 75–76, 85, 171–72
assessment. *See* evaluation and assessment
Attewell, Nadine, 75–76, 85
autobiography: about, 24, 75–88; authenticity, 87; collaborative method, 164, 170; coming-out processes, 128, 196, 200–207; course texts, 80–81, 117n6; curiosity, 87–88; ecstatic pedagogies, 93–96; embodiment of queerness, 24, 75–82; feminist cultural studies, 77, 82–88; film production, 348–49; first teaching experiences, 129–42; genealogy of learning, 24, 78, 82–88; lived experience as text, 102–104; nicknames, 79–82; queerness in *Fun Home*, 75–80; self-disclosure, 80; social location statements, 135; transnational and historical linkages, 84–86; trans teachers, 94–96; as unknowing yourself, 88; vulnerability and power, 24, 81–82, 88

Bakhtin, Mikhail, 235
Barker, Barbara, 340
Batraville, Nathalie, 212, 215–29, 381
BDSM, 222. *See also* kink and pedagogy
Beauchamp, Toby, 195
Bechdel, Alison, 75–80
Belcourt, Billy-Ray, 118
Bell, Nicole, 280
Bergson, Henri, 235
Berlant, Lauren, 109, 248, 361
Berne, Patty, 55
Bernstein, Elizabeth, 63–64
Better Practices (Kouri-Towe and Martel-Perry), xii–xiii
Bilge, Sirma, 139–40, 146, 156, 300–301
Billig, Michael, 235n1

biological determinism, 333, 338
BIPOC (Black, Indigenous, people of colour). *See* race and racism
Black feminist thought, 6, 76, 84–86, 113–15, 145–46, 153–54, 156–57, 212, 216, 317, 367–68
Black people: abolition campaign (#JusticeforMoka), 314–15, 319–25; abolition movement, 314, 316–19; anti-racism student riots (Sir George Williams Affair), 167–68, 174; Black studies, 29, 33, 86n6, 371–72; historical trauma of white supremacy, 217; history, 166; intersectionality, 113–15, 300–301; queer studies, 145–46, 153–54, 156–57; role-playing in *Harriet's Daughter*, 215–19; social devaluation in academia, 221–22, 267; students, 28, 29n1, 34–37, 164–74; theory in everyday life, 154–56; trauma, 215–19; unlearning colonial constructs, 156–59; unmappability of futures, 216; ways of knowing, 257; white gaze, 76; women, 221–22. *See also* anti-racism; queer theory, racism, and settler colonialism
Black people, racism and safe spaces in classrooms: about, 127, 163–76; agreements on safe spaces, 127, 170–76, 223, 225; anti-racism student riots (Sir George Williams Affair), 167–68, 174; balance between risk and safety, 272, 369; classroom ground rules, 127; collaborations, 127; collaborative autoethnographic method, 164, 170; Concordia University vitrine project (2019), 163–65, 166–69; critiques of institutional power, 28, 168–69, 301; critiques of pedagogies, 13–14; eye rolls as signals, 170–72; feminist seminar (FUS), 164–66, 172, 175, 176; harm vs. comfort, 127;

project work, 166, 168–69; racialized dynamics in white classes, 127, 149, 168–76; teacher positionalities, 164, 221. *See also* safe spaces in classrooms
Blackfoot people, 336, 338–39
bodies. *See* embodiment
Boler, Megan, 303, 363, 365
Bondi, Stephanie, 38
Bondy, Renée, 7
Bornstein, Kate, 198
Borrows, John, 342
Brant, Jennifer, 374
Brennan, Edward, 236
British Columbia. *See* Kamloops, British Columbia, region
Britzman, Deborah: on difficult knowledge, 115, 263–64, 363–64; on inclusive education, 9n9, 11n10; on knowledge and self, 12–13, 21–22, 369, 374
Brockenbrough, Ed, 201
Brophy, Sarah, 85
brown, adrienne maree, 104–105
Brown, Chester, 68
Butler, Judith, 80–81, 153, 155

Campbell, Maria, 284
canons, critiques of, 87, 149, 151–59
Carby, Hazel, 84
caring in pedagogies, 10–11, 275–78
Carter, Sarah, 288
Charania, Gulzar R., 127, 145–61, 381
Chatterjee, Sabina, 276, 295–311, 382
child and youth studies: playfulness in development, 269–71; trigger warnings, 127–28, 182, 183–84, 185, 187–89
Chisholm, Kami, 278, 347–59, 382
Christian, Barbara, 154, 157
cisnormativity, as term, 197–98
citational practices, 85–86, 86n6, 157, 238n3, 268, 285

Clarkson, Nicholas, 204–205
class, social: allyship power dynamics, 136–37; classism in higher education, 30; funding for artists in poverty, 350–51; intersectionality, 113–15, 300–301
coalitions: about, 15–17, 275–78, 361–77; across departments, 15–16; complicity and implication pedagogies, 369–72; contradiction in pedagogies, 375–76; defined, 365–67; embodied pedagogies, 367–69; power dynamics, 366–69; relationships, 367–69; self-reflection, 364–65; shared goals, 365–66; skills and capacities, 367–69, 372–73; as temporary, 365–66; transformative pedagogies, 15–16, 373–75. *See also* collaborations
codes of professionalization, 102
Cohen, Cathy, 149, 151–52
Cole, Jenn, 276, 279–94, 382
collaborations: about, 15–17, 275–78, 295–310, 372–73; assignments, 302–303, 308–309; autoethnographic methodology, 164, 170; coalitional work, 15–17, 377; in coalitions, 15–17, 377; course material selection, 306; creative celebrations, 308–309; critical thinking skills, 276, 305–306; ecstatic pedagogies, 103–105; in fields of study, 15–17, 372–73; handbook and toolkit, 296–97; in kink, 212, 218; in pedagogies, 15–17, 374–75, 377; pedagogies of discomfort, 141–42, 303–305; peer teaching, 212, 223–28; power dynamics, 276; for research funding, 373; in scholarly writing, xv; self-reflection, 302–303; team teaching, 297–300, 304; tutorials, 304–305. *See also* coalitions
Collins, Patricia Hill, 84, 146, 300–301

Colman, Andrew, 92n1
colonialism. *See* Indigenous peoples, settler colonialism; queer theory, racism, and settler colonialism; settler colonialism
colour, people of. *See* people of colour
Combahee River Collective, 149, 154
comedy: about, 212–13, 231–41; assignments, 240; course design, 212–13, 232–41; critical race humour, 237–41; feminism, 232–41; gendered comedy, 239; interdisciplinary approach, 234–38; intersectionality, 234, 240–41; marginalized comics, 236–37; objectives of courses, 239; playfulness, 233, 240–41; power dynamics, 213, 232–34, 236, 240–41; safe spaces, 239–41; scholarship on, 233, 234–38, 240; social criticism, 231–32, 239–41; stand-up comedy, 231–32, 234, 236–39; theoretical approaches, 235–38; trigger warnings, 233–34
coming-out processes, 128, 135, 196, 200–207
community-engaged learning: about, 104–105, 278, 339–44, 358–59; abolition activism (#JusticeforMoka), 276–77, 314–15, 319–25; ecstatic pedagogies, 103–105; film festivals (TQFF), 348–51, 354–59; gender and sexuality studies, 343–44; Indigenous connections, 289–91, 339–44; partnerships, 352; solidarity activism, 276–77; symposiums, 103–104, 353, 357–58. *See also* abolition; activism; guest speakers
complicity and implication: about, 25, 107–21, 369–72; accountability, 113, 119–21, 369–73; allyship dynamics, 137; assumptions of rationality, 108–10; collaborations, 373; as

concepts, 110–11, 370–71; conflict management, 369–70; course texts, 116–17; culpability, 119; cultural shifts, 3–5, 8–9, 14–15; difficult knowledge, 115–16, 118–21, 263–64, 363–64, 369–70; discomfort, 25, 121; fear and silences, 301–302; goals and objectives, 118–21; guilt and shame, 118–21, 369–73; historical events, 112–13; implication in structures, 107–109; impulse to innocence, 25, 109–10, 120–21, 371; intersectionality, 113–15, 120–21; multidirectional learning, 116–17; pedagogies of contradiction, 375–76; "repressive myths" of social justice, 107–10, 119; research processes, 114–15; resistance to learning, 116–21; romance of non-complicity, 110, 121; self-reflection, 25, 119–21, 364–65

Concordia University: anti-racism student riots (Sir George Williams Affair), 167–68, 174; Critical Feminist Activism and Research (CFAR), 166; Feminist University Seminar (FUS), 164–66, 172, 175, 176; Simone de Beauvoir Institute, 164, 170; vitrine project on anti-Black racism (2019), 163–69

consent: cultural shifts, 8; Indigenous teachings, 284, 285, 288; in kink, 218

content warnings. *See* trigger warnings

contradiction, pedagogies of, 375–76

Corntassel, Jeff, 303

correction, pedagogies of, 16–17

course design: canonical texts, 87, 149, 151–59; citational practices, 85–86, 86n6, 157, 238n3, 268, 285; collaborations, 147; course material selection, 306; critical consciousness course, 297; intersectionality, 113–15, 300–301, 306. *See also* coalitions; collaborations; critical pedagogies; evaluation and assessment; fields of study; fields of study, interdisciplinary

COVID-19 pandemic, 132, 258–59, 269

Crenshaw, Kimberlé, 113–14, 139–40

criminal justice system, 324–25. *See also* abolition

critical pedagogies: about, 133–34; accountability, 25; assumptions of rationality, 108–10; banking model (Freire's critique), 133, 205, 305; coalitions, 15–16, 275; complicity and implication, 25; critical thinking skills, 276; critique of impulse to innocence, 25, 109–10, 120–21, 371; cultural shifts, 3–5, 8–9, 14–15, 141–42, 264–65; historical contexts, 139–40; holistic approaches, 296; hooks's radical model, 133–34; implication and complicity, 107–10, 115–16, 118–21; "repressive myths" of social justice, 107–10, 119; strategies, 13; teaching about critique, 138–40; uncertainties, 12–13, 14, 17. *See also* discomfort, pedagogies of; power dynamics, disruption of

Cromwell, Jason, 95

cross-disciplinary studies, 247–49, 259–60. *See also* digital intimacies; fields of study, interdisciplinary

cultural studies: canon, 87; comedy, 234; digital cultural studies, 248–49, 252–53, 255–60; feminist cultural studies, 77, 82–88; multiplicity and openness, 87. *See also* comedy; digital intimacies; film and video; popular culture

Currah, Paisley, 203

Cuthand, TJ, 351

dance metaphor, 206–207
Danchuk, Jenna, 296n1
D'Arcangelis, Carol Lynne, 277–78, 331–44, 382–83
Davis, Angela, 317, 322–23
Davis, Dána-Ain, 37–38
Dawkins, Moka, 314–15, 319–25
Dean, Amber, 7
decolonization. *See* Indigenous peoples, decolonization
decriminalization. *See* abolition
DEI (diversity, equity, and inclusion) initiatives: about, 14–15; critiques, 27–28, 376; cultural shifts, 8–9, 14–15; institutional assignment of work, 23, 27–30. *See also* anti-racism; complicity and implication
Derrida, Jacques, 268
Desai, Chandni, 276–77, 313–29, 374, 383
desire and pleasure: about, 24–25, 373–75; assignments, 308–309; desire-based research, 307–309; passion for learning, 24–25, 100; transformative pedagogies, 373–75. *See also* ecstatic pedagogies; risks and pleasure
Deveau, Danielle, 237
D'Harlingue, Benjamin, 195
difficult knowledge, 115–16, 118–21, 185–87, 263–64, 363–64, 369–70
digital intimacies: about, 213, 247–60; archived materials, 257–58; artificial intelligence, 247–48, 255–56, 257; course design, 251–53; critical intimacy theory, 247–48, 252, 256, 259–60; cross-disciplinary pedagogies, 247–49, 259–60; early internet materials, 255; films, 255; identities, 251–54, 258; inquiry approach, 257; interpersonal communication, 253; materiality of, 251; medium theory, 249–50; platform ethnographies, 254; qualities of, 250–51; queer theory, 247–48, 253, 255, 257–58; remote learning, 258–59; robotics, 247–48, 255–59; sexuality, 247–48, 252–57, 259; specifications grading, 258–59; topics, 252–58; traditional local relationships, 248–49
digital technologies: artificial intelligence, 247–48, 255–56, 257; digital cultural studies, 248–49, 252–53, 255–60. *See also* digital intimacies; film and video; media
Dion, Susan, 301–302
disabilities: about, 23, 45–59; academic ableism, 23, 46, 49–55; access fatigue, 46–50, 53, 57; accommodations, 23, 51–53; collective access, 23, 46, 55–57; crip culture of access, 23, 46, 53–59; cultural shifts, 8–9, 14–15; desire for disability, 23, 45–46, 53–59; disability justice movement, 8, 23, 55, 58, 322; disability studies, 371–72; emotional labour, 48–51; filmmaking, 355; forced intimacy, 46, 48, 56–57; intersectionality, 47–48, 113–15; neoliberal culture, 57–58; power dynamics, 49, 53; self-advocacy, 48–49, 51–53, 55–56; statistics, 45; stigma, 50–51; strategies for instructors, 23, 55–59
discomfort, pedagogies of: about, 11–12, 141–42, 303–305; collaborative approach, 365–66; complicity and implication, 369–70; course design, 141–42, 303–305, 369–70; cultural shifts, 141–42; embodiment, 368–69; epistemological discomfort, 141–42; failures, 141–42; power dynamics, 370; safe spaces in classrooms, 191, 197, 370; student strategies, 304–305, 369–70; teacher's discomfort,

364–65, 368; uncertainties and change, 17, 206, 303–305, 369–70. *See also* complicity and implication; critical pedagogies
disruption of power dynamics. *See* power dynamics, disruption of
diversity initiatives. *See* DEI (diversity, equity, and inclusion) initiatives
Dolmage, Jay, 49
double binds, 267–69, 270
Duggan, Lisa, 37–38, 148–49, 362n1
Dyer, Hannah, 127–28, 177–93, 383

early teaching experience. *See* teaching, first experiences
ecstatic pedagogies: about, 25, 91–105; autobiography, 93–96; collaborative knowledge, 103–105; to counter resistance to learning, 24–25, 92–99, 100–105; course design, 96–97, 100–105; embodied knowledge, 93, 97–99, 103–105; evaluation and assessment, 104; key questions, 93; playfulness, 91–92; popular culture, 103; power dynamics, 24–25, 93–94, 97–100; self-reflection, 93–97, 101–102; student vulnerabilities, 97–99; symposium, 103–104. *See also* desire and pleasure
EDI. *See* DEI (diversity, equity, and inclusion) initiatives
Ellsworth, Elizabeth, 107–109, 116, 119
El-Tayeb, Fatima, 188
embodiment: about, 24–25, 101–102, 283–84, 367–69; coming out processes, 128, 196, 200–207; ecstatic pedagogies, 101–102; engaged pedagogy, 202–206; feminism as rooted in, 283; histories of violence and oppression, 367–68; Indigenous circle of care, 283–84, 290–91; learning as felt in body, 368–69; lived experience, 103, 202–206; pain narratives, 307–309; power dynamics, 367–68; queerness, 24, 75–78, 101–102; sensory connections with world, 283–84, 290–91; teachers, 283–84, 367–69; trauma, 283, 368. *See also* autobiography; ecstatic pedagogies; risks and pleasure; trauma
emotions: anxiety and fear, 92, 125, 131–35, 196, 368, 373; difficult knowledge, 115–16, 118–21, 263–64, 363–64, 369–70; digital intimacies studies, 252; embodied pedagogies, 367–69; emotional labour of forced intimacy, 46, 48, 56–57; first teaching experiences, 131–32; learning as feelings, 368–69; pedagogies of discomfort, 11–12, 141–42, 303–305; self-awareness, 368–69; student-teacher relationships, 100–101. *See also* desire and pleasure; discomfort, pedagogies of; ecstatic pedagogies; resistance to learning or knowledge
empowerment and anti-racism. *See* anti-racism
Emre, Merve, 361
engaged pedagogy: lived experience, 202–206; peer teaching, 212, 223–28
English literature courses: trauma, 187, 217–19; trigger warnings, 127–28, 180–81, 185–86, 189–91
equity initiatives. *See* DEI (diversity, equity, and inclusion) initiatives
ethics and implication, 115–16, 118–21
evaluation and assessment: of activism, 104; collaborations, 373; critiques of grading, 134, 168; ecstatic pedagogies, 100, 103–104; participation and attendance, 98; peer teaching, 224; specifications

grading, 258–59, 373; of teachers, 14, 86, 212; ungrading, 363. *See also* flipped classroom
experimentation. *See* playfulness

faculty. *See* teachers
failure as productive, 132, 138, 335. *See also* teaching, first experiences
fear. *See* emotions
Feinberg, Leslie, 81, 95
Felman, Shoshana, 116
feminism: abolition feminists, 314, 317, 322–23; autobiographical storytelling, 82–88; Black feminism, 84–86, 145–46, 153–54, 156–57, 317, 367–68; collaborative strategies, 147; comedy pedagogies, 233–37; consciousness-raising, 113; critical thinking, 232; embodiment overview, 283; historical contexts, 139–40; Indigenous thought, 146–47, 149, 154–56, 334–35, 339–40, 343; intersectionality, 113–15, 139–40, 154, 156–57; pedagogies of implication, 115; pleasurable approaches, 233; racism and settler colonialism, 156–57; standpoint theory, 82, 134–35, 141, 239, 367–68; as term, 110; trigger warnings, 233–34, 264–66; women's complicity with oppression, 110n4, 111–13
Ferguson, Roderick, xiv, 4n2, 15, 150, 156, 366, 372
Ferland, Nicki, 340–41
fields of study: about, 372–73; canons, critiques of, 87, 149, 151–59; citational practices, 85–86, 86n6, 157, 238n3, 268, 285; collaborative pedagogies, 15–17, 372–73; false universality of white theory, 146, 153–56; genealogies as contested, 146, 149–50, 152–54; theory in everyday life, 154–56; "waiting for Foucault" problem, 152–56. *See also* course design; critical pedagogies; gender and sexuality studies
fields of study, interdisciplinary: about, 4n3, 6; as coalitions, 15–16, 366; comedy pedagogies, 234–38; cross-disciplinary digital intimacy studies, 213, 247–49, 259–60; gender and sexuality studies, 4, 6; justice-based approaches, xii; minority subject areas, 366, 372. *See also* gender and sexuality studies
film and video: community-engaged learning, 348, 353–59; digital intimacies, 255; disabilities, 355; festivals as public pedagogies, 278, 353, 357–59; *Her*, 255; high- vs. low-budget work, 348–49, 354; Indigenous music videos, 286–87; *Pride Denied*, 149, 348; *Sense8*, 255; technology democratization, 348–49, 351–52. *See also* media; Toronto Queer Film Festival (TQFF)
first teaching experience. *See* teaching, first experiences
flipped classroom, 212, 223–28
flipped classroom, evaluation, 224
Floyd, George, 316
Foucault, Michel, 146, 152–53, 155–56, 158, 376
França de Souza Vasconcelos, Erika, 130
Franco-Métis people, 277–78, 331, 384
freewriting exercises, 197–98
Freire, Paolo, 6n5, 133, 205, 305, 327
Freud, Sigmund, 235, 268
Fritsch, Kelly, 23, 45–60, 383–84
fun. *See* comedy; ecstatic pedagogies; humour; playfulness; risks and pleasure
Fun Home (Bechdel), 75–80

Gagliardi, Meghan, 22–23, 27–43, 384
Gamache, Mylène Yannick, 277–78, 331–44, 384
games, online, 252, 253, 254
Gaudry, Adam, 303
Gay, Roxane, 189
Gaztambide-Fernández, Rubén, 374
Gehl, Lynn, 290
gender and sexuality: biological determinism, 333, 338; colonialism as structure vs. event, 147, 155–56; comedy performers, 234, 236–37; cultural shifts, 3–5, 8–9, 14–17; digital intimacies, 247–48, 252–59; embodiment overview, 283; film studies, 348–49; gender-based violence, 324–25; historical contexts, 111–12; homonationalism, 148–49, 348–49; homonormativity, 148, 151, 349; Indigenous gender fluidity, 155–56, 286–89, 342; intersectionality, 113–15, 149, 300–301, 362; languages without gendered words, 288; LGBTQ+ activism, 322, 349; queer, as term, 268n7; sex robots, 256, 257; sexual violence, 5–6; as terms, 4n4; women's complicity with oppression, 111–13. *See also* embodiment; feminism; gender identity; queerness; sex work; trans people
gender and sexuality studies: about, 4, 6, 361–62; abolition pedagogies, 276–77, 313; anti-oppression, 6; *Better Practices*, xii–xiii; coalitions for change, 15–17, 365–67, 376–77; complicity and implication, 107–108; critical sexuality studies, 91–92; cultural shifts, 3–5, 8–9, 14–17, 141–42, 361; discrediting of, 361–62, 376; embodied knowledge, 97–99; as field of study, 372–73; inclusive approaches, 6, 9; innovative strategies, 14; interdisciplinary studies, 4, 6; intersectionality, 6, 113–15, 300–301; justice-based approaches, xii, 6, 8–9; *My Gender Workbook*, 198; pedagogies for social change, 107; program name changes, 108; scholarship on, 7–8, 129–30; sexual violence topics, 5–6; trigger warnings research, 127–28, 179, 182–83, 184–88. *See also* critical pedagogies; fields of study; fields of study, interdisciplinary; queerness; sex work; trans pedagogies; trans teachers
gender identity: about, 195–200, 206–207; all subjects as gendered, 128, 196; benign diversity, 199–200; cisnormativity, as term, 197–98; coming-out processes, 128, 196, 200–207; embodied knowledge, 128, 195–96, 203–207; metaphor of dance floor, 206–207; naturalization of cis identities, 195–98; normalization of complexity, 198–200, 205–207; pronouns, 196, 197–98, 200, 206; self-reflection, 197–98, 205–206; trans identities, 195–96, 200–203, 205–206; visibility, 196, 200–201, 203–204, 206; writing exercises, 197–98. *See also* homonormativity; intersectionality
gender pronouns, 196, 197–98, 200, 206
George Williams Affair, 167–70, 174. *See also* Black people; race and racism
Georgis, Dina, 88, 213–14, 263–73, 369, 384–85
gifts of knowledge, 281–82, 284, 289–90
Gilbert, Jen, 200
Gilbert, Joanne, 236
Gillespie, Kelly, 325–26
Gilmore, Ruth Wilson, 317–18

global within the local, 342–43
Goldman, Nancy, 236
Görkem, Şenay Yavuz, 236
graduate students. *See* students, graduate
Greyeyes, Carol, 281
Grue, Jan, 52–53
guest speakers: about, 137–38, 204–205; on abolition movement, 137–38, 318–19, 323; as allyship, 67, 137–38, 339–40; alternative pedagogies, 339–40; critiques of uses, 67–68, 137–38, 204–205, 339–40; Indigenous community, 137–38, 339–40; power dynamics, 137–38; on sex work, 63, 67–68; on trans experience, 137–38, 196, 204–205
guilt for complicity and implication, 118–21, 369–73. *See also* complicity and implication

Haines, Staci, 218
Halberstam, Jack, 95, 132, 335
Hall, Stuart, 78, 80–81, 86–87
Halluci Nation, 286–87
Hanhardt, Christina, 177–78, 179, 181, 184
Hanson, Aubrey, 332
Hardy, Kate, 64–65
Harriet's Daughter (Philip, novel), 215–19
Her (film), 255
heteropatriarchy: colonial and settler colonial, 82, 85, 286–87; marriage, 148, 288, 332; oppression, 111–13
hierarchies in institutions. *See* power dynamics
higher education: about, 362; banking model (Freire's critique), 133, 205, 305; classism, 30; cultural shifts, 3–5, 8–9, 14–15, 141–42, 264–66, 361; Indigenization strategies, 335;

neoliberalization overview, 5, 28, 37–38; smaller institutions, 334. *See also* course design; critical pedagogies; DEI (diversity, equity, and inclusion) initiatives; fields of study; fields of study, interdisciplinary; gender and sexuality studies; neoliberalization of education; regional perspectives
Hillock, Susan, 7
Holmes, Kwame, 184
homonationalism, 148–49, 348–49
homonormativity, 148, 151, 349. *See also* same-sex marriage
hooks, bell: banking model of education, 133, 305; classrooms as radical spaces, 134, 305, 327; comedy in feminist studies, 232; critique of safe classrooms, 170; on her student life, 220; justice-based approach, xiin; labour of care and recognition, 222–23; passion for learning, 100, 221–23; on popular culture, 231, 232; power imbalances in classrooms, 221, 305; refusal of traditional pedagogies, 133; *Teaching to Transgress*, 100, 133–34; on vulnerability in classrooms, 202
hope and transformative pedagogies, 373–75
Hrynyk, Nicholas, 277–78, 331–44, 385
Hubrig, Adam, 49, 53, 58
humour: critical race humour, 238; reverse racism joke, 231–32; scholarship on, 233, 234–38; theoretical approaches, 235–38. *See also* comedy
Hyatt, Susan Brin, 28

identity: course texts, 80; in digital culture, 251, 252–53, 258; formation of, 80, 131; as good Canadian, 119; intersectionality overview, 113–15,

300–301; privilege of lived experience, 368. *See also* gender identity; intersectionality

implication. *See* complicity and implication

incarceration. *See* abolition

inclusion initiatives. *See* DEI (diversity, equity, and inclusion) initiatives

inclusive pedagogies, xii, 6, 9, 14–15, 127

Indigenous pedagogies: ancestral connections, 277, 331–32; Anishinaabe and Cree teachings and thinking, 288–89; community connections, 339–44; course design, 338–39, 340–41; critiques of colonialism, 154–57, 340–43; damage narratives, 335, 338–39; feminisms, 146–47, 149, 154–56, 334–35, 339–40, 343; filmmaking, 351–52; gender and sexuality, 154–57, 331–32, 340–42; gendered violence, 338–39; global within the local, 342–43; Indigenous law, 342; land connections, 339–42; local knowledges, 341–43; Mohawk territory, 288; place-based relationships, 339–42; stories, 341, 342

Indigenous pedagogies, circle of care: about, 276, 279–91; assignments, 285, 291; course texts, 289–90; gender fluidity, 286–290; gifts of knowledge, 280–82, 284, 289–91; intergenerational sharing, 276, 289–91; lack of extractivism and coercion, 281–82, 284–85; power dynamics, 276; principles of care, 279–81, 284, 290–91; protocols, 280–84; reciprocity and respect, 280, 284–85, 290–91; visions of futurities, 287–89

Indigenous peoples: animacy in languages, 288; Anishinaabe people, 279–83, 286–291; Blackfoot people, 336, 338–39; everyday life as theory, 154–56; gender and sexuality, 155, 286–89; Indigenous law, 342; Innu people, 335, 339, 343; Inuit, 335; kinship structures, 288; knowledge sharing, 289–91; land connections, 284, 290–91, 340–41; medicine circle, 283; Mi'kmaq people, 287, 332, 335, 340, 343; Missing and Murdered Indigenous Women and Girls, 338–39, 340; pre-colonial culture, 342; stories, 284, 289–91, 341, 342; Two-Spirit people, 155, 279, 286–89, 341, 351. *See also* Indigenous pedagogies; Métis

Indigenous peoples, decolonization: about, 154–57, 280, 285–86, 291; abolition campaign (#JusticeforMoka), 314–15, 319–25; allyship in activism, 136–37, 339–40; anti-racism responsibilities, 27–30; citational practices, 285; collective class agreements, 286; community-engaged learning, 339–44; course design, 300–301; critical thinking skills and bias, 305–306; critiques, 6n6, 154–57, 340–43; everyday life as theory, 154–56; global within the local, 342–43; guest speakers, 137–38, 339–40; Indigenous voices, 280, 285–86, 291; intersectionality, 113–15, 300–301; knowledge sharing, 289–91; media analysis of stereotypes (WD4), 287; multidirectional learning, 116–17; pedagogies of discomfort, 303–305; pedagogies of implication, 118–19; slowness and patience, 158; territorial acknowledgements, 6; Two-Spirit/Queer (2SQ) people, 286–89; unlearning colonial constructs, 154–59, 281, 283, 287–88, 342; visions of futurities, 287–89. *See also*

Index 401

anti-racism; Indigenous pedagogies; Indigenous pedagogies, circle of care
Indigenous peoples, settler colonialism: damage narratives, 335, 338–39; extractive research, 303; gender and sexuality, 154–57, 286–89, 340–42; gendered violence, 335, 338–39; historiography, 341–42; homogenization of culture, 342–43; marriage laws, 288; residential schools, 117n8, 118–20, 284, 301; trauma, 118–19, 285–87, 307–309, 335; white saviourism, 339
injustices and accountability. *See* accountability
Innu people, 335, 339, 343
institutions, academic. *See* higher education
interdisciplinary studies. *See* fields of study, interdisciplinary; gender and sexuality studies
intersectionality: about, 113–15, 139–40, 300–301; assignments, 302–303, 308–309; coming-out concerns, 201–202; complicity and implication, 113–15, 120–21; Crenshaw's theory, 113–14, 139–40; critiques of, 6n5, 139–40; disabilities, 47–48, 113–15; genealogy of, 113–14, 139–40; identity vectors, 113–15, 300–301; pain narratives, 307–309; power dynamics, 151–52; queer theory, 149–56; racism and colonialism, 154–57; zero-sum logics, 114
intimacy: about, 213, 247–48, 259–60; asexual intimacies, 92; critical intimacy theory, 247–48, 252, 256, 259–60; disabilities and forced intimacy, 46, 48, 56–57. *See also* digital intimacies

Inuit, 335
Irving, Dan, 24–25, 91–105, 385

Jaekel, Kathryn, 203–204
Joachim, Rebecca Gaëlle, 127, 163–76, 385–86
Johnson, Jennifer L., 7
jokes, 231–32, 236–37. *See also* comedy; humour
Justice, Daniel Heath, 289
justice, social. *See* social justice

Kaba, Mariame, 317, 374
Kamloops, British Columbia, region: community activism, 337–38; gender and sexuality studies, 334, 337–38, 344; student backgrounds, 334, 337–38; teacher's perspective, 333–34, 337–38, 344
Keenan, Harper Benjamin, 202–203, 205–207
Kelley, Robin D.G., 321
Khayatt, Didi, 201
Kimmerer, Robin Wall, 284
King, Tiffany Lethabo, 153–54
kink and pedagogy: about, 212, 215–28; abuse of power, 212, 227–28; peer teaching, 212, 223–28; playfulness, 212, 216–21; pleasure and pedagogies, 212, 221–23, 227–28; role-playing in *Harriet's Daughter*, 215–19; sadism and masochism (SM), 215–20, 222, 227–28; transparency and intent, 222
Kjellin, Harald, 226
Klein, Melanie, 270
Klement, Kristine, 276, 295–311, 386
knowledge production: about, 145, 266–67; curiosity and, 87–88, 265–67, 269, 271–72; as discovery, 269; double binds, 267–69, 270; learning as, 214, 266–67; neoliberalism, 57

Konrad, Annika, 48–49, 52–53, 58
Kouri-Towe, Natalie, xi–xvi, 127–28, 177–93, 347–59, 361–79, 386
Kovach, Margaret, 280
Kumashiro, Kevin, 13, 17, 21–22, 364

LaRocque, Emma, 343
Lau, Travis Chi Wing, 58
laughter. *See* comedy; humour; playfulness
learning, passion for. *See* desire and pleasure; ecstatic pedagogies; risks and pleasure
learning, power dynamics. *See* power dynamics; power dynamics, disruption of
learning, resistance to. *See* resistance to learning or knowledge
learning, trauma concerns. *See* safe spaces in classrooms; trauma; trigger warnings
Lenon, Suzanne, 277–78, 331–44, 386–87
Lenormand, Marie, 270
Lethbridge, Alberta, region: gender and sexuality studies, 336–37, 338–39; Indigenous resistances, 338–39; queer resistances, 336–37, 338; social conservatism, 336–37; student backgrounds, 335–36, 338–39; teacher's perspective, 277–78, 332–33, 335–37, 338–39
Leys, Ruth, 119
LGBTQ+. *See* gender and sexuality; gender identity
Light, Tracy Penny, 7
literature: *Fun Home*, 75, 77–79; *Harriet's Daughter*, 215–19; on sex work, 68. *See also* cultural studies; English literature courses; film and video

Long, Rebecca-Eli, 49–51, 53
Lorde, Audre, 84, 149, 157
love for learning. *See* desire and pleasure; ecstatic pedagogies; risks and pleasure
Lugones, Maria, 231, 233
Luhmann, Susanne, 7, 12, 25, 107–23, 369, 371, 387
Lypka, Celiese, 332

Mahrouse, Gada, 212–13, 231–45, 387
Makokis, James, 288
Malatino, Hilary, 199, 205
Manalansan, Martin, 153
Manitoba. *See* Winnipeg, Manitoba, region
Manning, Kimberley Ens, 127, 163–76, 387
Martell, Christopher, 337
masochism and sadism, 215–20, 222. *See also* kink and pedagogy
Mayo, Chris, 233, 239
McKegney, Sam, 284
McKinnon, Rachel, 136–37
McKittrick, Katherine: citational practices, 86n6; on curiosity, 267–68; "Freedom Is a Secret," 216–17; on historical formations, 217; on liberation, 267–68; on safe spaces, 170–71; on thinking the world anew, 333; on unknowing ourselves, 88; on white supremacy, 159
McLuhan, Marshall, 249
media: about, 249–50; as alternative form of education, 357–59; critical literacy skills, 357–58; early internet materials, 255; media analysis tools, 287, 356; medium theory, 249–50; technology democratization, 348–49, 351–52. *See also* digital intimacies;

Index   403

digital technologies; film and video; Toronto Queer Film Festival (TQFF)
Memorial University. *See* St. John's, Newfoundland, region
Métis: ancestral connections, 277, 331–32; embodied knowledge, 283–84; land-based education, 340–41; teacher's positionality, 277, 331–32
Mi'kmaq people, 287, 332, 335, 340, 343
Miller, Michelle, 127–28, 177–93, 387–88
Million, Dian, 154, 341–42
Mills, Brett, 235n2
Mingus, Mia, 48, 55, 58
Missing and Murdered Indigenous Women and Girls, 338–39, 340
Mitchell, David, 132
Montreal. *See* Concordia University; Quebec
morality and complicity, 115–16, 118–21
Morrill, Angie, 147, 154–55
Morrison, Danielle, 286
Morton, Katherine, 335
Movement for Black Lives, 27, 316, 316n3
multidirectional learning, 116–17
Mumford, Cara, 287
Mumford, Marrie, 283–84
Musial, Jennifer, 7
My Gender Workbook (Bornstein), 198

Naidoo, Leigh-Ann, 325–26
Napoleon, Val, 342
narratives: historiography, 341–42; pain narratives, 307–309; white saviourism, 339. *See also* stories and storytelling
Nash, Jennifer C., 6n5
National Inquiry into Missing and Murdered Indigenous Women and Girls, 338–39, 340
Nazi complicity, 111–12

neoliberalization of education: about, xiii, 5, 16, 28, 31–32, 37; ableist expectations, 57–58; allyship and accountability, 137; anti-racism work diminishment, 28–30, 32, 39–42; barriers to education, 357–58; characteristics of, 5, 28, 37–38; "empowered student" narrative, 28–34, 37–42; faculty responses to, 5, 7, 14, 16, 30; homonormativity, 148, 151, 349; precarious labour, 5, 32–33, 146, 358; and racism, 38–40
Nestle, Joan, 95
Nestojko, John, 226
Newfoundland and Labrador: Indigenous people, 335, 339–40. *See also* St. John's, Newfoundland, region
Nicholas, Jane, 7
Nicolazzo, Z., 203–204
Nixon, Kimberly, 333
non-human intimacies. *See* digital intimacies

online learning, 132, 258–59
Osorio, Ruth, 49, 53, 58

pandemic, COVID-19, 132, 258–59, 269
passion for learning. *See* ecstatic pedagogies; risks and pleasure
Patton, Lori, 38
Paying for It (Brown), 68
Payne, Nikki, 237
pedagogies: about, 5–9; additive approaches and minorities, 150; "best" practices, 7, 15; canonical texts and assumptions, 151–59; creative responses by students, 156, 308–309; cultural shifts, 3–5, 8–9, 14–15, 141–42; inclusive pedagogies, xii, 6, 9, 14–15, 127; key questions, 6–7;

legibility of theory, 154; pedagogies of correction, 16; recent scholarship on, 7–8; scholarship on, 7–8; slow and patient pedagogies, 158; structural harm in classrooms, 9; theory in everyday life, 154–56; uncertainties, 13, 14, 17. *See also* course design; critical pedagogies; discomfort, pedagogies of; evaluation and assessment; fields of study; fields of study, interdisciplinary; power dynamics, disruption of

peer teaching, 212, 223–28

peer teaching evaluation, 224

people of colour, 55, 99, 109, 154, 172, 303, 351. *See also* race and racism

Peterson, Micheal Nebeling, 248

Philip, M. NourbeSe, 215–19

Piepzna-Samarasinha, Leah Lakshmi, 53, 55

Pitt, Alice, 263n1

playfulness: about, 213–14, 263–72; comedy pedagogies, 233, 240–41; curiosity as, 265–67, 269, 271–72; ecstatic pedagogies, 91–92; in human development, 269–71; kink and pedagogy, 212, 216–21, 227–28; learning as knowledge-making, 214, 265, 269–72; as liberation, 269–72; new ideas outside binaries, 268–69; as non-compliance, 266–67, 270; power dynamics disruption, 216–21; as re/creation, 269–71; risk-taking capacity, 213–14, 266, 269–72; role-playing in *Harriet's Daughter*, 215–19; safe spaces for, 213–14, 271–72; Spivak on, 267–69; teacher's softening, 214, 271–72, 364–65; as therapy for trauma, 269; transformative pedagogies, 373–75; Winnicott on, 269–72. *See also* comedy; digital intimacies

pleasure. *See* desire and pleasure; ecstatic pedagogies; risks and pleasure

Poirier-Saumure, Alexis, 67, 126, 129–43, 388

police. *See* abolition

political correctness, 233

politics. *See* abolition; activism; allyship; community-engaged learning; Indigenous peoples, decolonization; public pedagogies

polymorphous perversity, 92

popular culture: assignments, 103; b. hooks on pedagogies, 231, 232; comedy overview, 231–38; Indigenous culture, 286–87. *See also* comedy; cultural studies; digital intimacies; film and video

power dynamics: about, 21–25, 97–100; in allyship, 136–37, 366; coalitions, 15–16, 365–67; disabilities, 49, 53; in disciplinarity, 375; embodied histories of violence, 367–68; "empowered student" narrative, 35, 37; epistemic power, 368, 370; Foucauldian power and resistance, 146, 376; Foucauldian theory as canonical, 152–53, 155–58; guest speakers, 137–38; hierarchies and inequalities, 35; implication in institutional injustices, 110; Indigenous relations, 154–56, 342; intersectionality, 151–52; pleasure and pedagogies, 221–23; precarious labour in teaching, 146; professional codes, 102; psychic resistance, 363–64; queer theory, 151–52; racialized dynamics in white classes, 127, 168–76; sadism and masochism (SM), 215–20, 222; safe space agreements, 127, 170–76, 223, 225; systemic power abuse, 227–28; trigger warnings, 179. *See also* accountability; complicity and implication

power dynamics, disruption of: about, 297–99, 363–64; abolition pedagogies, 276–77, 324, 326; accountability, 371–72; assessment (ungrading), 363; circles as non-hierarchical, 280, 290–91; classroom strategies, 363; collaborations, 297–300; community engagement, 363; consent and agency, 218, 227–28; critical analytic skills for, 370; discipline genealogies as contested, 146, 152–53; ecstatic pedagogies, 93–94, 100–105; peer teaching, 212, 223–28; playfulness as, 216–21; role-playing in *Harriet's Daughter*, 215–19; self-reflection, 364–65; softening of relationships, 214, 271–72, 364–65; specifications grading, 258–59; student-centred learning, 363; student vulnerabilities, 97–99, 370; team teaching, 297–300, 304. *See also* accountability; complicity and implication; self-reflection and self-reflexion
Pratt, Minnie Bruce, 112–13, 117n6
Price, Margaret, 50
Pride Denied (film), 149, 348
prison system, 324–25. *See also* abolition
professors. *See* teachers
pronouns, gender, 196, 197–98, 200, 206
psychoanalytic approaches: pedagogies of discomfort, 11–12; polymorphous perversity, 92; resistance to learning or knowledge, 12–13, 17, 92, 116–18, 127, 158, 178, 189, 213, 265n5, 272, 278, 363, 369; risk and playfulness, 213–14; self and otherness, 374; transformative pedagogies, 374–75. *See also* resistance to learning or knowledge
Puar, Jasbir, 148–49, 177–78
public pedagogies: critical race humour, 238; film festivals, 278, 353, 357–59; symposiums, 103–104, 353, 357–58. *See also* Toronto Queer Film Festival (TQFF)

Quebec: Bill 32 on academic freedom (2022), 3; politics, 141. *See also* Concordia University
queerness: about, 75–77, 147–52, 268n7; autobiography as pedagogy, 24, 75–78; canon in pedagogies, 149–50, 152–59; coming-out processes, 128, 196, 200–207; course design, 96–97; critical intimacy studies, 247–48, 253, 255, 257–58; critical sexuality studies, 91–92; embodied knowledge, 101–102; false universality of white theory, 146, 152–56; feminist approach, 146–47; in *Fun Home*, 75–80; gender nonconformity, 75–77, 202; genealogies of fields of study, 146, 149–50, 152–54; history of, 356; homonationalism, 148–49, 348–49; homonormativity, 148, 151, 349; Indigenous scholarship, 146; intergenerational friendships, 100–101; intersectionality, 113–15, 127, 149–56; liberation goals, 148; as more than sexuality, 146, 149–52; nicknames, 79–82; pedagogical approaches, 149–56; power dynamics, 146, 151–57; *Pride Denied* (film), 348; queer theory, 80, 97, 148, 153–55, 177, 253; representational politics, 356; terminology, 81, 268n7. *See also* autobiography; Toronto Queer Film Festival (TQFF)
queer theory, racism, and settler colonialism: about, 127, 145–59; canon in pedagogies, 146, 151–59; course design, 145–46, 149–50, 152–54, 156–59; course texts, 149–50; false universality of white theory, 146, 152–56;

genealogies of fields of study, 146, 149–50, 152–54; homonationalism, 148–49, 348–49; homonormativity, 148, 151, 349; Indigenous feminisms, 146–47, 149; Indigenous theory, 154–56; intersectionality, 127, 149–56; knowledge production, 145–46; power dynamics, 145–46, 151–57; queer theory, 97, 145–46, 154–56; racism, 146–47; settler colonialism, 146–47, 154–56; slow and patient pedagogies, 152, 154, 156, 158; teacher's positionality, 147, 156; theory in everyday life, 154–56; unlearning colonial constructs, 152, 156–59; "waiting for Foucault" problem, 146, 152–56; women of colour feminisms, 146–47, 149, 153–56

race and racism: about, 27–29; additive pedagogical approaches, 150; anti-Black racism, 49, 159, 296, 299, 307, 315; BIPOC (Black, Indigenous, people of colour), 55, 165, 238n3, 301; canonical texts and whiteness, 152–59; colour-blindness, 28, 37–38; "empowered student" narrative, 35–36; humour, 237–41; institutional and interpersonal racism, 35–36; intersectionality, 113–15, 300–301; neoliberalism's impacts, 28–33, 40; power dynamics, 215, 222–23; reverse racism joke, 231–32; role-playing in *Harriet's Daughter*, 215–19; structure vs. event, 147, 155, 158–59; trigger warnings, 188, 264–66. *See also* anti-racism; Black people, racism and safe spaces in classrooms; Indigenous peoples; queer theory, racism, and settler colonialism; students, racialized; white supremacy

Rahman, Aamer, 231–32

Rambukkana, Nathan, 213, 247–62, 388
Rancière, Jacques, 266, 269
Razack, Sherene, 322n7, 333
reading the room: cultural shifts, 3–5, 8–9, 14–15, 141–42
reflection and reflexion. *See* self-reflection and self-reflexion
Regan, Paulette, 303
regional perspectives: about, 277–78, 331–44; gender and sexuality studies, 278; global within the local, 342–43; Indigenous pedagogies, 277–78, 331–32, 334–35, 340–43; student backgrounds, 334–35, 337–38, 344; teachers' positionalities, 277–78, 331–35, 343–44; urban/rural divide, 277–78, 334, 344. *See also* Kamloops, British Columbia, region; Lethbridge, Alberta, region; St. John's, Newfoundland, region; Winnipeg, Manitoba, region
relational knowledge. *See* Indigenous pedagogies
remote areas, 277–78. *See also* regional perspectives
remote learning, 258–59
research processes: desire-based research, 307–309; extractive research, 303; intersectionality, 113–15; justice-oriented research agendas, 38; pain narratives, 307–309; research topics as non-neutral, 37–38; single vector analysis, 113–15; white denial of responsibilities for anti-racism, 37–38; zero-sum logics, 114
residential schools, 117n8, 118–20, 284, 301
resistance and power. *See* power dynamics, disruption of
resistance to learning or knowledge: about, 12–13, 24–25, 116–18, 213–14, 364–65; as affective power struggles,

266; cultural shifts, 3–5, 8–9, 92–93, 141–42, 264–65; ecstatic pedagogy as strategy, 24–25, 92–94, 100–105; existing knowledge as basis for resistance, 12–13; multidirectional learning, 116–17; over-identification, 120–21; paradox and political positions, 264n2; pedagogies of implication and complicity, 115–19, 369–72; power dynamics, 97–99; slowness and patience in pedagogies, 158; softening as response to, 214, 271–72, 364–65; strategies to counter, 24–25, 93–94, 100–105, 116–17, 364–65; student vulnerabilities, 97–99; unlearning colonial constructs, 156–59. *See also* power dynamics, disruption of; psychoanalytic approaches

responsibility. *See* accountability; complicity and implication

reverse racism joke, 231–32

risks and pleasure: about, 10, 221–23; transformative pedagogies, 373–75. *See also* comedy; digital intimacies; kink and pedagogy; playfulness

Rivers-Moore, Megan, 23–24, 61–73, 388–89

Robinson, Dylan, 283

robotics, 255–60. *See also* digital intimacies

Rodriguez, Dylan, 314–15

role-playing: in academia, 222–23; in *Harriet's Daughter*, 215–19

Rothberg, Michael, 117, 119, 121

rural areas, 277–78, 343–44. *See also* regional perspectives

Russo, Ann, 371

sadism and masochism (SM), 215–20, 222. *See also* kink and pedagogy

safe spaces in classrooms: about, 127, 169–76; accountability, 174–76; agreements on, 127, 170–76, 223, 225; class discussions on whiteness, 170; collaborative approaches, 127; comedy pedagogies, 239–41; critiques of, 13–14, 197, 223, 239, 263–64; cultural shifts, 3–5, 8–9, 14–15, 141–42, 264–65; eye rolls as signals, 170–72; as fantasy, 127, 170–71; gendered dynamics, 197; harm vs. comfort, 127; for playfulness and curiosity, 213–14, 271–72; political positions, 264n2; racialized dynamics, 127, 168–76, 197; resistance by students, 170–72; self-reflection, 101–102, 197–98, 205–206; statements in syllabi, 170–71, 239; teachers' fears, 170; transphobia, 197; writing exercises, 197–98. *See also* Black people, racism and safe spaces in classrooms

same-sex marriage, 148n1, 256, 333. *See also* homonormativity

Sanders, Teela, 64–65

Schumer, Amy, 234

Seikaly, Sherene, 181

self-advocacy: disabled people, 48–49, 51–53, 55–56; racialized students, 22–23, 27–43. *See also* anti-racism

self-reflection and self-reflexion: about, 13, 14, 24, 364–65, 367, 370, 377; accountability, 25; collaboration pedagogies, 16–17, 300, 302, 364–65, 377; course design, 302–303; critiques of, 364–65; ecstatic pedagogy, 91–96, 101–102; embodied experiences, 24–25, 277; first teaching experiences, 129–30; gender identity, 197–98, 205–206; Indigenous contexts, 277, 341; pedagogy of implication, 25; safe spaces, 197–98, 205–206; strategies, 13, 57, 93, 126, 130, 191, 197–98, 364–65, 367, 369–70, 377; teaching failures, 126, 140; trigger warnings,

191; tutorials, 304–305. *See also* accountability; autobiography; complicity and implication; Kumashiro, Kevin; teaching, first experiences

Sense8 (film), 255

settler colonialism: complicity in overview, 370–71; gender and sexuality, 155–56; historiography, 341–42; schools as colonial institutions, 220–21; structure vs. event, 147, 155, 158–59; unlearning colonial constructs, 156–59. *See also* Black feminist thought; complicity and implication; Indigenous peoples; settler colonialism; queer theory, racism, and settler colonialism; white supremacy

sexuality and gender. *See* gender and sexuality; gender and sexuality studies; gender identity

sex work: about, 23–24, 61–71; abolition campaign (#JusticeforMoka), 314–15, 319–25; campus resources for students, 65–66, 71; clients of sex workers, 68; courses on, 63, 68–71; cultural shifts, 23–24, 61–67, 69–71; digital industry, 64, 257, 259; financial issues, 64–66, 71; guest speakers, 63, 67–68; as labour, 67, 70; *Paying for It* (memoir), 68; scholarly literature on, 65; self-disclosure of status, 65, 71; sex work exclusionary radical feminists (SWERFs), 66, 68; stigma, 66, 68, 71; student resources, 66; students as sex workers, 23–24, 61–65, 69–71; terminology, 61, 71; trans sex workers, 319n6

shame and stigma. *See* stigma and shame

shame for complicity and implication, 118–21, 369–73. *See also* complicity and implication; stigma and shame

Sharpe, Christina, 217–18, 221
Shear, Boone, 28
Sheppard, Alice, 53–54
Shotwell, Alexis, 107, 121
Silin, Jonathan, 202
Simard, Fallon, 351
Simpson, Audra, 288
Simpson, Leanne Betasamosake, 153, 290, 339
Sinclair-Palm, Julia, 128, 195–209, 389
singularity (AI), 256
Sins Invalid, 55
Sir George Williams Affair, 167–70, 174. *See also* Black people; race and racism
"Sisters" (video, Halluci Nation), 286–87
slavery, 111–12, 215–19
Smith, Linda Tuhiwai, 280
Smollin, Leandra, 130–31
Snyder, Emily, 342
social class. *See* class, social
social justice: about, 108–10; abolition pedagogies overview, 276–77, 313–16, 326–27; allyship overview, 134–38; anti-apartheid movement, 314; assumptions of rationality and criticality, 108–10; classroom as activist space, 183, 188–89; complicity and implication, 109–11; ecstatic pedagogies, 103–105; failure of liberal ideals, 133; intersectionality, 113–15, 300–301; justice-based approaches, xii; queer pedagogies, 133; "repressive myths" of liberation, 107–10, 119; trigger warnings as response to, 182–83, 233–34, 264–66. *See also* abolition; transformative pedagogies
social location statements, 135
softening to student resistance, 214, 271–72, 364–65
Spivak, Gayatri, 267–69

Index   409

Stabler, Albert, 49–51, 53
standpoint theory, 82, 134–35, 141, 239, 367–68
Starblanket, Gina, 340–41
Stark, Heidi Kiiwetinepinesiik, 340–41
Stenfors, Terese, 226
Stevens, Kaylene, 337
stigma and shame: collective access model to counter, 56–57; comedy as challenge to, 237–38; disabilities, 50–51, 56–57; sex work, 66, 68, 71
St. John's, Newfoundland, region: Indigenous feminisms, 334–35, 339–40, 343; student backgrounds, 334–35, 339; teacher's perspective, 334–35, 339–40, 343
stories and storytelling: autobiographical storytelling, 88; damage narratives, 307–309; historiography, 341–42; Indigenous law, 342; Indigenous stories, 284, 289–91, 341, 342; pain narratives, 307–309; queer film festivals, 353–54. *See also* autobiography; narratives
Stryker, Susan, 79, 203
students: assumptions about, 23–24, 70; cultural shifts, 3–5, 8–9, 14–15, 141–42, 264–66, 361; financial pressures on, 64, 67. *See also* resistance to learning or knowledge; safe spaces in classrooms; student-teacher relationships
students, graduate: ableism and supervision of, 51; anti-racism program work, 36–37; first teaching experiences, 126, 129–32; self-reflection, 129–30; shift in status to professor, 95–96; teaching assistants (TAs), 297–300; training in collaboration pedagogies, 297. *See also* anti-racism; teaching, first experiences

students, racialized: health risks, 36; power dynamics in white spaces, 127, 168–76; responsibility to represent communities, 36–37; self-segregation as survival tactic, 167, 172. *See also* anti-racism; Black people; Indigenous peoples; queer theory, racism, and settler colonialism; race and racism
student-teacher relationships: accountability, 100–101; allyship overview, 134–38; coalitions, 15–16, 365–67; emotional labour, 100–101; Indigenous perspectives, 289–91; intergenerational friendships, 100–101; peer teaching, 212, 223–28; pleasure and pedagogies, 221–23; power dynamics, 220–21; schools as colonial institutions, 220–21. *See also* allyship; power dynamics; power dynamics, disruption of
study, fields of. *See* fields of study; fields of study, interdisciplinary
SWERFs (sex work exclusionary radical feminists), 66, 68
Sylliboy, Michelle, 340
symposiums, 103–104, 353, 357–58

TallBear, Kim, 288, 340
Taylor, Anne, 288
Taylor, Dorothy, 290
teachers: collective feminist practices, 147; coming-out processes, 128, 135, 196, 200–207; cultural shifts, 3–5, 8–9, 14–15; devaluation of Black women, 221–22; fears, 9; health risks of racialized teachers, 36; precarious employment, 5, 32–33, 146, 201, 358; professional codes, 102; reading the room, 9. *See also* autobiography; disabilities; regional perspectives;

teaching; teaching, first experiences; trans teachers
teacher-student relationships. *See* student-teacher relationships
teaching: about, 129–42; as allyship, 134–38; as knowledge production, 266; as knowledge transmission, 139; lived experiences and authority, 135; power dynamics, 130, 137; scholarship on, 129–30; social location statements, 135; as support for curiosity, 265–67, 269, 271–72; uncertainties, 13, 14, 17. *See also* critical pedagogies; discomfort, pedagogies of; pedagogies; power dynamics; power dynamics, disruption of; safe spaces in classrooms
teaching, first experiences: about, 126, 129–42; allyship, 130, 134–38; canonical learning expectations, 133–34; critical pedagogy, 133–34, 138–42; cultural shifts, 141–42; emotions, 131–32; failure as productive, 132–42, 335; graduate student liminality, 130–32; pedagogy of discomfort, 141–42; power dynamics, 130; scholarship on, 129–30; self-reflection, 129–30, 134–42; standpoint theory, 134–35, 141; teaching about critique, 138–40
teaching assistants (TAs). *See* students, graduate
team teaching, 297–300, 304. *See also* collaborations
technologies. *See* digital intimacies; media
Thomas, Rebecca, 287
Thompson Rivers University. *See* Kamloops, British Columbia, region
Thürmer-Rohr, Christina, 110–11, 113
Titchkosky, Tanya, 52, 54

topics of study. *See* fields of study; fields of study, interdisciplinary
Toronto Queer Film Festival (TQFF): about, 278, 347–59; collective structure, 349–50, 353; as community-engaged learning, 348–50, 354–55, 357–59; funding, 350–53; history of, 348–50, 356–57; knowledge sharing, 351–52; partnerships, 352; as queer activism, 353–54; symposiums, 353, 357–58; technology democratization, 348–49, 351–52; training and workshops, 347–48, 351–52
transformative justice, 317, 374
transformative pedagogies: about, 373–75; coalitions for change, 15–16, 376–77; hopefulness, 373–75; pedagogies of contradiction, 375–76; solidarity pedagogies, 374. *See also* ecstatic pedagogies; playfulness
trans pedagogies: about, 128, 195–207; course design, 195–99, 206–207; embodied knowledge, 128, 203–207; engaged pedagogy, 202–206; guest speakers, 137–38, 196, 204–205; metaphor of dance floor, 206–207; normalization of complexity, 198–200, 205–207; recommendations, 206–207; safe spaces, 197–99; scholarship on, 196, 206–207; self-reflection, 197–99, 205–206; students as allies, 196, 205–206; "teaching trans," 203–204; writing exercises, 197–99. *See also* ecstatic pedagogies
trans people: abolition campaign (#JusticeforMoka), 314–15, 319–25; Indigenous care, 288–89; Irving's story, 94–96; model for challenges to normalcy, 322–23; students as allies, 196, 205–206; targets of

violence, 319n6, 322–23, 324–25; transphobia, 116, 171, 195, 197, 205; trans youth, 195, 198–99, 205, 288–89

trans teachers: about, 128, 195–207; autobiographies, 94–96; coming-out processes, 128, 196, 200–207; course design, 195, 197–99; embodied knowledge, 94–96, 128; as expert authority, 200, 204; intersectionality, 201–202; metaphor of dance floor, 206–207; as object of knowledge, 96, 196, 200–202, 204; pronouns, 200; recommendations, 206–7; scholarship on, 196, 202; visibility of gender, 196, 200–201, 203–204, 206. *See also* ecstatic pedagogies

trauma: about, 179–87; child and youth studies, 187; complicity and implication, 115, 118–19, 179; course design, 187; cultural shifts, 118, 183; as difficult knowledge, 115–16, 118–21, 185–87; embodiment, 283, 368; in *Harriet's Daughter*, 215–19; historical trauma, 113, 115, 118–19, 187–88; Indigenous peoples, 118–19, 285, 307–309, 335; normalization of, 179; in pain narratives, 307–309; strategies, 308–309, 373–74; theories of, 181–82, 187–88; trigger warnings, 179, 181–87. *See also* complicity and implication; embodiment; safe spaces in classrooms; trigger warnings

trigger warnings: about, 127–28, 177–91, 264–66; as caring act, 180, 185–87, 189–91; in child and youth courses, 127–28, 182, 183–84, 185, 187–91; in comedy, 233–34, 239; courses without triggering content, 188–89; critiques of, 177–80, 189–91, 264–66; cultural shifts, 3–5, 8–9, 14–15, 183, 264–66; in gender and sexuality courses, 127–28, 179, 182–83, 184–88, 190–91; key questions, 178–79, 188; legal restrictions (Quebec's Bill 32), 3; in literature courses, 127–28, 180–81, 185–86, 189–91; in online spaces, 181; power dynamics, 179, 189; requests and expectations, 182–84, 188–91; research studies, 127–28, 178–79, 190–91; strategies, 127–28, 184–87, 190–91, 307–309; as student political location, 183, 188–89; trauma theory, 181–82, 187–88, 307–309; uncertainties, 189. *See also* trauma

Trimble, S., 24, 75–89, 81(f), 389

Trotz, Alissa, 145–46, 150

Tuck, Eve, 6n6, 147, 154–55, 307–308, 335, 339

tutorials, 304–305

Two-Spirit people, 155, 279, 286–89, 341, 351

universality, false: transness, 205; white theory, 146, 152–56

University, Concordia. *See* Concordia University

University, Memorial. *See* St. John's, Newfoundland, region

University, Thompson Rivers. *See* Kamloops, British Columbia, region

University of Lethbridge. *See* Lethbridge, Alberta, region

University of Manitoba. *See* Winnipeg, Manitoba, region

Valentine, Desiree, 52–54

Van der Wey, Delores, 303

Vest, Jennifer Lisa, 222

video. *See* film and video; media

virtual online learning, 132, 258–59

visual impairment, 57. *See also* disabilities

Walcott, Rinaldo, 153
war and robotics, 256–57
warnings, trigger. *See* trigger warnings
Watts, Vanessa, 341
Weaver, Simon, 237–38
Weheliye, Alexander G., 153
Weigman, Robyn, 375
Wekker, Gloria, 153
White, Melissa Autumn, 7
white gaze, 76
white people: assignment of anti-racism work, 22–23, 27–30; false universality of white theory, 146, 152–56; racialized dynamics in white classes, 127, 168–76; saviour narratives, 339; unlearning colonial constructs, 156–59. *See also* anti-racism; complicity and implication
white supremacy: capitalism, 49, 182; intersecting, 112, 150, 187, 336; racial violence, 156, 179, 370; reinforcement of, 23, 127, 147, 156–58, 173–75, 269, 281; resistance to, 351; settler colonialism, 99, 370
Wiegman, Robyn, xiv, 3, 12, 16, 110
Willet, Cynthia and Julie, 235n2
Williams, Alice Olsen, 279
Williams, Mollena, 222
Williams, Sir George, Affair (anti-racism student riots), 167–70, 174
Wilson, Alex, 340
Winnicott, D.W., 269–72
Winnipeg, Manitoba, region: Franco-Métis community, 331–32; as Indigenous centre, 341; Indigenous pedagogies, 340–43; teacher's perspective, 277, 331–32, 340–43
women: devaluation of Black teachers, 221–22; intersectionality, 113–15, 300–301; women of colour feminisms, 146–47, 149, 153–56; women's and gender studies, 108–109; women's complicity with oppression, 110n4, 111–13. *See also* feminism; gender and sexuality; gender and sexuality studies
Wynter, Sylvia, 84

Yalamarty, Harshita, 299n2
Yang, K. Wayne, 6n6, 155, 307–308, 335, 339
Yang, Mitchell Rae, 127, 163–76, 389
Yergeau, Remi, 57

Zembylas, Michalinos, 303
zero-sum logics, 114–15
Zoom classes, 258–59